# IHUM IIA
# The Making of the Modern World
# Europe & Latin America

### Edited by
### David Como

*Stanford University*

**University Readers™**
San Diego, CA

First published in the United States of America in 2010 by University Readers, Inc.

14 13 12 11 10          1 2 3 4 5

Printed in the United States of America

ISBN: 978-1-935551-85-0

 **University Readers**™
800.200.3908 I www.universityreaders.com

# Contents

# The Renaissance

Translated by Lydia G. Cochrane
Edited by Eric Cochrane and Julius Kirshner

## ALESSANDRA MACINGHI NEGLI STROZZI, *LETTERS TO FILIPPO DEGLI STROZZI*

Alessandra Macinghi negli Strozzi (b. 1407) was the daughter of Filippo de Niccolò Macinghi, one of the wealthiest citizens of Florence. Her mother, Caterina di Alberto Alberti, died when Alessandra was still a gift and was a descendent of the equally prominent Alberti family. (See the introduction to the selections in this volume from Leon Battista Alberti.) Nothing is known of Alessandra's childhood, although it is clear from her correspondence and account books that she learned how to read, write, and perform rudimentary arithmetic operations—abilities that proved indispensable for widows like Alessandra, who were responsible for administering the domestic household as well as their own patrimony. In 1422 she was married to Matteo di Simone Strozzi, a wealthy wool merchant, humanist, and member of another of the most wealthy and powerful families in Florence. Since she was only sixteen at the time and Matteo only twenty-five, this marriage was somewhat atypical. The average age of marriage for young women in Florence in this period was eighteen; for men, thirty-two. Similarly, the dowry of 1600 florins accompanying Alessandra to her husband was considerably higher than the 1000 to 1200-florin dowries characteristic of most upper-class Florentines. But one of the main purposes of marriage was amply fulfilled. From 1426 to 1436, Alessandra gave birth almost yearly: Andreoula in 1426, Simone in 1427, Filippo in 1428, Piero in 1429, Lorenzo in 1430, Caterina in 1432, Alessandra in 1434, Matteo in 1436.

Matteo's fortunes declined in 1434 when he, along with several other Strozzi, found themselves on the opposite side of the allies of Cosimo de' Medici. He suffered punitive taxation as well as exile. Alessandra joined her exiled husband in Pesaro, where they resided in comfort thanks to the generous hospitality of Archbishop Pandolfo Malatesta. After his death from plague in 1435, she returned to Florence, pregnant, with four surviving children, and with few financial resources beyond the dowry, which legally became hers again after the death of her husband. Her plight was similar to that of many other contemporary women. The census of Florence taken in 1427 and known as the *catasto* reveals that husbands tended to predecease their wives, and that one in four adult women were widows living in comparative poverty. By law all of a husband's estates went to his surviving sons, except for those portions earmarked for his daughters' dowries and special legacies, and except for that portion equivalent to his wife's dowry. Alessandra's financial hardship was compounded by the fact that first her sons inherited not their father's fortune but his tax debts, and second, that when they reached the age of eighteen they too fell under their father's ban of exile. Supported by their mother, who liquidated her property to provide them with capital, and by their relatives, who provided them with commercial opportunities, they eventually restored their family's lost wealth, and after their readmission to Florence, its former social position. Indeed the Strozzi Palace in Florence stands as testimony to the vision of grandeur and extraordinary wealth accumulated by Filippo Strozzi.

Trans. by Lydia G. Cochrane, Eric Cochrane and Julius Kirshner, eds., "Alessandra Macinghi negli Strozzi, *Letters to Filippo degli Strozzi*" from *University of Chicago Readings in Western Civilization: The Renaissance*, Vol. 5. pp. 105-117, 185-209. Copyright © 1986 University of Chicago Press. Permission to reprint granted by the publisher

The epistolary legacy of the Renaissance includes many letters of wives of merchants and public figures. Alessandra Strozzi's seventy-two letters, written to her sons between 1447 and just before her death in 1471, are an exceptional source for the social history of Renaissance Florence.

## Letter 2

To Filippo degli Strozzi in Naples
In the name of God, 4 November 1448

I have had your letter of August 8 in the last few days, and I haven't answered sooner because for a month now I've been suffering from intestinal problems *(la scesa)*. Writing bothers me these days, as I'm getting older and am in worse health day by day. But I don't yet have to worry about writing you, for I'm dictating to Matteo to give him practice in letter writing. When he writes slowly and puts his mind on what he's doing, he writes well. Antonio Strozzi[1] said as much, and Marco,[2] when I showed them some pages he had written, said that he writes a proper letter. But when he writes rapidly, you'd say it wasn't the same hand: there's a black and white difference between the two. I keep telling him that he should write more slowly. Mention to him when you write him to keep working on it; it will do him good. And that he should be good and respectful, because he is really impressed *(teme)* when you write him. And do write him often, so he can have a reason to write to you. And when you write Marco, put in a word for Matteo, and the same for Antonio degli Strozzi. That way, both of them will give him good guidance and he will pay more respectful attention to them than he does to me. May God give every one [of you] the grace and virtue I wish for you.

I had a letter today from Lorenzo dated 28 September, brought by Pagolo Salterelli, that tells me Lorenzo was supposed to leave for London on September 21; but the companions with whom he was going to travel left without saying a word to him, so he was left stranded.

This is what Lorenzo writes me, adding that he thinks it will be a while before he can find traveling companions. Now we're in winter and he still hasn't left. He could spend all winter waiting to leave, and winter is a poor time for such a long trip on horseback. I don't know how he's going to stay at Vignone until spring, if it comes to that. Besides, I really don't much like the idea of his going to London if he can be elsewhere, for I hear there's an epidemic *(la morìa)* there, and the same for Bruges. According to what Iacopo[3] writes, eight or ten people a day are dying there, so for the moment it's a poor idea. God give him [the wisdom] to make the right decision. Last August Granello Ricasoli[4] was here, and I asked him all about Lorenzo. He finally told me that Lorenzo had the right instincts but that he needed someone to guide him, because that would do him good. I have written Iacopo what I think needs to be said, and when I hear that he (Lorenzo) has left for London, I will write Lodovico[5] and get him to write to Antonio as needs be. A pen never seems so heavy to me as when I have to write something for your good and I don't do it. However, when it was necessary, I have always taken care of your interests and his, and in good time too. So enough of that.

This summer Piero de' Ricci, of whom I'm very fond, came to see me and I asked him about you. He told me you were very thin but well, that you did not have insomnia, as it should be, and that Niccolò[6] was in as good health as you, all of which pleases me. I beg you to be aware of the favors you have received from him and to be obedient to him even more than if he were your father, for you could never do as much good as to merit what he has done for you. So do your utmost not to be ungrateful to the person who made a man of you. May God give me reason to be pleased with you and with the others.

I haven't written you anything about the flax because I was making Matteo write you. It seems to me that if

---

1 Antonio di Benedetto Strozzi was a distant relative, but close to Alessandra and her sons whom he served as financial advisor.

2 Marco Parenti, who married Caterina Strozzi in 1447, was Alessandra's son-in-law.

3 Iacopo di Lionardo Strozzi was Matteo's second cousin with whom he had business dealings.

4 A friend of the family. Granello's father had been exiled in 1434.

5 Perhaps Lodovico di Francesco di Benedetto Strozzi, a distant relative.

6 Niccolò di Lionardo Strozzi was Matteo's second cousin with whom he had business dealings.

you have a mind to send it, you may have waited too long to buy it and won't have it as cheaply as you would have a month ago. Nor will you have as good a price for whoever ships it to me as a month ago when Favilla, the carter, promised to bring it to me without charge. Now I don't know what we'll do. Let me know how far you've gotten.

I've had letters from Rome from Andrea Bizeri saying he had sent you some fennel. You must have had it by now. Let him know so he can thank the person who sent it to you.

They say the king has returned there (to Naples). Tell me about it. May God send us peace everywhere.

Do write Lorenzo, who tells me it has been a good while since he's had news of you. Just write him a couple of lines, and remind him to do the right thing, because it always gets you farther.

The *morìa* (epidemic) is doing a good deal of harm here, with four or five a day [dying]. The 29th of last month they were saying that eleven had died of the plague *(segno)*. This is bad news for us, who have no way to flee. May it please God to provide for our needs.

You should know that a little house belonging to Messer Palla[1] has been sold in the Comune to Niccolò d'Arnolfo Popoleschi. The house abuts our own on two sides: it's on the corner of the back street—that is, between the stables and our own ground floor back room. The wall of the house gives onto our courtyard. On the right as you come into the courtyard there's our old house, next to the back entrance there's our stable, as you know, and on the left there's the wall of that house. Now Niccolò Popoleschi has resold it to Donato Rucellai, Giovanni's brother,[2] and he has advised me that I have to give written consent for him to buy the house since he cannot draw up a contract without my consent because the only contiguous property is mine. I have answered him that I am aware that I have right of first refusal, that I wanted to write to my in-laws and to you, and that what you decide to do we will do. Let me tell you that if I had ready money it wouldn't get out of my hands. On the other hand, if someone

else buys it and should decide to build a wall, it would cut off all the light from our ground floor kitchen, our courtyard, and all the land behind. This house would be worth nothing if the courtyard lost its sunlight. This is why I wanted to write you. Please show this part to Niccolò, who will understand better and remember the little house better than you. It should cost around 70 *fiorini* since it gets a rent of six *fiorini*. I can't write you the exact price because he sold it along with the house owned by Monna Maddalena—or rather the Conte di Poppi[3]—so the house has no set price of its own but will be priced in proportion to the rent. And if I am in 1450 as I am in 1448, I wouldn't let it slip out of my hands, but I would pay for it with the money we will have coming from the city. It would improve this house enormously. I don't say this for myself, as I have little time left to live, but for all of you and your children. It wouldn't take much work, and that little house would really improve this one and make it the handsomest house in the neighborhood. I wouldn't have neglected writing you about it for anything in the world. Let me hear your thoughts, and don't forget to show this to Niccolò, who will understand it all better than you. May God grant you his grace. Nothing more for now. God save you from harm. From your Alessandra in Florence.

We are all well, thank God.

## Letter 8

To Filippo degli Strozzi in Naples
In the name of God, 6 November 1450

I wrote you the 28th of last month and sent the letter by Bartolommeo Seragli, who I know will use it well. Since then I have had yours of the 10th of last month. This will be my answer to it, and to several other letters that you wrote me some time ago but that I didn't answer for lack of a trustworthy carrier.

First, I am sending you four shirts, six handkerchiefs, and a towel, all well wrapped as you shall see, by Favilla, the carter, who owes us about 2 *ducati*. The shirts are cut and sewn in our style and the handkerchiefs and the towel are as we do them here. I didn't

1 Messer Palla di Nofri Strozzi, relative, and a leading political figure as well as the wealthiest citizen of Florence before his exile in 1434.

2 The Rucellai were a prominent, wealthy family. Giovanni Rucellai had married Palla Strozzi's daughter in 1428.

3 Francesco de' Conti Guidi was Conte di Poppi, a fortified town in the mountains east of Florence.

make any more shirts because I don't know if you will like them, and the same with the other things. If they aren't to your liking, I can use them for my Matteo, and if you do like them, let me know what you want and I'll send it to you. If God gives me another year to live and if Lesandra leaves home [i.e., marries] I'll fill your house with linens and you'll be in fine shape. Really, as long as there are young girls in the house, you do nothing but work for them, so when she leaves I will have no one to attend to but you three. And when I get the house in a little better shape I would love it if you could think about coming home. You would have no cause to be ashamed with what there is now, and you could do honor to any friend who dropped in to see you at home. But two or three years from now it will all be much better. And I would love to get you a wife: you're of an age now to know how to manage the help and to give me some comfort and consolation. I have none, unless it is living in the hope of [consolation] from you and the others. May God in his mercy grant me my wish. When Niccolò was here he told me he wanted you to come back here soon and to have you take a wife. [He said] that they [Niccolò and his brother Iacopo, with whom Lorenzo was living] would help you get started so you could stay here (since they prefer that you work for them than someone else), and that they would do enough for you to make me consider myself very happy. [He said] all sorts of things that showed he loves you dearly, and to be sure, I think that he will do great things for you if you do well in the office (stanza) he opened in Barcelona and give him good reason to praise you. God give him grace to do so.

In a letter you wrote me some time ago you said that Messer Gianzzo,[1] who was ambassador there [in Naples], told you he wanted me to give Caterina to Franco's brother and that I was unwilling to do so. This is true; I was advised not to by someone who has our interests at heart. Although he is Franco's brother, he doesn't have half of Franco's qualities, which I don't have to spell out for you. And when a man puts himself in the hands of the gran maestri [roughly, big cheeses] and asks their advice, he had better do what they say, for better or for worse. If you don't, they say what Messer Giannozzo said to you. When Niccolò was here,

[Giannozzo] brought someone who doesn't ever spend a penny and does nothing to see me about Lesandra, and he urged me to give her to him. Niccolò can tell you all about it. I know that Giannozzo took it badly, and that's why he told you what he did. I plan to do my very best to give him [i.e., the daughter's eventual husband] a good amount of capital (capitate) so that he can accomplish something. I told Giovanni [della] Luna[2] and Antonio degli Strozzi as much; and if we can marry her well, I would be happy to add one or two hundred fiorini to the thousand she has in the Monte.[3] As long as he's a person who deserves her and who can help her and be good to her. If not, I don't want to spend a penny more than she has. For the moment, there's nothing promising on hand: when there is, you will be notified. May God have good fortune in store for her. When you write to Giovanni della Luna and Antonio Strozzi, put in a word for her, and with Marco too.

I think that if Agnolo can walk that far, old as he is, he will come to see you. He wants to, and I begged him to. If he comes, ask him about our affairs, and he'll be able to tell you everything because he takes care of everything for us. I'm giving him two fiorini larghi for his expenses from Rome to Naples, so when he heads back, make sure he has spending money and has good traveling companions. Otherwise he will stay too many days in Rome and come with Favilla. Also through Favilla I'm sending you four pair of lovely marzolini [fresh Tuscan sheep cheeses]. I sent you four others the 5th of this month by a carter that Avveduto in the Customs offices was sending down. I wasn't told the carter's name, but I'm sure he will gives good service. With the sack, they weighed a good fifteen pounds. There's nothing owing for the cartage. Here I gave him

---

1 Gianozzo Manetti. A friend of the family and leading humanist.

2 A prominent family and friends of the Strozzi, the Della Luna lived in Alessandra's neighborhood in Florence.

3 Alessandra is referring to the Monte delle doti or dowry fund. Established by the city of Florence in 1425, it provided dowries to girls for whom a premium had been paid into the fund. Payment of the dowry was actually made to the husband only after he had presents proof of consummation of marriage. Lesandra (Alessandra) di Matteo Strozzi was enrolled in the fund in 1438 when she was four years old. In 1450 she was married to Giovanni di Donato Bonsi who received 1,000 florins from the fund in partial payment of Lesandra's dowry.

one *grosso* for the customs, and I promised to write you to pay him something. Francesco di Batista[1] hasn't come back: I am sending you this *marzolino* for two people so as to avoid paying cartage. I would like you to send me by Favilla, if you have a chance, twenty pounds of almonds and ten pounds of capers, if they are ripe there. Favilla will bring me as much as thirty pounds without charge. Do it so I can have them for Lent.

As I told you in another letter, I had 154 pounds of flax (with the sack) from Giovanni Lorini—that is, twenty bunches of the coarse and nine of the finer. To tell you the truth, it was no less expensive than the first batch you sent me, which was 125 pounds and of which I still have several bunches left.

You know that some time ago I bought Cateruccia, our slave, and for several years now, though I haven't laid a hand on her, she has behaved so badly toward me and the children that you wouldn't believe it if you hadn't seen it. Our Lorenzo could tell you all about it. Matteo too, if it please God he come here, will tell you the truth of her behavior with us. I've always suffered it because I can't chastise her, and besides I thought you would come once a month so that we could come to a decision together or she could be brought to better obedience. For several months now she has been saying and is still saying that she doesn't want to stay here, and she is so moody that no one can do a thing with her. If it weren't for love of Lesandra, I would have told you to sell her, but because of her malicious tongue, I want to see Lesandra safely out of the house first. But I don't know if I can hold out that long: mark my words, I'm going to get her out of my sight because I don't want this constant battle. She pays no more attention to me than if I were the slave and she were the mistress, and she threatens us all so that Lesandra and I are both afraid of her. My Zanobi is coming back here with me. She doesn't want him and is having fits, but I have decided that he will stay with me as part of the staff here. Plus, here he has some supervision, for in Antella he was by himself and was having a hard time of it. So I have brought him with me. He's not the man to chastise her. I'd like her to have a good beating, but he wouldn't do it. Thus, seeing how she is, don't be surprised if I make up my mind to it myself, as I will do anything to live in peace. I beg you with all my might that on Niccolò's

return you take a leave for two months. I don't say this because of the slave woman, but for my own pleasure, as I think I will die of this yearning to see you. I thought of coming to Rome for the Jubilee[2] and to see you, but now, for Lesandra's sake, I don't want to leave here until she's settled. But be sure that if I had gone to Rome and you hadn't come, I think I would have gone all the way to Naples to see you. So do what you can to get Niccolò to give you leave, and come see me.

You have perhaps heard of Soldo's[3] death—God pardon him—and what a great shame it was. I went to pay a call on his wife, and she asked again and again to be remembered to Niccolò and to you, since you have all of Soldo's papers and account books in your hands and since there's so much money owed him [in Naples] that they would like to collect. She talked and talked. She has named Niccolò as her agent to collect it. Try to help those poor orphans; they're poorly off, and it's a work of charity. Put in a word for her with Niccolò when he gets back, and may God give them a good voyage.

You should know that Macigno di Giovacchino[4] has taken to wife the daughter of Agostino Capponi,[5] Luca Capponi's sister. She's a widow and has had two husbands but she is twenty-four years old with a dowry of a thousand *fiorini*. God give them long life.

Let me know which *marzolino* is best, the little one or the big one, so I'll know which to get for the coming year (and will send you in due time). Nothing else for this time. God save you from harm. From your Alessandra in Florence.

---

[1] The editors cannot identify this person.

[2] The practice of celebrating a Jubilee or Holy Year, when pilgrims flocked to Rome with a view to the Jubilee indulgence, began in 1300 with the pontificate of Boniface VIII. Before 1470 the Holy Year was celebrated every fifty years.

[3] Soldo di Bernardo Strozzi worked in Naples, where he was associated with Niccolò di Lionardo Strozzi.

[4] Macigno di Giovacchino was Alessandra's cousin.

[5] The Capponi were a socially and politically prominent family.

## Letter 17

To Filippo degli Strozzi in Naples
In the name of God, 6 September 1459

My dear, sweet son. The 11th of last month I had your letter of 29 July saying that my dear and beloved Matteo was down with some sickness, and not knowing from you what disease it was, the letter much distressed me and I was terribly afraid for him. I called on Francesco, and I sent [for word] through Matteo di Giorgio, and I heard from both of them that he had a tertian fever [usually, malaria]. This relieved me a good deal, since people don't die of a tertian fever unless some other sickness is added to it. Since then, I have been informed by you that his sickness was abating, which relieved my mind a bit, though I still was afraid for him. I heard after that on the 23rd it pleased Him who gave him to me to call him to Himself, in full presence of mind, in good grace, and with all the sacraments required of a good and faithful Christian. This was a bitter blow for me to be deprived of such a son, and I feel I have suffered a great loss in his death in more than his filial love. You, my other two sons, reduced to such a; small number as you are, [have suffered just as great a loss]. I praise and thank Our Lord for all that is of His will, and I am sure God took care of the salvation of his soul. I see from what you wrote me how well you are accepting this bitter, hard death, and I have heard as much from letters from others there. Although this has grieved my heart more than anything else ever has, I have taken comfort in two things. The first is that he was close to you, and I am sure that doctors, medicines, and whatever it was possible to do for his salvation as well as all available remedies were tried, and that no stone was left unturned to keep him in life. Nothing could have helped him because this was God's will. The other thought from which I have taken comfort is that Our Lord graced him with the strength, on the point of death, to give up his sins and request confession, communion, and extreme unction. I hear that he did all this with devotion, and all these are signs of hope that God has prepared a good place for him. For this reason, and knowing full well we all have to take that road, we know not how, and cannot be sure of doing so with as much grace as my Matteo (for some die of a sudden death and some are cut to pieces, so many die losing both body and soul), I am at peace when I consider that God could do much worse for me. If by His grace and mercy He leaves me you, my two sons, I will not add to my affliction. My only thought is to hear that you are not taking it too hard. It has undoubtedly been a terrible blow to you. But take care not to grieve to the point that it harms you: we don't want to throw the handle out with the broom. We have nothing to reproach ourselves for as far as his care is concerned. Quite the contrary, it was by the will of God that he left the tribulations of this care-laden world. I can see in your [letter] of the 26th that this has much afflicted both your mind and your body, which has grieved me so much (and still grieves me) that it threatens to do me harm, and I will continue to grieve until I have letters from you [saying] you have been consoled. May it please God that I not live long enough to go through another [sorrowful event] like this one! It seems to me that after having been upset by these bad nights and had the melancholy of his death and of other things, you must not be in very good health. I turn this thought over in my head so much day and night that I can't get any rest. I wish I hadn't asked anyone's advice and instead had done what seemed best to me and what I wanted to do. I would have arrived in time to have seen my dearest son alive and touched him, and I would have consoled him, and you, and taken consolation from him. I want to think it was all for the best. I beg you (if my prayers mean anything to you, as I think they do) to arm yourself with patience for love of me and to look after your health and put aside company business for a while. It would also be a good idea to purge yourself a bit, though with light things and particularly with some medicine, and then get some fresh air if you possibly can. Remember that your health should be dearer to you than material possessions since, as you see, all is left behind! And I, a mother laden with cares, what would I do without you? What does it mean to me to know you are making good money if it ruins your health with all these hardships and cares? It grieves me, my son, that I'm not near you to take some of these troublesome things off your hands. You should have told me the first day Matteo fell sick so I could have jumped on a horse and been there in just a few days. But I know that you didn't do it for fear I would get sick or would be put to trouble. But I have more trouble in my mind than it would have been for my body. Now God be praised for everything, and I will take it as all for the best.

I have been told that in the honors you arranged for the burial of my son you did honor to yourself as well as to him. You did all the better to pay him such honor there, since here they don't usually do anything for those who are in your condition [i.e., in exile]. Thus I am pleased that you did so. Here these two girls, who are unconsolable over the death of their brother, and I have gone into mourning, and because I had not yet gotten the woolen cloth to make a mantle for myself, I have gotten it now and I will pay for it. It will take thirteen *braccia* of cloth for each of them and will cost, in cash, 4¼ *fiorini* the *canna* [roughly 3 meters], or 6½ *canne* in all. I will have this paid to Matteo di Giorgio and you will hear from him about it.

I have seen a copy of his will, and it would be a good idea to carry out [the provisions] for the peace of his soul as quickly as possible. The rest can be done with more leisure. [There is one thing] I beg you to do and to let me know if there is anything I can do here: there is a sister here of the boy-servant you had here who is married but cannot go to her husband because she is in great poverty. I have mentioned her to you in other letters; but have never had an answer. Now that this has happened [e.g., Matteo's death], it would be good to help her and not fail her. [She needs] 15 *fiorini* in all. And in case [Matteo's estate] is less than that, we could take it and add the rest, from my money or from yours, which amounts to the same if any event. Be aware of this, and advise me how much it [Matteo's estate] if and what we can do.

I see that Niccolò was sick with the tertian fever, which added to my sorrow in many ways. May it please God in his mercy to liberate him from it.

I have had a letter from Messer Giannozzo, out of the kindness of his heart exhorting me with great charity to be patient and [citing me] a great number of examples. It has given me great comfort to see the affection and love he bears you. May God reward him for it. I do not feel strong enough (*di tale virtù*) to answer a man as important as he, so I won't, but will you please thank him for me [as warmly] as you can. Let me know, and often how you feel, and may God grant me what I wish. Although I was used to adversities in the past, these weigh heavily on me. Again, thank Bernardo de' Medici with a letter, because I can't tell you how lovingly he came to pay me a visit and console me and how much our loss and our trials grieve him. I will say no more now to avoid boring you, except that I am waiting for your letters to hear that you are taking comfort and are well. May the blessed Jesus concede us this grace, as I pray. From your poor little mother in Florence.

### Letter 65

To Filippo degli Strozzi, in Naples
In the name of God, 11 January 1465

I last wrote you the 4th. I have since [received] yours of the 28th of last month, and I can see that you write me more to give me the happiness of having your letters than out of need to write. This gives me great pleasure, now that-I cannot see you in person. I thank God for everything, which is perhaps for the best. To answer your letter:

I told you in my other [letter] what happened about 60,[1] and there's nothing new there. And you have been advised that there is no talk of 59[2] until we have placed the older girl. 13[3] believes we should do nothing further until we can see our way clearly concerning these two and see what way they will go. Considering their age, this shouldn't take too long. It's true that my wish would be to see both of you with a companion, as I have told you many times before. That way when I die I would think you ready to take the step all mothers want—seeing their sons married—so your children could enjoy what you have acquired with enormous effort and stress over the long years. To that end I have done my very best to keep up the little I have had, foregoing the things that I might have done for my soul's slake and for that of our ancestors. But for the hope I have that you will take a wife (in the aim of having children) I am happy to have done so. So what I would like would be what I told you. Since then I have heard what Lorenzo's wants are and how he was willing to take her to keep me happy, but that he would be just as glad to wait two years before binding himself to the lady. I have thought a good deal

---

1    The daughter of Francesco Tanagli.

2    A nubile woman who was perhaps a member of the Adimari family.

3    Marco Parenti.

about the matter, and it seems to me that since nothing really advantageous to us is available, and since we have time to wait these two years, it would be a good idea to leave it at that unless something really unexpected turns up. Otherwise, it doesn't seem to me something that requires immediate thought, particularly considering the stormy times we live in these days, when so many young men on this earth are happy to inhabit it without taking a wife. The world is in a sorry state, and never has so much expense been loaded on the backs of women as now. No dowry is so big that when the girl goes out she doesn't have the whole of it on her back, between silks and jewels. So we here cannot do him much good. Although I have not written anything to him about it, I am not searching around for anything for him, and we were waiting [to see] whether either of the two possibilities turns out to be for you. If 60 works out well, we could sound out the possibility of the other girl for him. There's good forage there if they were to give her, and at any [other] time it would have been a commendable move. As things are going now, it seems to me better to wait and see a while for him. Furthermore, according to what he writes me in all his letters, he is willing to wait two more years. With luck that will be all, and maybe by then people will have calmed down. This way something may come of it, and they will not offer a wife without money, as people are doing now, since it seems superfluous to those who are giving 50[1] to give her a dowry. 13 wrote you that 60's father touched on the matter with him in the way I wrote you about. He says that you should leave it to us to see to it and work it out. For my part, I've done my diligent best, and I can't think what more I could have done—for your consolation more than my own. My time is short, and yours should by rights be long. May it so please God. Marco is still looking out for you both diligently. May God make it all work out for the best. And tell Lorenzo to put his mind at ease as far as a wife is concerned.

Niccolò has gone out of office *(uscì)*, and although he did some good things, they weren't the ones I would have wanted. Little honor has been paid to him or to the other outgoing magistrates, either when they were in office, or now that they have stepped down. Our scrutineer[2] was quite upset about it, as were we, but I feel that what was done will collapse, and it is thought they will start fresh. This Signoria has spent days in deliberations, and no one can find out anything about them. They have threatened to denounce whoever reveals anything as a rebel, so things are being done in total secrecy. I have heard that 58[3] is everything and 54[4] doesn't stand a chance. For the moment, it looks to me as if they will get back to 56[5] in the runoffs *(ne' primi termini)*, if things continue to go as now. May God, who can do all, set this city right, for it is in a bad way. Niccolò went in proudly and then lost heart—as 14's[6] brother said, "He went in a lion and he will go out a lamb," and that's just what happened to him. When he saw the votes were going against him, he began to humble himself. Now, since he left office he goes about accompanied by five or six armed men for fear of the counts of Maremma27 or others. It would have been better for him if [he had never been elected], for he would never have made so many enemies.

You were advised of the 14 *fiorini* I had from the bank 5 November, and you answered me about them that same month.

Tell Giovacchino that on the 4th of this month I received the load of flax for the sisters. It came so late that I had already sealed my letter, so I didn't acknowledge it. I have since undone [the package]: there are 12 bundles. I have given four to that sister from [the convent of] San Domenico, I am waiting for the sister from Santa Marta to send for another four, and another four [are for] the sister from Polverosa. I expect them to send for it at any moment. I haven't weighed it, but each of them gets four bundles. They will let me know the weight. Included here is a letter from the sister from San Domenico. Give it to [Giovacchino], and when the others write I will send him [their letters].

I don't know what else to tell you. You must have heard of the new family alliances *(parentado)*: Messer Piero de' Pazzi's daughter and Braccio Martegli and

---

1   That is, a woman from an exiled family.

2   *Squittinante:* A member of a committee that periodically determined (scrutinized) the eligibility of candidates for office.

3   The Medici.

4   The Pitti. They were allies of the Medici.

5   The brother of Antonio Pucci. The Pucci were allies of the Medici.

6   Tommaso Soderini.

Antonio and Priore Pandolfini. Both girls have two thousand in dowry. Messer Piero's [daughter] has one eye that doesn't see well. I haven't heard a thing about Gianfrancesco's28 girl [granddaughter] here, but I hear from Pierantonio that she will be given in Mantua to Messer Benedetto Strozzi's son. I don't know where he heard it. Giovanni di ser Francesco told me the same thing when he returned. They should send news of this [to Naples], and if it turns out not to be true, think about having Niccolo Strozzi touch on the matter with Giovanfrancesco for 45,29 if you think it appropriate. Although I doubt that she would deign [to marry] so low, still, it sometimes happens that you look in places that in other times you wouldn't have dreamed of, by the force of events—deaths or other misfortunes. So think about it. Nothing else for now. God save you from harm. From your Alessandra Strozzi, Florence.

## MACHIAVELLI, *DISCOURSES ON THE FIRST TEN BOOKS OF TITUS LIVIUS*

Niccolò Machiavelli to Zanobi Buondelmonti and Cosimo Rucellai,[1] greetings.

I am sending you a gift which, even though it may not match the obligations I have to you, is, without a doubt, the best that Niccolò Machiavelli can send to you; in it I have expressed all I know and all that I have learned from long experience and continuous study of worldly affairs. And since it |s not possible for you or anyone else to ask more of me, you cannot complain if I have not given you more. You may very well complain about the poverty of my wit when my arguments are weak, and about the fallacious quality of my judgment if, in the course of my reasonings, I often manage to deceive myself. This being the case, I do not know which of us should be less obliged to the other: whether I should be so to you, who have

encouraged me to write, what I never would have written by myself, or you to me, since I may have written without satisfying you. Take this, then, as you would accept something from a friend: there one considers the intention of the sender more than the quality of the thing which is sent. And rest assured that in this venture I have one consolation, for I believe that although I may have deceived myself in many of its particulars, in one matter I know that I have not made an error; that is, to have chosen you above all others to whom I should dedicate these *Discourses* of mine, both because in so doing I believe that I have shown my gratitude for the benefits I have received and because I felt that I had departed from the common practice of those who write and always address their works to some prince and, blinded by ambition and by avarice, praise him for all his virtuous qualities when they ought to be blaming him for all his bad qualities. So, to avoid this mistake, I have chosen not those who are princes but those who, because of their numerous good qualities, deserve to be princes; not those who might shower me with offices, honors, and wealth, but those who, although unable, would like to do so. If men wish to judge correctly, they must esteem those who are generous, not those who are potentially generous; and, in like manner, they must esteem those who know how to rule a kingdom, not those who, without knowing how, have the power to do so. Thus, historians praise Hiero the Syracusan[2] more when he was a private citizen than they do Perseus of Macedonia[3] when he was king: for Hiero lacked nothing to be prince save a kingdom, while the other had no attribute of a king except his kingdom. Therefore, enjoy this good or bad work which you yourselves have requested; and if you persist in erroneously finding pleasure in my opinions, I shall not fail to follow this with the rest of the history, as I promised you in the beginning. Farewell.

---

1 Associates of Machiavelli in the city's chief literary circle in the Rucellai Gardens; they were implicated in a plot against the Medici regime in 1523.

2 King of Syracuse (Sicily), 265–215 B.C.
3 The last king of Macedon (179-168 B.C.), son of Philip V.

Niccolo Machiavelli; ed. and trans. by Peter Bondella and Mark Musa, *The Portable Machiavelli*, pp. 168-171, 175-181, 193-196, 200-213, 281-290, Copyright © 1979 Penguin USA. Permission to reprint granted by the publisher.

# BOOK I

## Introduction

Because of the envious nature of men, it has always been no less dangerous to discover new methods and institutions than to explore unknown oceans and lands, since men are quicker to criticize than to praise the deeds of others. Nevertheless, driven by that natural desire I have always felt to work on whatever might prove beneficial to everyone, I have determined to enter a path which has not yet been taken by anyone. Although it may bring me worry and difficulty, yet I may find my reward among those who study kindly the goal of these labors of mine. And if my feeble intelligence, my limited experience of current events, and my weak knowledge of ancient ones[1] should make this attempt of mine defective and of little use, it may, at least, show the way to someone with more ability, more eloquence, and more judgment who will be able to fulfill my intention; so that if I do not earn praise, I should not receive blame.

When we consider, then, how much honor is attributed to antiquity, and how many times (leaving aside numerous other examples) a fragment of an ancient statue has been bought at a great price so that the buyer may have it near him to decorate his house or to have it imitated by those who take pleasure in that art; and when we see, on the other hand, the powerful examples which history shows us that have been accomplished by ancient kingdoms and republics, by kings, captains, citizens, and legislators who have exhausted themselves for their fatherland, examples that have been more often admired than imitated (or so much ignored that not the slightest trace of this ancient ability remains), I cannot but be at the same time both amazed and sorry. And I am even more amazed when I see that in civil disputes which arise among citizens, or in sicknesses that break out, men always have recourse to those judgments or remedies which were pronounced or prescribed by the ancients. For civil law is nothing other than the judgments given by ancient jurists which, organized into a system, instruct our jurists today. Nor is medicine anything other than the experiments carried out by ancient doctors on which the doctors of today base

---

1  A paraphrase of the corresponding passage in the dedication to *The Prince*.

their diagnoses. Nevertheless, in instituting republics, maintaining states, governing kingdoms, organizing the army and administering a war, dispensing justice to subjects, and increasing an empire one cannot find a prince or a republic that has recourse to the examples of the ancients.

This, in my opinion, arises not so much from the weakness into which the present religion has brought the world or from the harm done to many Christian provinces and cities by an idle ambition as from not possessing a proper knowledge of histories, for in reading them we do not draw out of them that sense or taste that flavor which they have in themselves. Hence it happens that an infinite number of people read them and take pleasure in hearing about the variety of incidents which are contained in them without thinking to imitate them, for they consider imitation not only difficult but impossible; as if the heavens, the sun, the elements, and men had varied in their motion, their order, and their power from what they were in ancient times. Wishing, therefore, to free men of this erroneous way of thinking, I deemed it necessary to write about all those books by Livy which the malignity of time has not taken from us; I wish to write what I, according to my knowledge of ancient and modern affairs, judge necessary for a better understanding of them, so that those who read these statements of mine may more easily draw from them that practical knowledge one should seek from an acquaintance with history books. And although this undertaking is difficult, nevertheless, aided by those who have encouraged me to shoulder this burden, I believe I can carry it in such a manner that only a short distance will remain for another to bring it to the destined goal.

## Chapter 2.
## Of How Many Kinds of Republics There Are and of What Kind the Roman Republic Was

I wish to put aside a discussion of those cities which, at their beginnings, were subject to others; and I shall speak about those which have had their beginnings far from any foreign servitude and have been governed from the beginning by their own judgment, either as republics or as principalities, and which have had different laws and institutions just as they have had different origins. Some of them, either at their start or after very little time, were given laws by a single man and at one time, as Lycurgus did with the Spartans; others acquired their laws by chance, at different times and according to circumstances, as occurred in Rome. A republic can, indeed, be called fortunate if it produces a man so prudent that he gives it laws organized in such a manner that it can live securely under them without needing to revise them. And it seems that Sparta observed its laws more than eight hundred years without corrupting them or without any dangerous upheaval. Unfortunate, on the contrary, is the city which is forced to reorganize itself, not having chanced to encounter a prudent organizer. And of these cities, the one which is the furthest from order is the most unfortunate; and that one is furthest from it which in its institutions is completely off the straight path which could lead it to its perfect and true goal, because for those who find themselves in this state it is almost impossible that by any happening they can be set on the right path again. Those other cities that have had a good beginning and are capable of becoming better, even if they have not had a perfect constitution, can, by means of an unexpected course of events, become perfect. But it is very true that institutions are never established without danger; for most men never agree to a new law that concerns a new order in the city unless a necessity demonstrates to them that it is required; and since this necessity cannot arise without danger, the republic may easily be destroyed before it is brought to a perfection of organization. The Republic of Florence testifies to this: reorganized after what occurred at Arezzo in 1502, it was disorganized by what occurred at Prato in 1512.[1]

Since I wish to discuss what the institutions of the city of Rome were and the circumstances which led to their perfection, let me say that those who have written about republics declare that there are in them three kinds of governments, which they call principality, aristocracy, and democracy; and that those who organize a city most often turn to one of these, depending upon whichever seems more appropriate to them. Others—and wiser men, according to the judgment of many—are of the opinion that there are six types of government: three of these are very bad; three others are good in themselves but are so easily corruptible

that they, too, can become pernicious. Those which are good are the three mentioned above; those which are bad are three others which depend upon the first three, and each of them is, in a way, similar to its good counterpart, so that they easily jump from one form to another. For the principality easily becomes tyrannical; aristocrats can very easily produce an oligarchy; democracy is converted into anarchy with no difficulty. So that if a founder of a republic organizes one of these three governments in a city, he organizes it there for a brief period of time only, since no precaution can prevent it from slipping into its contrary on account of the similarity, in such a case, of the virtue and the vice.

These variations of government are born among men by chance: for in the beginning of the world, when its inhabitants were few, they lived at one time dispersed and like wild beasts; then, when their numbers multiplied, they gathered together and, in order to defend themselves better, they began to search among themselves for one who was stronger and braver, and they made him their leader and obeyed him. From this sprang the knowledge of what things are good and honorable, as distinct from the pernicious and the evil: for if someone were to harm his benefactor, this aroused hatred and compassion among men, since they cursed the ungrateful and honored those who showed gratitude; and thinking that the same injuries could also be committed against themselves, they made laws to avoid similar evils and instituted punishments for transgressors. Thus, the recognition of justice came about. The result was that, later on, when they had to elect a prince, they did not select the bravest man but rather the one who was most prudent and most just. But when they began to choose the prince by hereditary succession rather than by election, the heirs immediately began to degenerate from the level of their ancestors and, putting aside acts of valor, they thought that princes had nothing to do but to surpass other princes in luxury, lasciviousness, and in every other form of pleasure. So, as the prince came to be hated he became afraid of this hatred and quickly passed from fear to violent deeds, and the immediate result was tyranny.

From this there came next the destructions, the conspiracies, and the plots against princes, carried out not by those who were either timid or weak but by those who surpassed others in generosity, greatness of spirit, wealth, and nobility: these men could not stand

---

1 Cf. Luca Landucci, *Diary*, in this volume, pp. 162–66 and 166–71.

the disreputable life of such a prince. The masses, therefore, following the authority of these powerful men, took up arms against the prince, and after he had been eliminated they obeyed those men as their liberators. And since those men hated the very idea of a single ruler, they constituted for themselves a government; and in the beginning, since they remembered the past tyranny, they governed according to the laws instituted by themselves, subordinating their own interests to the common good, and they managed and maintained both their private and public affairs with the greatest of care. When this administration later passed to their sons, who did not understand the change ability of Fortune, had never experienced bad times, and could not be satisfied with equality among citizens, they turned to avarice, ambition, and the violation of other men's women, and they caused a government of the aristocrats to become a government of the few, with no regard to any civil rights; so that in a short time they experienced the same fate as the tyrant for as the masses were sick of their rule, they assisted, in any way the cold, anyone who might plan to attack these rulers, and thus there soon arose someone who, with the aid of the masses, destroyed them. And since the memory of the prince and of the injuries received from him was still fresh, they turned to a democratic form of government, having destroyed the government ruled by a few men and not wishing to return to that ruled by a prince; and they organized it in such a way that neither the few powerful men nor a prince might have any authority whatsoever in it. And because all governments are, at the outset, respected, this democratic government was maintained awhile, but not for a long time, particularly after the generation that organized it passed away; it immediately turned to anarchy, where neither the individual citizen nor the public official is feared; each individual lived according to his own wishes, so that every day a thousand wrongs were done; and so, constrained by necessity, either because of the suggestion of some good man or in order to flee such anarchy, it returned again to the principality; and from that, step by step, the government moved again in the direction of anarchy, in the manner and for the reasons just given.

And this is the cycle through which all states that have governed themselves or that now govern themselves pass; but rarely do they return to the same forms of government, for virtually no state can possess so much vitality that it can sustain so many changes and remain on its feet. But it may well happen that while a state lacking counsel and strength is in difficulty, it becomes subject to a neighboring state which is better organized; but if that were not the case, then a state might be liable to pass endlessly through the cycle of these governments.

Let me say, therefore, that all the forms of government listed are defective: the three good ones because of the brevity of their lives, the three bad ones because of their inherent harmfulness. Thus, those who were prudent in establishing laws recognized this fact and, avoiding each of these forms in themselves, chose one that combined them all, judging such a government to be steadier and more stable, for when there is in the same city-state a principality, an aristocracy, and a democracy, one form keeps watch over the other.

Among those who have deserved great praise for having established such constitutions is Lycurgus, who organized his laws in Sparta in such a manner that, assigning to the king, the aristocrats, and the people their respective roles, he created a state which lasted more than eight hundred years, to his everlasting credit, and resulted in the tranquillity of that city. The contrary happened to Solon, who organized the laws in Athens: for in organizing only a democratic state there he made it of such a brief existence that before he died he saw arise the tyranny of Pisistratus; and although forty years later the latter's heirs were driven away and Athens returned to its freedom, having reestablished the democratic state according to the institutions of Solon, it did not last more than a hundred years. In spite of the fact that many laws which were not foreseen by Solon were established in Athens in order to restrain the insolence of the upper class for the anarchy of the populace, nevertheless Athens lived a very brief tone in comparison to Sparta, because Solon did not mix democracy with the power of the principality and with that of the aristocrats.

But let us come to Rome. In spite of the fact that she never had a Lycurgus to organize her at the beginning so that she might exist free for a long time, nevertheless, because of the friction between the plebeians and the senate, so many circumstances attended her birth that chance brought about what a lawgiver had not acomplished. If Rome did not receive Fortune's first gift, she received the second: for her early institutions, although defective, nevertheless did not deviate from the right path that could lead them to perfection. Romulus and all the other kings passed many good laws in accordance with a free government; but since their goal was to found a kingdom and not a republic, when that city became free she lacked many institutions which were necessary to organize her under freedom, institutions which had not been set up by those kings. And when it happened that kings lost their power for the reasons and in the ways described earlier, nonetheless those who drove them out, having immediately established two in place of the king, drove out only the title of king and not royal power; so that, as there were in that republic the consuls and the senate, it came to be formed by only two of the three above-mentioned elements, that is, the principality and the aristocrats. There remained only to make a for the democratic part of the government. When the Roman nobility became insolent, for the reasons that will be listed below, the people rose up against them; in order not to lose everything, the nobility was forced to concede to the people their own share; and on the other hand, the senate and the consuls retained enough authority so that they could maintain their rank in that republic. And thus there came about the creation of the tribunes of the plebeians, after which the government of the republic became more stable, since each of the three elements of government had its share. And Fortune was so favorable to Rome that even though she passed from a government by kings and aristocrats to one by the people, through those same steps and because of those same reasons which were discussed above, nevertheless the kingly authority was never entirely abolished to give authority to the aristocrats, nor was the authority of the aristocrats diminished completely to give it to the people; but since these elements remained mixed, Rome was a perfect state; and this perfection was produced through the friction between the plebeians and the senate, as the two following chapters will demonstrate at greater length.

## Chapter 7.
### How the Right to Bring Public Charges Is Necessary for a Republic to Preserve Its Liberty

No more useful and necessary authority can be granted to those who are appointed to preserve a city's liberty than the capacity to bring before the people or before some magistrate or council charges against citizens who sin in any manner against the freedom of the government. This institution produces two very useful results in a republic: first, for fear of being accused, the citizens do not attempt anything against the government, or, if they do, they are immediately suppressed without regard to their station; second, it provides an outlet for those hatreds which grow up in cities, in whatever manner, against some particular citizen: and when these hatreds do not find a legal means of expression, they have recourse to illegal means, which cause the eventual ruin of the entire republic. And so, nothing makes a republic so stable and strong as organizing it in such a way that the agitation of the hatreds which excite it has a means of expressing itself provided for by the laws. This can be demonstrated by many examples, and especially by that which Livy brings forth concerning Coriolanus,[1] where he says that since the Roman nobility was angered at the plebeians because they felt that the plebeians had assumed too much authority as a result of the creation of the tribunes, who were to defend them, and since it happened that Rome then suffered a great scarcity of provision and the senate had sent to Sicily for grain, Coriolanus, enemy of the popular faction, advised that the time had come to punish the plebeians by keeping them hungry and not distributing the grain, and by taking away from them the authority which they had usurped from the nobility. When this advice reached the ears of the people, they were so angry at him that he would have been murdered by the crowd as he left the senate if the tribunes had not called him to appear before them in his own defense. What was said above can be applied to this event—that is, that it is useful and necessary for republics to provide with their laws a means of expression for the wrath that the multitude feels against a single citizen, for when these legal means do not exist the people turn to illegal ones, and without a doubt the latter produce much worse effects than do the former.

---

1   Livy, 2.33–35.

For, when a citizen is legally oppressed, even if this be unjust to him, little or no disorder in the republic follows; for the execution of the act is done without private or foreign forces, which are the ones that destroy free government; but it is done with public forces and institutions which have their specific limits nor do they transcend these limits to damage the republic. And as for corroborating this opinion with examples, that of Coriolanus from the ancients should suffice. Everyone should observe how much evil would have resulted for the Roman republic if he had been put to death by the crowd, for this would have created private grievances, which generate fear, and fear seeks defenses for which partisans are recruited, and from partisans are born the factions in cities, and from factions the ruin of the city. But since the matter was handled by those who had the authority to do so, all those evils which might have arisen by using private power were avoided.

We have witnessed in our own times what changes occurred in the Republic of Florence when the people were not able to vent their wrath legally against one of its citizens, as was the case when Francesco Valori[1] was almost like the prince of that city. He was regarded by many as ambitious, a man who would transgress lawful government because of his audacity and hot temper; and since there was no means within the republic's existing institutions of resisting him without establishing a rival party, it came about that he set out to enlist partisans, not fearing anything but illegal methods; on the other hand, since those who opposed him had no legal way to suppress him, they turned to illegal methods and eventually resorted to arms. Given the proper legal institutions, he might have been opposed and his authority destroyed, harming only himself, but because he had to be destroyed unlawfully, this resulted in harm not only to him but also to many other noble citizens. One could also cite, in support of the above conclusion, the incident which happened in connection with Piero Soderini, which came about entirely from the absence in that republic of any means of bringing charges against the ambition of powerful citizens. For it is not enough to accuse a powerful citizen before eight judges in a republic; there must be many judges, for the few always act in favor of the few. If these methods had existed in Florence, either the citizens would have accused him if his conduct was bad—by this means, without calling in a Spanish army, they would have vented their anger—or, if his conduct was not bad, they would not have dared to act against him for fear that they themselves might be accused; and thus, in either case the appetite for conflict, which was the cause of the quarrel, would have vanished.

The following conclusion can be drawn: whenever one finds foreign forces being called in by one faction of men living in a city, it may be taken for granted that the bad ordinances of that city are the cause, for it does not have an institution that provides an outlet for the malignant humors which are born among men to express themselves without their resorting to illegal means; adequate provision for this is made by making a number of judges available before whom public indictments may be made; and these accusations must be given proper importance. These means were so well organized in Rome that during the many conflicts between the plebeians and the senate neither the senate nor the plebeians nor any private citizen ever attempted to use outside forces; for they had a remedy at home and there was no need to search for it outside. And although the above examples are more than sufficient to prove this, I nevertheless wish to use another taken from Livy's history: there he relates how in Chiusi, a city which in those times was one of the most noble in Tuscany, a certain Lucumones raped the sister of Aruntes; unable to revenge himself because of the power of the rapist, Aruntes went to meet with the Gauls, who at that time ruled in the area which is now called Lombardy, and persuaded them to come with troops to Chiusi, showing them how they would profit by avenging the injustice he had suffered; Livy further explains how Aruntes would not have sought barbarian troops if he had seen a way to avenge himself through the city's institutions. But just as public accusations are useful in a republic, so false accusations are useless and harmful, as the discussion in the next chapter will show.

---

1 The head of the pro-Savonarola party in the Florentine government between 1495 and 1498. The events mentioned below are described in detail in the *Diary* of Luca Landucci in this volume.

## Chapter 9.
## How a Man Must Be Alone in order to Found a New Republic or to Reform Completely Its Ancient Institutions

It may appear to some that I have gone too far along in Roman history without mentioning the founders of that republic or those institutions which are concerned with her religion and her militia; therefore, no longer wishing to keep the minds that wish to hear about this matter in suspense, let me say that many will perhaps judge it to be a bad example for a founder of a constitutional state, as Romulus was, to have first murdered his brother and then to have consented to the death of Titus Tatius, the Sabine, whom he had elected as his companion in his rule. Judging from this, the citizens might, out of ambition and a desire to rule, follow the example of their prince and oppress those who are opposed to their authority. This opinion might be correct, were we not to consider the goal that led Romulus to commit such a murder.

And this should be taken as a general rule: it rarely or never happens that a republic or kingdom is well organized from the beginning, or completely reformed, with no respect for its ancient institutions, unless it is done by one man alone; moreover, it is necessary that one man provide the means and be the only one from whose mind any such organization originates; therefore, a prudent founder of a republic, one whose intention it is to govern for the common good and not in his own interest, not for his heirs but for the sake of the fatherland, should try to have the authority all to himself; nor will a wise mind ever reproach anyone for some extraordinary action performed in order to found a kingdom or to institute a republic. It is, indeed, fitting that while the action accuses him, the result excuses him; and when this result is good, as it was with Romulus, it will always excuse him: for one should reproach a man who is violent in order to destroy, not one who is violent in order to mend things.

The founder should be so prudent and able-minded as not to bequeath the authority he has taken to his heir; for, since men are more apt to do evil than good, his successor might use for ambitious ends what the founder had employed virtuously. Besides this, though one man alone is fit for founding a government, what he has founded will not last long if it rests upon his shoulders alone; it is lasting when it is left in the care of many and when many desire to maintain it. As the many are not fit to organize a government, for they cannot recognize the best means of doing so because of the diversity of opinion among them, just so, when they have realized that they have it they will not agree to abandon it. And that Romulus was among those who deserve to be pardoned for the death of his brother and his companion, and that what he did was for the common good and not for private ambition, is demonstrated by the fact that he immediately organized a senate with whom he would consult and whose opinions he deliberated; and anyone who would examine carefully the authority that Romulus reserved for himself will see that all he kept for himself was the power to command the army during wartime and to convoke the senate. Later, when Rome became free as a result of the expulsion of the Tarquins, we can see that the city was not given any new institutions by the Romans besides their ancient ones, except that in place of a permanent king there were two yearly consuls: this testifies to the fact that all the original institutions were more suitable to a free, self-governing state than to one which was absolutist and tyrannical.

Numerous examples could be cited in support of what I have written above, such as Moses, Lycurgus, Solon, and other founders of kingdoms and republics who were able to form laws for the common good because they had taken sole authority upon themselves, but I shall omit them since they are well known; instead, I shall present only one example, not so well known but worthy of examination by those who wish to be the organizers of good laws, and the example is: Agis, King of Sparta, who wished to return the Spartans to the bounds within which the laws of Lycurgus had enclosed them, for he felt that, having departed from them, his city had lost much of its former ability and, as a result, much of its strength and empire; but at the start of his efforts he was assassinated by the Spartan Ephors as a man who wanted to become a tyrant. But when Cleomenes succeeded him on the throne, the same desire, after a time, arose in him as a result of reading the memoirs and writings of Agis which he had discovered, wherein he saw what his real intentions were, and he realized that he could not do this good for his country if he did not possess sole authority; for it seemed impossible, on account of man's ambition, for him to be able to help the many against the wishes of the few; so, when the right occasion arose he had all the Ephors killed and anyone else who might oppose him; then he completely restored the laws of Lycurgus. This action might have been enough to revive Sparta and to give Cleomenes the same reputation that Lycurgus had if it had not been for the power of the Macedonians and the weakness of the other Greek republics; for, after such institutions had been established, Cleomenes was attacked by the Macedonians, and when he discovered he was weaker in numbers and had nowhere to go for help, he was defeated.[1] This plan of his, no matter how just and praiseworthy it might have been, was not carried out.

Considering all these matters, then, I conclude that it is necessary to be alone in establishing a republic; and that, concerning the death of Remus and Titus Tatius, Romulus deserves to be excused, not blamed.

## Chapter 10.
### Those Who Found a Republic or a Kingdom Deserve as Much Praise as Those Who Found a Tyranny Deserve Blame

Among all praiseworthy men, the most praiseworthy are those who were leaders and founders of religions; next come those who founded either republics or kingdoms; after these the most celebrated men are those who, commanding armies, have increased either their own kingdom or that of their native land; next to these may be placed men of letters, who, since they are of various types, are each praised according to their merits. To other men, whose number is infinite, some portion of praise may be attributed according to the skill they possess in their art or profession. On the other hand, men who have destroyed religions, wasted kingdoms and republics, and have been enemies of virtue, letters, and every sort of profession that brings gain and honor to the human race—such as the impious, the violent, the ignorant, the useless, the lazy, and the wicked—are considered infamous and detestable; and no one will ever be so mad or so wise, so sorry or so good that, given the choice between the two kinds of men, he will not praise those who merit praise and blame those who deserve blame.

Nevertheless, in the end nearly all men, deceived by a false appearance of good and a false sense of glory, allow themselves, either by their own choice or through their ignorance, to join the ranks of those who deserve more blame than praise; and while they have the possibility of establishing, to their perpetual honor, either a republic or a kingdom, they turn instead to tyranny, not realizing how much fame, glory, honor, security, tranquillity, and peace of mind they are losing by such a decision and, on the other hand, how much infamy, vituperation, blame, danger, and unrest they incur.

And if they read histories and make use of the records of ancient affairs, it is impossible for those who have lived as private citizens in a republic or who have become princes either because of Fortune or ability not to wish to live, if they are private citizens, in their native land like Scipio rather than like Caesar and, if they are princes, to live like Agesilaus, Timoleon, and Dion rather than like Nabis, Phalaris, and Dionysius;[2] for they would see how the latter are soundly condemned while the former are praised most highly; they would also see how Timoleon and the others had no less authority in their native lands than Dionysius and Phalaris had, and that they enjoyed, by far, greater security for a longer time.

Nor should anyone be deceived by Caesar's glory, so very celebrated by historians, for those who praised him were corrupted by his good fortune and amazed by the duration of the empire which, ruled in his name, did not allow writers to speak freely about him. But anyone who wishes to know what free historians would say about him should examine what they say about Catiline. And Caesar is even more blameworthy, just as a man who has committed an evil deed is more to be blamed than one who has only wished to do so; moreover, let the reader see how Brutus is so highly praised, as though, unable to criticize Caesar because of his power, they praise his enemy instead.[3]

Furthermore, let any man who has become a prince in a republic consider how much more praise those emperors deserved who lived under the laws and as

---

1   222 B.C.

2   Agesilaus (400–c. 360 B.C.) was a king of Sparta; Timoleon and Dion overthrew the tyranny of Dionysius II, who had invited Plato to Syracuse; Nabis (206–192 B.C.) and Phalaris (570–555 B.C.) were tyrants respectively of Sparta and Agrigento.

3   The opposite judgment in *The Prince,* 16.

good princes after Rome had become an empire than those who lived the opposite way, and he will see how Titus, Nerva, Trajan, Hadrian, Antoninus [Pius], and Marcus [Aurelius] had no need of Praetorian guards nor a multitude of legions to defend themselves, for their customs, the goodwill of the people, and the love of the senate protected them; the prince will also see how the Eastern and Western armies were not sufficient for Caligula, Nero, Vitellius, and other evil emperors to save themselves from the enemies that their wicked customs and evil lives had created for them. And if the history of these men were studied carefully, it would serve as an excellent lesson to show any prince the path to glory or to censure, to his security or to his peril, for of the twenty-six emperors between Caesar and Maximinus, sixteen were murdered and ten died a natural death; and if among those who were murdered there were several good men, like Galba and Pertinax, they were killed by the corruption which their predecessors had left behind in their soldiers; and if among those who died a natural death there was a wicked man, like Severus, this was the result of his very great fortune and ability—a combination of two things which few men enjoy. A prince will also observe, through the lesson of this history, how one can organize a good kingdom: for all the emperors who assumed the imperial throne by birth, except for Titus, were bad, and those who became emperors by adoption were all good, as were the five from Nerva to Marcus; and when the empire fell into hereditary succession, it returned again to its ruin.

Therefore, let a prince examine the times from Nerva to Marcus [Aurelius], and let him compare them with those which came before and afterward, and then let him choose during which period he would wish to be born or in which period he would like to be made emperor. In the times when good emperors governed, he will see a ruler secure in the midst of his secure citizens, and a world of peace and justice; he will see a senate with its full authority, the magistrates with their honors, the rich citizens enjoying their wealth, the nobles and ability exalted, and he will find tranquillity and well-being in everything; and on the other hand, he will see all rancor, licentiousness, corruption, and ambition extinguished; he will see a golden age in which a man can hold and defend whatever opinion he wishes. He will, in the end, see the world rejoicing: its prince endowed with respect and glory, its peoples with love and security. If next he studies carefully the times of the other emperors, he will see them full of the atrocities of war, the conflicts of sedition, and the cruelties of both peace and war, so many princes put to death by the sword, so many civil wars, so many foreign wars, all of Italy afflicted and full of previously unknown adversities, and her cities ruined and sacked. He will see Rome burned, the Capitoline destroyed by her own citizens, her ancient temples desolate, her rituals corrupted, and the cities full of adulterous conduct; he will see the seas covered with exiles and the earth stained with blood. He will find countless cruelties in Rome and discover that nobility, wealth, past honors, and especially virtue are considered capital crimes. He will see the rewarding of those who accuse falsely, the turning of servants against their masters and freedmen against their former owners, and he will see those who, lacking enemies, are oppressed by their friends. And then he will well understand how many obligations Rome, Italy, and the world owe to Caesar!

And the prince, without a doubt, if he is a man, will be frightened away from any imitation of the bad times and will burn with an ardent desire to follow the ways of the good times. If a prince truly seeks worldly glory, he should hope to possess a corrupt city—not in order to ruin it completely as Caesar did but to reorganize it as Romulus did. And the heavens cannot truly bestow upon men a greater opportunity for obtaining glory than this, nor can men desire a greater one. And if a man who wanted to reorganize a city well had, of necessity, to renounce the principality in order to do so, he might merit some excuse if he did not reform it in order not to lose his rank; but if he were able both to retain his principality and to reform it, he would deserve no excuse whatsoever.

In conclusion, then, let those to whom the heavens grant such opportunities observe that there are two paths open to them: one allows them to live securely and makes them famous after death; the other makes them live in continuous anxiety and, after death, allows them to leave behind an eternal reputation of infamy.

## Chapter 11.
## The Religion of the Romans

Even though Rome found its first institution builder in Romulus and, like a daughter, owed her birth and her education to him, nevertheless, as the heavens judged that the institutions of Romulus would not suffice for so great an empire, they inspired the Roman senate to elect Numa Pompilius as Romulus's successor so that those matters not attended to by Romulus could be seen to by Numa. Numa found the Roman people most undisciplined, and since he wanted to bring them to civil obedience by means of the arts of peace, he turned to religion as an absolutely necessary institution for the maintenance of a civic government, and he established it in such a way that for many centuries never was there more fear of God than in that republic—a fact which greatly facilitated any undertaking that the senate or those great Romans thought of doing.

Anyone who examines the many actions of the Roman people as a whole and of many individual Romans will discover how these citizens were more afraid of breaking an oath than of breaking the laws, since they respected the power of God more than that of man: this is most evident in the examples of Scipio and of Manlius Torquatus. After the rout inflicted upon the Romans by Hannibal at the battle of Cannae, many of the citizens assembled and, despairing for their native land, agreed to abandon Italy and to go to Sicily; when Scipio heard about this, he went to them, and with his bare sword in hand he forced them to swear not to abandon their fatherland. Lucius Manlius, the father of Titus Manlius (afterward called Torquatus), was accused of a crime by Marcus Pomponius, tribune of the plebeians; before the day of the trial arrived Titus went to Marcus and threatened to kill him if he did not swear to remove the indictment against his father; and when Marcus swore to do so, he withdrew the charge out of fear.

In this manner, those citizens whose love for the fatherland or its laws could not have kept them in Italy were restrained by an oath which they were forced to take; and that tribune set aside the hatred he had for the father and the injury he had suffered from the son and his own honor in order to obey the oath he had taken—all this came about from nothing other than the religion which Numa had introduced into that city.

Thus, anyone who examines Roman history closely will discover how much religion helped in commanding armies, encouraging the plebeians, keeping men good, and shaming the wicked. And so, if one were to argue about which prince Rome was more indebted to—whether Romulus or Numa—I believe that Numa would most easily be first choice; for where there is religion it is easy to introduce arms, but where there are arms without religion the latter can be introduced only with difficulty. It is evident that Romulus did not find divine authority necessary to found the senate and other civil and military institutions, but it was necessary for Numa, who pretended to have a relationship with a nymph who advised him what to say to the people; the reason was that he wanted to establish new and unfamiliar institutions in the city, and he doubted that his own authority would be sufficient to do so.

Actually, there never existed a person who could give unusual laws to his people without recourse to God, for otherwise such laws would not have been accepted: for the benefits they bring, although evident to a prudent man, are not self-explanatory enough to be evident to others. Therefore, wise men who wish to avoid this difficulty have recourse to God. Lycurgus did this, as did Solon and many others who had the same goal. Since the Roman people were amazed at the goodness and the prudence of Numa, they yielded to his every decision. It is, of course, true that those times were very religious ones and that the men with whom he had to deal were unsophisticated, thereby giving him a great deal of freedom to follow his own plans and to be able to impress upon them easily any new form he wished. And, without any doubt, anyone wishing to establish a republic in our present day would find it easier to do so among mountaineers, where there is no culture, than among men who are accustomed to living in cities where culture is corrupt; in like manner, a sculptor can more easily carve a beautiful statue out of a rough piece of marble than he can from one poorly blocked out by someone else.

Having considered everything, then, I conclude that the religion introduced by Numa was among the most important reasons for the success of that city, for it brought forth good institutions, and good institutions led to good fortune, and from good fortune came the felicitous successes of the city's undertakings. And as the observance of religious teaching is the reason for the greatness of republics, in like manner the disdain of the practice is the cause of their ruin; for where the fear of God is lacking a kingdom must either come to ruin or be sustained by the fear of a prince who makes up for the lack of religion. And since princes are short-lived, it is most likely that a kingdom will fail as quickly as the abilities of its prince fail; thus, kingdoms which depend upon the ability of a single man cannot last long, for such ability disappears with the life of the prince; and only rarely does it happen that this ability is revived by a successor, as Dante prudently declares:

> Not often in a family tree does virtue
> rise up to all its branches. This is what
> the Giver wills, that we may ask Him for it.[1]

The well-being, therefore, of a republic or a kingdom cannot rest upon a prince who governs prudently while he is alive, but rather upon one who organizes the government in such a way that it can be maintained in the event of his death. And, while it is true that uncultured men can be more easily persuaded to adopt a new institution or opinion, it is not, however, for this reason impossible to persuade cultured men or men who do not consider themselves uncultured to do the same. The people of Florence do not consider themselves ignorant or uncultured; nevertheless, they were persuaded by Brother Girolamo Savonarola that he spoke with God. I do not wish to judge if this were true or not, for of such a man as this one must speak with respect; but I do say that very many people believed him without ever having seen anything out of the ordinary to make them believe him, and this was the case because his life, his doctrines, and the topics about which he chose to preach from the Bible were enough to persuade them to have faith in him. No one, therefore, should despair of being able to accomplish what others have accomplished, for men—as I said in my preface—are born, live, and die always in the same way.

---

1 *Purgatorio,* 7.122–23.

## Chapter 12.
### How Much Importance Must Be Granted to Religion, and How Italy, Without Religion, Thanks to the Roman Church, Has Been Ruined

Princes or republics that wish to maintain themselves without corruption must, above all else, maintain free of corruption the ceremonies of their religion and must hold them constantly in veneration; for there is no greater indication of the ruin of a country than to see its religious worship not respected. This is easy to understand when one realizes upon what basis the religion of the place where a man was born is founded, because every religion has the foundation of its existence in one of its main institutions. The essence of the religion of the pagans resided in the responses of oracles and upon a sect of fortune-tellers and soothsayers: all their ceremonies, sacrifices, and rites depended upon these, for it was easy for them to believe that the god who could predict your future, good or evil, could also bring it about for you. From these arose their temples, their sacrifices, their supplications, and every other ceremony used in venerating them; from this arose the oracle of Delos, the temple of Jupiter Ammon, and other famous oracles which filled the world with admiration and devotion. Then, later, as these oracles began to speak on behalf of the powerful, their falsity was discovered by the people and men became unbelievers and were willing to upset every good institution.

Therefore, it is the duty of the rulers of a republic or of a kingdom to maintain the foundations of the religion that sustains them; and if this is done it will be easy for them to keep their republic religious and, as a consequence, good and united. And they must favor and encourage all those things which arise in favor of religion, even if they judge them to be false; the more they do this the more prudent and knowledgeable in worldly affairs they will be. And because this practice has been followed by wise men, there has arisen the belief in miracles that are celebrated even in false religions; for, no matter how they originated, men always gave them greater importance than they deserved, thus causing everyone to believe in them. There were many such miracles in Rome, among them the one that happened while the Roman soldiers were sacking the city of Veii: some of them entered the temple of Juno and, approaching the image of the goddesss, asked:

"Do you wish to come to Rome?"[1] It seemed to some that she nodded her head as if to say "yes" and to others that she actually replied that she did. Since these men were deeply religious (this Livy demonstrates, for he describes them entering the temple without a sound, devout and full of reverence), perhaps it seemed to them that they heard the reply to their question which they had expected from the start; this opinion and belief was carefully encouraged and cultivated by Camillus and the other leaders of the city. If the rulers of Christian republics had maintained this sort of religion according to the system set up by its founder, Christian states and republics would be more united and happier than they are at present. Nor can there be another, better explanation of its decline than to see how those people who are closer to the Roman church, the head of our religion, are less religious. And anyone who examines the principles upon which it was based and sees how different present practice is from these principles would conclude, without a doubt, that it is drawing near either to calamity or a scourge.

And since there are many who are of the opinion that the well-being of the Italian cities comes from the church of Rome, I wish to present some of my beliefs against such an opinion, very powerful ones which, I feel, cannot be refuted. The first is that because of the bad examples of that court of Rome this land has lost all its devotion and religion; this, in turn, brings about countless evils and countless disorders: for just as one takes for granted that all goes well where there is religion, just so, where religion is lacking one supposes the contrary. We Italians owe this first debt to the church and to the priests—we have become irreligious and wicked; but we owe them an even greater debt still, which is the second reason for our ruin: that the church has kept, and still keeps, this land of ours divided. And, in truth, no land is ever happy or united unless it is under the rule of one republic or one prince, as is the case with France and Spain. And the reason why Italy is not in the same condition and why she, too, has neither one republic nor one prince to govern her, lies solely with the Church: for although the Church possesses temporal power and has its seat in Italy, it has not been powerful enough nor has it possessed sufficient skill to be able to tyrannize Italy and make itself her ruler; and

it has not been, on the other hand, so feeble that, when in fear of losing its control of temporal affairs, it has been unable to bring in a foreign power to defend itself from those Italian states which have become too powerful. There are many instances of this in ancient times: when, with Charlemagne's aid, the Lombards—who were in control of almost all of Italy—were driven out; and when, in our own day, the Church took power away from the Venetians with the aid of France, and then when it drove out the French with the help of the Swiss. Therefore, since the Church has not been strong enough to take possession of Italy, nor has she permitted anyone else to do so, Italy has not been able to unite under one ruler. Rather, Italy has been under many rulers and lords, and from this has come so much disunity and so much weakness that she has continued to be at the mercy not only of powerful barbarians but of anyone who might attack her. This is the debt we Italians owe the Church and no one else! And anyone who might wish to see the truth of this borne out by actual experience need only have sufficient power to send the Roman court, with the authority it possesses in Italy, to live in the lands of the Swiss, who are today the only peoples living under both religious and military institutions organized according to ancient practices; and he would see that in a short time the wicked customs of that court would create more disorder in that land than any other event occurring at any time could possibly cause there.

## Chapter 58.
### The Masses[2] Are Wiser and More Constant Than a Prince

Nothing can be more unreliable and more inconstant than the masses, as our own Livy declares and as all other historians affirm. In the recounting of the actions of men, we often read that the masses condemn someone to death and then repent later, wishing that he were still alive, as is evident in what the Roman people did with Manlius Capitolinus, whom they first condemned to death and then wished to have back alive. And the words of the author are these: "As soon as he ceased to represent a danger, the people immediately were seized

---

1  Latin in the original, quoting from Livy, 5.22.

2  The Italian word is *moltitudine* which perhaps would be better rendered by the word multitude.—ED.

by remorse." And elsewhere, when he is explaining the events in Syracuse after the death of Hieronymus, the grandson of Hiero, he declares: "Such is the nature of the masses—either to obey humbly or to rule arrogantly."[1]

I do not know whether, in undertaking to defend an argument which, as I have mentioned, all writers have attacked, I may not be taking on a task so difficult and so full of problems that I shall either have to abandon it in shame or follow it with great pains. But be that as it may, I do not, nor shall I ever, think it wrong to defend an opinion with reasons without employing either authority or force. Let me say, therefore, that all men, and especially princes, can be accused individually of that fault for which writers blame the masses: for anyone not regulated by law will make the same errors that the uncontrolled masses will make. And this is obvious, for there are, and have been, many princes who have been able to break the bounds that could restrain them; nor shall we count among these the kings who arose in Egypt when, in that ancient time, the province was ruled by laws, nor those who arose in Sparta, nor those in our own times who arose in France, a kingdom more regulated by laws than any other kingdom that we have any knowledge of in our own day. The kings who arose under such constitutions are not to be considered among those whose individual nature we ought to consider here in order to see if it resembles that of the masses, for they should be compared to the masses regulated by laws in the same fashion as they are; and we shall find in the masses that same goodness we discover in such kings and shall see that the masses neither obey humbly nor rule arrogantly. The Roman people were like this, for while the Roman republic endured without corruption, it never obeyed humbly nor ruled arrogantly; on the contrary, it held its position honorably through its institutions and magistrates. And when it was necessary to band together against some powerful man, as in the case of Manlius, the decemvirs, and others who sought to oppress it, it did so; when it was necessary to obey the dictators and the consuls for the public welfare, it did so. And if the Roman people regretted the death of Manlius Capitolinus, it is not surprising, for they regretted the loss of his virtues, which were such that the memory of them aroused everyone's compassion;

and it would have had the power to produce the same effect in a prince, since all writers declare that ability is praised and admired even in one's enemies. If Manlius had been resurrected because of such an opinion, the people of Rome would have pronounced upon him the same sentence that they did when they had him removed from prison and shortly thereafter condemned him to death; nevertheless we see princes, reputed to be wise, who have had someone executed and then wished him returned to life, as Alexander did in the case of Clitus and his other friends and as Herod did with Mariamne. But when our historian speaks of the nature of the masses, he does not mean those who are regulated by law, as the Romans were; he speaks of the uncontrolled masses, like those of Syracuse, which committed crimes typical of undisciplined and infuriated men, as did Alexander the Great and Herod in the instances mentioned. But the nature of the masses is no more to be condemned than that of princes, for both err when there is nothing to control them. There are many examples of this, in addition to the ones I have mentioned, both among the Roman emperors and other tyrants and princes; and in them we witness as much lack of stability and variation of behavior as may ever be found in any multitude.

Therefore, I come to a conclusion contrary to the common opinion, which declares that when the people hold power they are unstable, changeable, and ungrateful; I affirm, rather, that the people are no more susceptible to these sins than are individual princes. And if one were to blame both the people and princes alike, he might be telling the truth, but if princes are to be excluded from this charge, then he would be deceiving himself, because a people which have power and are well organized will be no less stable, prudent, and grateful than a prince. In fact, they may be more so, even though the prince is thought wise; and, on the other hand, a prince freed from the restraint of law will be more ungrateful, changeable, and imprudent than the people. And the changeability of their behavior does not arise from a different nature, for it is the same in all men, and if there is one better than the other, it is the people; it comes, rather, from having greater or lesser respect for the laws under which they both live. And anyone who considers the Roman people will see that they were opposed to the very title of king for four hundred years and were lovers of the glory

---

1  Latin in the original, from Livy, 6.20 and 24.25.

and the common good of their city; and he will see many examples that testify to both characteristics. If anyone should cite, to the contrary, the ingratitude that the people showed toward Scipio, I would make the same reply I did earlier on this subject, where I showed that the people are less ungrateful than princes. But, concerning prudence and stability, let me say that the people are more prudent, more reliable, and have better judgment than a prince does. And it is not without reason that the voice of the people is likened to that of God: for it is evident that popular opinion has marvelous power in predicting, so much so that it would appear to foresee its own good and evil fortune through some occult ability. As for its judgment in various matters, when the people hear two equally able speakers, each arguing different opinions, only very rarely does it happen that they do not choose the better opinion and are incapable of understanding the truth of what they hear. And if they err in matters of courage or profit, as was mentioned above, a prince will often err because of his own passions, which are much stronger than those of the people. It is also evident that the people make better choices in electing magistrates than does a prince, for one can never persuade the people that it is good to elect to public office an infamous man of corrupt habits—something that a prince can easily be persuaded to do in a thousand ways; and when the people begin to feel an aversion for something, we see them persist in this aversion for many years—something we do not observe in a prince. For both of these characteristics I find it sufficient to cite the Roman people as evidence, for in so many hundreds of years, in so many elections of consuls and tribunes, the people did not make even four elections which they were forced to regret. And, as I have said, they so hated the very name of king that no amount of meritorious service rendered by one of their citizens seeking to gain the title could persuade the people to forget the just penalties he deserved for this ambition. Furthermore, it is evident that cities in which people are the rulers increase their territories in a very short time, much more so than cities which have always been under a prince, just as Rome did after the expulsion of the kings and Athens did after she freed herself of Pisistratus. This is the result of nothing other than the fact that government by the people is better than government by princes. Nor do I wish everything that our historian says in the aforementioned passage

and elsewhere to be cited against this opinion of mine, for if we were to discuss all the faults of the people and all those of princes, all the glories of the people and all those of princes, it would be evident that the people are far superior in goodness and in glory. And if princes are superior to the people in instituting laws, forming civic communities, and establishing statutes and new institutions, then the people are so much more superior in maintaining the things thus established that they attain, without a doubt, the same glory as those who established them.

And, in short, to conclude this subject, let me say that just as the states of princes have endured for a long time, so too have the states of republics; both have needed to be regulated by laws, for a prince who is able to do what he wishes is mad, and a people that can do what it wishes is not wise. If, therefore, we are talking about a prince obedient to the laws or a people restricted by them, we shall observe more ability in the people than in the prince; if we are discussing either one or the other as being free from these restrictions, we shall observe fewer errors in the people than in the prince; moreover, they are less serious ones and easier to remedy. For a licentious and unruly people can be spoken to by one good man and can easily be brought back to the right path; however, with an evil prince there is no one who can speak to him and no other remedy than the sword. From this fact one can draw a conclusion concerning the seriousness of their respective maladies: if words are enough to cure the malady of the people and the sword to cure that of the prince, there will never be anyone who will not conclude that the greater the faults, the greater the attention required. When a people is unrestrained, neither its mad actions nor the evil at hand need be feared, but rather the evil that may arise from them, since a tyrant may emerge from so much confusion. But with an evil prince the opposite happens: present evil is feared and one hopes for the future, since men persuade themselves that ending his evil life can result in an era of freedom. So you see the difference between the two: one concerns things as they are and the other concerns things that will be. The cruelties of the masses are directed against anyone who they fear might act against the public welfare; those of the prince are directed against anyone who he fears might act against his own interests. But the prejudice against the people arises because everyone speaks ill of them freely and without fear, even when they rule; one always speaks ill of princes only with great fear and apprehension. And this seems not to be beside the point, since this subject leads me ahead to discuss, in the following chapter, whether one may place more trust in alliances made with a republic or those made with a prince.

# BOOK 2

## Introduction

Men always praise ancient times and condemn the present, but not always with good reason; they are such advocates of the past that they celebrate not merely those ages which they know only through the memory of the historians but also those that they, now being old, remember having seen in their youth. And when this opinion of theirs is mistaken, as it is most of the time, I am persuaded that there are several reasons which lead them to make this mistake. First, I believe that we do not know the complete truth about antiquity; most often the facts that would discredit those times are hidden and other matters which bestow glory upon them are reported magnificently and most thoroughly. Most writers submit to the fortune of conquerors, and in order to render their victories glorious they not only exaggerate what they have ably achieved but also embellish the deeds of their enemies in such a way that anyone born afterward in either of the two lands—that of the victor or that of the vanquished—has reason to marvel at those men and those times and is forced to praise them and to love them to the greatest degree. Besides this, since men hate things either out of fear or envy, two very powerful reasons for hatred of things in the past are eliminated, for they cannot hurt you or give you cause for envy. But the contrary applies to those things you deal with and observe: they are known to you in every detail, you see in them what is good as well as the many things that displease you, and you are obliged to judge them most inferior to things of the past; while, in truth, those of the present may deserve even more glory and fame—I am not speaking of things pertaining to the arts here, for in themselves they possess so much brilliance that the times take away from them little and cannot bestow upon them much more glory than they intrinsically merit; I am speaking rather of those matters pertaining to the lives and customs of men, about which we do not witness such clear evidence.

I repeat, then, that this aforementioned custom of praising the old and condemning the new does exist, but it is not always wrong. Sometimes such a judgment has to be correct since human affairs are always in motion, either rising or declining. And so, one city or province can be seen to possess a government that was well organized by an excellent man; and for a time it may keep improving because of the ability of the founder. Anyone, then, who is born in such a state and praises ancient times more than modern times deceives himself, and his deception is caused by those things mentioned above. But those who are born afterward in that city or region at the time of its decline, do not, then, deceive themselves. As I reflect on why these matters proceed as they do, I believe that the world has always been in the same state and that there has always been as much good as evil in it; but this evil and this good changes from country to country, as we can see from what we know of ancient kingdoms that were different from each other according to the differences in their customs, while the world remained the same as it always had been. There is only this difference: the world's talents first found a home in Assyria, then moved to Media, later to Persia, and, in time, came into Italy and Rome; and if, after the Roman empire, no succeeding empire has lasted, nor has there been one where the world has retained all its talents in one place, nevertheless we can still see them scattered among many nations where men live ably, as in the kingdom of the Franks, the Turks—that of the Sultan—and today among the peoples of Germany; earlier there was that Turkish group which achieved so many grand things and seized so much of the world once it had destroyed the Eastern Roman Empire. In all these lands, then, after the Romans came to ruin, and in all those groups of people, such talents existed and still exist in some of them where they are desired and truly praised. And anyone who is born there and praises past times more than present ones may be deceiving himself, but anyone who is born in Italy or Greece and has not become an Ultramontane in Italy or a Turk in Greece has reason to condemn his own times and to praise others, for in them there were many things that made them marvelous, but in the present ones there is nothing to be seen but utter misery, infamy, and vituperation. There is no observance of religion, laws, or military discipline; all is stained with every kind of filth. Furthermore, these vices are the more detestable as they are found among those who sit on tribunals, command others, and expect to be worshiped.

But, returning to our subject, let me say that if the judgment of men is unfair in deciding which is better—the present age or the past—the latter of which, because of its antiquity, men cannot have as perfect a knowledge of as they can of their own times, this should not corrupt the judgment of old men in assessing the time of their youth and their old age, since they have known and observed both one and the other equally well. This would be true if men were all of the same opinion and had the same desires in all phases of their lives; but since these desires change, and the times do not, things cannot appear to men to be the same, since they have other desires, other pleasures, and other concerns in their old age than they had in their youth. For as men grow older they lose in vigor and gain in judgment and prudence, and the things that seemed acceptable and good to them in their youth become, later on, as they grow older, intolerable and bad; and although they should place the blame for this on their own judgment, they blame the times instead. Besides this, human desires are insatiable, for we are endowed by Nature with the power and the wish to desire everything and by Fortune with the ability to obtain little of what we desire. The result is an unending discontent in the minds of men and a weariness with what they possess: this makes men curse the present, praise the past, and hope in the future, even though they do this with no reasonable motive. I do not know, therefore, if I deserve to be considered among those who deceive themselves if, in these discourses of mine, I am too lavish with my praise of ancient Roman times and condemn our own. And certainly, if the excellence that existed then and the vice that rules now were not clearer than the sun, I would speak more hesitantly for fear that I might fall into the same error of which I accuse others. But since the matter is clear enough for all to see, I shall boldly declare in plain terms what I understand of those ancient times and of our own times, so that the minds of young men who read these writings of mine may be able to reject the present and prepare themselves to imitate the past whenever Fortune provides them with an occasion. For it is your duty as a good man to teach others whatever good you yourself have not been able to do, either because of the malignity of the times or because of Fortune, in order that—since many will thus be made aware of it—someone more beloved by Heaven may be prepared to put your truth into action.

In the discourse of the preceding book I have discussed the decisions the Romans made in matters concerning their internal affairs; now, in this one, I shall discuss what it was that the Roman people did concerning the expansion of their empire.

# The Four Voyages of Christopher Columbus

---ᴐX᭡ᴐ---

Translated and edited by J. M. Cohen

## LETTER OF COLUMBUS TO VARIOUS PERSONS DESCRIBING THE RESULTS OF HIS FIRST VOYAGE AND WRITTEN ON THE RETURN JOURNEY

### First Voyage: 1492-3

Since I know that you will be pleased at the great success with which the Lord has crowned my voyage, I write to inform you how in thirty-three days I crossed from the Canary Islands to the Indies, with the fleet which our most illustrious sovereigns gave me. I found very many islands with large populations and took possession of them all for their Highnesses; this I did by proclamation and unfurled the royal standard. No opposition was offered.

I named the first island that I found 'San Salvador', in honour of our Lord and Saviour who has granted me this miracle. The Indians call it 'Guanahani'. The second island I named 'Santa Maria de Concepción', the third 'Fernandina', the fourth 'Isabela' and the fifth 'Juana'; thus I renamed them all.

When I reached Cuba, I followed its north coast westwards, and found it so extensive that I thought this must be the mainland, the province of Cathay.[1]

Since there were no towns or villages on the coast, but only small groups of houses whose inhabitants fled as soon as we approached, I continued on my course, thinking that I should undoubtedly come to some great towns or cities. We continued for many leagues but found no change, except that the coast was bearing me northwards. This I wished to avoid, since winter was approaching and my plan was to journey south. As the wind was carrying me on I decided not to wait for a change of weather but to turn back to a remarkable harbour which I had observed. From here I sent two men inland to discover whether there was a king or any great cities. They travelled for three days, finding only a large number of small villages and great numbers of people, but nothing more substantial. Therefore they returned.

I understood from some Indians whom I had captured elsewhere that this was an island, and so I followed its coast for 107 leagues to its eastward point. From there I saw another island eighteen leagues eastwards which I then named 'Hispaniola'.[2] I crossed to this island and followed its northern coast eastwards for 188 leagues continuously, as I had followed the coast of Cuba. All these islands are extremely fertile and this one is particularly so. It has many large harbours finer than any I know in Christian lands, and many large rivers. All this is marvellous. The land is high and has many ranges of hills, and mountains incomparably finer than Tenerife. All are most beautiful and various in shape,

---

1   In the log-book and later in this letter Columbus accepts the native story that Cuba is an island which they can circumnavigate in something more than twenty-one days, yet he insists here and later, during the second voyage, that it is in fact part of the Asiatic mainland.

---

2   This is referred to in the log-book as Bohio or Bofio.

and all are accessible. They are covered with tall trees of different kinds which seem to reach the sky. I have heard that they never lose their leaves, which I can well believe, for I saw them as green and lovely as they are in Spain in May; some were flowering, some bore fruit and others were at different stages according to their nature. It was November but everywhere I went the nightingale[1] and many other birds were singing. There are palms of six or eight different kinds—a marvellous sight because of their great variety—and the other trees, fruit and plants are equally marvellous. There are splendid pine woods and broad fertile plains, and there is honey. There are many kinds of birds and varieties of fruit. In the interior are mines and a very large population.

Hispaniola is a wonder. The mountains and hills, the plains and meadow lands are both fertile and beautiful. They are most suitable for planting crops and for raising cattle of all kinds, and there are good sites for building towns and villages. The harbours are incredibly fine and there are many great rivers with broad channels and the majority contain gold.[2] The trees, fruits and plants are very different from those of Cuba. In Hispaniola there are many spices and large mines of gold and other metals. …[3]

The inhabitants of this island, and all the rest that I discovered or heard of, go naked, as their mothers bore them, men and women alike. A few of the women, however, cover a single place with a leaf of a plant or piece of cotton which they weave for the purpose. They have no iron or steel or arms and are not capable of using them, not because they are not strong and well built but because they are amazingly timid. All the weapons they have are canes cut at seeding time, at the end of which they fix a sharpened stick, but they have not the courage to make use of these, for very often when I have sent two or three men to a village to have conversation with them a great number of them have come out. But as soon as they saw my men all fled immediately, a father not even waiting for his son. And this is not because we have harmed any of them; on the contrary, wherever I have gone and been able to

---

1 Columbus was mistaken; he probably heard the mocking-bird

2 This did not prove to be true.

3 These statements are also inaccurate.

have conversation with them, I have given them some of the various things I had, a cloth and other articles, and received nothing in exchange. But they have still remained incurably timid. True, when they have been reassured and lost their fear, they are so ingenuous and so liberal with all their possessions that no one who has not seen them would believe it. If one asks for anything they have they never say no. On the contrary, they offer a share to anyone with demonstrations of heartfelt affection, and they are immediately content with any small thing, valuable or valueless, that is given them. I forbade the men to give them bits of broken crockery, fragments of glass or tags of laces, though if they could get them they fancied them the finest jewels in the world. One sailor was known to have received gold to the weight of two and a half *castellanos* for the tag of a breeches lace, and others received much more for things of even less value. For newly minted *blancas* they would give everything they possessed, even two or three *castellanos* of gold or an arroba or two of spun cotton. They even took bits of broken hoops from the wine barrels and, as simple as animals, gave what they had. This seemed to me to be wrong and I forbade it.

I gave them a thousand pretty things that I had brought, in order to gain their love and incline them to become Christians. I hoped to win them, to the love and service of their Highnesses and of the whole Spanish nation and to persuade them to collect and give us of the things which they possessed in abundance and which we needed. They have no religion and are not idolaters; but all believe that power and goodness dwell in the sky and they are firmly convinced that I have come from the sky with these ships and people. In this belief they gave me a good reception everywhere, once they had overcome their fear; and this is not because they are stupid—far from it, they are men of great intelligence, for they navigate all those seas, and give a marvellously good account of everything—but because they have never before seen men clothed or ships like these.

As soon as I came to the Indies, at the first island I discovered I seized some natives, intending them to inquire and inform me about things in these parts. These men soon understood us, and we them, either by speech or signs and they were very useful to us. I still have them with me and despite all the conversation they have had with me they are still of the opinion that

I come from the sky and have been the first to proclaim this wherever I have gone. Then others have gone running from house to house and to the neighbouring villages shouting: 'Come, come and see the people from the sky,' so, once they were reassured about us, all have come, men and women alike, and not one, old or young, has remained behind. All have brought us something to eat and drink which they have given with a great show of love. In all the islands they have very many canoes like oared *fustas*.

They are of various sizes, some as large as a *fusta* of eighteen benches. But they are not as broad, since they are hollowed out of a single tree. A *fusta* would not be able to keep up with them, however, for they are rowed at an incredible speed. In these they travel and transport their goods between the islands, which are innumerable. I have seen some of these canoes with eighty men in them, all rowing.

In all these islands I saw no great difference in the looks of the people, their customs or their language. On the other hand, all understand one another, which will be of singular assistance in the work of their conversion to our holy faith, on which I hope your Highnesses will decide, since they are very well disposed towards it.

I have already told of my voyage of 107 leagues in a straight line from west to east along the coast of Cuba, according to which I reckon that the island is larger than England and Scotland put together.[1]

One of these provinces is called Avan[2] and there the people are born with tails, and these provinces cannot have a length of less than fifty or sixty leagues, according to the information I received from those Indians whom I have with me and who know all the islands.

The other island, Hispaniola, is greater in circumference than the whole of Spain[3] from Collioure to Fuenterabia in the Basque province, since I travelled along one side for 188 great leagues[4] in a straight line from west to east.

These islands are richer than I yet know or can say and I have taken possession of them in their Majesties' name and hold them all on their behalf and as completely at their disposition as the Kingdom of Castile. In this island of Hispaniola I have taken possession of a large town which is most conveniently situated for the goldfields and for communications with the mainland both here,[5] and there in the territories of the Grand Khan, with which there will be very profitable trade. I have named this town Villa de Navidad and have built a fort there. Its fortifications will by now be finished and I have left sufficient men to complete them. They have arms, artillery and provisions for more than a year, and a *fusta;* also a skilled shipwright who can build more.

I have established warm friendship with the king of that land, so much so, indeed, that he was proud to call me and treat me as a brother. But even should he change his attitude and attack the men of La Navidad, he and his people know nothing about arms and go naked, as I have already said; they are the most timorous people in the world. In fact, the men that I have left there would be enough to destroy the whole land, and the island holds no dangers for them so long as they maintain discipline.

In all these islands the men are seemingly content with one woman, but their chief or king is allowed more than twenty. The women appear to work more than the men and I have not been able to find out if they have private property. As far as I could see whatever a man had was shared among all the rest and this particularly applies to food.

I have not found the human monsters which many people expected. On the contrary, the whole population is very well made. They are not Negroes as in Guinea, and their hair is straight, for where they live the sun's rays do not strike too harshly, but they are strong nevertheless, despite the fact that Hispaniola is 20 to 21 degrees from the Equator.

There are high mountains in these islands and it was very cold this winter but the natives are used to this and withstand the weather, thanks to their food, which they eat heavily seasoned with very hot spices. Not only have I found no monsters but I have had no reports of any

---

1 Cuba is actually considerably smaller than England without Scotland.

2 From which the Spaniards took the name La Habana, which they gave first to a town that they built on the southern coast of the island and afterwards to the present city of that name.

3 This also is an exaggeration.

4 Reckoned to be four (Roman) miles.

---

5 Columbus is apparently assuming now that Cuba is part of the mainland, but that a further part of the mainland of Asia is still to be discovered.

except at the island called 'Quaris',[1] which is the second as you approach the Indies from the east, and which is inhabited by a people who are regarded in these islands as extremely fierce and who eat human flesh. They have many canoes in which they travel throughout the islands of the Indies, robbing and taking all they can. They are no more ill-shaped than any other natives of the Indies, though they are in the habit of wearing their hair long like women. They have bows and arrows with the same canes as the others, tipped with splinters of wood, for lack of iron which they do not possess. They behave most savagely to the other peoples but I take no more account of them than the rest. It is these men who have relations with the women of Matinino,[2] where there are no men and which is the first island you come to on the way from Spain to the Indies, These women do not follow feminine occupations but use cane bows and arrows like those of the men and arm and protect themselves with plates of copper, of which they have much.

In another island, which I am told is larger than Hispaniola, the people have no hair. Here there is a vast quantity of gold, and from here and the other islands I bring Indians as evidence.

In conclusion, to speak only of the results of this very hasty voyage, their Highnesses can see that I will give them as much gold as they require, if they will render me some very slight assistance; also I will give them all the spices and cotton they want, and as for mastic, which has so far been found only in Greece and the island of Chios and which the Genoese authorities have sold at their own price, I will bring back as large a cargo as their Highnesses may command. I will also bring them as much aloes as they ask and as many slaves, who will be taken from the idolaters. I believe also that I have found rhubarb and cinnamon and there will be countless other things in addition, which the people I have left there will discover. For I did not stay anywhere unless delayed by lack of wind except at the town of La Navidad, which I had to leave secure and well established. In fact I should have done much more if the ships had been reasonably serviceable, but this is enough.

Thus the eternal God, Our Lord, grants to all those who walk in his way victory over apparent impossibilities, and this voyage was pre-eminently a victory of this kind. For although there was much talk and writing of these lands, all was conjectural, without ocular evidence. In fact, those who accepted the stories judged rather by hearsay than on any tangible information. So all Christendom will be delighted that our Redeemer has given victory to our most illustrious King and Queen and their renowned kingdoms, in this great matter. They should hold great celebrations and render solemn thanks to the Holy Trinity with many solemn prayers, for the great triumph which they will have, by the conversion of so many peoples to our holy faith and for the temporal benefits which will follow, for not only Spain, but all Christendom will receive encouragement and profit.

This is a brief account of the facts.

Written in the caravel off the Canary Islands.[3]

15 February 1493

At your orders
THE ADMIRAL

After this was written, when I was already in Spanish waters, I was struck by such a strong south-south-west wind that I was compelled to lighten ship, but today by a great miracle I made the port of Lisbon, from which I decided to write letters to their Highnesses. Throughout the Indies, I have always found weather like that of May; I went there in thirty-three days and returned in twenty-eight. I met with no storms except these which held me up for fourteen days, beating about in these seas. The sailors here say that there has never been so bad a winter nor so many ships lost.

Written on 4 March

---

1    Either Dominica or Maria Galante. Reports of monsters seem generally to refer to the Carabis

2    Martinique.

3    Actually Columbus was off Santa Maria in the Azores.

## THE LIFE OF THE ADMIRAL BY HIS SON, HERNANDO COLON

### Second Voyage 1493–6

*It is decided that the Admiral should return with a large fleet to settle the island of Hispaniola. The Pope confirms the conquest*

At Barcelona, orders were given with great care and dispatch for the Admiral's second expedition and return to Hispaniola. This second expedition was designed to relieve the men who had remained there, to settle more colonists and to conquer the island together with all the others that had been discovered and those that they hoped remained to be discovered. In order to make their title clear and good, the Catholic sovereigns on the Admiral's advice very promptly applied for the Supreme Pontiff's confirmation and gift: of the conquests of all these Indies.

The reigning Pope, Alexander VI, most liberally granted them not only all that they had conquered so far, but also everything that they should still discover further west as far as the Orient, in so far as no Christian prince had actual possession, and he forbade all others to encroach on these boundaries. In the following year the same Pope confirmed this gift, effectively defining it in a document of many clauses.[1]

Realizing that they owed the whole of this concession so kindly granted them by the Pope to the Admiral's labours and initiative, and that all their new rights and possessions were due to his voyage and discovery, the Catholic sovereigns were resolved to reward him for everything, and therefore at Barcelona on 28 May they granted him a new patent, or rather an explanation and amplification,[2] in which they reaffirmed the grants and concessions which they had originally made to him. In clear and precise language they declared that his jurisdiction as Admiral, his viceroyalty and governorship extended to the full limits of the concession granted to them by the Pope, and thus confirmed the patent granted to him at Santa Fé.

## THE LETTER WRITTEN BY DR CHANCA[3] TO THE CITY OF SEVILLE

Most Excellent Sir: Since the contents of the private letters which I have sent to others cannot be so generally communicated as those which I am writing here, I have decided to send the news from this place in one letter and my various requests to your lordship in another. My news is as follows:

The fleet which, by God's will, the Catholic Kings, our lords, sent to the Indies under the command of Christopher Columbus, their Admiral of the Ocean Sea, left Cadiz on 25 September 1493.[4] The weather and wind favoured our journey and continued to do so for two days, during which we were able to make about fifty leagues. The weather turned against us for the next two days, in which we made little or no progress. After this it pleased God to give us good weather, so that in another two days we reached Grand Canary, where we put into port; which we were compelled to do in order to repair a ship which was making much water. We remained there for the whole day, and set out on the morrow and met with some calms, so that we were four or five days in reaching Gomera. We had to remain for some time at Gomera, taking on all the stores we

---

1 The Pope issued several bulls in the course of the year. In the most important of them, *Inter coetera* of 4 May, he established the line of demarcation between the territories assigned to Spain and Portugal on the meridian passing 100 leagues west of the Azores and the Cape Verde Islands, granting to the Castilians everything that might be discovered to the west of it. In 1494, in direct negotiations with Portugal, the line was shifted to 370 leagues to the west of the Cape Verde Islands. By this grant, the Portuguese were later able to colonize Brazil and, at least in theory, the English and French were debarred from the New World.

---

2 In this document Columbus was appointed captain-general of the second fleet and given power to appoint any persons he might choose to the government of the Indies. A week before he had been given the highly prized right to wear a castle and lion in his coat of arms. [Hernando Colon's note.]

3 Chanca was one of Ferdinand and Isabela's physicians whom they sent as doctor to the expedition and whose salary they paid.

4 Columbus had a fleet of seventeen ships including caravels and lighter vessels for inshore work, and twelve to fifteen thousand men.

could of meat, wood and water for the long voyage we expected to make without sighting land.

So with our stay at these ports and a day's delay owing to calm after leaving Gomera, we were nineteen or twenty days in arriving at the island of Hierro. From here, by the kindness of God, we had good weather, the best that ever a fleet had on such a long voyage. Having left Hierro on 13 October in anchor, but could not find one anywhere. As much of the island as we could see was all very mountainous, very beautiful and very green down to the water's edge. It was a pleasure to look at, for at this season there is hardly any green in our own country.

Since we found no harbour there, the Admiral decided to steer for the other island, which lay on the right and was four or five leagues from this one. Meanwhile one ship remained off the first island for the whole day, continuing to look for a harbour, in case it should be necessary to return there. A good harbour was eventually found, and people and houses sighted. Later at night this ship rejoined the fleet, which had found a harbour on the other island, where the Admiral and many men had landed carrying the royal standard, and had taken formal possession of the land for their Highnesses. On this island the trees were amazingly dense, and were of a great variety of species known to none of us. Some were in fruit, some in flower, and all therefore were green. We found one tree, like a laurel but not so large, the leaves of which had the finest scent of clove that I have ever smelt. I think it must have been a species of laurel. There were wild fruit[1] of different kinds, which some rashly tried. But no sooner did they taste them than their faces swelled, growing so inflamed and painful that they almost went out of their minds. They cured themselves with cold compresses. We found no people on this island, nor any sign of them, and believed it to be uninhabited.

We remained only two hours, for when we got there it was late evening. Next day we departed in the morning for another island, which appeared beyond this one, very large and some seven or eight leagues away. At the point where we reached it, there was a great mountain mass which seemed to touch the sky, and in the middle a peak higher than all the rest. From here many streams flowed in different directions, particularly in the direction in which we lay. Three leagues away could be seen a waterfall of considerable breadth, which fell from so high that it seemed to come from the sky. It could be seen from so far off that many wagers were laid on board. Some said that it was white rock and others that it was water. When we got nearer, the truth was apparent. It was the most beautiful thing in the world to see the height from which it fell, and from how small a place such a force of water sprang. When we came near, the Admiral dispatched a light caravel to sail along the coast and look for a harbour. The caravel went ahead and, on reaching the land, sighted some houses. The captain went ashore in the boat and visited the houses, whose inhabitants fled as soon as they saw him. He went into the houses and saw their possessions, for they had taken nothing with them. He took two parrots, which were very large and very different from any previously seen. He saw much cotton, spun and ready for spinning, and some of their food. He took a little of everything, and in particular he took away four or five human arm and leg bones. When we saw these, we suspected that these were the Carib islands, whose inhabitants eat human flesh. For following the indications of their position given him by the Indians of the islands discovered in his previous voyage, the Admiral had set his course to discover them, since they were nearer to Spain and lay on the direct route to the island of Hispaniola, where he had left his men on the previous voyage. By the goodness of God, and thanks to the Admiral's skill and knowledge, we had reached them as directly as if we had been following a known and familiar course.

This island[2] is very large, and on this side the coast appeared to be twenty-five leagues in length. We sailed along it for more than two leagues looking for a harbour. On the side we approached there were very high mountains, and on the side from which we left wide plains appeared. On the seashore there were some small villages, and at the sight of our sails all the people fled. When we had gone two leagues and it was quite late, we found a harbour. That night the Admiral decided that some men should land early next morning and hold conversation with the natives, to find out what people they were, though he already suspected that they

---

1  This was probably the manchineal (manzanillo). The Caribs used the fruit of this tree to make poison for their arrows.

2  Guadalupe.

were Caribs and the people whom he had seen running away were naked, like those he had seen on his previous voyage.

Certain captains set out in the morning and some returned at dinner-time bringing a boy of about fourteen, who later told us that he was one of these people's captives. The other captains went in various directions. A few men returned with a boy whom a man had been leading by the hand, but had abandoned at their approach. Only these few were detached to bring him back, the rest remaining behind. These captured some women of the island, and also brought back other women who were prisoners and came of their own accord. One captain separated himself from the party with six men, not knowing that any information had been gained. He and his companions got lost and could not find their way back until, after four days, they struck the coast, which they followed until they rejoined the fleet. We thought that they were dead and eaten by these Caribs, for there seemed no other explanation of their disappearance, since among them were pilots, sailors capable of making the voyage to and from Spain by the stars, and we didn't think they could get lost in so small a space.

On the first day of our landing, many men and women walked along the seashore, gazing on the fleet and marvelling at the strange sight. And when a boat put ashore to speak with them saying 'Tayno Tayno', which means *good*, they waited so long as our men did not come ashore, remaining at the water's edge, ready to escape at any moment. Consequently none of these men could be taken, either by force or by persuasion, except two, who grew confident and were captured a little later. In addition to the two who were taken by force, more than twenty of the women prisoners and some other natives of the island came of their own accord. Some boy prisoners also fled to our men, escaping from the natives of the island who were guarding them.

We remained in this harbour for eight days because of the loss of the captain I have spoken of, and landed several times on the island, visiting the dwellings and villages on the coast, where we found great numbers of human bones and skulls hanging in the houses as vessels to hold things. Very few men appeared and the reason was, as we learned from the women, that ten canoes had gone to raid other islands. These people seemed to us more civilized than those elsewhere. All

have straw houses, but these people build them much better, and have larger stocks of provisions, and show more signs of industry practised by both men and women. They have much cotton, spun and ready for spinning, and much cotton cloth so well woven that it is no way inferior to the cloth of our own country. We asked the women who were held prisoners on this island what kind of people these were; and they replied that they were Caribs. When they understood that we hated these people on account of their cannibalism, they were highly delighted; and after that, if any Carib man or woman was brought in, they quietly told us that they were Caribs. For even here, where all were in our power, they showed the fear of a conquered people, and thus we learnt from the women which were Caribs and which were not. The Caribs wore round their legs two rings of woven cotton—one below the knee and one at the ankle. In this way they make their calves large and constrict the knee and ankle. They seem to regard this as attractive, and by this feature we distinguished the Caribs from the others.

The customs of these Carib people are beastly. There are three islands. This one they call Turuqueira; the first that we saw is Ceyre and the third Ayay.[1]

The people were all friendly to one another as if of one family. They do not harm each other but all make war against the neighbouring islands. They travel 150 leagues to make raids in their canoes, which are small *fustas* hewn out of a single tree. Instead of iron weapons they use arrows—for they have no iron. Some of their arrows are tipped with tortoise shell, but others on another island use fish bones which are naturally serrated like very strong saws. For an unarmed people, which they all are, they can kill and do great injury with these weapons, which are not very terrible, however, to men of our nation.

These people raid the other islands and carry off all the women they can take, especially the young and beautiful, whom they keep as servants and concubines. They had carried off so many that in fifty houses we found no males and more than twenty of the captives were girls. These women say that they are treated with a cruelty that seems incredible. The Caribs eat the male children that they have by them, and only bring up the

1 These are probably Guadelupe, Maria Galante and Santa Cruz, but the identification is not certain.

children of their own women; and as for the men they are able to capture, they bring those who are alive home to be slaughtered and eat those who are dead on the spot. They say that human flesh is so good that there is nothing like it in the world; and this must be true, for the human bones we found in their houses were so gnawed that no flesh was left on them except what was too tough to be eaten. In one house the neck of a man was found cooking in a pot. They castrate the boys that they capture and use them as servants until they are men. Then, when they want to make a feast, they kill and eat them, for they say that the flesh of boys and women is not good to eat. Three of these boys fled to us, and all three had been castrated.

After four days the captain who had been lost returned. We had abandoned all hope of his coming. For search parties had twice gone out to look for him, and only that day one party had returned with no certain news of him. We were as glad at his coming as if we had found him for the first time. In addition to the men who had gone with him, he brought in ten natives, boys and women. But neither this party nor those who had gone in search of them found any men, for they had all fled. But perhaps there were very few men left in the district, because as we learned from the women ten canoes had gone to raid the other islands. This captain and his companions returned so weary from the forest that they were a pitiful sight. When we asked how they had got lost, they answered that the trees were so thick they could not see the sky and that some of them who were sailors had climbed trees to look at the stars, but had not been able to see them, and if they had not found the sea it would have been impossible for them to rejoin the ships.

We left this island eight days after we arrived. Then at noon next day we saw another island which was not very large and was twelve leagues from this one.[1] We were becalmed for the greater part of the day after we left and remained near the coast of this island. The women whom we brought with us said that it was uninhabited, because the Caribs had removed the whole population. So we did not stay there. Then in the evening we sighted another island[2] and at nightfall found some shoals close to it, for fear of which we dropped anchor, nor daring to go further until daylight. Next morning another island of considerable size appeared.[3] We visited none of these, being anxious to relieve those who had been left on Hispaniola. But it did not please God that we should do so, as will appear later.

Next day at dinner-time we reached another island[4] which seemed to us to be a very good one, for, to judge by the many tracts of cultivation upon it, it was thickly inhabited. We went there and put into a coastal harbour. Then the Admiral sent a boat ashore with a landing party, whom he instructed to speak with the inhabitants and find out if possible what people they were. We also wished for information about our course, though, despite the fact that the Admiral had never sailed that way before, he had, as it appeared later, followed a very direct line. But because matters of doubt should always be looked into with the greatest possible care, he wished to make inquiries there also. Some of those in the boat landed and made their way to a village, whose inhabitants had all gone into hiding. The landing party took some women and boys, most of whom were the people's captives, for like the inhabitants of the other islands these people were Caribs, as we learnt from the women whom we took with us.

When this boat was about to return to the ships with the captures it had made down the coast below this place, there appeared along the coast a canoe with four men, two women and a boy, and when they saw the fleet they were so amazed that they remained motionless for a full hour about two lombard shots from the ships. The crew of the boat and indeed the whole fleet saw their stupefaction. Soon those in the boats went after them, keeping so close to the shore that these Indians, lost in amazement and wondering what the strange sight might be, failed to see them, until they were almost upon them and consequently could not escape though they tried hard to do so. Our men rowed after them so fast that they did not get far. When the Caribs saw that flight was useless they very boldly snatched up their bows, men and women alike; I say 'very boldly' because they were only four men and two women and there were twenty-five or more in our boat, but they succeeded in wounding two of them, one with two arrows in the chest and the other with an arrow

---

1 Montserrat.
2 Santa Maria la Redonda, the round island.

3 Santa Maria de la Antigua.
4 San Martin.

in his side. If our men had not carried shields of wood and leather and had not come close to the canoe and upset it, most of the others would have been wounded too. When the boat was upset, the Indians remained in the water, sometimes swimming and sometimes standing, since there were shallows there, and our men had some difficulty in catching them, for they continued to shoot when they could. There was indeed one that they could not take until he was mortally wounded with a spear-thrust and they brought him thus wounded to the ships.

[*An incident of this time recorded by one of the Admiral's Italian lieutenants, Michele de Cuneo, throws additional light on the Christians' behaviour to the Indians:*

'*While I was in the boat, I captured a very beautiful Carib woman, whom the said Lord Admiral gave to me. When I had taken her to my cabin she was naked—as was their custom. I was filled with a desire to take my pleasure with her and attempted to satisfy my desire. She was unwilling, and so treated me with her nails that I wished I had never begun. But—to cut a long story short—I then took a piece of rope and whipped her soundly, and she let forth such incredible screams that you would not have believed your ears. Eventually we came to such terms, I assure you, that you would have thought she had been brought up in a school for whores.*]

The difference in appearance between these Indians and the others is that the Caribs wear their hair very long and the others have it cut irregularly and decorate their heads in a great number of different patterns, each according to his fancy. They make these patterns—crosses and such-like devices—with sharpened reeds. Both the Caribs and the others are beardless; only very rarely will you find anyone with a beard. The Caribs who were captured there had their eyes and brows stained, which I think they do for show. It makes them look more terrifying. One of these Indians told us that in one of these islands, called Ceyre, which is the first we saw but did not visit, there is much gold.[1] They go there with studs and nails to build their canoes and bring away as much gold as they want.

Later that day we left this island after a stay of only six or seven hours and made for another land,[2] which came in sight on the course we were following. We came near to it at nightfall, and next morning followed its coast. There was much land though it was not very continuous, for there were more than forty islets: It was very high and unlike any of the islands we have seen before or since, and mostly barren. It seemed the sort of land in which there might be metals, but we did not go ashore, though a lateen-rigged caravel went to one of the islets where they found some fishermen's huts. The Indian women who were with us said they were uninhabited.

We followed this coast for the greater part of the day and in the evening of the next came in sight of another island called Burenquen[3] whose coast we followed for the whole of the next day. The island was reckoned to be thirty leagues long on this side. It is most beautiful and appears to be very fertile. The Caribs have come here on raids and taken many of the people. The natives have no canoes and no knowledge of navigation, but according to the Caribs whom we captured they use bows like their own, and if they manage to capture any of the raiders they eat them in the same way as the Caribs themselves. We stayed in a harbour on this island for two days, and many of our men landed, but we were never able to have speech with the people, for they were terrified of the Caribs and all fled.

All these islands were discovered on this voyage, for scarcely one of them had been seen by the Admiral when he came here before. They are all very beautiful and have good soil, and this one seemed the best of all. It was almost the last of the islands facing Spain which the Admiral had not already seen, but we consider it certain that there is land forty leagues nearer to Spain than these first islands, because two days before we sighted land we saw some of those birds called frigate-birds, sea-birds of prey, which never alight or sleep on the water, and towards evening they were circling high in the air and flying off in search of land on which to sleep. As it was now almost night they could not have been going to roost more than twelve or fifteen leagues away. We sighted them on our right as we sailed on our course from Spain and everyone reckoned therefore that there must be land there. But we did not go to look for it because this would have deflected us from

---

1   If this refers to Dominica it is not true. There is no gold but plenty of wood. There is perhaps a mistake in the text.

2   The island of Santa Cruz.

3   Puerto Rico.

our course. I hope that during the next few voyages it will be discovered.[1]

We left the island of Burenquen at dawn and at nightfall came within sight of land which was also unknown to those who had accompanied the Admiral on his previous voyage, but which, on the information of the Indian women whom we had aboard, we guessed must be Hispaniola, where we lie at present. Between this island and Burenquen there appeared another small one in the distance. When we reached Hispaniola the land on that side was at first low and very flat, and on seeing this everyone was uncertain what land it was, for neither the Admiral nor any of those who had sailed with him had seen this part of the island. It is so large that it is divided into provinces. This part which we reached first is called Haiti, the one next to it they call Jamana, and the one after that in which we now are is Bohio.[2] These provinces are themselves divided into districts, for Hispaniola is very large. Those who have seen the whole length of the coast suppose it to extend for 200 leagues. In my opinion it is not less than 150 leagues long, and its breadth is still unknown. Forty days ago a caravel left to circumnavigate it and has not yet returned.

The land is very remarkable; it contains many large rivers, great mountain ranges, wide open valleys and high mountains. I suspect that the vegetation remains green right through the year. I do not believe that there is winter either in this island or any of the others, for many birds' nests were found at Christmas, some containing fledglings and some eggs. No four-footed animal has been seen in any of them, except for some dogs of various colours like those in Spain, which are of the build of large mastiffs. There are no wild beasts, only a creature the size of a young rabbit, with a coat of the same kind and colour and a long tail and hind and forefeet like those of a rat. It climbs trees and many who have tried it say the flesh is very good to eat.[3]

There are many small snakes but only a few lizards, because the Indians consider them as great a delicacy as we do pheasants at home. They are of the same size as our native lizard but differently formed, though on one small island beside a harbour called Monte Christi, where we stayed for a day or two, a very large lizard was seen many times and was said to be as big as a calf and the length of a lance from tip to tail.[4] They often went out to hunt it, but owing to the thickness of the undergrowth it escaped into the sea and they never came face to face with it.

In Hispaniola and the other islands there are a great number of birds like those of our country and many others of kinds never seen there. No domestic fowls have been found here at all except in Zuruquia, where there were some ducks in the houses, most of them white as snow but a few black. They had flat crests and were larger, than those at home, though smaller than geese.

We sailed along the coast of this island for about a hundred leagues, to the place where the Admiral had left his people, which must have been about half-way along the island. As we coasted the province of Jamana, we put ashore one of the Indian captives of the previous voyage, clothed, and with a few small objects which the Admiral had given him. That day a Basque sailor died who had been wounded by the Caribs on the occasion when we surprised them by keeping close to the shore. Since we were near the coast the opportunity was taken of sending a boat ashore to bury him, and two caravels were sent in to escort it. Many Indians came out to meet the boat as it beached, some of whom had gold round their necks or in their ears. They wanted to come out to the ships with the Christians, but the sailors refused to bring them since they had no permission from the Admiral. When they realized that we were not going to row them out, two of them got into a small canoe and went to one of the caravels which had put in towards the shore.

They were kindly received and were then conveyed to the Admiral's ship, where they said through an interpreter that they had been sent by a certain king to learn who we were and to beg us to land because they had much gold and would give us some, as well as some food. The Admiral ordered that they should be given a shirt each and a cap and other trifles. He told them, however, that as he was going to the place where Guacamari[5] lived, he could not wait now, but would

---

1   The remaining Leeward Islands.

2   Haiti and Bohio were both native names for the whole island and Jamana was a district lying on the north coast.

3   Aguti, a kind of edible rat.

4   According to Oviedo an alligator.

5   Guacanagari.

be able to visit their king at some other time, and with that they went away. We sailed continuously along our course until we reached a harbour called Monte Christi, where we stayed two days to inspect the ground because the Admiral did not think that the place where he had left his people was suitable for a settlement. There was a large river of very good water, but the land around is all swampy and unsuitable for habitation. During their inspection of the river and the land some of our men found two corpses at a place near the bank, one with a noose round his neck and the other with his feet tied. This was on the first day. On the next they found two other corpses further upstream, one of which was so well preserved that it was possible to see that he had been heavily bearded. Some of our men suspected the worst and with justification, for the Indians have no beards, as has already been observed.

This harbour was two leagues away from the place where the Admiral had left his people and two days later we set sail for it. The Admiral had left them in the company of a king called Guacamari, who was I think one of the principal kings of this island. That day we arrived off the place, but it was already evening and because of the shoals on which the Admiral's ship had been lost on the previous voyage we did not dare to go inshore and enter the harbour until next day, when soundings could be taken and we could do so in safety. We remained that night rather less than a league from shore.

During the evening a canoe appeared in the distance with five or six Indians who were rowing rapidly after us, but, believing it was safer for us to keep our sails set, the Admiral would not allow us to wait for them. They pressed on, however, and came within a lombard shot of us, where they stopped to look at us and when they saw that we were not stopping they turned round and rowed back. After we had anchored offshore that evening, the Admiral ordered that two lombards should be fired in hope that the Christians who had remained with Guacamari would reply, for they also had lombards. But there was no reply and no sign of fires or houses in that place. This greatly disturbed our people, who drew the natural conclusion and were very sad.

Four or five hours after nightfall the same canoe returned. The Indians shouted to the captain of the first caravel they approached, asking for the Admiral. They were taken to his ship but would not go aboard until the Admiral himself had spoken to them. They asked for a light in order to recognize him, and when they had done so came on board. One of them was a cousin of Guacamari who had sent them on the previous occasion. When they had returned to him on that first evening, he had given them two gold masks, one to be taken as a present to the Admiral and the other to one of the captains who had accompanied him on his previous voyage. They remained aboard for three hours, talking with the Admiral in the presence of the whole crew, and seemed highly delighted. When the Admiral asked them about the Christians and how they were, Guacamari's cousin answered that they were all well, although some of them had died of disease and others of quarrels which had arisen between them. He said that Guacamari was lying at another village with a wound in his leg and for this reason had not come, but that he would come the next day. He said that two other kings, Caonabo and Mayreni, had attacked him and burned the village. And they went ashore later saying that they would return the next day with Guacamari, and so they left us comforted for that night.

Next morning we were waiting for Guacamari to come, and in the meantime several men landed, on the Admiral's orders, and went to the place where they had often been in the past. They found the palisaded blockhouse in which the Christians had been left, burnt, and the village demolished by fire, and also some clothes and rags that the Indians had brought to throw into the house.[1] The Indians whom they met there went about very warily and did not dare to come near us, but ran away. This seemed a bad sign, for the Admiral had told us that on our arrival so many canoes would put out to come alongside and see us that we should not be able to fend them off, as had been the case on the previous voyage. When we saw that they were now very shy with us, we came to the worst conclusions.

Nevertheless that day we made advances to them and threw them some small things, such as hawks' bells and beads, in order to reassure them. Two or three of them, including Guacamari's cousin, became sufficiently confident to enter the boat and came aboard the ship. When asked about the Christians, they answered that they were all dead. Although one of the Indians

---

1 These would have been thrown alight to set fire to the straw roofs; possibly they are the same as the clothing mentioned later.

who had come with us from Castile had reported that he had learned this from the two natives who had come to the ship and remained alongside in their canoe, we had not believed the story. Guacamari's cousin was asked who had killed them. He replied King Caonabo and King Mayreni and that they had burnt down the village. He said that many Indians had been wounded and that Guacamari himself had a wound in the thigh and was at present at another village where he proposed to go immediately and call him. He was given some presents and departed for the place where Guacamari was.

We waited all that day, and when we saw that they were not coming many of us suspected that the Indians who had done so on the day before had been drowned, because we had given them two or three glasses of wine and they had come in a small canoe which might easily have overturned. Next morning the Admiral and some of us landed and went to the site of the village. We found it completely burnt and the Spaniards' clothing lying on the grass. At that time, we did not see any corpses.

There are many opinions among us. Some of us suspected that Guacamari had taken part himself in the betrayal or murder of the Christians. Others thought not, since it was his village that had been burnt down. The whole matter was therefore extremely doubtful. The Admiral ordered that all the ground within the Christians' fortifications should be searched, since he had instructed them to bury any quantities of gold they might obtain. During this search he decided to inspect a place about a league away which seemed to us a suitable site for a town, since the time had now come to build. Some of us went with him along the coast, examining the country until we came to a small village of seven or eight houses which the Indians had abandoned when they saw us coming. They had taken what they could and hidden the rest of their possessions in the grass near them. These people are so like animals that they have not the intelligence to find a proper place to live. Those who live on the seashore build in a surprisingly primitive way. The houses there are so covered with green or damp that I am astonished they survive.

In these houses we found many possessions of the Christians, which it was incredible they should have bartered, among them a very fine Moorish cloak, which had not been unfolded since it had been brought from

Spain, and also stockings and pieces of cloth and an anchor from the ship which the Admiral had lost there on the previous voyage and other things which greatly strengthened our suspicions. On examining the contents of a wicker basket which they had carefully sewn up and well concealed, we found the head of a man, carefully wrapped. We concluded that this must be the head of a father or mother or of someone whom they greatly loved. I have since heard that many heads like this have been found, from which I conclude that our opinions that time was correct. After this we returned.

That day we again visited the place where the village had been and found many Indians there who had gained confidence and were bartering gold. They had bartered almost a mark's worth. We learnt that they had pointed out where eleven Christians lay covered with grass that had grown over them. They all told us through an interpreter that Caonabo and Mayreni had killed them, but complained at the same time that the Christians had taken three or four women apiece, from which we concluded that they had been murdered out of jealousy.

Next morning, since there was no suitable place for a settlement anywhere in that locality, the Admiral dispatched a caravel elsewhere to look for a site, and took some of us with him in another direction, where we found a very safe harbour and a very pleasant tract of land for a town. But as it was very far from the place where we wanted to be, which was near the goldfield, the Admiral decided not to make a settlement there but in another nearer place, assuming a suitable site might be found.

On our return we found the other caravel which had sailed in the opposite direction, with Melchior[1] and four or five important men. As they went along the coast in search of a suitable place a canoe had come out to them with two Indians, one of them Guacamari's brother, who was recognized by a pilot on that caravel. The Indians asked who were in the ship and had been told 'men of importance'. They then said that Guacamari invited them to land and come to a village of some fifty houses where he was staying. The Spaniards landed in the boat and went to the place where Guacamari was, and found him on his bed apparently suffering from a

_____

1 Melchior Maldonado, who had been sent on the expedition by the sovereigns Ferdinand and Isabela.

serious wound. They spoke with him and asked about the Christians, and he answered, telling the same story as the others, that it was Caonabo and Mayreni who had killed them, and that they had wounded him in the thigh, which he showed them bandaged. Seeing him in this state they believed that his story was true, and when they left he gave to each a golden jewel, small or great according to what he supposed to be their importance. These Indians beat their gold into very thin sheets from which they make masks, setting it in bitumen which they prepare for the purpose. They could not make their masks without it. They also shape gold to be worn as head ornaments or in the ears or nose. It always has to be beaten thin, since they do not prize it as riches but only for its ornamental uses. Guacamari intimated by signs as best he could that because of his wounded state we must ask the Admiral kindly to come and see him, and the Indians told this same story to the Admiral when he arrived.

Next morning the Admiral decided to go to that village, which was about three leagues from where we were, but as the journey would take just under three hours it would have been dinner-time when we arrived. So we ate before landing, and when we had finished the Admiral ordered that all the captains should come in their boats to go ashore, since earlier in the morning before we set out Guacamari's brother had visited the Admiral urging him to hasten his visit to Guacamari. The Admiral and all the chief officers landed so richly dressed that they could have graced a capital city. He took some presents, since he had already received a considerable amount of gold from Guacamari and it was right that he should respond to this demonstration of goodwill. Guacamari had himself prepared a further present for the Admiral and on our arrival we found him stretched on his bed, which was of their native kind, made of woven cotton mesh and hung above the ground. He did not get down but from his bed made the best gestures of courtesy that he could. He showed great feeling for the death of the Christians; the tears sprang to his eyes as he began to talk, demonstrating as best he could how some had died of disease and others had gone to Caonabo in search of the goldfield and had been killed there and how the rest had been killed in his own village. To judge from the condition of the bodies this had happened less than two months ago.

At this point Guacamari presented the Admiral with eight and a half marks worth of gold, and five or six hundred carved stones of various colours, and a head-dress of these same stones, of which I think they have great quantities. In this head-dress was a jewel to which they attached great value. It seems to me that they value copper more than gold.

I was present and so was a surgeon of the fleet. The Admiral said that we had knowledge of men's ailments and asked him to show us his wound. He agreed and I said that it would be best for him to go out of the house if he could, since the crowd of people inside made it dark and it was impossible to see clearly. He agreed to this, I think rather out of fear than goodwill, and left the house supported by an attendant. When he had sat down the surgeon went up and began to remove his bandages. Then Guacamari told the Admiral that he had been wounded by a *ciba*, which means a stone. When the bandages were off we began to examine him, and it was quite obvious that he was no more wounded in this thigh than in the other, although he made a cunning pretence of being in great pain.

What had occurred remained uncertain, for the facts were still not known, though there were many undoubted signs that some hostile people had attacked Guacamari. Consequently the Admiral could not decide what to do. He and many others thought that for the present and until the facts were better known it would be best to dissemble. When they learned the truth they could demand whatever reparation they chose from him.

That evening Guacamari accompanied the Admiral to the ships, where he was shown the horses and everything aboard, which greatly astonished him as things never seen before. He took supper on the ship and later in the evening returned to his house. The Admiral said that he wished to settle there with him and build houses, and Guacamari replied that this would please him but that the place was unhealthy because it was very damp, which it certainly was. All this conversation was conducted through two Indian interpreters, the only survivors of the seven who had been taken to Castile on the previous voyage. Five of them died on the way back and these two almost did so.

Next day we remained at anchor in that harbour and Guacamari inquired when the Admiral intended to depart. A reply was sent that we would leave on the following day, and on that day Guacamari's brother and some others came to the ship bringing gold for barter. This next day a fair amount of gold was exchanged.

There were ten women on board, who had been rescued from the Caribs, most of them from the island of Boriquen, and Guacamari's brother talked with them, and I think instructed them to do what they did that night, which was quietly to jump overboard during the first watch and swim ashore. By the time they were missed they had swum so far that only four were taken by the boats and not until they were just coming out of the water. They had swum a good half league. Next morning the Admiral went to Guacamari demanding that he should return the women who had escaped during the night, and sent to look for them immediately. When his messengers arrived they found the village deserted—not a person remained in it. Many people then reaffirmed their suspicions; others said that Guacamari had merely moved on to another village, as was their custom.

We remained anchored there that day because the weather was against us. On the morning of the next day the Admiral decided that since the weather was still unfavourable it would be a good idea to go and examine a harbour some two leagues up the coast and see if it offered a suitable site for settlement. We rowed there with all the boats, keeping close to the shore and leaving the ships in harbour. There too the natives were apprehensive. On arriving we discovered that the inhabitants of the village had all fled, but we found an Indian hidden in the undergrowth with a gaping dart wound in his back which had prevented him from escaping any further. The Indians of this island fight with darts which they shoot from slings like those with which small boys shoot in Castile. They can shoot both far and accurately, and for a people without iron weapons they can certainly do great damage. This man said that he had been wounded by Caonabo and his people and that they had burned Guacamari's houses. Since we understood them so little and their equivocal statements were so obscure, we have not yet been able to determine the truth about the death of our men, nor did we find a suitable site for a settlement near that harbour.

The Admiral decided that we should return up the coast in the direction from which we had come because he had news that there was gold there. But the weather was so much against us that to sail back thirty leagues was harder than to come from Castile. Indeed, it was so bad and the voyage so long that it was a full three months before we landed. By God's will, which prevented us going further, we had to land at the best and most favourable site we could find. Here there is a very good harbour and large fisheries, of which we were in great need, owing to lack of meat.

In this country the fish are very strange to us and more wholesome than those of Spain, Nevertheless the climate does not allow of their being kept from one day to the next, for it is hot and damp and perishable foods quickly go bad. The soil is most favourable for all crops. At this site there is one main river and another of moderate size with extremely good water.

A town[1] is being built beside the river and it stands immediately above the water at the top of a steep ravine, so that no defensive works are needed on this side. On the other side it is bounded by a forest so thick that a rabbit could hardly get through. The forest is so green that it would be impossible to burn it at any time of year. They have begun to divert an arm of the river which the workmen say they will bring through the centre of the town, and they intend to place mills and waterwheels on this channel and anything else that can be driven by water. They have sown many vegetables, which grow more in eight days than in twenty in Spain. Many Indians come here continually, among them *caciques*,[2] who are, so to speak, their chieftains, and many women as well.

They all bring yams, which are like turnips and very good food, and we prepare them for eating in a variety of ways. They are so nourishing that we are all greatly restored by them, for we have been living on the smallest possible rations during our months at sea. This was necessary, since we did not know what weather we should meet or how long it would please God that the voyage should take. So it was only prudent that we should limit our consumption in order to have enough to keep alive however long the voyage might last. The

---

1  The town was called Isabela, after the Queen. It was abandoned after two years in favour of Santo Domingo, and fell into ruins.

2  This word, Arawak in origin, was applied to chieftains throughout Spanish America, though the word was proper to the West Indies alone.

Indians barter gold and provisions and all that they bring for tags of laces, beads, pins and bits of dishes and plates. This yam is called by the Caribs *nabi* and by the Indians *hage*.

All the people go about as I have said, naked as their mothers bore them, except the women of this island, who cover their private parts with woven cotton which they tie round their hips or with grasses or the leaves of trees. Their way of decoration is to paint their faces black, or red and white, making themselves such sorry sights that we cannot help laughing at them. Their heads are partly shaved and partly covered with tangled locks in such a variety of patterns that it is impossible to describe them. In fact, the best of them delight to crop themselves in a way that in Spain we would only crop a madman. In their neighbourhood there are many goldfields, none of which, according to their reports, is more than twenty or twenty-five leagues away. Some are said to be in Niti, in the territory of Caonabo, who killed the Christians. Others are in another district called Cibao, and if it is God's pleasure we shall know and see all these with our own eyes before many days have passed. We would make the journey now were it not for the fact that there are so many things to be seen to that we cannot manage everything. For a third of the people have fallen sick in the last four or five days, most of them I think from hard work and the rigours of the voyage, and because of differences of climate. But I trust God that all will recover.

These Indians seem so well disposed that they could be converted if we had an interpreter, for they imitate everything that we do. They bend their knees at the altars, and at the *Ave Maria* and other moments, and cross themselves. They all say that they wish to be Christians, although actually they are idolaters. There are idols of all kinds in their houses. When I ask them what these are they answer that they belong to *Turey*, that is to say to the sky. I once made a show of wanting to throw these in the fire, which so upset them that they were on the point of tears. They also think that whatever we bring comes from the sky, for they call it all *Turey*, that is to say sky.

The first day on which I landed and slept ashore was Sunday. The short time that we have spent ashore has been devoted rather to preparing our settlement and searching for what we need than to exploring the land, but the little that we have seen is marvellous. We have seen trees that bear very fine wool, so fine that those who understand weaving say that good cloth could be woven from it.[1] These trees are so numerous that the caravels could be fully laden with the wool, though it is hard to gather, since they are very thorny, but some means of doing so could easily be devised. There is also an infinite amount of cotton growing on trees the size of peach trees, and there are trees that bear wax the colour and taste of bees' wax and as good for burning. Indeed, it is not very different. There are a great number of trees producing turpentine which are very remarkable and very fine; also much tragacanth, which is very good too, and some trees which I think bear nutmegs but at present no fruit. I say I think because the smell and taste of the bark is like that of nutmegs. I saw a root of ginger, which an Indian had tied round his neck. There is also aloe, and though not of a kind which has hitherto been seen in our country it is no doubt one of the species used by doctors. A kind of cinnamon has been found as well, though it is true that it is not so fine as the cinnamon we know at home. This may be because we do not know the right season to gather it, or possibly there are better trees in the land. Yellow mirabolans[2] have also been found, but at the time they were lying beneath the tree and as the soil is very damp they had gone rotten. They taste very bitter, I think because they are rotten. But in every respect except their taste, which is foul, they are the true mirabolan. There is also very good mastic.

None of the people we have met so far have iron. They have quantities of tools such as hatchets and axes, made of stone, which are so beautifully worked that it is a wonder they have been able to make them without iron. They live on bread made of the roots of a vegetable[3] which is half-way between a plant and a tree and on *age*, the turnip-like fruit, already mentioned, which is an extremely good food. They use as seasoning, a spice called *agi*,[4] with which they also season their fish and birds when they can get them. There are great numbers of birds of many different kinds. They have also some nuts like hazels, very good to eat. They eat any snakes, lizards or spiders and worms that they find

---

1  This is the Ceiba or silk cotton tree.

2  'Hog plum.'

3  Yucca.

4  Red pepper.

on the ground, and their habits seem to be more bestial than those of any beast in the world.

Although, on account of the many cases of sickness among his people, the Admiral had previously decided to postpone the search for the goldfields until he had dispatched the ships that were to go to Castile, he now resolved to send two parties under different captains, one to Cibao and the other to Niti, the residence of Caonabo. They went and returned, one on 20 January and the other on 21 January. The captain who went to Cibao found gold in so many places that no one dared to guess the number. Indeed, they found it in more than fifty streams and rivers, and on dry land also. He says that wherever you look, anywhere in this province, you will find gold. He bought samples from many parts from the sand of rivers and from springs on land. It is believed that, if we dig as we know how, it will be found in larger pieces, for the Indians cannot mine, since they have nothing with which to dig more than eight inches deep. The other captain who went to Niti also bought news of much gold in three or four places, and he too brought a sample.

Our sovereigns therefore can certainly consider themselves henceforth the richest and most prosperous on earth, for nothing comparable has ever been seen or read of till now in the whole world. On the next voyage which the ships make they will be able to carry away such quantities of gold that anyone who hears of it will be amazed. Here I think it will be well to end my story. I believe that those who do not know me and hear all this will consider me longwinded and exaggerative. But as God is my witness I have not departed one iota from the truth.

# Letters from a New World:
## Amerigo Vespucci's Discovery of America

Edited by Luciano Formisano and translated by David Jacobson

This text was originally published in 1502 or 1503, probably in Italy. It was then reprinted very quickly in Venice, Paris, Antwerp, Augsburg and several other European cities. It was then translated from Latin into several European languages and printed again. The *Mundus Novus* was one of the first international "bestsellers" in European history.

### LETTER V

### MUNDUS NOVUS

*Amerigo Vespucci to Lorenzo di Pierfrancesco de' Medici*, with many salutations.

In the past I have written to you in rather ample detail about my return from those new regions which we searched for and discovered with the fleet, at the expense and orders of His Most Serene Highness the King of Portugal,[1] and which can be called a new world,[2] since our ancestors had no knowledge of them and they are entirely new matter to those who hear about them. Indeed, it surpasses the opinion of our ancient authorities, since most of them assert that there is no continent south of the equator, but merely that sea which they called the Atlantic; furthermore, if any of them did affirm that a continent was there, they gave many arguments to deny that it was habitable land. But this last voyage of mine has demonstrated that this opinion of theirs is false and contradicts all truth, since I have discovered a continent in those southern regions that is inhabited by more numerous peoples and animals than in our Europe, or Asia or Africa,[3] and in addition I found a more temperate and pleasant climate than in any other region known to us, as you will learn from what follows, where we shall briefly write only of the main points of the matter, and of those things more worthy of note and record, which I either saw or heard in this new world, as will be evident below.

We set out from Lisbon under favorable conditions on 14 May 1501[4] by order of the aforesaid king, with three ships, to go in quest of new regions to the south, and we sailed steadily for twenty months,[5] and the route was as follows. We sailed to what were formerly called the Fortunate Islands and are now the Grand Canary Islands, which are in the third climate and at the bounds of the inhabited West.[6] From there, we travelled on the Ocean Sea along the entire African coast and part of the Ethiopian, as far as the Ethiopian promontory, as Ptolemy called it,[7] which is now called Cape Verde by our people, and Bezeguiche[8] by the Ethiopians. The region is Mandanga, fourteen degrees north of the equator within the Torrid Zone, and it is inhabited by black tribes and peoples. There, once we had recovered our strength and procured all the necessities for our voyage, we weighed anchor and spread our sails to the winds; and set our course across the very vast Ocean toward the Antarctic, steering somewhat to the west with the wind known as Vulturnus:[9] and from

Luciano Formisano, ed., David Jacobson, trans., "Letter V: Mundus Novus" from *Letters from a New World: Amerigo Vespucci's Discovery of America*, pp. 45-57. Published 1992 by Marsilio Publishers.

the day we left the aforesaid promontory, we sailed for two months and three days[10] before sighting any land. What we suffered in that vast expanse of sea, what dangers of shipwreck, what physical discomforts we endured, what anxieties beset our spirits, I leave to the understanding of those who have learned well and from much experience what it means to quest after uncertain things, things they have dared to investigate without prior knowledge of them. And that I might condense the whole story into one sentence, know that out of the sixty-seven days[11] we sailed, we had forty-four continuous days of rain, thunder, and lightning, so dark that we never saw sunlight in the day, nor clear sky at night. Fear so overwhelmed us that we had almost abandoned all hope of survival However, in those frequent, terrible tempests of sea and sky, it pleased the Most High to show us a nearby continent, and new regions and an unknown world. Sighting them, we were filled with joy, which, as one can well imagine, seizes those who have found safety after calamities and misfortunes. Thus, on 7 August 1501,[12] we dropped anchor off the shores of those regions, thanking our God with solemn prayer and the singing of a Mass. There we learned that the land was not an island but a continent, both because it extends over very long, straight shorelines, and because it is filled with countless inhabitants. For in it we encountered innumerable peoples and tribes, and all kinds of sylvan animals not found in our regions, and many other things we had never seen before, which would take too long to describe individually. God's mercy shone about greatly when we entered those regions; for our firewood and water supplies were dwindling, and in a few days we might have perished at sea. Honor be to Him, and glory, and thanks.

We decided to sail along the shore of that continent to the east, and never to lose sight of it. Soon we came to a bend where the shore curved to the south: the distance from where we first touched land to this bend was about three hundred leagues. In this phase of the voyage we landed on several occasions and conversed in friendly fashion with the people, as you will hear below. I had forgot to write to you that from the promontory of Cape Verde to the start of that continent is a distance of about seven hundred leagues, although I estimate that we sailed more than eighteen hundred, owing in part to our ignorance of the place and the ignorance of the pilot, and in part because of the storms and winds

which blocked our direct course and forced us to make frequent turns. For if my companions had not relied upon me and my knowledge of cosmography, there would have been no pilot or captain on the voyage to know within five hundred leagues where we were. Indeed, we were wandering with uncertainty, with only the instruments to show us accurate altitudes of the heavenly bodies: those instruments being the quadrant and astrolabe, as everyone knows. After this, everyone held me in great honor. For I truly showed them that, without any knowledge of sea charts, I was still more expert in the science of navigation than all the pilots in the world: for they know nothing of any places beyond those where they have often sailed before. In any case, where the aforementioned bend in the land curved southward on the coast, we agreed to sail beyond it and explore what was in those regions. Therefore we sailed along the shore, approximately six hundred leagues, and we often landed and conversed with the inhabitants of those regions, and were warmly received by them, and sometimes stayed with them fifteen or twenty days at a time, always in a very friendly and hospitable way, as you will hear in the following. Part of that new continent lies in the Torrid Zone beyond the equator and toward the Antarctic Pole; it starts eight degrees beyond the equator.[13] We sailed along the shore until we passed the Tropic of Capricorn and found the Antarctic Pole, fifty degrees above their horizon, and we were 17½ degrees from the Antarctic Circle itself; I shall now relate in due order what we saw there and what we learned of those peoples' nature, customs, and tractability, and of the fertility of soil, salubriousness of climate, the dispositions of the heavens and the heavenly bodies, and in particular of the fixed stars of the eighth sphere, which our ancestors never saw or described.

First, then, the people. We found such a great multitude of people in those regions that no one could count their number (as one reads in the book of the *Apocalypse*);[14] a gentle, tractable people. Everyone of both sexes goes about naked, covering no part of the body, and just as they issued from their mothers' wombs so they go about until their dying day. They have big, solid, well-formed and well-proportioned bodies, and their complexions tend toward red, which happens, I suppose, because in going about naked they are colored by the sun.[15] They also have long[16] black hair. They are nimble in gait and in their games, and have open, pleasant faces, which they themselves, however, disfigure. They pierce their own cheeks, lips, noses, and ears, and you must not imagine that these holes are small or that they have but one of them: indeed I saw several people who had seven holes in a single face, each big enough to hold a plum. They fill these holes with beautiful stones, cerulean, marblelike, crystalline, or alabaster, or with very white bones and other things artfully wrought in their fashion;[17] if you were to see such an unusual and monstrous thing as a man with seven stones just in his cheeks or jaws or lips, some of them half a palm long, you would be amazed. And I often considered this and judged that seven such stones must weigh sixteen ounces. Beyond that, in each ear, which they pierce with three holes, they carry more stones dangling from rings; this custom is only for the men: the women do not pierce their faces, but only their ears. They have another custom that is appalling and passes belief. Their women, being very lustful, make their husbands' members swell to such thickness that they look ugly and misshapen; this they accomplish with a certain device they have and by bites from certain poisonous animals. Because of this, many men lose their members, which rot through neglect, and they are left eunuchs. They have no cloth of wool, linen, or cotton, since they need none. Nor have they private property, but own everything in common: they live together without a king and without authorities, each man his own master. They take as many wives as they wish, and son may couple with mother, brother with sister, cousin with cousin, and in general men with women as they chance to meet. They dissolve marriage as often as they please, observing no order in any of these matters. Moreover, they have no temple and no religion, nor do they worship idols. What more can I say? They live according to nature, and might be called Epicureans rather than Stoics.[18] There are no merchants among them, nor is there any commerce. The peoples make war among themselves without art or order. The elders deliver orations to the young to sway their will, urging them on to wars in which they kill each other cruelly, and they take captives and keep them, not to spare them, but to kill them for food: for they eat each other, the victors eat the vanquished, and together with other kinds of meat, human flesh is common fare among them. This you may be sure of, because one father was known to have eaten his children and wife,[19]

and I myself met and spoke with a man who was said to have eaten more than three hundred+ human bodies; and I also stayed twenty-seven days in a certain city in which I saw salted human flesh hanging from house-beams, much as we hang up bacon and pork. I will say more: they marvel that we do not eat our enemies and use their flesh as food, for they say human flesh is very savory. Their weapons are bows and arrows, and when they charge into battle, they cover no part of their bodies to protect themselves, also in this respect like animals. We tried our best to dissuade them from these wicked customs, and they promised us that they would *give* them up. Their women, as I said, although they go naked and are exceedingly lustful, still have rather shapely and clean bodies, and are not as revolting as one might think, because, being fleshy, their shameful parts are less visible, covered for the most part by the good quality of their bodily composition. It seemed remarkable to us that none of them appeared to have sagging breasts, and also, those who had borne children could not be distinguished from the virgins by the shape or tautness of their wombs, and this was true too of other parts of their bodies, which decency bids me pass over.[21] When they were able to copulate with Christians, they were driven by their excessive lust to corrupt and prostitute all their modesty. The people live to be 150 years old,[22] seldom fall ill, and if they do happen to contract some sickness, they cure themselves with certain roots of herbs. These are the more remarkable things I noticed among them. The air there is very temperate and good, and, as I was able to learn by conversing with the people, there is no pestilence or illness there deriving from contaminated air, and unless they die a violent death, they live a long life: I think this is due to the southern winds blowing constantly there, especially the one we call Eurus,[23] which is to them as Aquilo[24] is to us. They are very zealous fishermen, and the sea there is full of fish of all sorts.[25] They are not hunters: I think this is because there are many kinds of forest animals there, especially lions,[26] bears, countless snakes, and other dreadful and ill-formed beasts, and forests on all sides with trees of enormous size, that they do not dare to expose themselves, naked and without any protection or weapons, to such dangers.

The land of those regions is very fertile and pleasant, abundant in hills and mountains, countless valleys and huge rivers, watered by healthful springs, and filled with broad, dense, barely penetrable forests and all sorts of wild beasts. Great trees grow there without cultivation, and many of them produce fruits delicious to taste and beneficial to the human body, though several indeed are the opposite, and none of the fruits there are like our own. Numberless kinds of herbs and roots grow there as well, from which the people make bread and excellent foods. They also have many seeds, totally different from ours. There are no kinds of metal there except gold, in which those regions abound, although we did not bring any back with us on this our first voyage. The inhabitants apprised us of it, and told us that in the interior there is great abundance of gold, which they do not at all value or consider precious. They are rich in pearls, as I wrote to you elsewhere.[27] If I wanted to mention separately all the things which are there, and to write about the numerous kinds of animals and their great numbers, I would grow too prolix with a matter so vast; and I certainly believe that our Pliny did not come within a thousandth part of the types of parrots and other birds and animals which are in those regions, with such great diversity of forms and colors that even Polycletus,[28] master of painting in all its perfection, would have failed to depict them adequately. All the trees there are fragrant, and all produce gum or oil or some liquor, and I do not doubt that their properties, if they were known to us, would be salubrious for the human body; and certainly, if anywhere in the world there exists an Earthly Paradise, I think it is not far from those regions, which lie, as I said, to the south, and in such a temperate climate that they never have either icy winters or scorching summers.

Sky and air are dear for most of the year and free from dense vapors. The rains there fall delicately and last three or four hours, then vanish like mist. The sky is adorned with very beautiful signs and figures, in which I noticed twenty stars as bright as we sometimes see Venus or Jupiter. I considered their movements and orbits and measured their circumferences and diameters with geometric methods, and determined that they are of great magnitude. I saw three Canopi[29] in that sky, two of which are bright indeed, and the third dim. The Antarctic Pole has no Ursa Major and Ursa Minor, as appear in our Arctic Pole, nor is any bright star seen near it; of the stars which are carried around it in smaller orbit, there are three which form the figure of an orthogonal triangle, of which half the

circumference, or the diameter, is 9½ degrees. As they rise, a white Canopus of extraordinary size can be seen to the left. When they reach mid-heaven they form this figure:

```
  *                          s s
                           s s s s
                          s s s s s s
                           s s s s
                                       Canopus
  *                        *
```

After these come two other stars, of which half the circumference, or diameter, is 12½ degrees, and with them can be seen another white Canopus. Another six stars, the brightest and most beautiful of all in the eighth sphere, follow them; on the surface of the firmament, these stars have a half-circumference, or diameter, of thirty-two degrees. A black Canopus of immense size soars up with them. They are seen in the Milky Way and form a figure like this when they are on the meridian line:

```
                              *
  *      *       *                            *
                    s s
                   s s s s s
                  s s s s s s
                   s s s
                      *
```

I encountered many other very beautiful stars during this voyage of mine, and I notated their movements carefully and have described them beautifully and graphically in a booklet of mine.[30] His Most Serene Highness the King has it at present, and I hope that he will return it to me. In that hemisphere I saw things which do not agree with the arguments of philosophers: a white rainbow was seen twice around midnight, not only by me, but also by all the sailors. Likewise, several times we saw a new moon on the day when it was in conjunction with the sun. Every night in that part of the sky, innumerable vapors and bright flares streak across. A bit earlier I spoke of the hemisphere, although, properly speaking, it is not fully a hemisphere with respect to ours; but since it approaches the shape of one, it is permissible to call it so.

Therefore, as I said, from Lisbon, our point of departure, 39½ degrees from the equator, we sailed

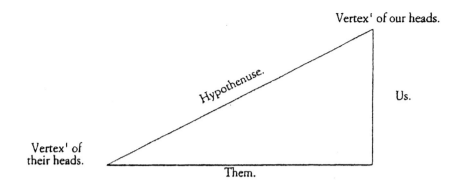

Vertex' of our heads.

Hypothenuse.

Us.

Vertex' of
their heads.

Them.

fifty degrees beyond the equator, which together make about ninety degrees, and since this sum makes a quarter of the great circle, according to the true reasoning of measurement passed on to us by the ancients, it is clear that we sailed around a quarter of the world. And by this logic, we who live in Lisbon, 39½ degrees this side of the equator in the northern latitude,[31] are at an angle of five degrees in the transverse line to those who live at the fiftieth degree beyond the same line in the southern latitude, or, so that you may understand more clearly: a perpendicular line, which hangs over our heads from a point directly above us while we stand upright, hangs pointing toward their sides or ribs: thus we are in an upright line, and they in a transverse line, and a kind of orthogonal triangle is formed thereby, of which we form, the perpendicular line, they the base, and the hypothenuse extends from our vertex to theirs, as is evident in the drawing. And let these words suffice for cosmography.

These were the more noteworthy things I saw on this last navigation of mine, which I call the "third journey." The other two "journeys" were my two other navigations, which I made toward the west on a mandate from the Most Serene King of the Spains;[32] on those voyages I noted the marvels accomplished by the sublime creator of all, our God: I kept a diary of the noteworthy things, so that, if ever I am granted the leisure, I may gather together all these marvels one by one and write a book, either of geography or of cosmography, so that my memory will live on for posterity, and so that the immense creation of almighty God, unknown in part to the ancients yet known to us, may be recognized. I

pray, therefore, to the most merciful God that He may prolong the days of my life, that by His good grace, and for the salvation of my soul, I may attain the fullest realization of my goals. The other two "journeys" I keep among my private papers, and when the Most Serene Highness returns the "third journey" to me, I shall try to return to tranquillity and my homeland, where I will be able to confer with experts and, with the help and encouragement of my friends, to complete that work.

I ask your forgiveness for not sending you this last navigation, or rather this last "journey," as I had promised to do in my last letter: you know the reason, since I could not yet have the original back from His Most Serene Highness. I still plan to make a fourth voyage, and have already received the promise of two ships together with their equipment, so that I may prepare to search for new regions to the south, travelling from the east with the wind called Africus;[33] on this voyage I think I will accomplish many things to the praise of God, the benefit of this kingdom, and the honor of my old age; and I await nothing but the consent of His Most Serene Highness. May God permit whatever is for the best. You will learn of whatever happens.

The interpreter Giocondo[34] has translated this letter from Italian to Latin, so that all the Latins may understand how many marvelous things are being discovered every day, and to curb the audacity of those people who wish to study the heavens and their majesty and to know more than they are permitted to know, for, ever since the world began, the earth's vastness and all things contained in it have been unknown.

Praise to God.

# Letters to the King of Portugal

## By Nzinga Mbemba (Afonso I)

The largest state in central West Africa by 1500 was the kingdom of Kongo, stretching along the estuary of the Congo River in territory that today lies within Angola and Zaire. In 1483 the Portuguese navigator Diogo Cao made contact with Kongo and several years later visited its inland capital. When he sailed home he brought with him Kongo emissaries, whom King Nzinga Kuwu dispatched to Lisbon to learn European ways. They returned in 1491, accompanied by Portuguese priests, artisans, and soldiers who brought with them numerous European goods, including a printing press. In the same year the king and his son, Nzinga Mbemba, were baptized as Catholic.

Around 1506 Nzinga Mbemba, whose Christian name was Afonso, succeeded his father and ruled until about 1543. Afonso promoted the introduction of European culture in his kingdom by adopting Christianity as the state religion (although most of his subjects, especially those in the hinterlands, were unaffected), imitating the etiquette of the Portuguese royal court, and using Portuguese as the language of state business. His son Henrique was educated in Portugal and returned to serve as West Africa's first black Roman Catholic bishop. European firearms, horses, and cattle, as well as new foods from the Americas, became common in Kongo, and Afonso dreamed of achieving a powerful and prosperous state through cooperation with the Europeans. By the time of his death, however, his kingdom verged on disintegration, in no small measure because of the Portuguese. As many later African rulers were to discover, the introduction of European products and customs caused widespread dissension and instability. Worse, the unceasing Portuguese pursuit of slaves undermined Afonso's authority and made his subjects restive. In 1526 the desperate king wrote the following three letters to King Joao III of Portugal, urging him to control his rapacious subjects. The documents are part of a collection of twenty-four letters that Afonso and his Portuguese-educated, native secretaries dispatched to the kings of Portugal on a variety of issues.

Sir, Your Highness should know how our Kingdom is being lost in so many ways that it is convenient to provide for the necessary remedy, since this is caused by the excessive freedom given by your agents and officials to the men and merchants who are allowed to come to this Kingdom to set up shops with goods and many things which have been prohibited by us, and which they spread throughout our Kingdoms and Domains in such an abundance that many of our vassals, whom we had in obedience, do not comply because they have the things in greater abundance than we ourselves; and it was with these things that we had them content and subjected under our vassalage and jurisdiction, so it is doing a great harm not only to the service of God, but the security and peace of our Kingdoms and State as well.

And we cannot reckon how great the damage is, since the mentioned merchants are taking every day our natives, sons of the land and the sons of our noblemen and vassals and our relatives, because the thieves and men of bad conscience grab them wishing to have the things and wares of this Kingdom which they are ambitious of; they grab them and get them to be sold; and so great, Sir, is the corruption and licentiousness that our country is being completely depopulated, and Your Highness should not agree with this nor accept it as in your service. And to avoid it we need from those (your) Kingdoms no more than some priests and a few people to reach in schools, and no other goods except wine and flour for the holy sacrament. That is why we beg of Your Highness to help and assist us in this matter, commanding your factors that they should not send here either merchants or wares, because it is *our will that in these Kingdoms there should not be any trade of slaves nor outlet for them.*[1] Concerning what is referred [to] above, again we beg of Your Highness to agree with it, since otherwise we cannot remedy such an obvious damage. Pray Our Lord in His mercy to have Your Highness under His guard and let you do forever the things of His service. …

* * *

Moreover, Sir, in our Kingdoms there is another great inconvenience which is of little service to God, and this is that many of our people, keenly desirous as they are of the wares and things of your Kingdoms, which are brought here by your people, and in order to satisfy their voracious appetite, seize many of our people, freed and exempt men, and very often it happens that they kidnap even noblemen and the sons of noblemen, and our relatives, and take them to be sold to the white men who are in our Kingdoms; and for this purpose they have concealed them; and others are brought during the night so that they might not be recognized.

And as soon as they are taken by the white men they are immediately ironed and branded with fire, and when they are carried to be embarked, if they are caught by our guards' men the whites allege that they have bought them but they cannot say from whom, so that it is our duty to do justice and to restore to the

freemen their freedom, but it cannot be done if your subjects feel offended, as they claim to be.

And to avoid such a great evil we passed a law so that any white man living in our Kingdoms and wanting to purchase goods in any way should first inform three of our noblemen and officials of our court whom we rely upon in this matter, and these are Dom Pedro Manipanza and Dom Manuel Manissaba, our chief usher, and Goncalo Pires our chief freighter, who should investigate if the mentioned goods are captives or free men, and if cleared by them there will be no further doubt nor embargo for them to be taken and embarked. But if the white men do not comply with it they will lose the aforementioned goods. And if we do them this favor and concession it is for the part Your Highness has in it, since we know that it is in your service too that these goods are taken from our Kingdom, otherwise we should not consent to this. …

* * *

Sir, Your Highness has been kind enough to write to us saying that we should ask in our letters for anything we need, and that we shall be provided with everything, and as the peace and the health of your Kingdom depend on us, and as there are among us old folks and people who have lived for many days, it happens we have continuously many and different diseases which put us very often in such a weakness that we reach almost the last extreme; and the same happens to Our children, relatives and natives owing to the lack in this country of physicians and surgeons who might know how to cure properly such diseases. And us we have got neither dispensaries nor drugs which might help us in this forlornness, many of those who had been already confirmed and instructed in the holy faith of Our Lord Jesus Christ perish and die; and the rest of the people in their majority cure themselves with herbs and breads and other ancient methods, so that they put all their faith in the mentioned herbs and ceremonies if they live, and believe that they are saved if they die; and this is not much in the service of God.

And to avoid such a great error and inconvenience, since it is from God in the first place and then from your Kingdoms and from Your Highness that all the good and drugs and medicines have come to save us, we beg of you to be agreeable and kind enough to send us two physicians and two apothecaries and one surgeon, so that they may come with their drugstores and all the necessary things to stay in our kingdoms, because we are in extreme need of them all and each of them. We shall do them all good and shall benefit them by all means, since they are sent by Your Highness, whom we thank for your work in their coming. We beg of Your Highness as a great favor to do this for us, because besides being good in itself it is in the service of God as we have said above.

every time he wants something he references God. Sly? or innocently naïve?

# Selections from
# Victors and Vanquished

## Edited by Stuart B. Schwartz

## BERNAL DÍAZ

### From *The True History of the Conquest of New Spain*

*Díaz's account provides an outline of events but also considerable detail about his companions and the political and personal factions among them. The descriptions of the battles with the Maya, the story of the Spanish castaways, and that of doña Marina are highlights of the narrative.*

After the return of the Captain Juan de Grijalva to Cuba, when the Governor Diego Velásquez understood how rich were these newly discovered lands, he ordered another fleet, much larger than the former one to be sent off, and he had already collected in the Port of Santiago, where he resided, ten ships, four of them were those in which we had returned with Juan de Grijalva, which had at once been careened, and the other six had been got together from other ports in the Island. He had them furnished with provisions, consisting of Cassava bread and salt pork, for at that time there were neither sheep nor cattle in the Island of Cuba, as it had been only recently settled. These provisions were only to last until we arrived at Havana, for it was at that port that we were to take in our stores, as was afterwards done.

I must cease talking of this and tell about the disputes which arose over the choice of a captain for the expedition. There were many debates and much opposition, for some gentleman said that Vasco Porcallo, a near relation of the Conde de Feria, should be captain, but Diego Velásquez feared that he would rise against him with the fleet, for he was very daring; others said that Agustin Bermudez or Antonio Velásquez Borrejo, or Bernadino Velásquez, kinsman of Diego Velásquez should go in command.

Most of us soldiers who were there said that we should prefer to go again under Juan de Grijalva, for he was a good captain, and there was no fault to be found either with his person or his capacity for command.

While things were going on in the way I have related, two great favourites of Diego Velásquez named Andrés de Duero, the Governor's Secretary, and Amador de Lares, His Majesty's accountant, secretly formed a partnership with a gentleman named Hernando Cortés, a native of Medellin, who held a grant of Indians in the Island. A short while before, Cortés had married a lady named Catalina Juarez la Marcayda; this lady was sister of a certain Juan Juarez who after the conquest of New Spain was a settler at Mexico. As far as I know, and from what others say, it was a love match. On this matter of the marriage other persons who saw it have had much to say, and for that reason I will not touch any more on this delicate subject.

I will go on to tell about this partnership, it came about in this manner:—These two great favourites of Velásquez agreed that they would get him to appoint Cortés Captain General of the whole fleet, and that they would divide between the three of them, the spoil of gold, silver and jewels which might fall to Cortés' share. For secretly Diego Velásquez was sending to trade and not to form a settlement, as was apparent afterwards from the instructions given about it, although it was announced and published that the expedition was for the purpose of founding a settlement.

When this arrangement had been made, Duero and the accountant went to work in such a way with Diego Velásquez, and addressed such honied words to him, praising Cortés highly, as the very man for the position of Captain, as in addition to being energetic he knew how to command and ensure respect, and as one who would be faithful in everything entrusted to him, both in regard to the fleet and in everything else, (pointing out too, that he was his godson, for Velásquez was his sponsor when Cortés married Doña Catalina Juarez), that they persuaded him to choose Cortés as Captain General.

Andrés de Duero, the Governor's Secretary, drew up the documents in very good ink[1] as the proverb says, in the way Cortés wished with very ample powers.

When the appointment was made public, some persons were pleased and others annoyed.

One Sunday when Diego Velásquez went to Mass,—and as he was Governor he was accompanied by the most distinguished persons in the town,—he placed Hernando Cortés on his right hand so as to pay him honour. A buffoon, called the mad Cervantes, ran in front of Diego Velásquez, making grimaces and cracking jokes and he cried out—

> The parade of my friend Diego, Diego,
> Who then is this captain of your choice?
> He comes from Medellin in Estremadura
> A very valiant captain indeed
> Have a care lest he run off with the fleet
> For all judge him a man to take care of his
> own. ...

Before going any further I wish to say that the valiant and energetic Hernando Cortés was a gentleman by birth (hijo-d'algo) by four lines of descent. The first through the Cortéses, for so his father Martin Cortés was named, the second through the Pizarros, the third through the Monroys and the fourth through the Altamiranos. Although he was such a valiant, energetic and daring captain, I will not from now on, call him by any of these epithets of valiant, or energetic, nor will I speak of him as Marqués del Valle, but simply as Hernando Cortés. For the name Cortés alone was held in as high respect throughout the Indies as well as in Spain, as was the name of Alexander in Macedonia, and those of Julius Caesar and Pompey and Scipio among the Romans, and Hannibal among the Carthaginians, or in our own Castille the name of Gonzalo Hernández, the Great Captain. And the valiant Cortés himself was better pleased not to be called by lofty titles but simply by his name, and so I will call him for the future. ...

As soon as Hernando Cortés had been appointed General in the way I have related, he began to search for all sorts of arms, guns, powder and crossbows and every kind of warlike stores which he could get together, and all sorts of articles to be used for barter, and other things necessary for the expedition.

Moreover he began to adorn himself and be more careful of his appearance than before, and he wore a plume of feathers with a medal, and a gold chain, and a velvet cloak trimmed with knots of gold, in fact he looked like a gallant and courageous Captain. However, he had no money to defray the expenses I have spoken about, for at that time he was very poor and much in debt, although he had a good *encomienda* of Indians who were getting him a return from his gold mines, but he spent all of it on his person and on finery for his wife whom he had recently married, and on entertaining some guests who had come to visit him. For he was affable in his manner and a good talker, and he had twice been chosen *Alcalde*[2] of the town of Santiago Baracoa where he had settled, and in that country it is esteemed a great honour to be chosen as *Alcalde*.

When some merchant friends of his named Jaime Tria, Jerónimo Tria and Pedro de Jerez saw that he had obtained this command as Captain General, they lent him four thousand gold dollars in coin and gave him merchandise worth another four thousand dollars secured on his Indians and estates. Then he ordered two standards and banners to be made, worked in gold with the royal arms and a cross on each side with a legend

---

1 De muy buena tinta: most efficiently.

2 Alcalde: Mayor.

which said, "Comrades, let us follow the sign of the holy Cross with true faith, and through it we shall conquer." And he ordered a proclamation to be made with the sound of drums and trumpets in the name of His Majesty and by Diego Velásquez in the King's name, and in his own as Captain General, to the effect that whatsoever person might wish to go in his company to the newly discovered lands to conquer them and to settle there, should receive his share of the gold, silver and riches which might be gained and an *encomienda* of Indians after the country had been pacified, and that to do these things Diego Velásquez held authority from His Majesty.

Although he put in the proclamation this about the authority of Our Lord the King, the Chaplain, Benito Martínez, had not yet arrived from Spain with the Commission which Diego Velásquez had sent him to obtain. …

We assembled at Santiago de Cuba, whence we set out with the fleet more than three hundred and fifty soldiers in number. From the house of Velásquez there came Diego de Ordás, the chief Mayordomo, whom Velásquez himself sent with orders to keep his eyes open and see that no plots were hatched in the fleet, for he was always distrustful of Cortés although he concealed his fears. There came also Francisco de Morla and an Escobar, whom we called The Page, and a Heredia, and Juan Ruano and Pedro Escudero, and Martin Ramos de Lares, and many others who were friends and followers of Diego Velásquez; and I place myself last on the list for I also came from the house of Diego Velásquez, for he was my kinsman. …

Cortés worked hard to get his fleet under way and hastened on his preparations, for already envy and malice had taken possession of the relations of Diego Velásquez who were affronted because their kinsman neither trusted them nor took any notice of them and because he had given charge and command to Cortés, knowing that he had looked upon him as a great enemy only a short time before, on account of his marriage, already mentioned by me; so they went about grumbling at their kinsman Diego Velásquez and at Cortés, and by every means in their power they worked on Diego Velásquez to induce him to revoke the commission.

Now Cortés was advised of all this, and for that reason never left the Governor's side, and always showed himself to be his zealous servant, and kept on telling him that, God willing, he was going to make him a very illustrious and wealthy gentleman in a very short time. Moreover Andrés de Duero was always advising Cortés to hasten the embarkation of himself and his soldiers, for Diego Velásquez was already changing his mind owing to the importunity of his family.

When Cortés knew this he sent orders to his wife that all provisions of food which he wished to take and any other gifts (such as women usually give to their husbands when starting on such an expedition) should be sent at once and placed on board ship.

He had already had a proclamation made that on that day by nightfall all ships, Captains, pilots and soldiers should be on board and no one should remain on shore. When Cortés had seen all his company embarked he went to take leave of Diego Velásquez, accompanied by his great friends and many other gentlemen, and all the most distinguished citizens of that town.

After many demonstrations and embraces of Cortés by the Governor, and of the Governor by Cortés, he took his leave. The next day very early after having heard Mass we went to our ships, and Diego Velásquez himself accompanied us, and again they embraced with many fair speeches one to the other until we set sail.

# ANDRÉS DE TAPIA

## *Another Spanish View of the Cholula Massacre*

*Cortés's own report of the events in Cholula gave little detail of his bloody actions, but another Spanish observer, the captain Andrés de Tapia, provides a succinct and frank record of the destruction of that city. Tapia was one of Cortés's captains and a man of great courage. In his mid-twenties during the conquest, he was often mentioned in Bernal Díaz's book as an able commander and companion. "Well-made and with a scanty beard," is the way Díaz remembered him. In the 1540s, Tapia was asked to give a deposition in an investigation of Cortés's actions. This deposition served as the basis for his "Relation of some things that happened to the Very Illustrious Don Hernando Cortés, Marqués del Valle. ..." A concise account by another eyewitness of the conquest, Tapia's brutally frank description of the two days of destruction wrought by the Spaniards and Tlaxcalans at Cholula was not published until the nineteenth century.*

...The marqués left Tlaxcala after gathering as much information as he could of the territory ahead, and the Indians said they would go with him to show the way as far as they knew it. They also said that about four leagues from here was an enemy city called Cholula which was a state in itself and a friend and ally of Moctezuma. And so the Spaniards set out for this city accompanied by forty thousand warriors who by order of the marqués marched at a distance from us.

The morning of the day we arrived at the city of Cholula, ten or twelve thousand men in squadrons came out to meet us, bringing maize bread and turkeys. Each squadron advanced toward the marqués to bid him welcome and then withdrew. The Cholulans earnestly begged the marqués not to allow the Tlaxcalans to enter their territory, so the marqués ordered them to go back, but the Tlaxcalans said: "Beware of the people of this city, who are traders and not men of war, and who have one heart and show another, resorting to trickery and lies. We dislike having to leave you, for we gave ourselves as your friends." In spite of this the marqués ordered that all their men were to go back, but that if some of the notables wished to stay they could be quartered outside the city with a few men to serve them, and that is the way it was done.

As we entered the city the rest of the men came out in their squadrons, greeting the Spaniards they met, who were marching in formation. After the squadrons came all the ministers who served the idols. They were dressed in sleeveless robes, some of which were closed in front like surplices, with heavy cotton fringe at the edges, and other kinds of dress. Many of them were

playing flutes and trumpets, and carrying certain idols that were covered, and many incense burners. They approached the marqués first and then the other men, perfuming them with a resin they burned in the censers.

In this city they had a principal god who at one time had been a man. They called him Quetzalcoatl. He is said to have founded this city, and to have commanded them not to kill men, but instead to build edifices to the creator of the sun and the heavens, in which to offer him quail and other things of the hunt. They were to wish no harm and do no harm to one another. Quetzalcoatl is supposed to have worn a white vesture like a monk's tunic, and over it a mantle covered with red crosses. They had certain green stones there, one of them a monkey's head, which they said had belonged to this man, and they regarded them as relics.

The marqués and his men stayed here several days, and he sent certain men as volunteers to explore a volcano we could see on a high ridge five leagues away, and which gave out much smoke. They were to look out from there in all directions and bring back news of the disposition of the land.

Certain persons of rank came to this city as messengers of Moctezuma and made their speeches over and over again. Sometimes they said there was no reason for us to go on, and where would we go anyway, since they had no provisions for us to eat where they lived. At other times they told us Moctezuma said that if we went to see him he would die of fright. Also they said there was no road by which to go. When they saw that the marqués was undisturbed by all this, they made the people of the city tell us that where Moctezuma lived there were great numbers of lions and tigers and other wild beasts that he let loose any time he wanted to, and that they were enough to tear us to pieces and eat us.

When they saw that none of this served to deter us, Moctezuma's messengers plotted with the people of the city to kill us. The way they proposed to do it was to take us to the left of the road leading to Mexico, where there were dangerous crossings formed by the waters flowing from the ridge where the volcano was. Since the earth there is soft and sandy, a little water can make a big ravine, and some of them are more than a hundred *estados* deep. They are also so narrow that there is timber tall enough to make bridges across the ravines, and these exist, because we later saw them.

As we were preparing to leave, an Indian woman of this city of Cholula, the wife of one of the notables, told the woman who was our interpreter along with the Christian, that she would like her to stay there because she was very fond of her and would be grieved to see her killed. Then she told her what they were plotting and thus the marqués learned of it and delayed his departure two days. He repeatedly told the Cholulans that it caused him no surprise or anger when men fought, even if they fought against him; but that he would be greatly displeased if they told him lies, so he warned them not to lie in their dealings with him, nor to resort to treachery. They assured him they were his friends and always would be, and that they would never lie to him. Then they asked him when he wished to leave, and he said that on the following day. They said they wanted to assemble many men to send with him, but the marqués said he wanted only slaves to carry the Spaniards' baggage. They still insisted on giving him warriors, and he refused, repeating that he wanted only enough men to carry the baggage.

Next day there came unbidden many men with weapons of the kind they use, saying they were slaves and bearers, though it later turned out that they were among the bravest of their warriors. The marqués said he wished to take his leave of all the lords, and asked that they be summoned. There was no one lord of this city, but only captains of the republic, since it was in the nature of a dominion and they governed themselves in that way. The dignitaries then arrived, and the marqués took about thirty of them, those who looked most important, into a courtyard of the house where he was lodged, and he said to them: "In everything have I spoken the truth to you, and I have given orders to all the Christians of my company to do you no harm, and no harm has been done you, yet with evil intention you asked that the Tlaxcalans be kept from entering your territory. And although you have not given me to eat as you should, I have not allowed so much as a chicken to be taken from you. Also I have asked you not to lie to me. But in payment for these good deeds you have conspired to kill me and my companions, bringing men to fight me as soon as we have reached the bad terrain over which you plan to lead us. For this wickedness you shall all die, and as a sign that you are traitors I shall destroy your city so that no edifice remains. It is

needless for you to deny this, for I know it as well as I am saying it to you."

They were astonished, and kept looking at one another. There were guards to keep them from escaping and there were also men guarding the people that would carry our baggage, who were outside in the large courtyards of the idols. The marqués then said to these dignitaries: "I wish to have you tell me the truth, though I already know it, so that these messengers and all the rest hear it from your mouths and not think that I have accused you falsely."

Five or six were taken aside, and each confessed separately, without torture of any kind, that it was as the marqués had said. When he saw that they were in agreement with one another he brought everyone together again and they all confessed that it was so, and said among themselves: "He is like our gods, who know all; there is no use in denying it to him."

The marqués had Moctezuma's messengers brought, and said to them: "These people wanted to kill me, and they say that Moctezuma was behind it, but I do not believe it because I hold him as friend and know that he is a great lord, and a lord does not lie. I believe they wanted to do me this injury by treachery, as scoundrels that they are, and people who have no lord; and for this they shall die. But you have nothing to fear, for besides being messengers you are the envoys of that lord I regard as friend, who I have reason to believe is very good, and nothing will I hear to the contrary."

Then he ordered most of those lords killed, leaving a few of them fettered, and ordered the signal given the Spaniards to attack the men in the courtyards and kill them all, and so it was done. They defended themselves the best they could, and tried to take the offensive, but since they were walled inside the courtyards with the entrances guarded, most of them died anyway.

This done, the Spaniards and Indians in our company went out in squads to different parts of the city, killing warriors and burning houses. In a short time a number of the Tlaxcalans arrived, and they looted the city and destroyed everything possible, making off with a great amount of plunder.

Certain priests of the devil climbed to the top of the principal idol's tower and would not give themselves up but stayed there to be burned, lamenting and complaining to their idol how wrong of him it was to forsake them. So everything possible was done to destroy this city, but the marqués ordered us to refrain from killing women and children. The destruction took two days, during which many of the inhabitants went to hide in the hills and fields, and others took refuge in surrounding enemy country.

At the end of two days the marqués ordered the destruction ceased, and within another two or three days, it later appeared, many of the natives of the city must have gathered together, for they sent word to the marqués begging for pardon and for permission to reoccupy the city, offering themselves protectorate of the Tlaxcalans.

# FRAY BERNARDINO DE SAHAGÚN

## From the *Florentine Codex*

*The Nahua accounts collected by Sahagún emphasize the progress of the Spaniards toward Tenochtitlan and the treachery of the Tlaxcalans. Here the Cholula massacre is presented as an unprovoked act of violence. Once again we turn to the modern translations from the Nahuatl in Lockhart's* We People Here.

Tenth chapter, where it is said how the Spaniards landed uncontested and came on their way in this direction, and how Moteucçoma left the great palace and went to his personal home.

Then Moteucçoma abandoned his patrimonial home, the great palace, and came back to his personal home.

When at last [the Spaniards] came, when they were coming along and moving this way, a certain person from Cempoallan, whose name was Tlacochcalcatl, whom they had taken when they first came to see the land and the various altepetl, also came interpreting for them, planning their route, conducting them, showing them the way, leading and guiding them.

And when they reached Tecoac, which is in the land of the Tlaxcalans, where their Otomis lived, the Otomis met them with hostilities and war. But they annihilated the Otomis of Tecoac, who were destroyed completely. They lanced and stabbed them, they shot them with guns, iron bolts, crossbows. Not just a few but a huge number of them were destroyed.

After the great defeat at Tecoac, when the Tlaxcalans heard it and found out about it and it was reported to them, they became limp with fear, they were made faint; fear took hold of them. Then they assembled, and all of them, including the lords and rulers, took counsel among themselves, considering the reports.

They said, "How is it to be with us? Should we face them? For the Otomis are great and valiant warriors, yet they thought nothing of them, they regarded them as nothing; in a very short time, in the blink of an eyelid, they destroyed the people. Now let us just submit to them, let us make friends with them, let us be friends, for something must be done about the common people."

Thereupon the Tlaxcalan rulers went to meet them, taking along food: turkey hens, eggs, white tortillas, fine tortillas. They said to them, "Welcome, our lords."

[The Spaniards] answered them back, "Where is your homeland? Where have you come from?"

They said, "We are Tlaxcalans. Welcome, you have arrived, you have reached the land of Tlaxcala, which is your home."

(But in olden times it was called Texcallan and the people Texcalans.)

Eleventh chapter, where it is said how the Spaniards reached Tlaxcala, [also] called Texcallan.

[The Tlaxcalans] guided, accompanied, and led them until they brought them to their palace(s) and placed them there. They showed them great honors, they gave them what they needed and attended to them, and then they gave them their daughters.

Then [the Spaniards] asked them, "Where is Mexico? What kind of a place is it? Is it still far?"

Fray Bernardino de Sahagun; trans and ed by James Lockhart, "Fray Bernardino de Sahagun: Florentine Codex" from *We People Here: Nahuatl Accounts of the Conquest of Mexico*, pp. 90, 92, 94, 96, 106, Copyright © 1993 University of California Press. Permission to reprint granted by the publisher.

They answered them, "It's not far now. Perhaps one can get there in three days. It is a very favored place, and [the Mexica] are very strong, great warriors, conquerors, who go about conquering everywhere."

Now before this there had been friction between the Tlaxcalans and the Cholulans. They viewed each other with anger, fury, hate, and disgust; they could come together on nothing. Because of this they put [the Spaniards] up to killing them treacherously.

They said to them, "The Cholulans are very evil; they are our enemies. They are as strong as the Mexica, and they are the Mexicans friends."

When the Spaniards heard this, they went to Cholula. The Tlaxcalans and Cempoalans went with them, outfitted for war. When they arrived, there was a general summons and cry that all the noblemen, rulers, subordinate leaders, warriors, and commoners should come, and everyone assembled in the temple courtyard. When they had all come together, [the Spaniards and their friends] blocked the entrances, all of the places where one entered. Thereupon people were stabbed, struck, and killed. No such thing was in the minds of the Cholulans; they did not meet the Spaniards with weapons of war. It just seemed that they were stealthily and treacherously killed, because the Tlaxcalans persuaded [the Spaniards] to do it.

And a report of everything that was happening was given and relayed to Moteucçoma. Some of the messengers would be arriving as others were leaving; they just turned around and ran back. There was no time when they weren't listening, when reports weren't being given. And all the common people went about in a state of excitement; there were frequent disturbances, as if the earth moved and (quaked), as if everything were spinning before one's eyes. People took fright.

And after the dying in Cholula, [the Spaniards] set off on their way to Mexico, coming gathered and bunched, raising dust. Their iron lances and halberds seemed to sparkle, and their iron swords were curved like a stream of water. Their cuirasses and iron helmets seemed to make a clattering sound. Some of them came wearing iron all over, turned into iron beings, gleaming, so that they aroused great fear and were generally seen with fear and dread. Their dogs came in front, coming ahead of them, keeping to the front, panting, with their spittle hanging down.

Twelfth chapter, where it is said how Moteucçoma sent a great nobleman along with many other noblemen to go to meet the Spaniards, and what their gifts of greeting were when they greeted the Captain between Iztactepetl and Popocatepetl.

Thereupon Moteucçoma named and sent the noblemen and a great many other agents of his, with Tzihuacpopocatzin as their leader, to go meet [Cortés] between Popocatepetl and Iztactepetl, at Quauhtechcac. They gave [the Spaniards] golden banners, banners of precious feathers, and golden necklaces.

And when they had given the things to them, they seemed to smile, to rejoice and be very happy. Like monkeys they grabbed the gold. It was as though their hearts were put to rest, brightened, freshened. For gold was what they greatly thirsted for; they were gluttonous for it, starved for it, piggishly wanting it. They came lifting up the golden banners, waving them from side to side, showing them to each other. They seemed to babble; what they said to each other was in a babbling tongue.

And when they saw Tzihuacpopocatzin, they said, "Is this one then Moteucçoma?" They said it to the Tlaxcalans and Cempoalans, their lookouts, who came among them, questioning them secretly. They said, "It is not that one, o our lords. This is Tzihuacpopocatzin, who is representing Moteucçoma."

[The Spaniards] said to him, "Are you then Moteucçoma?" He said, "I am your agent Moteucçoma."

Then they told him, "Go on with you! Why do you lie to us? What do you take us for? You can't lie to us, you can't fool us, (turn our heads), flatter us, (make faces at us), trick us, confuse our vision, distort things for us, blind us, dazzle us, throw mud in our eyes, put muddy hands on our faces. It is not you. Moteucçoma exists; he will not be able to hide from us, he will not be able to find refuge. Where will he go? Is he a bird, will he fly? Or will he take an underground route, will he go somewhere into a mountain that is hollow inside? We will see him, we will not fail to gaze on his face and hear his words from his lips."

… They spent the night at Amaquemecan, then came straight on along the road and reached Cuitlahuac, where they also spent the night. They assembled the rulers from each of the kingdoms among the chinampa people: Xochimilco, Cuitlahuac, Mizquic. They told them what they had told the rulers of Chalco. And the rulers of the chinampa people also submitted to them.

And when the Spaniards were satisfied, they moved on this way and made a halt in Itztapalapan. Then they summoned, had summoned the rulers there as well, called the Four Lords, of Itztapalapan, Mexicatzinco, Colhuacan, and Huitzilopochco. They talked with them in the same way they had spoken to [the chinampa people] (as was said). And they too peacefully submitted to the Spaniards.

Moteucçoma did not give orders for anyone to make war against them or for anyone to meet them in battle. No one was to meet them in battle. He just ordered that they be strictly obeyed and very well attended to.

And at this time there was silence here in Mexico. No one went out any more; mothers no longer let [their children] go out. The roads were as if swept clean, wide open, as if at dawn, with no one crossing. People assembled in the houses and did nothing but grieve. The people said, "Let it be that way; curses on it. What more can you do? For we are about to die and perish, we are awaiting our deaths."

## TENOCHTITLAN

After the massacre at Cholula, Cortés and his companions continued toward the Mexica capital, ignoring both the attempts to have them turn back and the hardships of the march. The entry of the Spaniards into Tenochtitlan on November 8, 1519 was one of the quintessential moments of world history. It represents the encounter and clash of two worlds that until that moment had developed in ignorance of each other. From the European side it was a moment of marvel and wonder. "And some of our soldiers asked whether the things we saw were not a dream," wrote Bernal Díaz. Some Spaniards who had been to Rome or Venice could compare Tenochtitlan to those cities, but most like Bernal Díaz thought that what they were seeing could only compare to the popular books of chivalry filled with fantasies, dreams, and dangers. And on the Mexica side, the Spanish entry seemed just as wondrous. Thousands of people lined the causeways, stood on the rooftops, or took to the thousands of canoes that filled the lake to catch a glimpse of the strange "deer" and the bearded men dressed in metal. They also wondered

and worried about the meaning of the thousands of Tlaxcalan and other auxiliaries, their traditional enemies who, with the Spaniards, also entered the city.

A ritualized meeting took place between Moctezuma and Cortés at the entrance to the city, which both Spanish and Nahuatl accounts recorded, and then the Spaniards were lodged in the palaces within the main temple complex at the heart of the city. Within a week, Cortés imprisoned Moctezuma in his own palaces. The seizure of the Mexica leader, even a hospitable one, was a treachery to be sure, but a tactic that had already been used effectively against other indigenous leaders in the Caribbean. During the following eight months the Spaniards resided in Tenochtitlan as guests and invaders. While the city was restive, there was no overt resistance against them in the city. It was during this period that both Spaniards and Mexica had an opportunity to observe each other closely. Bernal Díaz's account is filled with details about Moctezuma and his court. But in reality, neither the Spanish nor the Nahua accounts provide much detail of the day-to-day interactions of the two peoples. The Spanish used this time to install Catholic images in the temples and prohibit the practice of human sacrifice. They also discovered treasure in the palaces and seized it. Their delight and greed caught the notice of the Mexica.

What might have happened had this situation continued we cannot tell, but events were soon to change conditions leading to open Mexica resistance (called rebellion by Cortés).

The Nahua accounts (see pp. 130–132) gathered by Sahagún describe the Spanish entry into the city. The observations about the panting of the Spanish dogs, the sweating of the horses, and the strange weapons of the Spaniards contain both details and a sense of awe that convey the feel of eyewitness observation. The excerpts from Bernal Díaz (see pp. 133–155) are some of his most colorful writing and provide us with the sense of awe that he felt. Moreover, they are filled with ethnographic details that make his account so valuable as a limited vision of Mexica life, especially that of the palace. Included here also are Bernal Díaz's discussions of Moctezuma's reactions to the Spanish attempts at conversion as well as Díaz's description of Moctezuma's personality and the curious relationship that began to develop between the emperor and his Spanish captors.

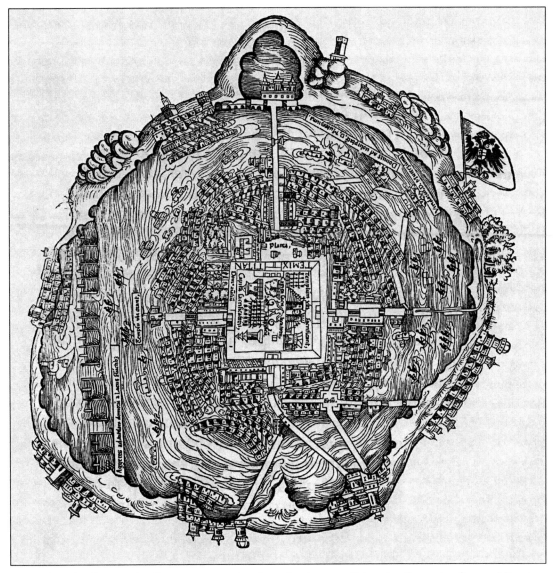

**Map.**  Tenochtitlan in the European imagination. An image of the city from the first publication of Cortés's letters.

*Source:* From *Praeclara Fernandi Cortesii de Nova Maris Oceani Hispana Narratio* (Nuremberg, 1524).

## FRAY BERNARDINO DE SAHAGÚN

### From the *Florentine Codex*

*The Spaniards approached Tenochtitlan from the south, crossing to the city along the causeway from Ixtapalapa (see map). The Nahua accounts concentrate on those things that were new and strange like horses and crossbows but also seek to find parallels and comparisons between their own practices and customs and the ways of the strangers. Here, for example, Cortés is compared to the* tlacatecatl *or military commander. The welcoming coming "speech" of Moctezuma and his concession of authority to Cortés is particularly interesting and raises questions about the nature of "polite" political discourse among the Nahua as well as the possibility of later interpretations and explanations being placed in the historical record after the conquest.*

Fray Bernardino de Sahagun; trans and ed by James Lockhart, "Fray Bernardino de Sahagun: Florentine Codex" from *We People Here: Nahuatl Accounts of the Conquest of Mexico*, pp. 108-118, Copyright © 1993 University of California Press. Permission to reprint granted by the publisher.

Fifteenth chapter, where it is said how the Spaniards came from Itztapalapan when they reached Mexico.

Then they set out in this direction, about to enter Mexico here. Then they all dressed and equipped themselves for war. They girded themselves, tying their battle gear tightly on themselves and then on their horses. Then they arranged themselves in rows, files, ranks.

Four horse [men] came ahead, going first, staying ahead, leading. They kept turning about as they went, facing people, looking this way and that, looking sideways, gazing everywhere between the houses, examining things, looking up at the roofs.

Also the dogs, their dogs, came ahead, sniffing at things and constantly panting.

By himself came marching ahead, all alone, the one who bore the standard on his shoulder. He came waving it about, making it spin, tossing it here and there. It came stiffening, rising up like a warrior, twisting and turning.

Following him came those with iron swords. Their iron swords came bare and gleaming. On their shoulders they bore their shields, of wood or leather.

The second contingent and file were horses carrying people, each with his cotton cuirass, his leather shield, his iron lance, and his iron sword hanging down from the horse's neck. They came with bells on, jingling or rattling. The horses, the deer, neighed, there was much neighing, and they would sweat a great deal; water seemed to fall from them. And their flecks of foam splattered on the ground, like soapsuds splatting. As they went they made a beating, throbbing, and hoof-pounding like throwing stones. Their hooves made holes, they dug holes in the ground wherever they placed them. Separate holes formed wherever they went placing their hindlegs and forelegs.

The third file were those with iron crossbows, the crossbowmen. As they came, the iron crossbows lay in their arms. They came along testing them out, brandishing them, (aiming them). But some carried them on their shoulders, came shouldering the crossbows. Their quivers went hanging at their sides, passed under their armpits, well filled, packed with arrows, with iron bolts. Their cotton upper armor reached to their knees, very thick, firmly sewn, and dense, like stone. And their heads were wrapped in the same cotton armor, and on their heads plumes stood up, parting and spreading.

The fourth file were likewise horse [men]; their outfits were the same as has been said.

The fifth group were those with harquebuses, the harquebusiers, shouldering their harquebuses; some held them [level]. And when they went into the great palace, the residence of the ruler, they repeatedly shot off their harquebuses. They exploded, sputtered, discharged, thundered, (disgorged). Smoke spread, it grew dark with smoke, everyplace filled with smoke. The fetid smell made people dizzy and faint.

And last, bringing up the rear, went the war leader, thought to be the ruler and director in battle, like [among us] a *tlacateccatl* Gathered and massed about him, going at his side, accompanying him, enclosing him were his warriors, those with devices, his [aides], like [among us] those with scraped heads [*quaquachictin*] and the Otomi warriors, the strong and valiant ones of the altepetl, its buttress and support, its heart and foundation.

Then all those from the various altepetl on the other side of the mountains, the Tlaxcalans, the people of Tliliuhquitepec, of Huexotzinco, came following behind. They came outfitted for war with their cotton upper armor, shields, and bows, their quivers full and packed with feathered arrows, some barbed, some blunted, some with obsidian points. They went crouching, hitting their mouths with their hands and yelling, singing in Tocuillan style, whistling, shaking their heads.

Some bore burdens and provisions on their backs; some used [tump lines for] their foreheads, some [bands around] their chests, some carrying frames, some board cages, some deep baskets. Some made bundles, perhaps putting the bundles on their backs. Some dragged the large cannons, which went resting on wooden wheels, making a clamor as they came.

Sixteenth chapter, where it is said how Moteucçoma went in peace and quiet to meet the Spaniards at Xoloco, where the house of Alvarado is now, or at the place they call Huitzillan.

And when they [the Spaniards] had come as far as Xoloco, when they had stopped there, Moteucçoma dressed and prepared himself for a meeting, along with other great rulers and high nobles, his rulers and nobles. Then they went to the meeting. On gourd bases they set out different precious flowers, in the midst of the shield flowers and heart flowers stood popcorn flowers, yellow tobacco flowers, cacao flowers, [made into] wreaths for the head, wreaths to be girded around. And they carried golden necklaces, necklaces with pendants, wide necklaces.

And when Moteucçoma went out to meet them at Huitzillan, thereupon he gave various things to the war leader, the commander of the warriors; he gave him flowers, he put necklaces on him, he put flower necklaces on him, he girded him with flowers, he put flower wreaths on his head. Then he laid before him the golden necklaces, all the different things for greeting people. He ended by putting some of the necklaces on him.

Then [Cortés] said in reply to Moteucçoma, "Is it not you? Is it not you then? Moteucçoma?"

Moteucçoma said, "Yes, it is me." Thereupon he stood up straight, he stood up with their faces meeting. He bowed down deeply to him. He stretched as far as he could, standing stiffly. Addressing him, he said to him,

"O our lord, be doubly welcomed on your arrival in this land; you have come to satisfy your curiosity about your altepetl of Mexico, you have come to sit on your seat of authority, which I have kept a while for you, where I have been in charge for you, for your agents the rulers—Itzcoatzin, the elder Moteucçoma, Axayacatl, Ticocic, and Ahuitzotl—have gone, who for a very short time came to be in charge for you, to govern the altepetl of Mexico. It is after them that your poor vassal [myself] came. Will they come back to the place of their absence? If only one of them could see and behold what has now happened in my time, what I now see after our lords are gone! For I am not just dreaming, not just sleepwalking, not just seeing it in my sleep. I am not just dreaming that I have seen you, have looked upon your face. For a time I have been concerned, looking toward the mysterious place from which you have come, among clouds and mist. It is so that the rulers on departing said that you would come in order to acquaint yourself with your altepetl and sit upon your seat of authority. And now it has come true, you have come. Be doubly welcomed, enter the land, go to enjoy your palace; rest your body. May our lords be arrived in the land."

And when the speech that Moteucçoma directed to the Marqués had concluded, Marina reported it to him, interpreting it for him. And when the Marqués had heard what Moteucçoma had said, he spoke to Marina in return, babbling back to them, replying in his babbling tongue,

"Let Moteucçoma be at ease, let him not be afraid, for we greatly esteem him. Now we are truly satisfied to see him in person and hear him, for until now we have greatly desired to see him and look upon his face. Well, now we have seen him, we have come to his homeland of Mexico. Bit by bit he will hear what we have to say."

Thereupon [the Spaniards] took [Moteucçoma] by the hand. They came along with him, stroking his hair to show their good feeling. And the Spaniards looked at him, each of them giving him a close look. They would start along walking, then mount, then dismount again in order to see him. …

## BERNAL DÍAZ

### From *The True History of the Conquest of New Spain*

*Bernal Díaz provides not only a description of the Spanish entry to the city, the encounter between Cortés and Moctezuma, and the reception by the population, but also an account of the life of the Mexica* tlatoani *and a great deal about his personality. Díaz's description of the buildings, gardens, the zoo, the temples, and religious practices convey a combination of appreciation and disgust, but his report of Moctezuma's defense of his religion and of the ruler's conversations with Cortés are not unsympathetic.*

Early next day we left Iztapalapa with a large escort of those great Caciques whom I have already mentioned. We proceeded along the Causeway which is here eight paces in width and runs so straight to the City of Mexico that it does not seem to me to turn either much or little, but, broad as it is, it was so crowded with people that there was hardly room for them all, some of them going to and others returning from Mexico, besides those who had come out to see us, so that we were hardly able to pass by the crowds of them that came; and the towers and cues were full of people as well as the canoes from all parts of the lake. It was not to be wondered at, for they had never before seen horses or men such as we are.

Gazing on such wonderful sights, we did not know what to say, or whether what appeared before us was real, for on one side, on the land, there were great cities, and in the lake ever so many more, and the lake itself was crowded with canoes, and in the Causeway were many bridges at intervals, and in front of us stood the great City of Mexico, and we,—we did not even number four hundred soldiers! and we well remembered the words and warnings given us by the people of Huexotzingo and Tlaxcala and Tlamanalco, and the many other warnings that had been given that we should beware of entering Mexico, where they would kill us, as soon as they had us inside.

Let the curious readers consider whether there is not much to ponder over in this that I am writing. What men have there been in the world who have shown such daring? But let us get on, and march along the Causeway. When we arrived where another small causeway branches off (leading to Coyoacan, which is another city) where there were some buildings like towers, which are their oratories, many more chieftains and Caciques approached clad in very rich mantles, the brilliant liveries of one chieftain differing from those of another, and the causeways were crowded with them. The Great Montezuma had sent these great Caciques in advance to receive us, and when they came before Cortés they bade us welcome in their language, and as a sign of peace, they touched their hands against the ground, and kissed the ground with the hand.

There we halted for a good while, and Cacamatzin, the Lord of Texcoco, and the Lord of Iztapalapa and the Lord of Tacuba and the Lord of Coyoacan went on in advance to meet the Great Montezuma, who was approaching in a rich litter accompanied by other great Lords and Caciques, who owned vassals. When we arrived near to Mexico, where there were some

other small towers, the Great Montezuma got down from his litter, and those great Caciques supported him with their arms beneath a marvellously rich canopy of green coloured feathers with much gold and silver embroidery and with pearls and chalchihuites suspended from a sort of bordering, which was wonderful to look at. The Great Montezuma was richly attired according to his usage, and he was shod with sandals [cotoras], for so they call what they wear on their feet, the soles were of gold and the upper part adorned with precious stones. The four Chieftains who supported his arms were also richly clothed according to their usage, in garments which were apparently held ready for them on the road to enable them to accompany their prince, for they did not appear in such attire when they came to receive us. Besides these four Chieftains, there were four other great Caciques, who supported the canopy over their heads, and many other Lords who walked before the Great Montezuma, sweeping the ground where he would tread and spreading cloths on it, so that he should not tread on the earth. Not one of these chieftains dared even to think of looking him in the face, but kept their eyes lowered with great reverence, except those four relations, his nephews, who supported him with their arms.

When Cortés was told that the Great Montezuma was approaching, and he saw him coming, he dismounted from his horse, and when he was near Montezuma, they simultaneously paid great reverence to one another. Montezuma bade him welcome and our Cortés replied through Doña Marina wishing him very good health. And it seems to me that Cortés, through Doña Marina, offered him his right hand, and Montezuma did not wish to take it, but he did give his hand to Cortés and Cortés brought out a necklace which he had ready at hand, made of glass stones, which I have already said are called Margaritas, which have within them many patterns of diverse colours, these were strung on a cord of gold and with musk so that it should have a sweet scent, and he placed it round the neck of the Great Montezuma and when he had so placed it he was going to embrace him, and those great Princes who accompanied Montezuma held back Cortés by the arm so that he should not embrace him, for they considered it an indignity.

Then Cortés through the mouth of Doña Marina told him that now his heart rejoiced at having seen such a great Prince, and that he took it as a great honour that he had come in person to meet him and had frequently shown him such favour.

Then Montezuma spoke other words of politeness to him, and told two of his nephews who supported his arms, the Lord of Texcoco and the Lord of Coyoacan, to go with us and show us to our quarters, and Montezuma with his other two relations, the Lord of Cuitlahuac and the Lord of Tacuba who accompanied him, returned to the city, and all those grand companies of Caciques and chieftains who had come with him returned in his train. As they turned back after their Prince we stood watching them and observed how they all marched with their eyes fixed on the ground without looking at him, keeping close to the wall, following him with great reverence. Thus space was made for us to enter the streets of Mexico, without being so much crowded. But who could now count the multitude of men and women and boys who were in the streets and on the azoteas,[1] and in canoes on the canals, who had come out to see us. It was indeed wonderful, and, now that I am writing about it, it all comes before my eyes as though it had happened but yesterday. Coming to think it over it seems to be a great mercy that our Lord Jesus Christ was pleased to give us grace and courage to dare to enter into such a city; and for the many times He has saved me from danger of death, as will be seen later on, I give Him sincere thanks, and in that He has preserved me to write about it, although I cannot do it as fully as is fitting or the subject needs. Let us make no words about it, for deeds are the best witnesses to what I say here and elsewhere.

Let us return to our entry to Mexico. They took us to lodge in some large houses, where there were apartments for all of us, for they had belonged to the father of the Great Montezuma, who was named Axayaca, and at that time Montezuma kept there the great oratories for his idols, and a secret chamber where he kept bars and jewels of gold, which was the treasure that he had inherited from his father Axayaca, and he never disturbed it. They took us to lodge in that house, because they called us Teules, and took us for such, so that we should be with the Idols or Teules which were kept there. However, for one reason or another, it was there they took us, where there were great halls

_____
1  Rooftops.

and chambers canopied with the cloth of the country for our Captain, and for every one of us beds of matting with canopies above, and no better bed is given, however great the chief may be, for they are not used. And all these palaces were [coated] with shining cement and swept and garlanded.

As soon as we arrived and entered into the great court, the Great Montezuma took our Captain by the hand, for he was there awaiting him, and led him to the apartment and saloon where he was to lodge, which was very richly adorned according to their usage, and he had at hand a very rich necklace made of golden crabs, a marvelous piece of work, and Montezuma himself placed it round the neck of our Captain Cortés, and greatly astonished his [own] Captains by the great honour that he was bestowing on him. When the necklace had been fastened, Cortés thanked Montezuma through our interpreters, and Montezuma replied—"Malinche you and your brethren are in your own house, rest awhile," and then he went to his palaces which were not far away, and we divided our lodgings by companies, and placed the artillery pointing in a convenient direction, and the order which we had to keep was clearly explained to us, and that we were to be much on the alert, both the cavalry and all of us soldiers. A sumptuous dinner was provided for us according to their use and custom, and we ate it at once. So this was our lucky and daring entry into the great city of Tenochtitlan Mexico on the 8th day of November the year of our Saviour Jesus Christ 1519.

Thanks to our Lord Jesus Christ for it all. And if I have not said anything that I ought to have said, may your honours pardon me, for I do not know now even at the present time how better to express it.

Let us leave this talk and go back to our story of what else happened to us, which I will go on to relate.

* * *

Let us leave this and go on to another great house, where they keep many Idols, and they say that they are their fierce gods, and with them many kinds of carnivorous beasts of prey, tigers and two kinds of lions, and animals something like wolves which in this country they call jackals and foxes, and other smaller carnivorous animals, and all these carnivores they feed with flesh, and the greater number of them breed in the house. They give them as food deer and fowls, dogs and other things which they are used to hunt, and I have heard it said that they feed them on the bodies of the Indians who have been sacrificed. It is in this way: you have already heard me say that when they sacrifice a wretched Indian they saw open the chest with stone knives and hasten to tear out the palpitating heart and blood, and offer it to their Idols in whose name the sacrifice is made. Then they cut off the thighs, arms and head and eat the former at feasts and banquets, and the head they hang up on some beams, and the body of the man sacrificed is not eaten but given to these fierce animals. They also have in that cursed house many vipers and poisonous snakes which carry on their tails things that sound like bells. These are the worst vipers of all, and they keep them in jars and great pottery vessels with many feathers, and there they lay their eggs and rear their young, and they give them to eat the bodies of the Indians who have been sacrificed, and the flesh of dogs which they are in the habit of breeding. We even knew for certain that when they drove us out of Mexico and killed over eight hundred of our soldiers that they fed those fierce animals and snakes for many days on their bodies, as I will relate at the proper time and season. And those snakes and wild beasts were dedicated to those savage Idols, so that they might keep them company.

Let me speak now of the infernal noise when the lions and tigers roared and the jackals and the foxes howled and the serpents hissed, it was horrible to listen to and it seemed like a hell. Let us go on and speak of the skilled workmen he [Montezuma] employed in every craft that was practiced among them. We will begin with lapidaries and workers in gold and silver and all the hollow work, which even the great goldsmiths in Spain were forced to admire, and of these there were a great number of the best in a town named Azcapotzalco, a league from Mexico. Then for working precious stones and chalchihuites, which are like emeralds, there were other great artists. Let us go on to the great craftsmen in feather work, and painters and sculptors who were most refined; from what we see of their work to-day we can form a judgment of what they did then, for there are three Indians to-day in the City of Mexico named Marcos de Aquino, Juan de la Cruz and El Crespillo, so skilful in their work as sculptors and painters, that had they lived in the days of the ancient and famous Apelles, or of Michael Angelo Buonarotti, in our times, they would be placed in the same company. Let us go

on to the Indian women who did the weaving and the washing, who made such an immense quantity of fine fabrics with wonderful feather work designs; the greater part of it was brought daily from some towns of the province on the north coast near Vera Cruz called Cotaxtla, close by San Juan de Ulua, where we disembarked when we came with Cortés.

In the house of the Great Montezuma himself, all the daughters of chieftains whom he had as mistresses always wore beautiful things, and there were many daughters of Mexican citizens who lived in retirement and wished to appear to be like nuns, who also did weaving but it was wholly of feather work. These nuns had their houses near the great Cue of Huichilobos and out of devotion to it, or to another idol, that of a woman who was said to be their mediatrix in the matter of marriage, their fathers placed them in that religious retirement until they married, and they were [only] taken out thence to be married.

Let us go on and tell about the great number of dancers kept by the Great Montezuma for his amusement, and others who used stilts on their feet, and others who flew when they danced up in the air, and others like Merry-Andrews, and I may say that there was a district full of these people who had no other occupation. Let us go on and speak of the workmen that he had as stone cutters, masons and carpenters, all of whom attended to the work of his houses, I say that he had as many as he wished for. We must not forget the gardens of flowers and sweet-scented trees, and the many kinds that there were of them, and the arrangement of them and the walks, and the ponds and tanks of fresh water where the water entered at one end and flowed out at the other; and the baths which he had there, and the variety of small birds that nested in the branches, and the medicinal and useful herbs that were in the gardens. It was a wonder to see, and to take care of it there were many gardeners. Everything was made in masonry and well cemented, baths and walks and closets, and apartments like summer houses where they danced and sang. There was as much to be seen in these gardens as there was everywhere else, and we could not tire of witnessing his great power. Thus as a consequence of so many crafts being practiced among them, a large number of skilled Indians were employed. …

hints at a very advanced civilization.

As we had already been four days in Mexico and neither the Captain nor any of us had left our lodgings except to go to the houses and gardens, Cortés said to us that it would be well to go to the great Plaza and see the great Temple of Huichilobos, and that he wished to consult the Great Montezuma and have his approval. For this purpose he sent Jerónimo de Aguilar and the Doña Marina as messengers, and with them went our Captain's small page named Orteguilla, who already understood something of the language. When Montezuma knew his wishes he sent to say that we were welcome to go; on the other hand, as he was afraid that we might do some dishonour to his Idols, he determined to go with us himself with many of his chieftains. He came out from his Palace in his rich litter, but when half the distance had been traversed and he was near some oratories, he stepped out of the litter, for he thought it a great affront to his idols to go to their house and temple in that manner. Some of the great chieftains supported him with their arms, and the tribal lords went in front of him carrying two staves like scepters held on high, which was the sign that the Great Montezuma was coming. (When he went in his litter he carried a wand half of gold and half of wood, which was held up like a wand of justice.) So he went on and ascended the great Cue accompanied by many priests, and he began to burn incense and perform other ceremonies to Huichilobos.

Let us leave Montezuma, who had gone ahead as I have said, and return to Cortés and our captains and soldiers, who according to our custom both night and day were armed, and as Montezuma was used to see us so armed when we went to visit him, he did not look upon it as anything new. I say this because our captain and all those who had horses went to Tlaltelolco on horseback, and nearly all of us soldiers were fully equipped, and many Caciques whom Montezuma had sent for that purpose went in our company. When we arrived at the great market place, called Tlaltelolco, we were astonished at the number of people and the quantity of merchandise that it contained, and at the good order and control that was maintained, for we had never seen such a thing before. The chieftains who accompanied us acted as guides. Each kind of merchandise was kept by itself and had its fixed place marked out. Let us begin with the dealers in gold, silver, and precious stones, feathers, mantles, and embroidered goods. Then there were other wares consisting of Indian slaves both men

and women; and I say that they bring as many of them to that great market for sale as the Portuguese bring negroes from Guinea; and they brought them along tied to long poles, with collars round their necks so that they could not escape, and others they left free. Next there were other traders who sold great pieces of cloth and cotton, and articles of twisted thread, and there were *cacahuateros* who sold cacao. In this way one could see every sort of merchandise that is to be found in the whole of New Spain, placed in arrangement in the same manner as they do in my own country, which is Medina del Campo, where they hold the fairs, where each line of booths has its particular kind of merchandise, and so it is in this great market. There were those who sold cloths of henequen and ropes and the *cotaras*[1] with which they are shod, which are made from the same plant, and sweet cooked roots, and other tubers which they get from this plant, all were kept in one part of the market in the place assigned to them. In another part there were skins of tigers and lions, of otters and jackals, deer and other animals and badgers and mountain cats, some tanned and others untanned, and other classes of merchandise.

Let us go on and speak of those who sold beans and sage and other vegetables and herbs in another part, and to those who sold fowls, cocks with wattles, rabbits, hares, deer, mallards, young dogs and other things of that sort in their part of the market, and let us also mention the fruiterers, and the women who sold cooked food, dough and tripe in their own part of the market; then every sort of pottery made in a thousand different forms from great water jars to little jugs, these also had a place to themselves; then those who sold honey and honey paste and other dainties like nut paste, and those who sold lumber, boards, cradles, beams, blocks and benches, each article by itself, and the vendors of *ocote*[2] firewood, and other things of a similar nature. I must furthermore mention, asking your pardon, that they also sold many canoes full of human excrement, and these were kept in the creeks near the market, and this they use to make salt or for tanning skins, for without it they say that they cannot be well prepared. I know well that some gentlemen laugh at this, but I say that it is so, and I may add that on all the roads it is a usual

1  Sandals.
2  Pitch-pine for torches.

thing to have places made of reeds or straw or grass, so that they may be screened from the passers by, into these they retire when they wish to purge their bowels so that even that filth should not be lost. But why do I waste so many words in recounting what they sell in that great market, for I shall never finish if I tell it all in detail. Paper, which in this country is called *Amal*, and reeds scented with *liquidambar*, and full of tobacco, and yellow ointments and things of that sort are sold by themselves, and much cochineal is sold under the arcades which are in that great market place, and there are many vendors of herbs and other sorts of trades. There are also buildings where three magistrates sit in judgment, and there are executive officers like *Alguacils* who inspect the merchandise. I am forgetting those who sell salt, and those who make the stone knives, and how they split them off the stone itself; and the fisherwomen and others who sell some small cakes made from a sort of ooze which they get out of the great lake, which curdles, and from this they make a bread having a flavour something like cheese. There are for sale axes of brass and copper and tin, and gourds and gaily painted jars made of wood. I could wish that I had finished telling of all the things which are sold there, but they are so numerous and of such different quality and the great market place with its surrounding arcades was so crowded with people, that one would not have been able to see and inquire about it all in two days.

Then we went to the great Cue, and when we were already approaching its great courts, before leaving the market place itself, there were many more merchants, who, as I was told, brought gold for sale in grains, just as it is taken from the mines. The gold is placed in thin quills of the geese of the country, white quills, so that the gold can be seen through, and according to the length and thickness of the quills they arrange their accounts with one another, how much so many mantles or so many gourds full of cacao were worth, or how many slaves, or whatever other thing they were exchanging.

Now let us leave the great market place, and not look at it again, and arrive at the great courts and walls where the great Cue stands. Before reaching the great Cue there is a great enclosure of courts, it seems to me larger than the plaza of Salamanca, with two walls of masonry surrounding it and the court itself all paved with very smooth great white flagstones. And where

there were not these stones it was cemented and burnished and all very clean, so that one could not find any dust or a straw in the whole place. …

When we arrived there Montezuma came out of an oratory where his cursed idols were, at the summit of the great Cue, and two priests came with him, and after paying great reverence to Cortés and to all of us he said: "You must be tired, Señor Malinche, from ascending this our great Cue," and Cortés replied through our interpreters who were with us that he and his companions were never tired by anything. Then Montezuma took him by the hand and told him to look at his great city and all the other cities that were standing in the water, and the many other towns on the land round the lake, and that if he had not seen the great market place well, that from where they were they could see it better.

So we stood looking about us, for that huge and cursed temple stood so high that from it one could see over everything very well, and we saw the three causeways which led into Mexico, that is the causeway of Iztapalapa by which we had entered four days before, and that of Tacuba, along which later on we fled on the night of our great defeat, when Cuitlahuac the new prince drove us out of the city, as I shall tell later on, and that of Tepeaquilla, and we saw the fresh water that comes from Chapultepec which supplies the city, and we saw the bridges on the three causeways which were built at certain distances apart through which the water of the lake flowed in and out from one side to the other, and we beheld on that great lake a great multitude of canoes, some coming with supplies of food and others returning loaded with cargoes of merchandise; and we saw that from every house of that great city and of all the other cities that were built in the water it was impossible to pass from house to house, except by drawbridges which were made of wood or in canoes; and we saw in those cities Cues and oratories like towers and fortresses and all gleaming white, and it was a wonderful thing to behold; then the houses with flat roofs, and on the causeways other small towers and oratories which were like fortresses.

After having examined and considered all that we had seen we turned to look at the great market place and the crowds of people that were in it, some buying and others selling, so that the murmur and hum of their voices and words that they used could be heard more than a league off. Some of the soldiers

Proof positive that, in some ways, the
Aztecs were as advanced or more advanced
than Europeans were.

among us who had been in many parts of the world, in Constantinople, and all over Italy, and in Rome, said that so large a market place and so full of people, and so well regulated and arranged, they had never beheld before.

Let us leave this, and return to our Captain, who said to Fray Bartolomé de Olmedo, who has often been mentioned by me, and who happened to be near by him: "It seems to me, Senor Padre, that it would be a good thing to throw out a feeler to Montezuma, as to whether he would allow us to build our church here"; and the Padre replied that it would be a good thing if it were successful, but it seemed to him that it was not quite a suitable time to speak about it, for Montezuma did not appear to be inclined to do such a thing.

Then our Cortés said to Montezuma through the interpreter Doña Marina: "Your Highness is indeed a very great prince and worthy of even greater things. We are rejoiced to see your cities, and as we are here in your temple, what I now beg as a favour is that you will show us your gods and Teules. Montezuma replied that he must first speak with his high priests, and when he had spoken to them he said that we might enter into a small tower and apartment, a sort of hall, where there were two altars, with very richly carved boardings on the top of the roof. On each altar were two figures, like giants with very tall bodies and very fat, and the first which stood on the right hand they said was the figure of Huichilobos their god of War; it had a very broad face and monstrous and terrible eyes, and the whole of his body was covered with precious stones, and gold and pearls, and with seed pearls stuck on with a paste that they make in this country out of a sort of root, and all the body and head was covered with it, and the body was girdled by great snakes made of gold and precious stones, and in one hand he held a bow and in the other some arrows. And another small idol that stood by him, they said was his page, and he held a short lance and a shield richly decorated with gold and stones. Huichilobos had round his neck some Indians' faces and other things like hearts of Indians, the former made of gold and the latter of silver, with many precious blue stones.

There were some braziers with incense which they call copal, and in them they were burning the hearts of the three Indians whom they had sacrificed that day, and they had made the sacrifice with smoke and copal. All

the walls of the oratory were so splashed and encrusted with blood that they were black, the floor was the same and the whole place stank vilely. Then we saw on the other side on the left hand there stood the other great image the same height as Huichilobos, and it had a face like a bear and eyes that shone, made of their mirrors which they call *Tezcat,* and the body plastered with precious stones like that of Huichilobos, for they say that the two are brothers; and this Tezcatepuca was the god of Hell and had charge of the souls of the Mexicans, and his body was girt with figures like little devils with snakes' tails. The walls were so clotted with blood and the soil so bathed with it that in the slaughter houses in Spain there is not such another stench.

They had offered to this Idol five hearts from that day's sacrifices. In the highest part of the Cue there was a recess of which the woodwork was very richly worked, and in it was another image half man and half lizard, with precious stones all over it, and half the body was covered with a mantle. They say that the body of this figure is full of all the seeds that there are in the world, and they say that it is the god of seed time and harvest, but I do not remember its name, and everything was covered with blood, both walls and altar, and the stench was such that we could hardly wait the moment to get out of it.

They had an exceedingly large drum there, and when they beat it the sound of it was so dismal and like, so to say, an instrument of the infernal regions, that one could hear it a distance of two leagues, and they said that the skins it was covered with were those of great snakes. In that small place there were many diabolical things to be seen, bugles and trumpets and knives, and many hearts of Indians that they had burned in fumigating their idols, and everything was so clotted with blood, and there was so much of it, that I curse the whole of it, and as it stank like a slaughter house we hastened to clear out of such a bad stench and worse sight. Our Captain said to Montezuma through our interpreter, half laughing: "Señor Montezuma, I do not understand how such a great Prince and wise man as you are has not come to the conclusion, in your mind, that these idols of yours are not gods, but evil things that are called devils, and so that you may know it and all your priests may see it clearly, do me the favour to approve of my placing a cross here on the top of this tower, and that in one part of these oratories

Their place of
holy worship is satanical
to the Europeans regardless of their
civilized
other qualities.

where your Huichilobos and Tezcatepuca stand we may divide off a space where we can set up an image of Our Lady (an image which Montezuma had already seen) and you will see by the fear in which these Idols hold it that they are deceiving you."

Montezuma replied half angrily, (and the two priests who were with him showed great annoyance,) and said: "Señor Malinche, if I had known that you would have said such defamatory things I would not have shown you my gods, we consider them to be very good, for they give us health and rains and good seed times and seasons and as many victories as we desire, and we are obliged to worship them and make sacrifices, and I pray you not to say another word to their dishonour."

When our Captain heard that and noted the angry looks he did not refer again to the subject, but said with a cheerful manner: "It is time for your Excellency and for us to return," and Montezuma replied that it was well, but that he had to pray and offer certain sacrifices on account of the great *tatacul*, that is to say sin, which he had committed in allowing us to ascend his great Cue, and being the cause of our being permitted to see his gods, and of our dishonouring them by speaking evil of them, so that before he left he must pray and worship.

Then Cortés said "I ask your pardon if it be so," and then we went down the steps, and as they numbered one hundred and fourteen, and as some of our soldiers were suffering from tumours and abscesses, their legs were tired by the descent.

## THINGS FALL APART: TOXCATL AND THE *NOCHE TRISTE*

After installing themselves in the palaces, invited by Moctezuma, the Spaniards settled into a routine. Relations with Moctezuma remained cordial and visits between him and Cortés were done with considerable courtesy and formality. Meanwhile, the Spaniards began to reconnoiter the city, examining the markets, the temples, and the crowds. The Spaniards also built a small chapel for their prayers and discovered a secret vault filled with treasure in one of the temple walls. Bernal Díaz tells of this period in some detail. He also claims that some of the Spanish captains and soldiers prevailed upon Cortés to place Moctezuma under arrest in order

to forestall any rebellion against them. The plans were already under way for this move when justification for it arrived from the coast. Word was brought of a battle near Vera Cruz in which the Totonacs supported by the Spaniards had resisted a Mexica army aimed at restoring the Totonacs to a tributary status. Cortés used the incident as an excuse to take Moctezuma hostage and to demand the execution of the Mexica captains responsible for the attack. With this audacious and treacherous act, barely a week after the Spanish entry into Tenochtitlan, Cortés seized the initiative, making Moctezuma a prisoner in his own city. While some of the other leaders like Cacamatzin, ruler of Texcoco, advocated resistance to the strangers, with Moctezuma still alive, many of the Mexica were reluctant to act against his wishes, although Cortés and Bernal Díaz both suggested that Moctezuma was himself secretly organizing a resistance. In any case, for dynastic, ethnic, and personal reasons, the Mexica city–states and the various factions inside Tenochtitlan were still not able to mount a resistance and Moctezuma retained his role as a Spanish captive and puppet, albeit a reluctant one.

At the end of April 1520, news arrived from Vera Cruz that a large expedition had been sent by Diego Velázquez, governor of Cuba, to arrest Cortés for his disobedience. Almost a thousand soldiers with artillery and horses had been sent against Cortés under Pánfilo Narváez. Whereas divisions among the native peoples had until this moment hindered their actions against the Spaniards, divisions among the Europeans now threatened Cortés's program. Leaving a small garrison under Pedro de Alvarado in control of the palaces and of Moctezuma, and pretending that the newly arrived Spaniards were his friends (although Moctezuma's spies had probably informed him of the truth), Cortés marched with about two hundred men and many Tlaxcalan allies to meet this new threat. In a quick, surprise attack, Cortés routed Narváez and his forces. He then offered to let Narváez's men return to Cuba (in disgrace) or to join him in the conquest of a great and wealthy empire. By this stroke of good luck and skill, Cortés converted a potential disaster into reinforcements and marched back to Tenochtitlan with about 1,400 new recruits. Despite various promises he had made to win the support of the newcomers, a division developed between the men of the original band

and those later recruited from Narváez's forces. That division would continue to plague Spanish operations.

Meanwhile in Tenochtitlan, the situation had darkened. Alvarado was brave but impulsive. The accounts of Bernal Díaz and those of the Nahua observers differ on what happened, but apparently in Cortés's absence, the Mexica approached Alvarado and asked permission to celebrate the festival of Toxcatl in honor of Huitzilopochtli. Permission was given, but during the festival when "song was linked to song" (see Figure 12), as the Nahua accounts retell it, Alvarado staged a surprise attack on the unarmed celebrants. Hundreds of the leading nobles and warriors were brutally slain and the city then rose in open revolt, surrounding the Spaniards in the temple precinct and placing them under siege. Alvarado forced Moctezuma to try to stop the siege but his authority was weakening. Cortés, learning of the situation, made a forced march back to Tenochtitlan and on June 24 reentered the city. No crowds of curious Mexica awaited the Spaniards this time, but rather abandoned streets and a sullen population. Moctezuma was already dead. Spanish and Nahua accounts differ on what had happened to the Mexica ruler. The Spanish versions claim that he was struck by a stone as he tried from a rooftop to dissuade his people from attacking. The Nahua accounts state that he was murdered by the Spaniards. In any case, his brother Cuitlahuac, lord of Iztapalapa, began to organize the resistance and was soon recognized as the new *tlatoani*. There is no dispute over what happened to the nobles who waited on Moctezuma in captivity. They were simply put to death by the Spaniards.

The Spanish position had become untenable, surrounded as they were in the heart of the city, besieged and cut off from food and water.

Bernal Díaz describes the conditions and the discussions on a plan of action. On the rainy night of June 30, 1520, Cortés, his men and allies stealthily broke out. Discovered, a savage battle ensued. Hundreds of Spaniards and thousands of Tlaxcalans were killed before the Spanish force reached the lakeshore. The escape from the city had been made but the event was always remembered by the Spaniards thereafter as the *"Noche triste"* (Sad Night).

## FRANCISCO LÓPEZ DE GÓMARA

### From *Istoria de la conquista de Mexico*

*The question of responsibility for the Toxcatl massacre is addressed first in a chapter from* Istoria de la conquista de Mexico *(Zaragoza, 1552) by Francisco López de Gómara, Cortés's secretary and biographer. Gómara had access to Cortés's private papers and his biography was always favorable to the conqueror's interests. Neither Bernal Díaz nor Cortés were in Tenochtitlan during the Toxcatl massacre so their accounts are based on hearsay rather than on their own observation.*

*Francisco López de Gómara—cleric, Renaissance scholar, and author of great stylistic ability—became Cortés's confessor. His history of the conquest published in 1552 was essentially a defense and* apologia *for Cortés and was, in fact, dedicated to Cortés's son. By this time Cortés was in disfavor because of his political ambitions and so López de Gómara's book, like Cortés's letters, was banned. Bernal Díaz particularly objected to its unceasing pro-Cortés stance, the artistic license of the author in reporting apparitions of various saints during the battles, and probably, most of all, by the fact that López de Gómara had published first. Still, López de Gómara knew how to tell a story.*

Cortés wanted to get at the root of the rebellion of the Mexicans. He interrogated all the Spaniards together, and some said it was caused by the message sent by Narváez; others, by the desire of the people to drive them out of Mexico, as had been planned, as soon as there were ships in which to sail, for during the fighting they kept shouting "Get out!" Others said it was to liberate Moctezuma, because the Indians said "Free our god and king if you wish to live!" Still others said it was because the Indians wanted to steal the gold, silver, and jewels of the Spaniards, for they heard the Indians say: "Here you shall leave the gold you took from us!" Again, some said it was to keep the Tlaxcalans and other mortal enemies out of Mexico. Many, finally, believed it was because the images of the gods had been cast down and [the Indians] wished to give themselves to the devil.

Any of these things could have caused the rebellion, let alone all of them together; but the principal one was this: A few days after Cortés had left to encounter Narváez, there was a solemn festival, which the Mexicans wished to celebrate in their traditional fashion. They begged Pedro de Alvarado (who had stayed behind to act as warden and Cortés, lieutenant) to give his permission, so that he would not think they were gathering to massacre the Spaniards. Alvarado consented, with the proviso that they were not to kill men in sacrifice or bear arms. More than six hundred (some say more than a thousand) gentlemen, and even several lords, assembled in the yard of the main temple, where that night they made a great hubbub with their drums, conches, trumpets, and bone fifes, which emit a loud whistle. They were naked, but covered with precious stones, pearls, necklaces, belts, bracelets, jewels of gold, silver, and mother-of-pearl, wearing many rich plumes on their heads. They performed the dance called *macehualixtli,* which means "reward through work" (from *macehaulli,* a farmer).

… [T]hey spread mats in the temple yard and placed drums upon them. They danced in rings, grasping hands, to the music of the singers, to which they responded. The songs were sacred, not profane, and were sung to praise the god whose feast was being celebrated, to induce him to give them water or grain, health or victory, or to thank him for giving them peace, children, health, and the like. Those who knew the language and these ceremonial rites said that, when the people danced in the temple [on this occasion], they performed very differently from those who danced the *netotelixtli,* in voice, movement of the body, head, arms, and feet, by which they manifest their concepts of good and evil. The Spaniards called this dance an *areyto,* a word they brought from the islands of Cuba and Santo Domingo.

While the Mexican gentlemen were dancing in the temple yard of Huitzilopochtli, Pedro de Alvarado went there, whether of his own notion or following the decision of the rest, I cannot say. Some say he had been warned that the Indian nobles of the city had assembled to plot the mutiny and rebellion which they later carried out; others, that [the Spaniards] went to see them perform this much-praised and famous dance, and, seeing them so rich, they coveted the gold the Indians were wearing, so he [Alvarado] blocked the entrances with ten or twelve Spaniards at each one, himself went in with more than fifty, and cruelly and pitilessly stabbed and killed the Indians, and took what they were wearing. Cortés, who must have felt badly about the affair, dissembled his feelings so as not to irritate the perpetrators, for it happened at a time when he had need of them, either against the Indians, or to put down trouble among his own men.

*makes it look like Alvarado's fault + Cortés backed into a corner.*

## FROM THE *FLORENTINE CODEX* AND THE *CODEX AUBIN*

*Miguel León-Portilla, the great Mexican scholar, gathered together a number of postconquest indigenous texts on the Toxcatl incident in his volume* Broken Spears. *Included here are his renditions of the* Florentine Codex *accounts and a small section from the* Codex Aubin, *a manuscript post-conquest collection of Nahuatl writings preserved in Paris. The indigenous sources give no indication that any "rebellion" was coordinated with the festival. These sources make the shock of these events clear.*

### The Preparations for the Fiesta

The Aztecs begged permission of their king to hold the fiesta of Huitzilopochtli. The Spaniards wanted to see this fiesta to learn how it was celebrated. A delegation of the celebrants came to the palace where Motecuhzoma

Ed. Miguel Leon-Portilla, excerpts from: Florentine Codex & Codex Aubin in *The Broken Spears: The Aztec Account of the Conquest of Mexico, 2nd ed.,* pp. 71-78, 80-81, Copyright © 1992 Beacon Press. Permission to reprint granted by the publisher.

was a prisoner, and when their spokesman asked his permission, he granted it to them.

As soon as the delegation returned, the women began to grind seeds of the chicalote.[1] These women had fasted for a whole year. They ground the seeds in the patio of the temple.

The Spaniards came out of the palace together, dressed in armor and carrying their weapons with them. They stalked among the women and looked at them one by one; they stared into the faces of the women who were grinding seeds. After this cold inspection, they went back into the palace. It is said that they planned to kill the celebrants if the men entered the patio.

### The Beginning of the Fiesta

Early the next morning, the statue's face was uncovered by those who had been chosen for that ceremony. They gathered in front of the idol in single file and offered it gifts of food, such as round seedcakes or perhaps human flesh. But they did not carry it up to its temple on top of the pyramid.

All the young warriors were eager for the fiesta to begin. They had sworn to dance and sing with all their hearts, so that the Spaniards would marvel at the beauty of the rituals.

The procession began, and the celebrants filed into the temple patio to dance the Dance of the Serpent. When they were all together in the patio, the songs and the dance began. Those who had fasted for twenty days and those who had fasted for a year were in command of the others; they kept the dancers in file with their pine wands. (If anyone wished to urinate, he did not stop dancing, but simply opened his clothing at the hips and separated his clusters of heron feathers.)

If anyone disobeyed the leaders or was not in his proper place they struck him on the hips and shoulders. Then they drove him out of the patio, beating him and shoving him from behind. They pushed him so hard that he sprawled to the ground, and they dragged him outside by the ears. No one dared to say a word about this punishment, for those who had fasted during the year were feared and venerated; they had earned the exclusive title "Brothers of Huitzilopochtli."

The great captain, the bravest warriors, danced at the head of the files to guide the others. The youths followed at a slight distance. Some of the youths wore their hair gathered into large locks, a sign that they had never taken any captives. Others carried their headdresses on their shoulders; they had taken captives, but only with help.

Then came the recruits, who were called "the young warriors." They had each captured an enemy of two. The others called to them: "Come, comrades, show us how brave you are! Dance with all your hearts!"

### The Spaniards Attack the Celebrants

At this moment in the fiesta, when the dance was loveliest and when song was linked to song, the Spaniards were seized with an urge to kill the celebrants. They all ran forward, armed as if for battle. They closed the entrances and passageways, all the gates of the patio: the Eagle Gate in the lesser palace, the Gate of the Canestalk and the Gate of the Serpent of Mirrors. They posted guards so that no one could escape, and then rushed into the Sacred Patio to slaughter the celebrants. They came on foot, carrying their swords and their wooden or metal shields.

They ran in among the dancers, forcing their way to the place where the drums were played. They attacked the man who was drumming and cut off his arms. Then they cut off his head, and it rolled across the floor.

They attacked all the celebrants, stabbing them, spearing them, striking them with their swords. They attacked some of them from behind, and these fell instantly to the ground with their entrails hanging out. Others they beheaded: they cut off their heads, or split their heads to pieces.

They struck others in the shoulders, and their arms were torn from their bodies. They wounded some in the thigh and some in the calf. They slashed others in the abdomen, and their entrails all spilled to the ground. Some attempted to run away, but their intestines dragged as they ran; they seemed to tangle their feet in their own entrails. No matter how they tried to save themselves, they could find no escape.

Some attempted to force their way out, but the Spaniards murdered them at the gates. Others climbed the walls, but they could not save themselves. Those who ran into the communal houses were safe there for

---

1  *Argemone mexicana,* an edible plant, also used in medicines.

a while; so were those who lay down among the victims and pretended to be dead. But if they stood up again, the Spaniards saw them and killed them.

The blood of the warriors flowed like water and gathered into pools. The pools widened, and the stench of blood and entrails filled the air. The Spaniards ran into the communal houses to kill those who were hiding. They ran everywhere and searched everywhere; they invaded every room, hunting and killing.

### The Aztecs Retaliate

When the news of this massacre was heard outside the Sacred Patio, a great cry went up: "Mexicanos, come running! Bring your spears and shields! The strangers have murdered our warriors!"

This cry was answered with a roar of grief and anger: the people shouted and wailed and beat their palms against their mouths. The captains assembled at once, as if the hour had been determined in advance. They all carried their spears and shields.

Then the battle began. The Aztecs attacked with javelins and arrows, even with the light spears that are used for hunting birds. They hurled their javelins with all their strength, and the cloud of missiles spread out over the Spaniards like a yellow cloak.

The Spaniards immediately took refuge in the palace. They began to shoot at the Mexicans with their iron arrows and to fire their cannons and arquebuses. And they shackled Motecuhzoma in chains.

### The Lament for the Dead

The Mexicans who had died in the massacre were taken out of the patio one by one and inquiries were made to discover their names. The fathers and mothers of the dead wept and lamented.

Each victim was taken first to his own home and then to the Sacred Patio, where all the dead were brought together. Some of the bodies were later burned in the place called the Eagle Urn, and others in the House of the Young Men.

### Motecuhzoma's Message

At sunset, Itzcuauhtzin climbed onto the roof of the palace and shouted this proclamation: "Mexicanos! Tlatelolcas! Your king, the lord Motecuhzoma, has sent me to speak for him. Mexicanos, hear me, for these are his words to you: 'We must not fight them. We are not their equals in battle. Put down your shields and arrows.'

"He tells you this because it is the aged who will suffer most, and they deserve your pity. The humblest classes will also suffer, and so will the innocent children who still crawl on all fours, who still sleep in their cradles.

"Therefore your king says: 'We are not strong enough to defeat them. Stop fighting, and return to your homes.' Mexicanos, they have put your king in chains; his feet are bound with chains."

When Itzcuauhtzin had finished speaking, there was a great uproar among the people. They shouted insults at him in their fury, and cried: "Who is Motecuhzoma to give us orders? We are no longer his slaves!" They shouted war cries and fired arrows at the rooftop. The Spaniards quickly hid Motecuhzoma and Itzcuauhtzin behind their shields so that the arrows would not find them.

The Mexicans were enraged because the attack on the captains had been so treacherous: their warriors had been killed without the slightest warning. Now they refused to go away or to put down their arms.

### The Massacre According to the *Codex Aubin*

Motecuhzoma said to La Malinche: "Please ask the god to hear me. It is almost time to celebrate the fiesta of Toxcatl. It will last for only ten days, and we beg his permission to hold it. We merely burn some incense and dance our dances. There will be a little noise because of the music, but that is all."

The Captain said: "Very well, tell him they may hold it." Then he left the city to meet another force of Spaniards who were marching in this direction. Pedro de Alvarado, called The Sun, was in command during his absence.

When the day of the fiesta arrived, Motecuhzoma said to The Sun: "Please hear me, my lord. We beg your permission to begin the fiesta of our god."

The Sun replied: "Let it begin. We shall be here to watch it."

The Aztec captains then called for their elder brothers, who were given this order: "You must celebrate the fiesta as grandly as possible."

The elder brothers replied: "We will dance with all our might"

Then Tecatzin, the chief of the armory, said: "Please remind the lord that he is here, not in Cholula. You know how they trapped the Cholultecas in their patio! They have already caused us enough trouble. We should hide our weapons close at hand!"

But Motecuhzoma said: "Are we at war with them? I tell you, we can trust them."

Tecatzin said: "Very well."

Then the songs and dances began. A young captain wearing a lip plug guided the dancers; he was Cuatlazol, from Tolnahuac.

But the songs had hardly begun when the Christians came out of the palace. They entered the patio and stationed four guards at each entrance. Then they attacked the captain who was guiding the dance. One of the Spaniards struck the idol in the face, and others attacked the three men who were playing the drums. After that there was a general slaughter until the patio was heaped with corpses.

A priest from the Place of the Canefields cried out in a loud voice: "Mexicanos! Who said we are not at war? Who said we could trust them?"

The Mexicans could only fight back with sticks of wood; they were cut to pieces by the swords. Finally the Spaniards retired to the palace where they were lodged.

# BERNAL DÍAZ

### From *The True History of the Conquest of New Spain*

*In his account, Bernal Díaz, who had gone with Cortés to attack Narváez, reported on the return to a Tenochtitlan in arms. Cortés, he reported, was furious with Alvarado but also with Moctezuma, whom he suspected had been in contact with Narváez. The intercession of various Spanish captains in favor of the captive ruler did not pacify him. It quickly became apparent that the Spaniards were besieged. Three excerpts are presented here; first, Díaz's account of the battle to control the major* cue, *the pyramid and temple of Huitzilopochtli; second, the death of Moctezuma; and lastly the escape of the* Noche triste *and the disastrous (for the Spaniards and Tlax-calans) fighting at the Tolteca canal.*

… We passed the night in dressing wounds and in mending the breaches in the walls that they [the enemy] had made, and in getting ready for the next day. Then, as soon as it was dawn, our Captain decided that all of us and Narváez' men should sally out to fight with them and that we should take the cannon and muskets and crossbows and endeavour to defeat them, or at least to make them feel our strength and valour better than the day before. I may state that when we came to this decision, the Mexicans were arranging the very same thing. We fought very well, but they were so strong, and had so many squadrons which relieved each other from time to time, that even if ten thousand Trojan Hectors and as many more Roldans had been there, they would not have been able to break through them.

So that it may now be understood, I will relate how it happened. We noted [their] tenacity in fighting, but I declare that I do not know how to describe it, for neither cannon nor muskets nor crossbows availed, nor hand-to-hand fighting, nor killing thirty or forty of them every time we charged, for they still fought on in as close ranks and with more energy than in the beginning. Sometimes when we were gaining a little ground or a part of the street, they pretended to retreat, but it was [merely] to induce us to follow them and cut us off from our fortress and quarters, so as to fall on us in greater safety to themselves, believing that we could not return to our quarters alive, for they did us much damage when we were retreating.

Then, as to going out to burn their houses, I have already said in the chapter that treats of the subject, that between one house and another, they have wooden drawbridges, and these they raised so that we could only pass through deep water. Then we could not endure the rocks and stones [hurled] from the roofs, in such a way that they damaged and wounded many of our men. I do not know why I write thus, so lukewarmly, for some three or four soldiers who were there with us and who had served in Italy, swore to God many times that they had never seen such fierce fights, not even when they had taken part in such between Christians, and against the artillery of the King of France, or of the Great Turk, nor had they seen men like those Indians with such courage in closing up their ranks.

However, as they said many other things and gave explanations of them, as will be seen further on, I will leave the matter here, and will relate how, with great difficulty we withdrew to our quarters, many squadrons of warriors still pressing on us with loud yells and whistles, and trumpets and drums, calling us villains and cowards who did not dare to meet them all day in battle, but turned in flight.

On that day they killed ten or twelve more soldiers and we all returned badly wounded. What took place during the night was the arrangement that in two days' time all the soldiers in camp, as many as were able, should sally out with four engines like towers built of strong timber, in such a manner that five and twenty men could find shelter under each of them, and they were provided with apertures and loopholes through which to shoot, and musketeers and crossbowmen accompanied them, and close by them were to march the other soldiers, musketeers and crossbowmen and the guns, and all the rest, and the horsemen were to make charges.

When this plan was settled, as we spent all that day in carrying out the work and in strengthening many breaches that they had made in the walls, we did not go out to fight.

I do not know how to tell of the great squadrons of warriors who came to attack us in our quarters, not only in ten or twelve places, but in more than twenty, for we were distributed over them all and in many other places, and while we built up and fortified [ourselves], as I have related, many other squadrons openly endeavoured to penetrate into our quarters, and neither with guns, crossbows nor muskets, nor with many charges and sword-thrusts could we force them back, for they said that not one of us should remain [alive] that day

and they would sacrifice our hearts and blood to their gods, and would have enough to glut [their appetites] and hold feasts on our arms and legs, and would throw our bodies to the tigers, lions, vipers and snakes, which they kept caged, so that they might gorge on them, and for that reason they had ordered them not to be given food for the past two days. As for the gold we possessed, we would get little satisfaction from it or from all the cloths; and as for the Tlaxcalans who were with us, they said that they would place them in cages to fatten, and little by little they would offer their bodies in sacrifice; and, very tenderly, they said that we should give up to them their great Lord Montezuma, and they said other things. Night by night, in like manner, there were always many yells and whistles and showers of darts, stones and arrows.

As soon as dawn came, after commending ourselves to God, we sallied out from our quarters with our towers (and it seems to me that in other countries where I have been,[1] in wars where such things were necessary, they were called "Buros" and "Mantas") with the cannon, muskets and crossbows in advance, and the horsemen making charges, but, as I have stated, although we killed many of them it availed nothing towards making them turn their backs, indeed if they had fought bravely on the two previous days, they proved themselves far more vigorous and displayed much greater forces and squadrons on this day. Nevertheless, we determined, although it should cost the lives of all of us, to push on with our towers and engines as far as the great Cue of Huichilobos.

I will not relate at length, the fights we had with them in a fortified house, nor will I tell how they wounded the horses, nor were they [the horses] of any use to us, because although they charged the squadrons to break through them, so many arrows, darts and stones were hurled at them, that they, well protected by armour though they were, could not prevail against them [the enemy], and if they pursued and overtook them, the Mexicans promptly dropped for safety into the canals and lagoons where they had raised other walls against the horsemen, and many other Indians were stationed with very long lances to finish killing them. Thus it benefited us nothing to turn aside to burn or demolish

1   The text says "donde me he hallado en guerra," but Bernal Díaz had not been in any wars except wars in America.

a house, it was quite useless, for, as I have said, they all stood in the water, and between house and house there was a movable bridge, and to cross by swimming was very dangerous, for on the roofs they had such store of rocks and stones and such defences, that it was certain destruction to risk it. In addition to this, where we did set fire to some houses, a single house took a whole day to burn, and the houses did not catch fire one from the other, as, for one reason, they stood apart with the water between; and, for the other, were provided with flat roofs (azoteas); thus it was useless toil to risk our persons in the attempt, so we went towards the great Cue of their Idols. Then, all of a sudden, more than four thousand Mexicans ascended it, not counting other Companies that were posted on it with long lances and stones and darts, and placed themselves on the defensive, and resisted our ascent for a good while, and neither the towers nor the cannon or crossbows, nor the muskets were of any avail, nor the horsemen, for, although they wished to charge [with] their horses, the whole of the courtyard was paved with very large flagstones, so that the horses lost their foothold, and they [the stones] were so slippery that they [the horses] fell. While from the steps of the lofty Cue they forbade our advance, we had so many enemies both on one side and the other that although our cannon [shots] carried off ten or fifteen of them and we slew many others by sword-thrusts and charges, so many men attacked us that we were not able to ascend the lofty Cue. However with great unanimity we persisted in the attack, and without taking the towers (for they were already destroyed) we made our way to the summit.

Here Cortés showed himself very much of a man, as he always was. Oh! what a fight and what a fierce battle it was that took place; it was a memorable thing to see us all streaming with blood, and covered with wounds and others slain. It pleased our Lord that we reached the place where we used to keep the image of Our Lady, and we did not find it, and it appears, as we came to know, that the great Montezuma paid devotion to Her, and ordered it [the image] to be preserved in safety.

We set fire to their Idols and a good part of the chamber with the Idols Huichilobos and Tezcatepuca was burned. On that occasion the Tlaxcalans helped us very greatly. After this was accomplished, while some of us were fighting and others kindling the fire, as I have related, oh! to see the priests who were stationed on this great Cue, and the three or four thousand Indians, all men of importance. While we descended, oh! how they made us tumble down six or even ten steps at a time! And so much more there is to tell of the other squadrons posted on the battlements and recesses of the great Cue discharging so many darts and arrows that we could face neither one group of squadrons nor the other. We resolved to return, with much toil and risk to ourselves, to our quarters, our castles being destroyed, all of us wounded and sixteen slain, with the Indians constantly pressing on us and other squadrons on our flanks.

However clearly I may tell all this, I can never [fully] explain it to any one who did not see us. So far, I have not spoken of what the Mexican squadrons did who kept on attacking our quarters while we were marching outside, and the great obstinacy and tenacity they displayed in forcing their way in.

In this battle, we captured two of the chief priests, whom Cortés ordered us to convey with great care.

Many times I have seen among the Mexicans and Tlaxcalans, paintings of this battle, and the ascent that we made of the great Cue, as they look upon it as a very heroic deed. And although in the pictures that they have made of it, they depict all of us as badly wounded and streaming with blood and many of us dead they considered it a great feat, this setting fire to the Cue, when so many warriors were guarding it both on the battlements and recesses, and many more Indians were below on the ground and the Courts were full of them and there were many more on the sides; and with our towers destroyed, how was it possible to scale it? …

Let us return to the great attacks they made on us; Montezuma was placed by a battlement of the roof with many of us soldiers guarding him, and he began to speak to them [his people], with very affectionate expressions [telling them] to desist from the war, and that we would leave Mexico. Many of the Mexican Chieftains and Captains knew him well and at once ordered their people to be silent and not to discharge darts, stones or arrows, and four of them reached a spot where Montezuma could speak to them, and they to him, and with tears they said to him: "Oh! Señor, and our great Lord, how all your misfortune and injury and that of your children and relations afflicts us, we make known to you that we have already raised one of your kinsmen to be our Lord," and there he stated his name, that he was called Cuitlahuac, the Lord of Ixtapalapa, (for it was not Guatemoc, he who was Lord soon after,) and moreover they said that the war must be carried through, and that they had vowed to their Idols not to relax it until we were all dead, and that they prayed every day to their Huichilobos and Texcatepuca to guard him free and safe from our power, and that should it end as they desired, they would not fail to hold him in higher regard as their Lord than they did before, and they begged him to forgive them. They had hardly finished this speech when suddenly such a shower of stones and darts was discharged that (our men who were shielding him having neglected their duty [to shield him] for a moment, because they saw how the attack ceased while he spoke to them) he was hit by three stones, one on the head, another on the arm and another on the leg, and although they begged him to have the wounds dressed and to take food, and spoke kind words to him about it, he would not. Indeed, when we least expected it, they came to say that he was dead. Cortés wept for him, and all of us Captains and soldiers, and there was no man among us who knew him and was intimate with him, who did not bemoan him as though he were our father, and it is not to be wondered at, considering how good he was. It was stated that he had reigned for seventeen years and that he was the best king there had ever been in Mexico, and that he had conquered in person, in three wars which he had carried on in the countries he had subjugated. Let us continue.

I have already told about the sorrow that we all of us felt about it when we saw that Montezuma was dead. We even thought badly of the Fraile de la Merced because he had not persuaded him to become a Christian, and he gave as an excuse that he did not think that he would die of those wounds, but that he ought to have ordered them to give him something to stupefy him. At the end of much discussion Cortés ordered a priest and a chief from among the prisoners to go and tell the Cacique whom they had chosen for Lord, who was named Cuitlahuac, and his Captains, that the great Montezuma was dead, and they had seen him die, and about the manner of his death and the wounds his own people had inflicted on him, and they should say how grieved we all were about it, and that they should bury him as the great king that he was, and they should raise

the cousin of Montezuma who was with us, to be king, for the inheritance was his, or one of his (Montezuma's) other sons, and that he whom they had raised to be king was not so by right, and they should negotiate a peace so that we could leave Mexico; and if they did not do so, now that Montezuma was dead, whom we held in respect and for that reason had not destroyed their city, we should sally out to make war on them and burn all their houses and do them much damage. So as to convince them that Montezuma was dead, he ordered six Mexicans who were high chieftains, and the priests whom we held as prisoners, to carry him out on their shoulders and to hand him [the body] over to the Mexican Captains, and to tell them what Montezuma had commanded at the time of his death, for those who carried him out on their backs were present at his death; and they told Cuitlahuac the whole truth, how his own people killed him with blows from three stones.

When they beheld him thus dead, we saw that they were in floods of tears and we clearly heard the shrieks and cries of distress that they gave for him, but for all this, the fierce assault they made on us with darts, stones and arrows never ceased, and then they came on us again with greater force and fury, and said to us: "Now for certain you will pay for the death of our King and Lord, and the dishonour to our Idols; and as for the peace you sent to beg for, come out here and we will settle how and in what way it is to be made," and they said many things about this and other matters that I cannot now remember and I will leave them un-reported, and [they said] that they had already chosen a good king, and he would not be so fainthearted as to be deceived with false speeches like their good Montezuma, and as for the burial, we need not trouble about that, but about our own lives, for in two days there would not be one of us left;—so much for the messages we had sent them. With these words [they fell on us] with loud yells and whistles and showers of stones, darts and arrows, while other squadrons were still attempting to set fire to our quarters in many places.

When Cortés and all of us observed this, we agreed that next day we would all of us sally out from our camp and attack in another direction, where there were many houses on dry land, and we would do all the damage we were able and go towards the causeway, and that all the horsemen should break through the squadrons and spear them with their lances or drive them into the water, even though they [the enemy] should kill the horses. This was decided on in order to find out if by chance, with the damage and slaughter that we should inflict on them, they would abandon their attack and arrange some sort of peace, so that we could go free without more deaths and damage. Although the next day we all bore ourselves very manfully and killed many of the enemy and burned a matter of twenty houses and almost reached dry land, it was all of no use, because of the great damage and deaths and wounds they inflicted on us, and we could not hold a single bridge, for they were all of them half broken down. Many Mexicans charged down on us, and they had set up walls and barricades in places which they thought could be reached by the horses, so that if we had met with many difficulties up to this time, we found much greater ones ahead of us.

Let us leave it here, and go back to say that we determined to get out of Mexico. …

Now we saw our forces diminishing every day and those of the Mexicans increasing, and many of our men were dead and all the rest wounded, and although we fought like brave men we could not drive back nor even get free from the many squadrons which attacked us both by day and night, and the powder was giving out, and the same was happening with the food and water, and the great Montezuma being dead, they were unwilling to grant the peace and truce which we had sent to demand of them. In fact we were staring death in the face, and the bridges had been raised. It was [therefore] decided by Cortés and all of us captains and soldiers that we should set out during the night, when we could see that the squadrons of warriors were most off their guard. In order to put them all the more off their guard, that very afternoon we sent to tell them, through one of their priests whom we held prisoner and who was a man of great importance among them and through some other prisoners, that they should let us go in peace within eight days and we would give up to them all the gold; and this [was done] to put them off their guard so that we might get out that night.

… I will relate how the order was given to make a bridge of very strong beams and planks, so that we could carry it with us and place it where the bridges were broken. Four hundred Tlaxcalan Indians and one hundred and fifty soldiers were told off to carry this bridge and place it in position and guard the passage until the army and all the baggage had crossed. Two hundred Tlaxcalan Indians and fifty soldiers were told off to carry the cannon, and Gonzalo de Sandoval, Diego de Ordás, Francisco de Sauzedo, Francisco de Lugo and a company of one hundred young and active soldiers were selected to go in the van to do the fighting. It was agreed that Cortés himself, Alonzo de Ávila, Cristóbal de Olid, and other Captains should go in the middle and support the party that most needed help in fighting. Pedro de Alvarado and Juan Velásquez de Leon were with the rearguard, and placed in the middle between them [and the preceding section] were two captains and the soldiers of Narvaez, and three hundred Tlaxcalans, and thirty soldiers were told off to take charge of the prisoners and of Doña Marina and Doña Luisa; by the time this arrangement was made, it was already night.

In order to bring out the gold and divide it up and carry it, Cortés ordered his steward named Cristóbal de Guzman and other soldiers who were his servants to bring out all the gold and jewels and silver, and he gave them many Tlaxcalan Indians for the purpose, and they placed it in the Hall. Then Cortés told the King's officers named Alonzo Dávila and Gonzalo Mejía to take charge of the gold belonging to His Majesty, and he gave them seven wounded and lame horses and one mare, and many friendly Tlaxcalans, more than eighty in number, and they loaded them with parcels of it, as much as they could carry, for it was put up into very broad ingots, as I have already said in the chapter that treats of it, and much gold still remained in the Hall piled up in heaps. Then Cortés called his secretary and the others who were King's Notaries, and said: "Bear witness for me that I can do no more with this gold. We have here in this apartment and Hall over seven hundred thousand pesos in gold, and, as you have seen, it cannot be weighed nor placed in safety. I now give it up to any of the soldiers who care to take it, otherwise it will be lost among these dogs [of Mexicans]."

When they heard this, many of the soldiers of Narvaez and some of our people loaded themselves with it. I declare that I had no other desire but the desire to save my life, but I did not fail to carry off from some small boxes that were there, four chalchihuites, which are stones very highly prized among the Indians, and I quickly placed them in my bosom under my armour, and, later on, the price of them served me well in healing my wounds and getting me food.

After we had learnt the plans that Cortés had made about the way in which we were to escape that night and get to the bridges, as it was somewhat dark and cloudy and rainy, we began before midnight to bring along the bridge and the baggage, and the horses and mare began their march, and the Tlaxcalans who were laden with the gold. Then the bridge was quickly put in place, and Cortés and the others whom he took with him in the first [detachment], and many of the horsemen, crossed over it. While this was happening, the voices, trumpets, cries and whistles of the Mexicans began to sound and they called out in their language to the people of Tlaltelolco, "Come out at once with your canoes for the Teules are leaving; cut them off so that not one of them may be left alive." When I least expected it, we saw so many squadrons of warriors bearing down on us, and the lake so crowded with canoes that we could not defend ourselves. Many of our soldiers had already crossed [the bridge] and while we were in this position, a great multitude of Mexicans charged down on us [with the intention of] removing the bridge and wounding and killing our men who were unable to assist each other; and as misfortune is perverse at such times, one mischance followed another, and as it was raining, two of the horses slipped and fell into the lake. When I and others of Cortés's Company saw that, we got safely to the other side of the bridge, and so many warriors charged on us, that despite all our good fighting, no further use could be made of the bridge, so that the passage or water opening was soon filled up with dead horses, Indian men and women, servants, baggage and boxes.

Fearing that they would not fail to kill us, we thrust ourselves ahead along the causeway, arid we met many squadrons armed with long lances waiting for us, and they used abusive words to us, and among them they cried "Oh! villains, are you still alive?" and with the cuts and thrusts we gave them, we got through, although they then wounded six of those who were going along [with me]. Then if there was some sort of plan such as we had agreed upon it was an accursed one; for Cortés and the captains and soldiers who passed first on horseback, so as to save themselves and reach dry land and make sure of their lives, spurred on along the causeway, and

they did not fail to attain their object, and the horses with the gold and the Tlaxcalans also got out in safety. I assert that if we had waited, (the horsemen and the soldiers, one for the other,) at the bridges, we should all have been put an end to, and not one of us would have been left alive; the reason was this, that as we went along the causeway, charging the Mexican squadrons, on one side of us was water and on the other azoteas,[1] and the lake was full of canoes so that we could do nothing. Moreover the muskets and crossbows were all left behind at the bridge, and as it was night time, what could we do beyond what we accomplished? which was to charge and give some sword-thrusts to those who tried to lay hands on us, and to march and get on ahead so as to get off the causeway.

Had it been in the day-time, it would have been far worse, and we who escaped did so only by the Grace of God. To one who saw the hosts of warriors who fell on us that night and the canoes [full] of them coming along to carry off our soldiers, it was terrifying. So we went ahead along the causeway in order to get to the town of Tacuba where Cortés was already stationed with all the Captains. Gonzalo de Sandoval, Cristóbal de Olid and others of those horsemen who had gone on ahead were crying out: "Señor Capitan, let us halt, for they say that we are fleeing and leaving them to die at the bridges; let us go back and help them, if any of them survive"; but not one of them came out or escaped. Cortés's reply was that it was a miracle that any of us escaped. However, he promptly went back with the horsemen and the soldiers who were unwounded, but they did not march far, for Pedro de Alvarado soon met them, badly wounded, holding a spear in his hand, and on foot, for they [the enemy] had already killed his sorrel mare, and he brought with him four soldiers as badly wounded as he was himself, and eight Tlaxcalans, all of them with blood flowing from many wounds.

While Cortés was on the causeway with the rest of the captains, we repaired to the courtyard in Tacuba. Many squadrons had already arrived from Mexico, shouting out orders to Tacuba and to the other town named Azcapotzalco, and they began to hurl darts, stones, and arrows [and attack] with their long lances. We made some charges and both attacked [them] and defended ourselves. …

---

1   The flat roofs of the houses.

Let us go on and I will relate how, when we were waiting in Tacuba, many Mexican warriors came together from all those towns and they killed three of our soldiers, so we agreed to get out of that town as quickly as we could, and five Tlaxcalan Indians, who found out a way towards Tlaxcala without following the [main] road, guided us with great precaution until we reached some small houses placed on a hill, and near to them a Cue or Oratory [built] like a fort, where we halted. …

## FRAY BERNARDINO DE SAHAGÚN

### From the *Florentine Codex*

*Before reading this Mexica account of* Noche triste, *take a look at Figures 14 and 15 (from* Lienzo de Tlaxcala) *to see how the Tlaxcalan view is presented. There are some striking images of the battle to escape the city in which Cortés, doña Marina, and the Tlaxcalan warriors are carefully shown in European style; however, indigenous pictorial conventions like the symbols for temples and water are also used effectively. This selection by the city's defenders is drawn from the* Florentine Codex. *It reports the death of Moctezuma and then the fighting in the city. These descriptions convey the intensity of the battles from the Mexica point of view. It should be remembered that many of Sahagún's informants were Tlatelolcans, who had their own complaints against Moctezuma's leadership.*

Twenty-third chapter, where it is said how Moteucçoma and a great nobleman of Tlatelolco died, and the Spaniards threw their bodies out at the entryway of the house where they were.

Four days after people had been cast down from the temple, [the Spaniards] removed [the bodies of] Moteucçoma and Itzquauhtzin, who had died, to a place at the water's edge called Teoayoc [Place of the Divine Turtle], for an image of a turtle was there, carved in stone; the stone represented a turtle.

And when they were seen and recognized as Moteucçoma and Itzquauhtzin, they hastened to take Moteucçoma up in their arms and brought him to the place called Copolco. Then they placed him on a pile of wood and set fire to it, ignited it. Then the fire crackled and roared, with many tongues of flame, tongues of flame like tassels, rising up. And Moteucçoma's body lay sizzling, and it let off a stench as it burned.

And when it was burning, some people, enraged and no longer with goodwill, scolded at him, saying, "This miserable fellow made the whole world fear him, in the whole world he was dreaded, in the whole world he inspired respect and fright. If someone offended him only in some small way, he immediately disposed of him. He punished many for imagined things, not true, but just fabricated tales." And there were many others who scolded him, moaning, lamenting, shaking their heads.

But Itzquauhtzin they put in a boat; they took his body in a boat until they got him here to Tlatelolco. They grieved greatly, their hearts were desolate; the tears flowed down. Not a soul scolded him or cursed him.

They said, "The lord Tlacochcalcatl Itzquauhtzin has suffered travail, for he suffered and was afflicted along with Moteucçoma. What tribulations he endured on our behalf in the past, during all of Moteucçoma's time!" Then they outfitted him, equipping him with the lordly banner and other items of paper, and they gave him provisions. Then they took him and burned him in the temple courtyard at the place called Quauhxicalco. It was with great splendor that his body was burned.

After four days of fighting, for seven days the Spaniards were just enclosed in the house. But when the seven days were past, they came back out for a while to take a look, looking around here and there; they went as far as Maçatzintamalco. They gathered stalks of green maize, beginning to form ears. They just gathered the maize leaves as one does in war, going in great haste. Hardly had they got where they were going when they quickly went back into the building. When they had come out the sun was already off to one side, about to set.

Fray Bernardino de Sahagun; trans and ed by James Lockhart, "Fray Bernardino de Sahagun: Florentine Codex" from *We People Here: Nahuatl Accounts of the Conquest of Mexico*, pp. 150, 152, 154, 156, Copyright © 1993 University of California Press. Permission to reprint granted by the publisher.

Twenty-fourth chapter, where it is said how the Spaniards and Tlaxcalans came out and fled from Mexico by night.

When night had fallen and midnight had come, the Spaniards came out. They formed up, along with all the Tlaxcalans. The Spaniards went ahead, and the Tlaxcalans went following, bringing up the rear, like their wall of protection. [The Spaniards] went carrying a wooden platform [or platforms]; they laid it down at a canal and crossed over on it.

At this time it was drizzling and sprinkling, the rain was gently dripping down. They were able to cross some other canals, at Tecpantzinco, Tzapotla, and Atenchicalco. But when they got to Mixcoatechialtitlan, at the fourth canal, there they were seen coming out. It was a woman fetching water who saw them; then she shouted, saying, "O Mexica, come running, your enemies have come out, they have emerged secretly!" Then another person shouted, on top of [the temple of] Huitzilopochtli; his crying spread everywhere, everyone heard it. He said, "O warriors, o Mexica, your enemies are coming out, let everyone hasten with the war boats and on the roads!"

When it was heard, there was a clamor. Everyone scrambled; the operators of the war boats hastened and paddled hard, hitting one another's boats as they went in the direction of Mictlantonco and Macuilcuitlapilco. The war boats came upon them from both directions; the war boats of the Tenochca and the war boats of the Tlatelolca converged on them. And some people went on foot, going straight to Nonoalco, heading toward Tlacopan to try to cut them off there. Then the war-boat people hurled barbed darts at the Spaniards; from both sides the darts fell on them. But the Spaniards also shot at the Mexica, shooting back with iron bolts and guns. There were deaths on both sides. Spaniards and Tlaxcalans were hit, and Mexica were hit.

When the Spaniards reached Tlaltecayoacan, where the Tolteca canal is, it was as though they had fallen off a precipice; they all fell and dropped in, the Tlaxcalans, the people of Tliliuhquitepec, and the Spaniards, along with the horses, and some women. The canal was completely full of them, full to the very top. And those who came last just passed and crossed over on people, on bodies.

When they reached Petlacalco, where there was yet another canal, they passed gently, slowly, gradually,

with caution, on the wooden platform. There they restored themselves, took their breath, regained their vigor. When they reached Popotlan, it dawned, light came. They began to go along with spirit, they went heading into the distance.

Then the Mexica went shouting at them, surrounding them, hovering about them. They captured some Tlaxcalans as they went, and some Spaniards died. Also Mexica and Tlatelolca were killed; there was death on both sides. They drove and pursued [the Spaniards] to Tlacopan. And when they had driven them to Tiliuhcan, to Xocotliiyohuican, at Xoxocotla, Chimalpopoca, son of Moteucçoma, died in battle. They came upon him lying hit by a barbed dart and struck [by some hand weapon]. At the same place died Tlaltecatzin, a Tepaneca lord who had been guiding the Spaniards, pointing out the way for them, conducting them, showing them the road.

Then they crossed the Tepçolatl (a small river); they forded and went over the water at Tepçolac. Then they went up to Acueco and stopped at Otoncalpolco, [where] wooden walls or barricades were in the courtyard. There they all took a rest and caught their breath, there they restored themselves. There the people of Teocalhueyacan came to meet them and guide them.

## THE SIEGE AND FALL OF TENOCHTITLAN

The final stage of the military conquest of Mexico took place in roughly a year, between the arrival of the Spaniards in Tlaxcala on July 11, 1520, after their flight from Tenochtitlan and their destruction of the Mexica capital and the surrender of the last emperor Cuahtemoc on August 13, 1521. During the first ten of those thirteen months, both the Mexica and the Spaniards maneuvered to find allies and to muster their forces. These months were filled with campaigns and battles around the valley of Mexico. The final siege of Tenochtitlan lasted about three months (Bernal Díaz says ninety-three days). It ended with the fall of Tenochtitlan.

The fighting in these last few months was bitter, and at the end it was often house-by-house combat. The Mexica had to contend not only with the reinforced Spanish troops and the thousands of native allies that accompanied them, but also with another enemy: epidemic disease in the form of smallpox. The Nahua accounts mention the effects of the disease that decimated the population and devastated their leadership. Cuitlahuac, the brother of Moctezuma who became the *tlatoani* when the latter died and who directed the attacks of the *Noche triste,* lived for only three months before succumbing to smallpox. He was then replaced by Cuahtemoc, who directed the final defense. Historian Ross Hassig has argued that the plague strengthened the Spanish position, although the native allies of the Spanish also suffered from its effects. Cortés exploited these gaps in the leadership of other cities by backing new leaders who were loyal to him. Meanwhile, Cuahtemoc tried to win support by lowering the tribute demands on the Mexica dependents, but his attempts only made Tenochtitlan seem weak. This contributed to the number of native groups which collaborated with the Spaniards.

As the Spaniards consolidated their position and more soldiers arrived on the coast, Cortés demonstrated considerable ability in cajoling, convincing, and bullying various cities into joining him for the final effort against Tenochtitlan. Key in this effort was the continued allegiance of Tlaxcala, which, even after the *Noche triste* when the Spaniards were at their weakest, maintained its loyalty.

The final battle for Tenochtitlan was a combined naval and land operation. First Cortés sought to isolate the city from its support. Texcoco, another major city on the shores of the lake and a traditional ally of Tenochtitlan, was in the midst of a dynastic crisis and civil war. Cortés was able to gain its loyalty without a battle. The Spaniards seized Iztapalapa but were later forced out again. Eventually, however, the Spaniards were able to win over or neutralize many of the lakeside towns and cities and to secure access to the coast by defeating Mexica armies operating outside the lake area. In the final battles, Tenochtitlan and its subdivision Tlatelolco were effectively left to fight on their own.

The city's peculiar location on an island in the midst of a lake had defensive advantages as long as the defenders could control access across the lake. Cortés realized this, and so upon return to Tlaxcala he began the construction of thirteen small (about forty feet long), shallow-draught ships, or brigantines. The timber for these was then dragged back to the lake by his native allies. These ships were then outfitted with small cannon, sails, and rigging that the Spaniards had saved from the original ships scuttled at Vera Cruz.[1] Although the Mexica developed various barriers and traps to impede the Spanish naval operations, once these ships were on the lake, the Mexica war canoes were outmatched. Cortés was able to cut the city off from its supply sources, tightening a noose around the throat of the city.

Meanwhile, the Mexica took advantage of the structure of their city with its many canals and its streets intersected by bridges. The Mexica would draw Spanish troops into the city and then cut off their retreat by removing the bridges over which they had crossed. The Spanish eventually learned to avoid these situations by not advancing beyond secured areas or by carrying small portable bridges along with their forces. When on the causeways, the Spanish found the mobility and effectiveness of their horses hampered and the Mexica war canoes effectively harassed the Spanish forces. On a number of occasions, Spanish forces were routed withstanding great losses. The spirited Mexica defense, however, was almost helpless against the Spanish brigantines, which could attack at any point and were not limited to the streets and causeways where the Mexica could plan their defense. In the final days of fighting, the Spaniards destroyed houses to eliminate their rooftops as platforms from which the Mexica could fire arrows or hurl stones. The Spaniards also used the rubble to fill in the water gaps created by the Mexica in the streets to cut off the enemy. The result of these tactics was the leveling of large parts of the city. Even Cortés regretted the loss. In a moment of explanation and self-justification he told his king why he had burned many of the palaces and great houses in an attempt to bring the Mexica to submission: "I was much grieved to do this," he wrote, "but since it was still more grievous to them I determined on burning them." Such tactics had little effect on the Mexica will to fight. The admiration of Cortés and Bernal Díaz for

---

1   The naval aspects of the final siege are the subject of C. Harvey Gardiner, *Naval Power in the Conquest of Mexico* (Austin: University of Texas Press, 1956).

the bravery and resilience of the Mexica defenders is evident throughout their accounts.

This chapter includes both indigenous and Spanish accounts. Included here is an excerpt from the Tarascan neighbors of the Mexica, the Nahua accounts drawn from the *Florentine Codex,* and some elegies preserved in Nahuatl after the conquest about the fall of the city. The Spanish side is represented both by Bernal Díaz and by another conquistador, Francisco de Aguilar.

## FRAY BERNARDINO DE SAHAGÚN

### From the *Florentine Codex*

*Included here are excerpts from Book Twelve of the* Florentine Codex *as translated in* We People Here. *The agonies of the defeat are apparent, beginning with the report of the smallpox epidemic that was spreading through the city. These excerpts give particular attention to the places where the battles took place and the specific conditions of the combat. Sometimes, as in the case of Tzilacatzin, the names and exploits of the warriors involved are given as well as the victories and defeats. In one noteworthy selection a retelling of the capture and sacrifice of the Spaniards is described in detail. Sahagún's informants for these accounts were men from Tlatelolco, the quarter of Tenochtitlan which had once been a separate city and was politically subordinate. The excerpts indicate the strength of local pride and perhaps a Tlatelolcan bias against the political and military failure of Tenochtitlan. Just as the first arrival of the Spaniards had been accompanied by supernatural signs in the Nahua accounts, the final defeat is also presaged by an omen, a blood-colored sky. The Nahua texts do not fail to mention in matter-of-fact directness the Spanish actions after the surrender, the search for gold, and the taking of women and of slaves.*

Twenty-ninth chapter, where it is said how, at the time the Spaniards left Mexico, there came an illness of pustules of which many local people died; it was called "the great rash" [smallpox].

Before the Spaniards appeared to us, first an epidemic broke out, a sickness of pustules. It began in Tepeilhuitl. Large bumps spread on people; some were entirely covered. They spread everywhere, on the face, the head, the chest, etc. [The disease] brought great desolation; a great many died of it. They could no longer walk about, but lay in their dwellings and sleeping places, no longer able to move or stir. They were unable to change position, to stretch out on their sides or face down, or raise their heads. And when they made a motion, that called out loudly. The pustules that covered people caused great desolation; very many people died of them, and many just starved to death; starvation reigned, and no one took care of others any longer.

On some people, the pustules appeared only far apart, and they did not suffer greatly, nor did many of them die of it. But many people's faces were spoiled by it, their faces and noses were made rough. Some lost an eye or were blinded.

This disease of pustules lasted a full sixty days; after sixty days it abated and ended. When people were convalescing and reviving, the pustules disease began to move in the direction of Chalco. And many were disabled or paralyzed by it, but they were not disabled forever. It broke out in Teotleco, and it abated in Panquetzaliztli. The Mexica warriors were greatly weakened by it.

And when things were in this state, the Spaniards came, moving toward us from Tetzcoco. They appeared from the direction of Quauhtitlan and made a halt at Tlacopan. There they gave one another assignments and divided themselves. Pedro de Alvarado was made responsible for the road coming to Tlatelolco. The Marqués considered the Tenochca great and valiant warriors.

And it was right in Nextlatilco, or in Ilyacac, that war first began. Then [the Spaniards] quickly reached

Fray Bernardino de Sahagun; trans and ed by James Lockhart, "Fray Bernardino de Sahagun: Florentine Codex" from *We People Here: Nahuatl Accounts of the Conquest of Mexico*, pp. 180, 182, 184, 192, 194, 198, 200, 214, 216, 218, 242, 244, 246, 248, 185, Copyright © 1993 University of California Press. Permission to reprint granted by the publisher.

Nonoalco, and the warriors came pursuing them. None of the Mexica died; then the Spaniards retreated. The warriors fought in boats; the war-boat people shot at the Spaniards, and their arrows sprinkled down on them. Then [the main force of the Mexica] entered [Nonoalco]. Thereupon the Marqués sent [his men] toward the Tenochca, following the Acachinanco road. Many times they skirmished, and the Mexica went out to face them.

Thirty-first chapter, where it is said how the Spaniards came with the brigantines, pursuing those who were in boats. When they were done contending with them, they drew close and reached all the houses.

And when they had finished adjusting [the guns], they shot at the wall. The wall then ripped and broke open. The second time it was hit, the wall went to the ground; it was knocked down in places, perforated, holes were blown in it. Then, like the other time, the road stood clear. And the warriors who had been lying at the wall dispersed and came fleeing; everyone escaped in fear. And then all the different people [who were on the side of the Spaniards] quickly went filling in the canals and making them level with stones, adobes, and some logs, with which they closed off the water.

And when the canals were stopped up, some horse[men] came, perhaps ten of them; they came going in circles, spinning, turning, twisting. Another group of horse[men] came following behind them. And some Tlatelolca who had quickly entered the palace that had been Moteucçoma's residence came back out in alarm to contend with the horse[men]. They lanced one of the Tlatclolca, but when they had lanced him, he was able to take hold of [the Spaniard's] iron lance. Then his companions took it from [the Spaniard's] hands, throwing him on his back and unhorsing him. When he fell to the ground, they struck him repeatedly on the back of the neck, and he died there.

Then the Spaniards sent everyone, they all moved together; they reached Quauhquiahuac [Eagle Gate]. As they went they took the cannon and its gear and set it down at Quauhquiahuac. (The reason it is so called is that an eagle stood there, carved of stone, some seven feet tall, and enclosing it were a jaguar standing on one side, and a wolf standing on the other, likewise carved in stone.) And when things were in this state the great warriors tried to take shelter behind the stone pillars; there were two rows of them, eight altogether. And the roof of the Coacalli was also full of warriors. None of them ventured to cross into the open.

And the Spaniards did not move at all; when they fired the cannon, it grew very dark, and smoke spread. Those who had been taking shelter behind the stone pillars fled; all who had been lying on the roof jumped down and ran far away. Then they brought the cannon up and set it down at the round stone [of gladiatorial sacrifice]. On top of [the temple of] Huitzilopochtli they were still trying to keep watch, beating the log drums, as though the air were full of them. Then two Spaniards climbed up and struck [the drummers]; after they had struck them they cast them aside, threw them down.

And those with scraped heads, all the warriors who were fighting in boats, came onto dry land, and only the youths who poled the others conducted the boats. And at this point the warriors inspected the passageways, with much running and shouting, saying "O warriors, let everyone come running!" …

Thirty-second chapter, where it is said how the Mexica left their altepetl in fear and came here when they dreaded the Spaniards.

And at this time the Tenochca came entering into Tlatelolco here, weeping and shouting. Many were the tears of the women; the men came accompanying their women, and some of them carried their children on their shoulders. In just one day they abandoned their altepetl. But the Tlatelolca still went to Tenochtitlan to fight.

And at this point Pedro de Alvarado hurled his forces at Ilyacac, toward Nonoalco, but they could do nothing; it was as though they had hit against a stone, because the Tlatelolca made great efforts. There was fighting on both sides of the road and in the water with war boats. When Alvarado tired, he returned and established himself in Tlacopan. But just two days later they sent out all the boats; at first only two came, then afterward all of them, and formed beside the houses in Nonoalco. Then they came onto dry land, and then they began to follow the narrow road between the houses; they came toward the center of them.

When the Spaniards landed it fell silent; not one of the people came out. But then Tzilacatzin, who was a great warrior and very valorous, hurled three stones he was carrying, huge round stones, wall stones or white stones; he had one in his hand and two on his shield. Then he went pursuing the Spaniards, scattering them, forcing them into the water. They went right into the water; those who went down in the water got thoroughly wetted.

(This Tzilacatzin had the warrior [rank] of Otomi, for which reason he wore the Otomi hairstyle, so he looked down on his enemies, even though they be Spaniards, thinking nothing of them. He inspired general fear. When our enemies saw Tzilacatzin, they would hunch down. They strove greatly to kill him, whether shooting him with iron bolts or with guns. But Tzilacatzin disguised himself in order not to be recognized. Sometimes he would put on [his own] device, with his lip pendant and his golden earplugs, and he would put on his shell necklace. He would go with his head uncovered, showing that he was an Otomi. But sometimes he put on only cotton upper armor and covered his forehead with a little narrow cloth. Sometimes to disguise himself he put on a feather hairpiece or wig, with eagle feathers tied at the back of the neck. This was the way in which those who threw people in the fire were attired; he went about looking like one of them, imitating them. He had golden arm bands on both sides, on both arms, shimmering, and he also had shining golden bands on the calves of his legs.)

Thirty-fifth chapter, where it is told how the Mexica took captives again—according to the count of the Spaniards they captured, there were fifty-three, as well as many Tlaxcalans and people of Tetzcoco, Chalco, and Xochimilco—and how they killed all of them before their former gods.

And at this point they let loose with all the warriors who had been crouching there; they came out and chased [the Spaniards] in the passageways, and when the Spaniards saw it they [the Mexica] seemed to be intoxicated. Then captives were taken. Many Tlaxcalans, and people of Acolhuacan, Chalco, Xochimilco, etc., were captured. A great abundance were captured and killed. They made the Spaniards and all the others go right into the water. And the road became very slippery; one could no longer walk on it, but would slip and slide. …

Then they took the captives to Yacacolco, hurrying them along, going along herding their captives together. Some went weeping, some singing, some went shouting while hitting their hands against their mouths. When they got them to Yacacolco, they lined them

all up. Each one went to the altar platform, where the sacrifice was performed. The Spaniards went first, going in the lead; the people of all the different altepetl just followed, coming last. And when the sacrifice was over, they strung the Spaniards' heads on poles [on the skull rack]; they also strung up the horses' heads. They placed them below, and the Spaniards' heads were above them, strung up facing east. But they did not string up the heads of all the various [other] people from far away. There were fifty-three of the Spaniards they captured, along with four horses.

Nevertheless, watch was kept everywhere, and there was fighting. They did not stop keeping watch because of [what had happened]. The people of Xochimilco went about in boats surrounding us on all sides; there were deaths and captives taken on both sides.

And all the common people suffered greatly. There was famine; many died of hunger. They no longer drank good, pure water, but the water they drank was salty. Many people died of it, and because of it many got dysentery and died. Everything was eaten: lizards, swallows, maize straw, grass that grows on salt flats. And they chewed at colorin wood, glue flowers, plaster, leather, and deerskin, which they roasted, baked, and toasted so that they could eat them, and they ground up medicinal herbs and adobe bricks. There had never been the like of such suffering. The siege was frightening, and great numbers died of hunger. And bit by bit they came pressing us back against the wall, herding us together. …

Thirty-ninth chapter, where it is said how when [the Spaniards] had forced the Mexica to the very wall, there appeared and was seen a blood-colored fire that seemed to come from the sky. It appeared like a great blazing coal as it came.

When night came, it rained and sprinkled off and on. It was very dark when a fire appeared. It looked and appeared as if it was coming from the sky, like a whirlwind. It went spinning around and around, turning on itself; as it went it seemed to explode into coals, some large, some small, some just like sparks. It seemed to take on the aspect of a "wind-axe." It sputtered, crackled, and snapped. It circled the walls at the water, heading toward Coyonacazco, then it went into the midst of the water and disappeared there. No one struck his hand against his mouth, no one uttered a sound. …

Then they took Quauhtemoctzin in a boat. In it were only two people accompanying him, going with him: Tepotzitoloc, a seasoned warrior, and Iaztachimal, Quauhtemoctzin's page, with one person who poled them along, named Cenyaotl. When they were about to take Quauhtemoctzin, all the people wept, saying, "There goes the lord Quauhtemoctzin, going to give himself to the gods, the Spaniards."

Fortieth chapter, where it is said how the Tlatelolca and Tenochca and their ruler submitted to the Spaniards, and what happened when they were among them.

And when they had gotten him there and put him on land, all the Spaniards were waiting. They came to take him; the Spaniards grasped him by the hand, took him up to the roof, and stood him before the Captain, the war leader. When they stood him before him, he looked at Quauhtemoctzin, took a good look at him, stroked his hair; then they seated him next to him. And they fired off the guns; they hit no one, but they aimed over the people, the [shots] just went over their heads. Then they took a [cannon], put it in a boat, and took it to the home of Coyohuehuetzin. When they got there, they took it up on the roof. Then again they killed people; many died there. But [the Mexica] just fled, and the war came to an end.

Then everyone shouted, saying, "It's over! Let everyone leave! Go eat greens!" When they heard this, the people departed; they just went into the water. But when they went out on the highway, again they killed some people, which angered the Spaniards; a few of them were carrying their shields and war clubs. Those who lived in houses went straight to Amaxac, where the road forks. There the people divided, some going toward Tepeyacac, some toward Xoxohuiltitlan, some toward Nonoalco. But no one went toword Xoloco and Maçatzintamalco.

And all who lived in boats and on platforms [in the water] and those at Tolmayeccan just went into the water. The water came to the stomachs of some, to the chests of others, to the necks of others, and some sank entirely into the deep water. The little children were carried on people's backs. There was a general wail; but some rejoicing and amusing themselves as they went along the road. Most of the owners of boats left at night, though some left by day. They seemed to knock against one another as they went.

And along every stretch [of road] the Spaniards took things from people by force. They were looking for gold; they cared nothing for green-stone, precious feathers, or turquoise. They looked everywhere with the women, on their abdomens, under their skirts. And they looked everywhere with the men, under their loin-cloths and in their mouths. And [the Spaniards] took, picked out the beautiful women, with yellow bodies. And how some women got loose was that they covered their faces with mud and put on ragged blouses and skirts, clothing themselves in rags. And some men were picked out, those who were strong and in the prime of life, and those who were barely youths, to run errands for them and be their errand boys, called their *tlamaca-zque* [priests, acolytes]. Then they burned some of them on the mouth [branded them]; some they branded on the cheeks, some on the mouth.

And when the weapons were laid down and we collapsed, the year count was Three House, and the day count was One Serpent. ...

# The Devastation of the Indies:
# A Brief Account

By Bartolomé De Las Casas

## NEW SPAIN

In the year one thousand five hundred and seven New Spain[18] was discovered and during the discovery great outrages were perpetrated against the Indians and some of the discoverers were slain. In the year one thousand five hundred and eighteen, Spaniards who called themselves Christians went there to massacre and kill, although they said their aim was to settle Christians in the province. And from that year to this day (we are in the year one thousand five hundred and forty-two), the climax of injustice and violence and tyranny committed against the Indians has been reached and surpassed. Because the Spaniards have now lost all fear of God and of the King, they have ceased to know right from wrong. Because among so many and such different nations they have committed and continue to commit so many acts of cruelty, such terrible ravages, massacres, destructions, exterminations, thefts, violences and tyrannies of all kinds that all the things we have related are as nothing by comparison. But were we to describe all the infinite number of such acts they would be as nothing when compared to what they have done this day and year of one thousand five hundred and forty-two, and today in this month of September are doing, for they continue to commit acts of the most abominable kind. As we have said above, the rule is always this: from the beginning the Spaniards have always continually increased and expanded their infernal acts and outrages.

Thus, from the beginning of their discovery of New Spain, that is to say, from the eighteenth of April in the year one thousand five hundred and eighteen until the year thirty, a period of twelve whole years, there were continual massacres and outrages committed by the bloody hands and swords of the Spaniards against the Indians living on the four hundred and fifty leagues of land surrounding the city of Mexico, which comprised four or five great kingdoms as large as and more felicitous than Spain. Those lands were all more densely populated than Toledo or Seville and Valladolid and Zaragoza all combined, along with Barcelona. Never has there been such a population as in these cities which God saw fit to place in that vast expanse of land having a circumference of more than a thousand leagues. The Spaniards have killed more Indians here in twelve years by the sword, by fire, and enslavement than anywhere else in the Indies. They have killed young and old, men, women, and children,[19] some four million souls during what they call the Conquests, which were the violent invasions of cruel tyrants that should be condemned not only by the law of God but by all the laws of man (since they were much worse than the deeds committed by the Turks in their effort to destroy the Christian Church). And this does not take into account those Indians who have died from ill treatment or were killed under tyrannical servitude.

In particulars, no tongue would suffice, nor word nor human efforts, to narrate the frightful deeds committed simultaneously by the Spaniards in regions far distant from each other, those notorious hellions, enemies of humankind. And some of their deeds committed in the Indies, in their quality and circumstances, truly they could not, even with much time and diligence and writing, could not be explained. I will narrate, along with protests and sworn statements by eyewitnesses, only some portions of the story, for I could not hope to explain a thousandth part.

Among other massacres there was the one in a big city of more than thirty thousand inhabitants, which is called Cholula. The people came out to welcome all the lords of the country and the earth; first of all came the priests with the head priest of the Christians in procession and received them with great respect and reverence, and took them to lodge in the center of the town, where they would reside in the houses of the most important nobles.

Soon after this the Spaniards agreed to carry out a massacre, or as they called it a punitive attack, in order to sow terror and apprehension, and to make a display of their power in every corner of that land. This was always the determination of the Spaniards in all the lands they conquered: to commit a great massacre that would terrorize the tame flock and make it tremble.

With this aim, therefore, they sent a summons to all the caciques and nobles of the city and in the localities subject to it, and also the head chieftain, and as they arrived to speak with the Spanish captain they were taken prisoner, so unexpectedly that none could flee and warn the others. The Spaniards had asked for five or six thousand Indians to carry their cargo. When all the chiefs had come, they and the burden-bearers were herded into the patios of the houses. What a grievous thing it was, to see those Indians as they prepared to carry the loads of the Spaniards: it was a grievous sight for they came naked, stark naked except for their private parts, which were covered. And they had a netting bag slung over their shoulders, holding their meager nourishment. They were all made to squat down on their haunches like tame sheep.

When they were all placed close together they were bound and tied. At the closed doorways armed guards took turns to see that none escaped. Then, at a command, all the Spaniards drew their swords or pikes and while their chiefs looked on, helpless, all those tame sheep were butchered, cut to pieces. At the end of two or three days some survivors came out from under the corpses, wounded but still alive, and they went,

weeping, to the Spaniards, imploring mercy, which was denied. The Spaniards had no compassion but drove them back and cut them down. Then the Spaniards had the chiefs, a total of more than a hundred, who were already shackled, burned at the stakes that had been driven into the ground.

But one of the caciques, and who knows, he may have been the ruler of that land, managed to escape with twenty or thirty of his followers. They took refuge in the great temple that was there, which was like a fortress, and was called *Cuu,* and there he defended himself for the greater part of the day. But the Spaniards, against whom there is no protection, especially no protection for these unarmed people, set fire to the temple and burned them there as they cried out: "Oh, wicked men! What have we done against you? Why are you killing us? Go to the city of Mexico, where our lord and master, Montezuma, will revenge us!"

It is said that when the Spaniards were putting the five or six thousand Indians in the patios to the sword one captain sang out: "Nero of Tarpeia watched Rome burn and the cries of the young and the old did not move him."

They carried out another great massacre in the city of Tepeaca, which was much larger and more densely populated than Cholula. Many perished, too many to count, and great acts of particular cruelty were committed.

From Cholula they marched toward the city of Mexico, and the great Montezuma sent them thousands of presents and an assembly of chiefs and people celebrated fiestas on the road, and as the Spaniards reached the pavements of the city at a distance of two leagues, the great ruler sent them his own brother accompanied by many nobles, bearing gifts of silver and gold and rich garments. At the entrance to the city he himself greeted them and accompanied them to the palace in which he had arranged for them to be lodged. And that very day, as I was told by some of those who were there, the Spaniards deceitfully set a guard of eighty men to capture the great King Montezuma and put him in chains.

But I leave all this, even though there are many important events to relate, and shall only summarize what those tyrants did. The captain-general took his troops down to the sea to encounter and defeat a certain other Spanish captain[20] who was marching against him, but

*look at the rhetoric in vocabulary.*

left a number of his officers in Mexico City and about a hundred men to guard the captive King and gave them permission to commit an outstanding crime, with the aim of increasing and spreading terror throughout the land, using their utmost methods of cruelty.

The Indians, nobles and commoners alike, throughout the city, thinking only of giving pleasure to their lord imprisoned within the palace assembled nearby to celebrate a fiesta[21] in a public square, singing and dancing the dance they called *mitote* which is like the *arieta* of the islands. At this fiesta the nobles donned their gala costumes to display their wealth, and some of these nobles were of royal lineage. Celebrating this fiesta were more than a thousand nobles, the flower of Indian youth, the elite of Montezuma's empire.

The Spanish captain set out toward this fiesta with a company of his men and sent out other squadrons to the other fiestas being celebrated in other parts of the city, with orders that at a certain set time they were to attack the celebrants mercilessly, after pretending at first merely to be enjoying the fiestas.

Being a little drunk and having safely penetrated to the very center of the fiesta nearest the palace, he called out, "Now, Santiago be with us, and at them!" And with naked swords they attacked those delicate bodies, letting that generous blood flow, leaving not one of the Indian nobles to survive. While in other parts of the city the same atrocities were committed.

This was an event that spread terror throughout those kingdoms and filled the people with bitterness, anguish, and revolt. That calamity, which deprived them of the flower of the nobility, meant, for them, the end of the world, and they have never ceased lamenting and recounting the story in their songs and the dances called *ariettas*, as in their stories called "romances." They have never recovered from that loss of succession to all the nobility, which had been for many years their glory.

The unheard-of cruelty and injustice of this massacre stirred up the Indians to revolt, although until that time they had tolerated the imprisonment of their universal ruler, because Montezuma himself had commanded them not to plot against the Spanish conquerors. Now, throughout the city they took up arms, attacked the Christians, wounding and killing many of those who did not manage to escape. And when Montezuma came out into the corridors of the palace and commanded the Indians to go away in peace, their leader set his dagger against the King's breast and they all swore henceforth not to obey him and that they would consult together and elect another lord who would guide them in their battles.

For they intended to wage war against the captain-general when he should return from Veracruz, victorious. But when he did return, it was with a larger army of Christians, and the Indian uprising, which had lasted three or four days, was coming to an end.

The attack made by the augmented army against all the Indians of that land produced a battle so fierce that, fearing all the Christians would be slain, in self-defense they declared a truce and left the city. The Indians had killed a great many Christians on the bridges of the lagoon, in this righteous war.

After this, there followed the battle for the city, the Christians having returned in full strength and they created great havoc. In this strange and admirable kingdom of the Indies, they slew a countless number of people and burned alive many great chiefs.

Later, when the Spaniards had inflicted extraordinary abominations on the city of Mexico and the other cities and towns, over a surface of fifteen or twenty leagues, killing countless Indians, they pressed forward to spread terror and lay waste the province of Pánuco, where an amazing number of people were slain.

Likewise, they destroyed the province of Tututepec, and then the province of Ipilcingo, and after that the province of Colima, each of those lands being more vast than the kingdoms of León and Castile.[22] To recount the ravages and massacres and cruelties they perpetrated in each of those lands would no doubt be difficult if not impossible and would be a story unbearable to hear.

At this point we should take note of the reason the Spaniards gave for conquering these lands and why they tried to destroy all those innocents and to devastate those regions where the aspect of the joy and happiness of a numerous population should have caused them to become veritable Christians. Their aim, they said, was to subject the people to the King of Spain, who had commanded them to kill and to enslave. And the Indians who did not obey stupid messages and would not put themselves in the hands of the iniquitous and ruthless Christians would be considered rebels unwilling to serve His Majesty. And their argument was set down in letters addressed to our lord the King. And the blindness of those who ruled the Indies prevented them

Similar to Afonso's argument "not in the sense of God."

from understanding that in the King's laws is expressed the following: that no one is or can be called a rebel if, to begin with, he is not a subject of the King. The Christians (who know something of God and of reason and of human laws) should realize how astounding all this is to simple people, living peacefully on their lands and who have their own chiefs, to be told by the Spaniards of a new Spanish ruler never seen or heard of before, and that if they do not subject themselves to that King they will be cut to pieces. It makes their hearts stand still, for they have seen from experience that this will be done. And the most horrifying thing is that the Indians who do obey are placed in servitude where with incredible hard labor and torments even harder to endure and longer lasting than the torments of those who are put to the sword they are finally, with their wives and children and their entire generation exterminated. And now that, with these fears and under threats, these peoples and others in the New World have come to obey and to recognize the authority of the foreign King, these rotten and inconstant Viceroys, blinded and confused by ambition and diabolical greed, do not see that they have not acquired one jot of right as veritable representatives of the King, that both natural and human and divine right are something quite different, that they have acquired nothing when the Indians are terrorized into giving submission and tribute to the foreign King but have earned the punishment of the devil and of the eternal fires of hell. They do not see that they are even committing offenses against the King of Castile in destroying these kingdoms and in annihilating the inhabitants. Yet such are the services the Spaniards in the Indies have rendered to their King and are still rendering today.

It was with this supposedly just cause that the tyrant-Governors sent out two other tyrants[23] even more cruel and ferocious, of even less piety and mercy, to several flourishing and happy kingdoms. One of them went to Guatemala toward the southern sea, while the other proceeded to Naco and its bordering kingdoms of Honduras and Guaimura on the northern sea, which are, at a distance of three hundred leagues from Mexico. One of the captains went by land, the other by sea, each captain in command of many horsemen and foot soldiers.

I am stating the truth when I say that both captains committed wrongs, most notably the one who went to Guatemala, for the other one came to a bad end before he could commit so many ferocious deeds. But the injustices, cruelties, exterminations committed in Guatemala comprise a story that horrifies the centuries, past, present, and to come, and these alone would swell a very big book. Because the campaign of that captain surpassed in vile deeds all others past and present, both in quality and quantity, the people he exterminated and the lands he laid waste were countless.

# The Essays of Michel de Montaigne

Translated and Edited by M.A. Screech

## 27.
## THAT IT IS MADNESS TO JUDGE THE TRUE AND THE FALSE FROM OUR OWN CAPACITIES

[Curiosity when applied to strange or miraculous events is both vain and arrogant. Since men are lulled by habit, they cease to wonder at the glory of the heavens yet they claim to know the limits of the whole order of Nature—and so to judge from their own parochial experience what is miraculous and what is not. Only the authority of the Church and of God's saints can recognize miracles for what they are and vouch for them. Once the Church has decided any issue of fact or doctrine, Roman Catholics must never deviate from her teachings. A man may reject her authority altogether, but he is not free to pick and choose among doctrines, especially during discussions with heretics.]

[A] It is not perhaps without good reason that we attribute to simple-mindedness a readiness to believe anything and to ignorance the readiness to be convinced, for I think I was once taught that a belief is like an impression stamped on our soul: the softer and less resisting the soul, the easier it is to print anything on it: [C] 'Ut necesse est lancem in libra ponderibus impositis deprimi, sic animum perspicuis cedere.' ['For just as a weight placed on a balance must weigh it down, so the

mind must yield to clear evidence.']¹ The more empty a soul is and the less furnished with counterweights, the more easily its balance will be swayed under the force of its first convictions. [A] That is why children, the common people, women and the sick are more readily led by the nose.

On the other hand there is a silly arrogance in continuing to disdain something and to condemn it as false just because it seems unlikely to us. That is a common vice among those who think their capacities are above the ordinary.

I used to do that once: if I heard tell of ghosts walking or of prophecies, enchantments, sorcery, or some other tale which I could not get my teeth into—

*Somnia, terrores magicos, miracula, sagas,*
*Nocturnos lemures portentaque Thessala*

[Dreams, magic terrors, miracles, witches, nocturnal visits from the dead or spells from Thessaly]²

—I used to feel sorry for the wretched folk who were taken in by such madness. Now I find that I was at least as much to be pitied as they were. It is not that experience has subsequently shown me anything going beyond my original beliefs (nor is it from any lack of curiosity on my part), but reason has taught me that, if you condemn in this way anything whatever as definitely false and quite impossible, you are claiming to know the frontiers and bounds of the will of God and

---

1  Cicero, *Academica*, II, ii, 127.
2  Horace, *Epistles*, II, ii, 208–9.

the power of Nature our Mother; it taught me also that there is nothing in the whole world madder than bringing matters down to the measure of our own capacities and potentialities.

How many of the things which constantly come into our purview must be deemed monstrous or miraculous if we apply such terms to anything which outstrips our reason! If we consider that we have to grope through a fog even to understand the very things we hold in our hands, then we will certainly find that it is not knowledge but habit which takes away their strangeness;

> [B] *jam nemo, fessus satiate vivendi,*
> *Suspicere in cœli dignatur lucida templa;*

[Already now, tired and satiated with life, nobody bothers to gaze up at the shining temples of the heavens:]

[A] such things, if they were newly presented to us, would seem as unbelievable as any others;

> *si nunc primum mortalibus adsint*
> *Ex improviso, ceu sint objecta repente,*
> *Nil magis his rebus poterat mirabile dici,*
> *Aut minus ante quod auderent fore credere*
> *gentes.*

[supposing that now, for the first time, they were suddenly shown to mortal men: nothing could be called more miraculous; such things the nations would not have dared to believe.][1]

He who had never actually seen a river, the first time he did so took it for the ocean, since we think that the biggest things that we know represent the limits of what Nature can produce in that species.

> [B] *Scilicet et fluvius, qui non est maximus,*
> *eii est Qui non ante aliquem majorem vidit, et*
> *ingens Arbor homoque videtur;* [A] *et omnia de*
> *genere omni Maxima quæ vidit quisque, hæc*
> *ingentia fingit.*

[Just as a river may not be all that big, but seems huge to a man who has never seen a bigger one, so, too, the biggest tree or biggest man or biggest thing of any kind which we know is considered huge by us.]

[C] '*Consuetudine oculorum assuescunt animi, neque admirantur, neque requirunt rationes earum rerum quas semper vident.*' [When we grow used to seeing anything it accustoms our minds to it and we cease to be astonished by it; we never seek the causes of things like that.][2] What makes us seek the cause of anything is not size but novelty.

[A] We ought to judge the infinite power of [C] Nature [A] with more reverence[3] and a greater recognition of our own ignorance and weakness. How many improbable things there are which have been testified to by people worthy of our trust: if we cannot be convinced we should at least remain in suspense. To condemn them as impossible is to be rashly presumptuous, boasting that we know the limits of the possible. [C] If we understood the difference between what is impossible and what is unusual, or between what is against the order of the course of Nature[4] and what is against the common opinion of mankind, then the way to observe that rule laid down by Chilo, *Nothing to excess*, would be, Not to believe too rashly: not to disbelieve too easily.

[A] When we read in Froissart that the Comte de Foix knew the following morning in Béarn of the defeat of King John of Castille at Juberoth, and when we read of the means he is alleged to have used, we can laugh at that;[5] we can laugh too when our annals tell how Pope Honorius, on the very same day that King Phillip-Augustus died at Mante, celebrated a public requiem for him and ordered the same to be done throughout

---

1  Lucretius, II, 1037–8; 1032–5.

2  Lucretius, VI, 674–7; Cicero, De natura deorum, II, XXXVIII, 96.

3  '80: power of *God* with more reverence …

4  In Christian theology it is only an event which occurs against the *whole order* of Nature which constitutes a miracle.

5  In 1385 the Comte de Foix took to his rooms and then was able to announce that there had just occurred in Portugal a huge slaughter of soldiers from Béarn. It was believed that he had a familiar spirit, either one called Orthon or another like him, who, in an earlier period, had deserted the local *curé* to serve the Seigneur de Corasse (Froissart, III, 17).

Italy;[1] for the authority of such witnesses is not high enough to rein us back.

But wait. When Plutarch (leaving aside the many examples which he alleges from Antiquity) says that he himself knows quite definitely that, at the time of Domitian, news of the battle lost by Antony several days' journey away in Germany was publicly announced in Rome and spread through all the world on the very day that it was lost; and when Caesar maintains that it was often the case that news of an event actually anticipated the event itself: are we supposed to say that they were simple people who merely followed the mob and who let themselves be deceived because they saw things less clearly than we do![2]

Can there be anything more delicate, clear-cut and lively than the judgement of Pliny when he pleases to exercise it? Is there anything further from triviality? (I am not discussing his outstanding erudition; I put less store by that: but in which of those two qualities are we supposed to surpass him?) And yet every little schoolboy convicts him of lying and lectures him about the march of Nature's handiwork.[3]

When we read in Bouchet about miracles associated with the relics of Saint Hilary we can shrug it off:[4] his right to be believed is not great enough to take away our freedom to challenge him. But to go on from there and condemn all similar accounts seems to me to be impudent in the extreme. Such a great saint as Augustine swears that he saw:[5] a blind child restored to sight by the relics of Saint Gervaise and Saint Protasius at Milan; a woman in Carthage cured of a cancer by the sign of the cross made by a woman who had just been baptised; his close friend Hesperius driving off devils (who were infesting his house) by using a little soil taken from the sepulchre of our Lord, and that same soil, borne into the Church, suddenly curing a paralytic; a woman who, having touched the reliquary of Saint Stephen with a posy of flowers during a procession, rubbed her eyes with them afterwards and recovered her sight which she had recently lost—as well as several other miracles which occurred in his presence. What are we to accuse him of—him and the two holy bishops, Aurelius and Maximinus, whom he calls on as witnesses? Is it of ignorance, simple-mindedness, credulity, deliberate deception or imposture? Is there any man in our century so impudent as to think he can be compared with them for virtue, piety, scholarship, judgement and ability? [C] 'Qui, ut rationen nulam afferent, ipsa authoritate me frangerent.' [Why, even if they gave no reasons, they would convince me by their very authority.][6]

[A] Apart from the absurd rashness which it entails, there is a dangerous boldness of great consequence in despising whatever we cannot understand. For as soon as you have established the frontiers of truth and error with that fine brain of yours and then discover that you must of necessity believe some things even stranger than the ones which you reject, you are already forced to abandon these frontiers.

Now it seems to me that what brings as much disorder as anything into our consciences during our current religious strife is the way Catholics are: prepared to treat some of their beliefs as expendable. They believe they are being moderate and well-informed when they surrender to their enemies some of the articles of faith which are in dispute. But, apart from the fact that they cannot see what an advantage you give to an adversary when you begin to yield ground and beat a retreat, or how much that excites him to follow up his attack, the very articles which they select as being less weighty are sometimes extremely important ones.

We must either totally submit to the authority of our ecclesiastical polity or else totally release ourselves from it. It is not for us to decide what degree of obedience we owe to it.

Moreover I can say that for having assayed it; in the past I made use of that freedom of personal choice and private selection in order to neglect certain details in the observances of our Church because they seemed to be rather odd or rather empty; then, when I came to tell some learned men about it, I discovered that those

---

1  Nicole Gilles, *Annales des moderateurs des belliqueuses Gaulles;* the event 'happened' in 1233.

2  Plutarch, *Life of Paulus Aemilius.* The reference to Caesar is puzzling.

3  Such works as the *De Plini erroribus* of Nicolaus Leonicenus had helped spread criticisms of Pliny.

4  Jean Bouchet, *Annates d'Acquitaine,* Poitiers, 1567 etc., pp. 21—30.

5  St Augustine, *City of God,* XII, viii.

6  Cicero, *Tusc. disput.,* I, xxi, 49, adapted: Cicero wrote, 'For even though Plato gave no reasons—note what tribute I pay to him—he would convince me by his very authority.'

very practices were based on massive and absolutely solid foundations, and that it is only our ignorance and animal stupidity which make us treat them with less reverence than all the rest.

Why cannot we remember all the contradictions which we feel within our own judgement, and how many things which were articles of belief of us yesterday are fables for us today?

Vainglory and curiosity are the twin scourges of our souls. The former makes us stick our noses into everything: the latter forbids us to leave anything unresolved or undecided.

## 31. ON THE CANNIBALS

*[The cannibals mentioned in this chapter lived on the coasts of Brazil. Montaigne had read many accounts of the conquest of the New World, including Girolamo Benzoni's* Historia del mondo novo *(Venice, 1565) in the French translation by Urbain Chauveton, the very title of which emphasizes the dreadful treatment of the natives by the Conquistadores:* A New History of the New World containing all that Spaniards have done up to the present in the West Indies, and the harsh treatment which they have meted out to those peoples yonder … Together with a short History of a Massacre committed by the Spaniards on some Frenchmen in Florida *(two editions in 1579).*

*Montaigne's 'primitivism' (his respect for barbarous peoples and his admiration for much of their conduct, once their motives are understood) has little in common with the 'noble savages' of later centuries. These peoples are indeed cruel: but so are we. Their simple ways have much to teach us: they can serve as a standard by which we can judge Plato's* Republic, *the myth of the Golden Age, the cruelty, the corruption and the culture of Europe, and show up that European insularity which condemns peoples as barbarous merely because their manners and their dress are different.]*

[A] When King Pyrrhus crossed into Italy, after noting the excellent formation of the army which the Romans had sent ahead towards him he said, 'I do not know what kind of Barbarians these are' (for the Greeks called all foreigners Barbarians) 'but there is nothing barbarous about the ordering of the army which I can see!' The Greeks said the same about the army which Flaminius brought over to their country, [C] as did Philip when he saw from a hill-top in his kingdom the order and plan of the Roman encampment under Publius Sulpicius Galba.[1] [A] We should be similarly wary of accepting common opinions; we should judge them by the ways of reason not by popular vote.

I have long had a man with me who stayed some ten or twelve years in that other world which was discovered in our century when Villegaignon made his landfall and named it *La France Antartique.*[2] This discovery of a boundless territory seems to me worthy of reflection. I am by no means sure that some other land may not be discovered in the future, since so many persons, [C] greater than we are, [A] were wrong about this one! I fear that our eyes are bigger than our bellies, our curiosity more[3] than we can stomach. We grasp at everything but clasp nothing but wind.

Plato brings in Solon to relate that he had learned from the priests of the town of Saïs in Egypt how, long ago before the Flood, there was a vast island called Atlantis right at the mouth of the Straits of Gibraltar, occupying an area greater than Asia and Africa combined; the kings of that country, who not only possessed that island but had spread on to the mainland across the breadth of Africa as far as Egypt and the length of Europe as far as Tuscany, planned to stride over into Asia and subdue all the peoples bordering on the Mediterranean as far as the Black Sea. To this end they had traversed Spain, Gaul and Italy and had reached as far as Greece when the Athenians withstood them; but soon afterwards those Athenians, as well as

---

1   Plutarch, *Life of Pyrrhus* and *Life of Flaminius.*

2   Durand de Villegagnon struck land, in Brazil, in 1557. Cf. *Lettres sur la navigation du chevalier de Villegaignon es terres de l'Amérique,* Paris, 1557, by an author who calls himself simply N.B.

3   '80: our bellies, *as they say, applying it to those whose appetite and hunger make them desire more meat than they can manage: I fear that we too have* curiosity *far more …*

the people of Atlantis and their island, were engulfed in that Flood.[1]

It is most likely that that vast inundation should have produced strange changes to the inhabitable areas of the world; it is maintained that it was then that the sea cut off Sicily from Italy—

[B] *Hæc loca, vi quondam et vasta convulsa ruina, Dissiluisse ferunt, cum protinus utraque tellus Una foret.*

[Those places, they say, were once wrenched apart by a violent convulsion, whereas they had formerly been one single land.][2]

[A] as well as Cyprus from Syria, and the island of Negropontus from the Boeotian mainland, while elsewhere lands once separated were joined together by filling in the trenches between them with mud and sand:

*sterilisque diu palus aptaque remis Vicinas urbes alit, et grave sentit aratrum,*

[Barren swamps which you could row a boat through now feed neighbouring cities and bear the heavy plough.][3]

Yet there is little likelihood of that island's being the New World which we have recently discovered, for it was virtually touching Spain; it would be unbelievable for a flood to force it back more than twelve hundred leagues to where it is now; besides our modern seamen have already all but discovered that it is not an island at all but a mainland, contiguous on one side with the East Indies and on others with lands lying beneath both the Poles—or that if it is separated from them, it is by straits so narrow that it does not deserve the name of 'island' on that account.

[B] It seems that large bodies such as these are subject, as are our own, to changes, [C] some natural, some [B] feverish.[4] When I consider how my local river the Dordogne has, during my own lifetime, been encroaching on the right-hand bank going downstream and has taken over so much land that it has robbed many buildings of their foundation, I realize that it has been suffering from some unusual upset: for if it had always gone on like this or were to do so in the future, the whole face of the world would be distorted. But their moods change: sometimes they incline one way, then another: and sometimes they restrain themselves. I am not discussing those sudden floodings whose causes we know. By the coast-line in Médoc, my brother the Sieur d'Arsac can see lands of his lying buried under sand spewed up by the sea: the tops of some of the buildings are still visible: his rents and arable fields have been changed into very sparse grazing. The locals say that the sea has been thrusting so hard against them for some time now that they have lost four leagues of land. These sands are the sea's pioneer-corps: [C] and we can see those huge shifting sand-dunes marching a half-league ahead in the vanguard, capturing territory.

[A] The other testimony from Antiquity which some would make; relevant to this discovery is in Aristotle—if that little book about unheard wonders is really his.[5] He tells how some Carthaginians struck out across the Atlantic beyond the Straits of Gibraltar, sailed for a long time and finally discovered a large fertile island entirely clothed in woodlands and watered by great deep rivers but very far from any mainland; they and others after them, attracted by the richness and fertility of the soil, emigrated with their wives and children and started living there. The Carthaginian lords, seeing that their country was being gradually depopulated, expressly forbade any more to go there on pain of death and drove out those new settlers, fearing it is said that they would in time increase so greatly that they would supplant them and bring down their State.

But that account in Aristotle cannot apply to these new lands either.

That man of mine was a simple, rough fellow— qualities which make for a good witness: those clever chaps notice more things more carefully but are always adding glosses; they cannot help changing their story a little in order to make their views triumph and be more persuasive; they never show you anything purely as it

---

1  Plato *Timaeus,* 24E etc., and Girolamo Benzoni, *Historia del mondo novo,* Venice 1565. Cf. also Plato, *Critias,* 113 A ff.

2  Virgil, *Aeneid,* III, 414–17.

3  Horace, *Ars poetica,* 65–6.

4  '88: changes *sickly* and feverish. When …

5  The *Secreta secretorum* is supposititious. Montaigne is following Girolamo Benzoni.

is: they bend it and disguise it to fit in with their own views. To make their judgement more credible and to win you over they emphasize their own side, amplify it and extend it. So you need either a very trustworthy man or else a man so simple that he has nothing in him on which to build such false discoveries or make them plausible; and he must be wedded to no cause. Such was my man; moreover on various occasions he showed me several seamen and merchants whom he knew on that voyage. So I am content with what he told me, without inquiring what the cosmographers have to say about it.

What we need is topographers who would make detailed accounts of the places which they had actually been to. But because they have the advantage of visiting Palestine, they want to enjoy the right of telling us tales about all the rest of the world! I wish everyone would write only about what he knows—not in this matter only but in all others. A man may well have detailed knowledge or experience of the nature of one particular river or stream, yet about all the others he knows only what everyone else does but in order to trot out his little scrap of knowledge he will write a book on the whole of physics! From this vice many great inconveniences arise.

*extrapolating based on data narrow experiences*

Now to get back to the subject, I find (from what has been told me) that there is nothing savage or barbarous about those peoples, but that every man calls barbarous anything he is not accustomed to; it is indeed the case that we have no other criterion of truth or right-reason than the example and form of the opinions and customs of our own country. There we always find the perfect religion, the perfect polity, the most developed and perfect way of doing anything! Those 'savages' are only wild in the sense that we call fruits wild when they are produced by Nature in her ordinary course: whereas it is fruit which we have artificially perverted and misled from the common order which we ought to call savage. It is in the first kind that we find their true, vigorous, living, most natural and most useful properties and virtues, which we have bastardized in the other kind by merely adapting them to our corrupt tastes. [C] Moreover, there is a delicious savour which even our taste finds excellent in a variety of fruits produced in those countries without cultivation: they rival our own. [A] It is not sensible that, artifice should be reverenced more that. Nature, our great and powerful Mother.

We have so overloaded the richness and beauty of her products by our own ingenuity that we have smothered her entirely. Yet wherever her pure light does shine, she wondrously shames our vain and frivolous enterprises:

> [B] *Et veniunt ederæ sponte sua melius,*
> *Surgit et in solis formosior arbutus antris,*
> *Et volucres nulla dulcius arte canunt.*

[Ivy grows best when left untended; the strawberry tree flourishes more beautifully in lonely grottoes, and birds sing the sweeter for their artlessness.][1]

[A] All our strivings cannot even manage to reproduce the nest of the smallest little bird, with its beauty and appropriateness to its purpose; we cannot even reproduce the web of the wretched spider. [C] Plato says that all things are produced by nature, fortune or art, the greatest and fairest by the first two, the lesser and least perfect by the last.[2] *here he calls the original state the truest + the best.*

[A] Those peoples, then, seem to me to be barbarous only in that they have been hardly fashioned by the mind of man, still remaining close; neighbours to their original state of nature. They are still governed by the laws of Nature and are only very slightly bastardized by ours; but the purity is such that I am sometimes seized with irritation at their not having been discovered earlier, in times when there were men who could have appreciated them better than we do. It irritates me that neither Lycurgus; nor Plato had any knowledge of them, for it seems to me that what experience has taught us about those peoples surpasses not only all the descriptions with which poetry has beautifully painted the Age of Gold[3] and all its ingenious fictions about Man's blessed early state, but also the very conceptions and yearnings of philosophy. They could not even imagine a state of nature so simple and so pure as the one we have learned about from experience; they could not even believe that societies of men could be maintained with so little artifice, so little in the way of human solder. I would tell Plato that those people have no trade of any kind, no acquaintance with writing, no

---

1 Propertius, I, ii, 10–12.

2 Plato, *Laws*, X, 888A–B.

3 Cf. Elizabeth Armstrong, *Ronsard and the Age of Gold*, Cambridge, 1968.

knowledge of numbers, no terms for governor or political superior, no practice of subordination or of riches or poverty, contracts, no inheritances, no divided estates, no occupation but leisure, no concern for kinship—except such as is common to them all—no clothing, no agriculture, no metals, no use of wine or corn. Among them you hear no words for treachery, lying, cheating, avarice, envy, backbiting or forgiveness. How remote from such perfection would Plato find that Republic which he thought up—[C] 'viri a diis recentes' [men fresh from the gods].[1]

[B] *Hos natura modos primum dedit.*

[These are the ways which Nature first ordained.][2]

[A] In addition they inhabit a land with a most delightful countryside and a temperate climate, so that, from what I have been told by my sources, it is rare to find anyone ill there;[3] I have been assured that they never saw a single man bent with age, toothless, bleary-eyed or tottering. They dwell along the sea-shore, shut in to landwards by great lofty mountains, on a stretch of land some hundred leagues in width. They have fish and flesh in abundance which bear no resemblance to ours; these they eat simply cooked. They were so horror-struck by the first man who brought a horse there and rode it that they killed him with their arrows before they could recognize him, even though he had had dealings with them on several previous voyages. Their dwellings are immensely long, big enough to hold two or three hundred souls; they are covered with the bark of tall trees which are fixed into the earth, leaning against each other in support at the top, like some of our barns where the cladding reaches down to the ground and acts as a side. They have a kind of wood so hard that they use it to cut with, making their swords from it as well as grills to cook their meat. Their

beds are woven from cotton and slung from the roof like hammocks on our ships; each has his own, since wives sleep apart from their husbands. They get up at sunrise and have their meal for the day as soon as they do so; they have no other meal but that one. They drink nothing with it, [B] like those Eastern peoples who, according to Suidas,[4] only drink apart from meals. [A] They drink together several times a day, and plenty of it. This drink is made from a certain root and has the colour of our claret. They always drink it lukewarm; it only keeps for two or three days; it tastes a bit sharp, is in no ways heady and is good for the stomach; for those who are not used to it it is laxative but for those who are, it is a very pleasant drink. Instead of bread they use a certain white product resembling coriander-cakes. I have tried some: it tastes sweet and somewhat insipid.

They spend the whole day dancing; the younger men go off hunting with bow and arrow. Meanwhile some of the women-folk are occupied in warming up their drink: that is their main task. In the morning, before their meal, one of their elders walks from one end of the building to the other, addressing the whole barnful of them by repeating one single phrase over and over again until he has made the rounds, their building being a good hundred yards long. He preaches two things only: bravery before their enemies and love for their wives. They never fail to stress this second duty, repeating that it is their wives who season their drink and keep it warm. In my own house, as in many other places, you can see the style of their beds and rope-work as well as their wooden swords and the wooden bracelets with which they arm their wrists in battle, and the big open ended canes to the sound of which they maintain the rhythm of their dances. They shave off all their hair, cutting it more cleanly than we do yet with razors made of only wood or stone. They believe in the immortality of the soul: souls which deserve well of the gods dwell in the sky where the sun rises; souls which are accursed dwell where it sets. They have some priests and prophets or other, but they rarely appear among the people since they live in the mountains. When they do appear they hold a great festival and a solemn meeting of several villages—each of the barns which have described constituting a village situated about one

---

1 Seneca, *Epist. moral.*, XC, 44. (This epistle is a major defence of the innocence of natural man before he was corrupted by philosophy and progress.)

2 Virgil *Georgics*, II, 208.

3 One of Montaigne's sources was Simon Goulart's *Histoire du Portugal*, Paris, 1587, based on a work by Bishop Jeronimo Osorio (da Fonseca) and others.

---

4 Suidas, *Historica, caeteraque omnia quae ad cognitionem rerum spectant*, Basle, 1564.

French league distant from the next. The prophet then addresses them in public, exhorting them to be virtuous and dutiful, but their entire system of ethics contains only the same two articles: resoluteness in battle and love for their wives. He foretells what is to happen and the results they must expect from what they under take; he either incites them to war or deflects them from it, but only on condition that if he fails to divine correctly and if things turn out other than he foretold, then—if they can catch him—he is condemned as a false prophet and hacked to pieces. So the prophet who gets it wrong once is seen no more.

[C] Prophecy is a gift of God.[1] That is why abusing it should be treated as a punishable deceit. Among the Scythians, whenever their soothsayers got it wrong they were shackled hand and foot and laid in ox-carts full of bracken where they were burned.[2] Those who treat subjects under the guidance of human limitations can be excused if they have done their best; but those who come and cheat us with assurances of powers beyond the natural order and then fail to do what they promise, should they not be punished for it and for the foolhardiness of their deceit?

[A] These peoples have their wars against others further inland beyond their mountains; they go forth naked, with no other arms but their bows and their wooden swords sharpened to a point like the blades of our pigstickers. Their steadfastness in battle is astonishing and always ends in killing and bloodshed: they do not even know the meaning of fear or flight. Each man brings back the head of the enemy he has slain and sets it as a trophy over the door of his dwelling. For a long period they treat captives well and provide them with all the comforts which they can devise; afterwards the master of each captive summons a great assembly of this acquaintances; he ties a rope to one of the arms of his prisoner [C] and holds him by it, standing a few feet away for fear of being caught in the blows, [A] and allows his dearest friend to hold the prisoner the same way by the other arm: then, before the whole assembly, they both hack at him with their swords and kill him. This done, they roast him and make a common meal of him, sending chunks of his flesh to absent friends. This is not as some think done for food—as the Scythians used do in antiquity—but to symbolize ultimate revenge. As a proof of this, when they noted that the Portuguese who were allied to their enemies practiced a different kind of execution on them when taken prisoner—which was to bury them up to the waist, to shoot showers of arrows at their exposed parts and then to hang them—they thought that these men from the Other World, who had scattered a knowledge of many a vice throughout their neighbourhood and who were greater masters than they were of every kind of revenge, which must be more severe than their own; began to abandon their ancient method and adopted that one. It does not sadden me that we should note the horrible barbarity in a practice such as theirs: what does sadden me is that, while judging correctly of their wrong-doings we should be so blind to our own. I think there is more barbarity in eating a man alive than in eating him dead; more barbarity in lacerating by rack and torture a body still fully able to feel things, in roasting him little by little and having him bruised and bitten by pigs and dogs (as we have not only read about but seen in recent memory, not among enemies in antiquity but among our fellow-citizens and neighbours and, what is worse, in the name of duty and religion) than in roasting him and eating him after his death.

Chrysippus and Zeno, the leaders of the Stoic school, certainly thought that there was nothing wrong in using our carcasses for whatever purpose we needed, even for food—as our own forebears did when, beleaguered by Caesar in the town of Alesia, they decided to relieve the hunger of the besieged with the flesh of old men, women and others who were no use in battle:

[B] *Vascones, fama est, alimentis talibus usi*
*Produxere animas.*

[By the eating of such food it is notorious that the Gascons prolonged their lives.][3]

[A] And our medical men do not flinch from using corpses in many ways, both internally and externally, to

---

1   Cf. Cicero, *De divinatione*, I,i.1; I Peter 1:2; I Corinthians 12:20; 13:2.

2   Herodotus, *History*, IV, lxix.

3   Sextus Empiricus, *Hypotyposes*, III, xxiv; Caesar, *Gallic Wars*, VII, lvii–lviii; Juvenal, *Satires*, XV, 93–4.

cure us.[1] Yet no opinion has ever been so unruly as to justify treachery, disloyalty, tyranny and cruelty, which are everyday vices in us. So we can indeed call those folk barbarians by the rules of reason but not in comparison with ourselves, who surpass them in every kind of barbarism. Their warfare is entirely noble and magnanimous; it has as much justification and beauty as that human malady allows: among them it has no other foundation than a zealous concern for courage. They are not striving to conquer new lands, since without toil or travail they still enjoy that bounteous Nature who furnishes them abundantly with all they need, so that they have no concern to push back their frontiers. They are still in that blessed state of desiring nothing beyond what is ordained by their natural necessities: for them anything further is merely superfluous. The generic term which they use for men of the same age is 'brother'; younger men they call 'sons'. As for the old men of they are the 'fathers' of everyone else; they bequeath all their goods indivisibly, to all these heirs in common, there being no other entitlement than that with which Nature purely and simply endows all her creatures by bringing them into this world. If the neighbouring peoples come over the mountains to attack them and happen to defeat them, the victors' booty consists in fame and in the privilege of mastery in virtue and valour: they have no other interest in the goods of the vanquished and so return home to their own land, which lacks no necessity; nor do they lack that great accomplishment of knowing how to enjoy their mode-of-being in happiness and to be content with it. These people do the same in their turn: they require no other ransom from their prisoners-of-war than that they should admit and acknowledge their defeat—yet there is not one prisoner in a hundred years who does not prefer to die rather than to derogate from the greatness of an invincible mind by look or by word; you cannot find one who does not prefer to be killed and eaten than merely to ask to be spared. In order to make their prisoners love life more they treat them generously in every way,[2] but occupy their thoughts with the menaces of the death awaiting all of them, of the tortures they will have to undergo and of the preparations being made for it, of limbs to be lopped off and of the feast they will provide. All that has only one purpose: to wrench some weak or unworthy word from their lips or to make them wish to escape, so as to enjoy the privilege of having frightened them and forced their constancy.[3] Indeed, if you take it the right way, true victory[4] consists in that alone:

[C] *victoria nulla est*
*Quam quæ confessos animo quoque subjugat*
*hostes.*

[There is no victory unless you subjugate the minds of the enemy and make them admit defeat.][5]

In former times those warlike fighters the Hungarians never pressed their advantage beyond making their enemy throw himself on their mercy. Once having wrenched this admission from him, they let him go without injury or ransom, except at most for an undertaking never again to bear arms against them.[6]

[A] Quite enough of the advantages we do gain over our enemies are mainly borrowed ones not truly our own. To have stronger arms and legs is the property of a porter not of Valour; agility is a dead and physical quality, for it is chance which causes your opponent to stumble and which makes the sun dazzle him; to be good at fencing is a matter of skill and knowledge which may light on a coward or a worthless individual. A man's worth and reputation lie in the mind and in the will: his true honour is found there. Bravery does not consist in firm arms and legs but in firm minds and souls: it is not a matter of what our horse or our weapons are worth but of what we are. The man who is struck down but whose mind remains steadfast, [C] '*si succiderit, de genu pugnat* [if his legs give way then on his knees doth he fight];[7] [B] the man who relaxes none of his mental assurance when threatened with imminent death and who faces his enemy with inflexible scorn as he gives up the ghost is beaten by

---

1  Mummies were imported for use in medicines. (Othello's handkerchief was steeped in 'juice of mummy'.)

2  '80: generously in every way, *and furnish them with all the comforts they can devise* but …

3  '80: their *virtue and their* constancy …

4  '80: true *and solid* victory …

5  Claudian, *De sexto consulatu Honorii*, 248–9.

6  Nicolas Chalcocondylas (tr. Blaise de Vigenère), *De la décadence de l'empire grec*, V, ix.

7  Seneca, *De constantia*, II.

Fortune not by us: [C] he is slain but not vanquished.[1] [B] Sometimes it is the bravest who may prove most unlucky. [C] So there are triumphant defeats rivaling victories; Salamis, Plataea, Mycale and Sicily are the fairest sister-victories which the Sun has ever seen, yet they would never dare to compare their combined glory with the glorious defeat of King Leonidas and his men at the defile of Thermopylae.[2] Who has ever run into battle with a greater desire and ambition for victory than did Captain Ischolas when he was defeated? Has any man ever assured his safety more cleverly or carefully than he assured his destruction?[3] His task was to defend against the Arcadians a certain pass in the Peleponnesus. He realized that he could not achieve this because of the nature of the site and of the odds against him, concluding that every man who faced the enemy must of necessity die in the battlefield; on the other hand he judged it unworthy of his own courage, of his greatness of soul and of the name of Sparta to fail in his duty; so he chose the middle path between these two extremes and acted thus: he saved the youngest and fittest soldiers of his unit to serve for the defence of their country and sent them back there. He then determined to defend that pass with men whose loss would matter less and who would by their death, make the enemy purchase their breakthrough as dearly possible. And so it turned out. After butchering the Arcadians who beset them on every side, they were all put to the sword. Was ever a trophy raised to a victor which was not better due to those who were vanquished? True victory lies in your role in the conflict, not in coming through safely: it consists in the honour of battling bravely not battling through.

[A] To return to my tale, those prisoners, far from yielding despite all that was done to them during the two or three months of their captivity, maintain on the contrary a joyful countenance: they urge their captors to hurry up and put them to the test; they defy them, insult them and put them for cowardice and for all the battles they have lost against their country. I have a song made by one such prisoner which contains the

following: Let them all dare to come and gather to feast on him, for with him they will feast on their own fathers and ancestors who have served as food and sustenance for his body. 'These sinews,' he said, 'this flesh and these veins—poor fools that you are—are your very own; you do not graze that they still contain the very substance of the limbs of your forebears: savour them well, for you will find that they taste of your very own flesh!' There is nothing 'barbarous' in the contriving of that topic. Those who tell how they die and who describe the act of execution show the prisoners spitting at their killers and pulling faces at them. Indeed, until their latest breath, they never stop braving them and defying them with word and look. It is no lie to say that these men are indeed savages—by our standards; for either they must be or we must be: there is an amazing gulf between their [C] souls [A] and ours.[4]

The husbands have several wives: the higher their reputation for valour the more of them they have. One beautiful characteristic of their marriages is worth noting: just as our wives are zealous in thwarting our love and tenderness for other women, theirs are equally zealous in obtaining them for them. Being more concerned for their husband's reputation than for anything else, they take care and trouble to have as many fellow-wives as possible, since that is a testimony to their husband's valour.

—[C] Our wives will scream that that is a marvel, but it is not: it is a virtue proper to matrimony, but at an earlier stage. In the Bible Leah, Rachel, Sarah and the wives of Jacob all made their fair handmaidens available to their husbands; Livia, to her own detriment, connived at the lusts of Augustus, and Stratonice the consort of King Deiotarus not only provided her husband with a very beautiful chambermaid who served her but carefully brought up their children and lent a hand in enabling them to succeed to her husband's rank.[5]

—[A] Lest anyone should think that they do all this out of a simple slavish subjection to convention or because of the impact of the authority of their ancient customs without any reasoning or judgement on their part having minds so dulled that they could never

---

1  '80: by us: *he is vanquished in practice but not by reason; it is his bad luck which we may indict not his cowardice.* Sometimes …

2  Cf. Cicero, *Tust. Disput.*, I, xli, 100 for the glory of Leonidas' death in the details of Thermopylae.

3  Diodorus Siculus, XV, xii.

4  '80 their constancy and ours …

5  Standard examples: cf. Tiraquellus, *De legibus connubialibus*, XIII, 35, for all these un-jealous wives. (But Leah and Sarah were in fact Jacob's wives.)

decide to do anything else, I should cite a few examples of what they are capable of.

*← importance of pre-meditation*

Apart from that war-song which I have just given an account of, I have another of their songs, a love-song, which begins like this:

> O Adder, stay: stay O Adder! From your colours let my sister take the pattern for a girdle she will make for me to offer to my love;
> So may your beauty and your speckled hues be for ever honoured above all other snakes.

This opening couplet serves as the song's refrain. Now I know enough about poetry to make the following judgement: not only is there nothing 'barbarous' in this conceit but it is thoroughly anacreontic.[1] Their language incidentally is [C] a pleasant one with an agreeable sound [A] and has terminations[2] rather like Greek.

Three such natives, unaware of what price in peace and happiness they would have to pay to buy a knowledge of our corruptions, and unaware that such commerce would lead to their downfall—which I suspect to be already far advanced—pitifully allowing themselves to be cheated by their desire for novelty and leaving the gentleness of their regions to come and see ours, were at Rouen at the same time as King Charles IX.[3] The King had a long interview with them: they were shown our manners, our ceremonial and the layout of a fair city. Then someone asked them what they thought of all this and wanted to know what they had been most amazed by. They made three points; I am very annoyed with myself for forgetting the third, but. I still remember two of them. In the first place they said (probably referring to the Swiss Guard) that they found it very odd that all those full-grown bearded men, strong and bearing arms in the King's entourage, should consent to obey a boy rather than choosing one of themselves as a Commander; secondly—since they have an idiom in their language which calls all men 'halves' of one another—that they had noticed that there were among us men fully bloated with all sorts of comforts while their halves were begging at their doors, emaciated with poverty and hunger: they found it odd that those destitute halves should put up with such injustice and did not take the others by the throat or set fire to their houses.

I had a very long talk with one of them (but I used a stupid interpreter who was so bad at grasping my meaning and at understanding my ideas that I got little joy from it). When I asked the man (who was a commander among them, our sailors calling him a king) what advantage he got from his high rank, he told me that it was to lead his troops into battle; asked how many men followed him, he pointed to an open space to signify as many as it would hold—about four or five thousand men; questioned whether his authority lapsed when the war was over, he replied that he retained the privilege of having paths cut for him through the thickets in their forests, so that he could easily walk through them when he visited villages under his sway.

Not at all bad, that. —Ah! But they wear no breeches …

## 11. ON THE LAME

*[The human mind is capable of great self-deception. It can find reasons for anything—even for non-existent phenomena and unreal 'facts'. Experience is no guard against error: it can be conditioned by prior expectations. That is one of the considerations which led Montaigne never to discuss alleged miracles and to remain unimpressed by judicial certainties.*

*For us today Montaigne's scepticism about the reality of the powers of male and female witches is arresting. (He was not alone in holding such views, though he remained in the minority.) But he is determined to subordinate his own opinions to the teachings of the Roman Catholic Church. For him the value of his opinions is that they are opinions and that they are his: they tell us of his* forma mentis. *But since men's opinions are never certainties, should we ever burn people on account of them, unless God directly intervenes to order us to do so?]*

---

1  Anacreon was the great love-poet of Teos (*fl.* 540 b c).

2  '80: their language *is the pleasantest language in the world; its* sound *is agreeable to the ear* and has terminations …

3  In 1562, when Rouen was retaken by Royalist forces.

[B] In France, some two or three years ago now, they shortened the year by ten days.[1] What changes were supposed to result from that reform! It was, quite literally, to move both the heavens and the earth at the same time. Yet nothing has been shoved out of place. My neighbours find that seed-time and harvest, auspicious times for business, as well as ill-omened or propitious days, come at precisely the same second to which they have ever been assigned. The error of our practices was never felt beforehand: no amendment is felt there now, so much uncertainty is there everywhere, so gross is our faculty of perception, [C] so darkened and so blunt.

[B] They say that this adjustment could have been made less awkwardly by following the example of Augustus and omitting the extra day over a period of several leap-years—it is a source of trouble and confusion anyway—until we had paid back the missing time (something which we have not even achieved by this correction: we are still a day or two in arrears). By this means we could also have provided for the future, declaring that after a specified number of years had rolled by that extra day would be banished for ever, with the result that our miscalculation from then on could not exceed twenty-four hours.

Years are the only measure we have for time. The world has been using 'years' for many centuries, yet it is a unit which we have never succeeded in standardizing, so that we live in daily uncertainty about the incompatible forms given to it by other nations, and about how they apply them.

And what if (as some say) the heavens as they grow old are contracting downwards towards us, thereby casting our very hours and days into confusion? And what of our months too, since Plutarch says that even in his period the science of the heavens had yet to fix the motions of the moon?[2]

A fine position we are in to keep chronicles of past events!

I was recently letting my mind range wildly (as I often do) over our human reason and what a rambling and roving instrument it is. I realize that if you ask people to account for 'facts', they usually spend more time finding reasons for them than finding out whether they are true. They ignore the *whats* and expatiate on the *whys*. [C] Wiseacres!

To know causes belongs only to Him who governs things, not to us who are patients of such things and who, without penetrating their origin or essences, have complete enjoyment of them in terms of our own nature. Wine is no more delightful to the man who knows its primary qualities. Quite the reverse: by bringing in pretensions to knowledge the body infringes, and the soul encroaches upon, the rights which both of them have to enjoy the things of this world. To define, to know and to allow belong to professors and schoolmasters: to enjoy and to accept belong to inferiors, subordinates and apprentices.

Let us get back to that custom of ours.

[B] They skip over the facts but carefully deduce inferences. They normally begin thus: 'How does this come about?' But does it do so? That is what they ought to be asking. Our reason has capacity enough to provide the stuff for a hundred other worlds, and then to discover their principles and construction! It needs neither matter nor foundation; let it run free: it can build as well upon the void as upon the plenum, upon space as upon matter:

*dare pondus idonea fumo.*

[meet to give heaviness even to smoke.][3]

I find that we should be saying virtually all the time, 'It is not at all like that!' I would frequently make that reply but I dare not, since folk bellow that it is a dodge produced by ignorance and by weakness of intellect; so I am usually obliged to be a mountebank for the sake of good company, and to discuss trivial subjects and tales which I totally disbelieve. Moreover it is rather rude and aggressive flatly to deny a statement of fact; and (especially in matters where it is difficult to convince others) few people fail to assert that 'they have seen it themselves' or to cite witnesses whose authority puts a stop to our contradictions. By following this practice we know the bases and causes of hundreds of things which never were; the world is involved in duels about

---

1  A further allusion to the Gregorian reform of the calendar (1562). Cf. III, 10; note 23. The previous reform was that of the Emperor Augustus.

2  Plutarch (tr. Amyot), *Demandes des choses Romaines*, 464 B, drawing the same conclusions as Montaigne.

3  Persius, *Satires*, I, 20.

hundreds of questions where both the for and the against are false: [C] '*Ita finitima sunt falsa veris, ut in prœcipitem locum non debeat se sapiens committere.*' [The false and the true are in such close proximity that the wise man should not trust himself to so steep a slope.][1] [B] Truth and falsehood are both alike in form of face and have identical stances, tastes and demeanours. We look on them with the same eye. I find that we are not merely slack about guarding ourselves from dupery, but we actually want to fall on its sword. We love to be entangled with vanity, since it corresponds in form to our own being.

I have seen in my time the birth of several miracles. Even if they are smothered at birth, that does not stop us from predicting the course they would have taken if they had grown up! We only need to get hold of the end of the thread: we then reel off whatever we want. Yet the distance is greater from nothing to the minutest thing in the world than it is from the minutest thing to the biggest. Now when the first people who drank their fill of the original oddity come to spread their tale abroad, they can tell by the opposition which they arouse what it is that others find difficult to accept; they then stop up the chinks with some false piece of oakum. [C] Moreover, '*insita hominibus libidine alendi de industria rumores*' [by man's inborn tendency to work hard at feeding rumours][2] we naturally feel embarrassed if what was lent to us we pass on to others without some exorbitant interest of our own. At first the individual error creates the public one: then, in its turn, the public error creates the individual one. [B] And so, as it passes from hand to hand, the whole fabric is padded out and reshaped, so that the most far-off witness is better informed about it than the closest one, and the last to be told more convinced than the first. It is a natural progression. For whoever believes anything reckons that it is a work of charity to convince someone else of it; and to do this he is not at all afraid to add, out of his own invention, whatever his story-needs to overcome the resistance and the defects which he thinks there are in the other man's ability to grasp it. I myself am particularly scrupulous about lying and can scarcely be bothered to quote authority for what I say in order to make it believable: yet even I notice that when I get heated about a matter I have in hand, [C] either because of another's resistance to it or else because of the excitement of the actual telling, [B] I increase the importance of my subject and puff it up by tone of voice, gestures, powerful and vigorous words—and also by stretching it a bit and exaggerating it, not without some damage to native truth. But I do so with the proviso that I immediately give up the attempt for the first man who summons me back and demands the truth, bare and bold, which I then give to him without exaggeration, without bombast and without embroidery. [C] A loud and lively gab, such as mine habitually is, soon flies off into hyperbole.

[B] There is nothing over which men usually strain harder than when giving free run to their opinions: should the regular means be lacking, we support them by commands, force, fire and sword. It is wretched to be reduced to the point where the best touchstone of truth has become the multitude of believers, at a time when the fools in the crowd are so much more numerous than the wise: [C] '*quasi vero quidquam sit tam valde quam nil sapere vulgare*' [as though anything whatsoever were more common than lack of wisdom].[3] '*Sanitatis patrocinium est, insanientium turba.*' [A mob of lunatics now form the authority for sane truth.]

[B] It is hard to stiffen your judgement against widely held opinions. At first simple folk are convinced by the event itself: it sweeps over them. From them it spreads to the more intelligent folk by the authority of the number and the antiquity of the testimonies. Personally, what I would not believe when one person says it, I would not believe if a hundred times one said it. And I do not judge opinions by their age.

Not long ago one of our princes, whose excellent natural endowments and lively constitution had been undermined by the gout, allowed himself to be so strongly convinced by the reports which were circulating about the wonderful treatments of a priest who, by means of words and gestures, cured all illnesses, that he made a long journey to go and consult him. By the force of his imagination he convinced his legs for a few hours to feel no pain, so that he made them serve him as they had long since forgotten how to do. If Fortune

---

1  Cicero, *Academica*, II (Lucullus), XXI, 68.

2  Livy, XXVIII, xxiv.

3  Cicero, *De divinatione*, II, xxxix, 81; then, St Augustine, *City of God*, VI, x. (Montaigne's context echoes Seneca, *Epist. moral.*, LXXXI, etc.)

had allowed some five or six such events to happen one on top of the other, they would have sufficed to give birth to a miracle. Afterwards, there was found such simplemindedness and such little artifice in the inventor of this treatment that he was not judged worthy of any punishment. We would do the same for most such things if we examined them back in their burrows. [C] 'Miramur ex intervallo fallentia.' [We are astounded by things which deceive us by their remoteness.]¹ [B] Thus does our sight often produce strange visions in the distance which vanish as we draw near. 'Nunquam ad liquidum fama perducitur.' [Rumour never stops at what is crystal-clear.]

It is wonderful how such celebrated opinions are born of such vain beginnings and trivial causes. It is precisely that which makes it hard to inquire into them: for while we are looking for powerful causes and weighty ends worthy of such great fame we lose the real ones: they are so tiny that they escape our view. And indeed for such investigations we need a very wise, diligent and subtle investigator, who is neither partial nor prejudiced.

To this hour all such miracles and strange happenings hide away when I am about. I have not seen anywhere in the world a prodigy more expressly miraculous than I am. Time and custom condition us to anything strange: nevertheless, the more I haunt myself and know myself the more my misshapenness amazes me and the less I understand myself.

The right to promulgate and to publish such phenomena is mainly reserved to Fortune. The day before yesterday I was on my way through a village two leagues from home when I found the market-place still hot and excited about a miracle which had just come to grief there. All the neighbourhood had been preoccupied with it for months; the excitement had spread to the neighbouring provinces and great troops of people of all classes came pouring in. One night a local youth had larked about at home, imitating the voice of a ghost; he intended no trickery beyond enjoying the immediate play-acting. He succeeded somewhat beyond his hopes, so, to heighten the farce and thicken the plot, he brought in a village maiden who was absolutely stupid and simple. Eventually there were three of them, all of the same age, all equally stupid. From sermons in people's homes they progressed to sermons in public, hiding under the altar in church, delivering them only at night and forbidding any lights to be brought in. They started with talk directed towards the conversion of the world and the imminence of the Day of Judgement (for imposture can more readily crouch behind our reverence for the authority of such subjects) and then progressed on to several visions and actions so silly and laughable there is hardly anything more crude in the games of little children. Yet if Fortune had chosen to lend them a little of her favour, who knows what that play-acting might have grown into? Those poor devils are even now in gaol and may easily have to pay the penalty for the public's gullibility. And who knows whether some judge or other may not revenge his own upon them?

This incident has been uncovered: we can see clearly into it this time; but in many similar kinds of case which surpass our knowledge I consider that we should suspend our judgement, neither believing nor rejecting. Many of this world's abuses are engendered—[C] or to put it more rashly, all of this world's abuses are engendered—[B] by our being schooled to fear to admit our ignorance [C] and because we are required to accept anything which we cannot refute. [B] Everything is proclaimed by injunction and assertion. In Rome, the legal style required that even the testimony of an eye-witness or the sentence of a judge based on his most certain knowledge had to be couched in the formula, 'It seems to me that ... '²

You make me hate things probable when you thrust them on me as things infallible. I love terms which soften and tone down the rashness of what we put forward, terms such as 'perhaps', 'somewhat', 'some', 'they say', 'I think' and so on. And if I had had sons to bring up I would have trained their lips to answer with [C] inquiring and undecided [B] expressions such as, 'What does this mean?' 'I do not understand that', 'It might be so', 'Is that true?' so that they would have been more likely to retain the manners of an apprentice at sixty than, as boys do, to act like learned doctors at ten. Anyone who wishes to be cured of ignorance must first admit to it: [C] Iris is the daughter of Thaumantis:

---

1 Seneca, *Epist. moral.*, CVIII, 7; then, Quintus Curtius, IX, ii.

2 Cicero, *Academica*, II (Lucullus), xlvii, 146.

amazement is the foundation of all philosophy; inquiry, its way of advancing; and ignorance is its end.[1]

[B] Yes indeed: there is a kind of ignorance, strong and magnanimous, which in honour and courage is in no wise inferior to knowledge; [C] you need no less knowledge to beget such ignorance than to beget knowledge itself.

[B] When I was a boy I saw the account of a trial of a strange event printed by Coras, a learned counsel in Toulouse, concerning two men who each passed himself off for the other. What I remember of it (and I remember nothing else) is that it seemed to me at the time that Coras had made the impersonation on the part of the one he deemed guilty to be so miraculous and so far exceeding our own experience and his own as judge, that I found a great deal of boldness in the verdict which condemned the man to be hanged.[2] Let us (more frankly and more simply than the judges of the Areopagus, who when they found themselves hemmed in by a case which they could not unravel decreed that the parties should appear before them again a hundred years later) accept for a verdict a formula which declares, 'The Court does not understand anything whatever about this case.'[3]

My local witches go in risk of their lives, depending on the testimony of each new authority who comes and gives substance to their delusions. The Word of God offers us absolutely certain and irrefragable examples of such phenomena,[4] but to adapt and apply them to things happening in our own times because we cannot understand what caused them or how they were done needs a greater intelligence than we possess. It may perhaps be the property of that almighty Witness[5] alone to say to us: 'This is an example of it; so is that; this is not.' We must believe God—that really is right—but not, for all that, one of ourselves who is amazed by his own narration—necessarily amazed if he is not out of his senses—whether testifying about others or against himself. I am a lumpish fellow and hold somewhat to solid probable things, avoiding those ancient reproaches: *Majorem fidem homines adhibent iis quae non intelligunt'* [Men place more trust in whatever they do not understand] and, *'Cupidine humani ingenii libentius obscura creduntur.'* [There is a desire in the mind of Man which makes it more ready to believe whatever is obscure.][6] I am well aware that folk get angry and and forbid me to have any doubts about witches on pain of fearsome retribution. A new form of persuasion! Thanks be to God my credo is not to be managed by thumps from anyone's fists. Let them bring out the cane for those who maintain that their opinions are wrong; I merely maintain that their opinions are bold and hard to believe, and I condemn a denial as much as they

1 The Scholastic axiom, *Admiratio parit scientiam.* (Consult Signoriello, *Lexicon peripateticum philosophico-theologicum,* s.v. *Admiratio,* citing Thomas Aquinas.) The saying derives from Plato, *Theaetetus,* 155 D. (Plato derived the name of Thaumas, Isis' father, from *thauma,* wonder, prodigy. Montaigne's name for him, Thaumantis, is in fact the name of Isis herself.)

2 The case of Martin Guerre (now well-known from a film thanks to the scholarship of Professor Nathalie Zemon Davies). Cf. the *Arrest memorable du Parlement de Tholose contenant une histoire prodigieuse d'un supposé mary, advenüe de nostre temps … par M. Iean de Coras,* Paris, 1582. Coras (p. 129) justifies the sentence of strangulation by hanging followed by the public burning of the body but (pp. 130–3) makes a passionate plea against burning anyone alive and against cruel torturings as unworthy of Christians, since they are partly based on a desire to purge one's own guilt.

3 The Areopagus in Athens had to judge a wife who murdered her second husband who, with his own son, had murdered her child by her dead husband. (This became the classical example of a *casus perplexus,* a case with the maximum degree of moral difficulty.) The Areopagus decreed that the parties concerned were to return to the Court, in person, one hundred years later! Tiraquellus evokes this well-known *exemplum* in his treatise *De poenis temperandis* (Opera, 1597, VII, 14). Cf. Rabelais *(Tiers Livre,* TLF, XLIIII, 6–44).

4 Cf. II Chronicles 33; II Kings 9; I Samuel 28 (the Witch of Endor consulted by Saul).

5 The Holy Ghost who, for Montaigne, was the author of Scripture.

6 The second from Tacitus, *Hist.,* I, xxu; the first is attributed by Marie de Gournay to Pliny, but remains untraced.

do, though less imperiously. [C] *'Videantur sane: ne affirmentur modo.'* [Let us grant that things so appear, provided they be not affirmed.][1]

[B] Any man who supports his opinion with challenges and commands demonstrates that his reasons for it are weak. When it is a question of words, of scholastic disputations, let us grant that they apparently have as good a case as that of their objectors: but in the practical consequences that they draw from it the advantages are all with the latter. To kill people, there must be sharp and brilliant clarity; this life of ours is too real, too fundamental, to be used to guarantee these supernatural and imagined events.

As for the use of compounds and potions, I leave it out of account: that is murder of the worst sort.[2] Yet even there it is said that we should not always be content with the confessions of such folk, for they have been known to accuse themselves of killing people who have later been found alive and well. As for those other accusations which exceed the bounds of reason I would like to say that it is quite enough for any man—no matter how highly esteemed he is—to be believed about matters human: in the case of whatever is beyond his comprehension and produces supernatural results he should be believed only when supernatural authority confirms it.

That privilege which God has granted to some of our testimonies must not be debased or lightly made common.[3] They have battered my ears with hundreds of stories like this: three men saw him in the east on a particular day; the following morning, in such-and-such a time and place and dress, he was seen in the west. I would certainly never trust my own testimony over such a matter: how much more natural and probable it seems to me that two men should lie, rather than that, in twelve hours, one man should go like the wind from east to west; how much more natural that our mind should be enraptured from its setting by the whirlwind of our own deranged spirit than that, by a spirit from beyond, one of us humans, in flesh and blood, should be sent flying on a broomstick up the flue of his chimney. We, who are never-endingly confused by our own internal delusions, should not go looking for unknown external ones. It seems to me that it is excusable to disbelieve any wonder, at least in so far as we can weaken its proof by diverting it along some non-miraculous way. I am of Saint Augustine's opinion, that in matters difficult to verify and perilous to believe, it is better to incline towards doubt than certainty.[4]

A few years ago I was passing through the domains of a sovereign prince who, as a courtesy to me and to overcome my disbelief, graciously allowed me to see, in a private place when he was present, ten or a dozen of this kind of prisoner, including one old woman, truly a witch as far as ugliness and misshapenness was concerned, and who had long been most famous for professing witchcraft. I was shown evidence and voluntary confessions as well as some insensitive spot or other on that wretched old woman;[5] I talked and questioned till I had had enough, bringing to bear the most sane attention that I could—and I am hardly the man to allow my judgement to be muzzled by preconceptions—but in the end, and in all honesty, I would have prescribed not hemlock for them but hellebore:[6] [C] *'Captisque res magis mentibus, quam consceleratis similis visa.'* [Their case seemed to be more a matter of insane minds rather

---

1  Cicero, *Academica*, II (Lucullus), xxvii, 87.

2  In law a *maleficus* (a witch, an 'evil-doer') was taken in general as one who harmed another and was not necessarily restricted to *incantatores* (workers of spells). (Cf. Spiegel, *Lexicon Juris, s.v.*) Montaigne here excludes those not allegedly working their evil through magic; thus strengthening and limiting his argument. The crucial biblical authority is Exodus 22:18, 'Thou shalt not suffer a witch to live.' But what does it mean? The Greek Septuagint uses the word *pharmakous* here, the Clementine Vulgate uses *maleficos*. Both words apply to both sexes. But Hebraists, since at least Nicolas of Lyra, insisted that the original term *kashaph* is used in the feminine. Liberal theologians clung to the Greek term and insisted that it means sorcerers who use potions to produce their wicked effects.

3  As Montaigne is about to talk of physical rapture from one place to another he is doubtless thinking of the rapture of Philip (Acts 8:39) when the 'Spirit of the Lord caught away' Philip from the road to Gaza so that he was found at Azotus.

4  St Augustine, *City of God*, XIX, xviii, contrasting scriptural truth with human testimony. Vives comments that no human knowledge, since it is known through the senses, can have the certainty of Scripture.

5  The so-called *witches' spot;* when pricked the true witch felt no sensation there. Inquisitors made painful searches for such a spot on the body of anyone charged with witchcraft.

6  Hemlock *(cicuta)* was used by the Greeks to poison criminals—hence Socrates' death by it; hellebore was used to purge madness.

than of delinquents.][1] [B] Justice has its own remedies for such maladies.[2]

As for the objections and arguments put to me there, and often elsewhere, by decent men, none ever seemed to tie me fast: all seemed to have a solution more convincing than their conclusions. It is true, though, that I never attempt to unknot 'proofs' or 'reasons' based on [C] experience nor on [B] a fact: they have no ends that you can get hold of; so, like Alexander cutting his knot, I often slice through them.[3] After all, it is to put a very high value on your surmises to roast a man alive for them.

[C] Praestantius—and we have various examples of similar accounts—tells how his father fell into a profound sleep, deeper far than normal sleep at its best: he thought that he was a mare, serving soldiers as a beast of burden. And he actually became what he thought he was.[4] Now even if wizards dream concrete dreams like that; even if dreams can at times take on real bodies: still I do not believe that our wills should be held responsible to justice for them. [B] I say that, as one who am neither a king's judge nor counsellor, and who consider myself far from worthy of being so; I am an ordinary man, born and bred to obey State policy in both word and deed. Anyone who took account of my ravings, to the prejudice of the most wretched law, opinion or custom of his village, would do great wrong to himself and also to me. [C] I warrant you no certainty for whatever I say, except that it was indeed my thought at the time ... my vacillating and disorderly thought. I will talk about anything by way of conversation, about nothing by way of counsel '*Nec me*

*pudent, ut istos, fateri nescire quod nesciam.*' [Nor, like those other fellows, am I ashamed to admit that I do not know what I do not know.][5]

[B] I would not be so rash of speech if it were my privilege to be believed on this matter. And I replied thus to a great nobleman who complained of the sharpness and tension of my exhortations: 'Knowing that you are braced and prepared on one side, I set out the other side for you as thoroughly as I can, not to bind your judgement but to give it some light. God holds sway over your mind: he will allow you a choice. I am not so presumptuous as to desire that my opinions should weigh even slightly in a matter of such importance: it is not my lot to groom them to influence such mighty and exalted decisions.'

It is certain that I have not only a great many humours but also quite a few opinions which I would willingly train a son of mine to find distasteful, if I had one that is. Why! What if even the truest of them should not always be the most appropriate for Man, given that his make-up is so barbarous?

On the point or off the point, no matter; it is said as a common proverb in Italy that he who has not lain with a lame woman does not know Venus in her sweet perfection. Chance, or some particular incident, long ago put that saying on the lips of the common people. It is applied to both male and female, for the Queen of the Amazons retorted to the Scythian who solicited her: Ἄριστα χολός οἰφεῖ: 'The lame man does it best.'[6]

In that Republic of women, in order to avoid the dominance of the male, they crippled their boys in childhood—arms, legs and other parts which give men the advantage over women—and exploited men only for such uses as we put women to in our part of the world.

Now I would have said that it was the erratic movements of the lame woman which brought some new sensation to the job and some stab of pleasure to those who assayed it: but I have just learned that ancient philosophy itself has decided the matter: it says that

---

1 Livy, VIII, xviii.

2 From the earliest times, Roman law placed the insane in the primary care of their blood relations.

3 It was said that whoever undid the untieable knot in the temple of Gordius would conquer the East: Alexander sliced it through with his sword. Cf. Erasmus, *Adages*, I, I, VI, *Nodum solvere* and, I, IX, XLVIII, *Heraculanus nodus*. (Throughout this passage Montaigne plays on the double meaning of *solutio* in Latin: 'unloosening' and 'resolving'.)

4 St Augustine, *City of God*, XVIII, xviii, suggesting that the cause was diabolical deception working through a Platonizing philosopher. Vives has a long theological note on the subject, rejecting as fictional Apuleius' metamorphosis into a donkey in his *Golden Ass*.

5 Cicero, *Tusc. dispute* I, xxv, 60.

6 Erasmus, *Adages*, II, DC, XLIX, *Claudus optime virum agit.* Cf. also Septalius' note in his edition of Aristotle's (or Pseudo-Aristotle's) *Problemata* X, 25 (26); Coelius Richerius Rhodiginus, *Antiquae Lectiones*, XIV, v, *Cur claudi salaciores.* Cf. also Erasmus, *Apophthegmata*, VIII, *Thrasea*, second hundred, XXI.

a) you must know both sides of an argument to be able to pick "the better" one.

I thought he didn't care about how old thoughts are?

the legs and the thighs of lame women cannot receive (being imperfect) the nourishment which is their due, with the result that the genital organs which are sited above them become more developed, better fed and more vigorous. Alternatively, since this defect discourages exercise, those who are marked by it dissipate their strength less and so come more whole to Venus' sports which is also why the Greeks disparaged women who worked at the loom, saying they were lustier than others because of their sedentary occupation which is without much physical exertion.

At this rate, what can we *not* reason about! Of those women weavers I could just as well say that the shuttling to and fro which their work imposes on them while they are squatting down stimulates and arouses them just as the jerking and shaking of their coaches do for our ladies.

Do not these examples serve to prove what I said at the outset: that our reasons often run ahead of the facts and enjoy such an infinitely wide jurisdiction that they are used to make judgements about the very void and nonentity. Apart from the pliancy of our inventive powers when forging reasons for all sorts of idle fancies, our imagination finds it just as easy to receive the stamp of false impressions derived from frivolous appearances: for on the sole authority of the ancient and widespread currency of that saying, I once got myself to believe that I had derived greater pleasure from a woman because she was deformed, even counting her deformity among her charms.

In his comparison between France and Italy Torquato Tasso says that he had noticed that we have skinnier legs than the gentlemen of Italy and attributes the cause of it to our being continually on our horses. Now that is the very same 'cause' which leads Suetonius to the opposite conclusion: for he says, on the contrary, that Germanicus had fattened his legs by the constant practice of that same exercise![1]

There is nothing so supple and eccentric as our understanding. It is like Theramenes' shoe: good for either foot.[2] It is ambiguous and faces both ways; matters, too,

are ambiguous and facing both ways: 'Give me a silver penny,' said a Cynic philosopher to Antigonus. 'That is no present from a king,' he replied. 'Give me half a hundredweight of gold then'—'That is no present for a Cynic!'[3]

*Seu plures calor ille vias et cœca relaxat*
*Spiramenta, novas venial qua succus in herbas;*
*Seu durat magis et venas astringit hiantes,*
*Ne tenues pluviæ, rapidive potentia solis*
*Acrior, aut Boreæ penetrabile frigus adurat.*

[It is either because the heat opens up new ways through the secret pores in the soil, along which the sap rises to the tender plants, or else because it hardens that soil and constricts its gaping veins, thus protecting it from the drizzling rain, the heat of the burning sun and the penetrating cold of the north wind.][4]

'*Ogni medaglia ha suo riverso.*' [Every medal has its obverse.] That is why Clitomachus said in ancient times that Carneades had surpassed the labours of Hercules by having wrenched assent away from Man (that is, conjecturing and rashness in judging).[5]

That idea of Carneades—such a vigorous one—was born, I suggest, in antiquity because of the shamelessness of those whose profession was knowledge and their overweening arrogance.

Aesop was put on sale with two other slaves. The purchaser asked the first what he could do: he, to enhance his value, answered mountains and miracles: he could do this and he could do that. The second said as much or more of himself. When it was Aesop's turn to be asked what he could do he said, 'Nothing! These two have got in first and taken the lot: they know everything!'[6]

That is what happened in the school of philosophy. The arrogance of those who attributed to Man's mind

---

1 Torquato Tasso, *Paragon dell' Italia alia Francia;* Suetonius, *Life of Caligula,* III.

2 Cf. Erasmus, *Adages,* I, I, XCIV, *Cothurno versatilior.* Theramenes was an Athenian rhetorician who could find arguments for either party.

3 Erasmus, *Apophthegmata,* IV, *Antigonus Rex Macedonum,* XV.

4 Virgil, *Georgics,* I, 89–93 (two of several reasons why burning stubble is good for crops).

5 Translated from Cicero, *Academica,* II (*Lucullus*), xxxiv, 108: '*adsensionem, id est, opinationem et temeritatem.*'

6 From Maximus Planudes' *Life of Aesop,* frequently printed with the *Fables.*

a capacity for everything produced in others (through irritation and emulation) the opinion that it has a capacity for nothing. Some went to the same extreme about ignorance as the others did about knowledge, so that no one may deny that Man is immoderate in all things and that he has no stopping-point save necessity, when too feeble to get any farther.

# Selections from Colonial Lives:
## Documents on Latin American History, 1550-1850

### Edited by Richard Boyer and Geoffrey Spurling

## CHAPTER 5

"In the Service of God, I Order These Temples of Idolatrous Worship Razed to the Ground": Extirpation of Idolatry and the Search for the *Santuario Grande* of Iguaque (*Colombia, 1595*)

### J. Michael Francis

## INTRODUCTION

In 1595, the Audiencia of New Granada (modern-day Colombia) launched a brief campaign aimed to extirpate Indian idolatry in the province of Tunja. It appointed one of its own judges (*oidores*), Egas de Guzmán, to inspect the province (a region roughly the size of the State of Maryland) inhabited by a group of Indians known as the Muisca.[1] Among his many responsibilities, Guzmán received instructions to assess the status of the spiritual conversion of the Indians to Catholicism and to eradicate all physical remnants of Muisca religion.

The following document, housed in Colombia's National Archive, is part of the material Guzmán gathered during a nine-day inspection of the *pueblo* of Iguaque (located in Colombia's Eastern Highlands). Iguaque was one of the province's largest *encomiendas,*

with a tributary population of 157 Indians.[2] Guzmán's inspection of the province was brief, and he rarely spent more than a few days in a given town. Iguaque, however, was an exception. Rumors had reached the *visitador* that the *pueblo* was the site of an important Muisca shrine, the *santuario grande,* and Guzmán hoped to discover its location. The proceedings open with the confessions of seven Indian nobles from Iguaque, six of whom confessed that they possessed *cucas,* or holy houses. However, when the *cucas* yielded no great treasure, Guzmán began his inquisition of the *pueblo's* inhabitants. Dozens of Iguaque's Indians were then arrested, questioned, and tortured, as Guzmán attempted to determine the nature of local religious practices and the location of the *pueblo's* hidden shrines. In the end, two dozen Indians from Iguaque were found guilty and sentenced for the possession of pagan sanctuaries and for practicing idolatry. The *santuario grande* of Iguaque was never found.

It is worth noting that the looting of Muisca sanctuaries was a common occurrence throughout the early colonial period. In fact, in 1569 such practices were officially condoned by the *audiencia* which, in 1577, launched its own crusade against Indian idolatry. It too was a brief campaign, but it proved remarkably profitable. In only ten *pueblos,* an estimated 44,129 pesos (a conservative estimate since most of this loot was never officially declared) were confiscated from Muisca sanctuaries.[3]

# THE DOCUMENT[4]

## 5.1 *The Campaign Begins*

On October 25, 1595, in the *pueblo* and *repartimiento* of Iguaque of the *encomienda* of Juan de Otalora, señor Egas de Guzmán, counsel to our Lord the King, his senior judge on the *audiencia* of this kingdom and *visitador-general* of the province of the city of Tunja, addressed the assembled Indian men, women, *principales,* and *caciques.* Speaking through the interpreter Cristóbal de Sanabria, his honor told the Indians that he came on a visit of inspection, to procure that they be good Christians, and to see that they did not keep old shrines and idols. To this effect and to extirpate all idolatrous practices, he commanded that anyone among them who maintained such shrines or temples dedicated to the devil declare it openly. In the name of His Majesty the King he promised to forgive those who told the truth, but vowed that all who concealed such practices would be dealt with and brought to justice in accord with the will of God and His Majesty.

There immediately appeared before the judge an Indian *principal* named Pedro Conba, who stated that he possessed a shrine known as a *cuca,* or holy house. Don Juan, the *cacique* of this *repartimiento,* promptly declared that he too had a house referred to as a *cuca* that was left to him by an uncle. The *principal* don Fernando then declared that he had no such house. Don Diego Unbayan stated that he had a house known as a *cuca,* meaning a holy house, left to him by his forebears. Juan Ribe declared that he possessed a house called a *cuca,* bequeathed to him by his forebears, but that he did not know what was inside. An Indian named Ventura said that he had a house called a *cuca* that he inherited from his father but that he did not know what was inside. Sebastián Sepaquen then declared that he had a house known as a *cuca* left to him by his forebears but did not know what was inside. No further Indians testified in the opening proceedings and these were closed and the record signed by the judge, the notary, and the interpreter.

## 5.2 *Interrogations, Confessions, the Collection of Evidence*

Accompanied by me [the notary], as well as the interpreter and others, the judge and *visitador-general* went directly to inspect the houses and huts referred to by the Indians and searched each one thoroughly in order to see if they contained idols or shrines. He discovered none, and given that there were no shrines in any of these huts, he ordered that one of the Indians be threatened. Producing a rope, on the orders of Judge Guzmán, Alonso de Molina began to tie the hands of the Indian Ventura, who begged them do him no harm and said that he wanted to declare what he knew. Through the interpreter Cristóbal de Sanabria the Indian stated that the *principal* Pedro Conba was the one who knew who possessed shrines, after which no further questioning was undertaken with the Indian.

Thereupon the judge ordered that the Indian Pedro Conba be stripped of his clothing and asked him to state and declare if he or other Indians have any such shrines. Conba said that he knew nothing, and in light of the Indian's reticence and previous declaration, the judge, to intimidate and frighten him, ordered Alonso de Molina to tie the man's arms with a rope, telling the Indian through the interpreter that he should speak the truth, because if he did not he would have to be tortured. In order to strike fear in Conba, his arms were tied and the rope thrown over a beam in the hut and pulled slightly, in a manner such that it did him no physical harm. He said that an Indian woman named Clara kept a cotton idol but that he did not know what was inside it.

The judge ordered the woman to appear before him and through the interpreter ordered her to reveal this shrine, which she said was hidden in a distant field and which she would show him. The judge ordered me [the notary] and the interpreter to go with her to see what was there. We were led by the Indian woman to a field some five hundred strides from the village, where she pointed to some stones under which there was a small clay pot containing two hollow figurines made of unrefined gold wrapped in a bit of cotton and colored cloth and filled with earth. Beneath other stones shown us by the Indian woman was found a piece of white cloth the width of the palm of the hand and a bit of cotton, within which was wrapped a figurine of unrefined gold filled with earth and six tiny emerald-like gems of no value. Apart from myself [the notary], the witnesses to these proceedings—the interpreter Cristóbal de Sanabria, the *alguacil* Diego Gómez, and Antonio

*[margin, handwritten:]* clearly these are old customs that no longer have religious significance.

de Porras—removed the figurines. As notary I hereby attest that no other things were found or removed.

The judge, noting the clear proof of the *principal* Pedro Conba's dissembling, ordered the Indian brought to his lodgings to be able to deal with him as he saw fit and to learn the truth regarding the whereabouts of the great shrine reputed to exist in this *repartimiento*. At the hour of evening prayers, the judge had Pedro Conba formally detained as a prisoner under the custody of the interpreter Cristóbal de Sanabria, who led him away. The next morning, Sanabria announced that Pedro Conba had fled in the night, escaping by way of a hole in 'the roof of the hut where he was being held. Despite a thorough search for Pedro Conba, the Indian has not appeared.

Following the events described above, on October 27 of the same year in the aforementioned *repartimiento* of Iguaque, an Indian called Aguicha, speaking through the interpreter Cristóbal de Sanabria, voluntarily testified before the judge that he had a shrine in his house that had been left to him by his forebears. The judge went in person to the Indian's hut, and in my presence as notary, García produced two figurines of unrefined gold wrapped in a small cloth that also contained a few tiny emeralds. These were of such low quality that they were worthless.

The same day, the *alguacil* Bartolomé de Ospino brought to the judge two small figurines of unrefined gold wrapped in a cloth, given him by an Indian named Juan Pirasaque on behalf of the *capitán* don Fernando.

Also on October 27, there appeared before the judge an Indian named Diego Sipaquencha, who voluntarily testified through the interpreter Cristóbal de Sanabria that he had in his house two figurines of unrefined gold. The figurines were found in the Indian's house, wrapped in a cotton cloth along with several tiny, worthless emerald-like stones, to which fact I attest as notary.

In the *repartimiento* of Iguaque on October 27 of the same year, an Indian named Juan Neaquenchia voluntarily appeared before the judge and through the interpreter Cristóbal de Sanabria said that on a hill outside this pueblo there is a shrine that was bequeathed to him by an uncle and that he would reveal to them if they would accompany him. After reading the testimony of the Indian, the judge ordered me as notary, along with the *alguacil* Bartolomé de

Ospino, the interpreter Cristóbal de Sanabria, Alonso de Molina and the *corregidor* don Pedro de Orellano, to investigate. We went with the Indian to the place he indicated, [which was located] on the former site of the *pueblo*, on a hill nearly a league and a half away. The final third of the way, given the steep and uneven terrain, we went on foot. Among some stones at the top of the hill the Indian showed us a white pouch, within which there was found a gold figurine and two eagles of thin gold leaf, the beaks of which appeared to be made of fine quality gold. There was also a small figurine and another figurine of unrefined gold designed as a clasp, as well as five moldy cotton blankets, which were of no value. The gold and blankets were brought to the judge, who found that the metal was worth seventy pesos. The Indian stated that the shrine referred to also belonged in part to Pedro Conba.

In the *pueblo* of Iguaque on October 27, 1595, the judge and *visitador*, his honor Egas de Guzmán, in order to discover and verify the truth relating to the shrines, rites, and ceremonies of the Indians of this *pueblo*, ordered to come before him a certain Hernán Sanchez, resident of this district. The judge administered the witness with the legal oath, which he took and by which he swore on his life to speak the truth, and being asked by his honor, he said that about a year and a half ago he had been appointed by the former *corregidor* as *teniente de corregidor* for this *pueblo* and that of Chiquisa. The witness, having been in this *pueblo* at that time, saw the Indian Juan Cacaria, who was then *gobernador*, exchange heated words with the *capitán* Pedro Conba. Having separated the two, the witness overheard Cacaria speaking with other Indians from this *pueblo*, saying that Pedro Conba possessed too much gold in his shrine and that it would be good to inform the *corregidor* of this fact, in order to take the gold from Conba, who made no good use of it. In this regard the witness to the statements made by Cacaria (who is now in custody) adds that the same day as the events described above he heard a Spanish-speaking Indian named Juan Saisipa say that the principal shrine in this *pueblo* contained a great quantity of gold, a fact he had learned from an Indian named Neaquenchia, who claimed to be *jeque* of the shrine. The witness states that this is the truth and is all he knows regarding what he has been asked.

The same day, following the testimony of Hernán Sánchez in which he claimed that Juan Cacaria—who is now being held in custody—knew the location of the shrine, the judge called the Indian prisoner before him. The Indian was asked to state and declare what had happened. Cacaria replied that it was true that some two years ago, when a certain Luis was *corregidor*, the present witness had fought with Pedro Conba and other *principales* of this *repartimiento*, and for this reason had threatened to expose [the location of] the shrine. But afterwards they became friends, and for this reason he had not revealed the shrine, nor does he know anything about it, not even its location. The judge therefore ordered the Indian, who seemed to be about forty years old, to be taken back to jail.

On the same day the judge had the Indian again brought from the jail in order to learn the truth from him. As soon as the Indian appeared, and as he seemed to be a strong and robust man, the judge ordered him stripped of his clothes and had his upper arms tied with a rope. Thus bound he was hoisted to a height of more than two *palmos* off the floor and was then commanded to declare the truth and to reveal the whereabouts of the great shrine and the bones of the old *cacique*. The Indian promised that if they let him down he would tell the truth, and having been lowered to the ground stated that an Indian named Diego Raga knew where the shrine was and said that they should call him to testify.

The judge summoned the Indian Diego Raga to appear before him, and once he had appeared and had been informed through the interpreter that Juan Cacaria alleged that he had the bones of the old *cacique* and the shrine, the Indian Diego stated that that was a lie and that he knew nothing. After this refutation the order was given to again hoist the Indian Juan Cacaria with the rope, and again he was raised two *palmos* above the floor and warned that he was to speak the truth. He immediately said that they should let him down and call for his mother, because she and Diego knew where the bones of the old *cacique* were. The Indian woman was promptly summoned, and once all three were together, with Juan Cacaria on the floor bound only by the arms, they—and in particular Diego—said he [Diego] knew where the bones of the old *cacique* lay and that he would take them there and give them the bones. Asked where they were, he stated that they were

in this *repartimiento* on a hill some two leagues away. As it was now nearly vespers and too late to depart, the judge ordered the *alguacil* Bartolomé de Ospino to take Juan Cacaria, Diego, and the Indian woman into custody and to go to look for the bones of the old *cacique* early the next morning. The *alguacil* then led the Indians away.

After the events described above, on the same day of October 27, 1595, the judge, in the use of his faculties to discover the truth and in view of the evidence against the *capitán* don Alvaro, who is now in custody, ordered the man brought before him. Once in his honor's presence, don Alvaro was commanded to speak and declare the truth regarding the shrine that he possessed or whether he knew of another person who had one. He said that he knew nothing about any shrine nor about people who might have one. The judge ordered his shirt removed and had him laid on his back, naked and tied firmly to two benches. Without further tightening the cords, the judge then ordered water poured into his mouth and nostrils. After one jug of water had been poured on him, he was warned to tell the truth and immediately said that he had no shrine but that an Indian named Pirama had six figurines and should be called to testify.

The judge then summoned the Indian Pirama, who declared without being pressed that he had in his house six gold figurines and that he would surrender them, adding that don Alvaro was innocent. I as notary, and in the company of several others, went immediately to the house of the Indian Pirama, who removed from his hut seven figurines of unrefined gold and a few small emeralds of no value. After further proceedings involving don Alvaro, the Indian Pirama testified that in another of his fields he had two other figurines of gold and four of cloth, which he will produce in the morning because at this hour it was already dark. With this the judge ordered the *alguacil* Bartolomé de Ospino to take don Alvaro and the Indian Pirama into custody and to keep them closely confined.

In this *repartimiento* on October 27 of the same year, the judge, using his powers to discover the truth and in the light of the evidence against don Fernando, the *principal* of this *repartimiento*, ordered the latter brought before him. Through the interpreter Cristóbal de Sanabria, don Fernando was commanded many times to testify regarding the shrine that he possessed as well as any idols of gold or cloth or of any other form,, and to reveal whether he knew of any other Indians who may have such things. Fernando replied that he had no shrine, nor knew of any Indians who did. In view of this denial the judge ordered him stripped of his clothing and bound by the thighs to two benches; the cords were then tightened [in the manner of a tourniquet] by two and a half turns and a jug of water was poured into his mouth and nostrils. Since after all of these measures and other procedures and threats the Indian refused to confess to anything, the judge ordered him untied and sent back to jail, noting that if it seemed worthwhile or necessary, the judge, as was his customary right, would have him tortured again.

On October 28 of the same year, and obeying the orders of the judge, I as notary, along with the *alguacil* Bartolomé de Ospino, the interpreter Cristóbal de Sanabria, and Alonso de Molina, left this *repartimiento* for the site of the old *pueblo*[5] in the company of the Indian man and woman Diego Raga and Francisca Fusgay, those named by Juan Cacaria. There, more or less one league from this *repartimiento,* in some stone caves facing a hill and impossible to reach on horseback, Diego indicated a cave inside which there was found a large *tunjo* of cotton cloth. Wrapped within it were bones and a skull that Diego Raga said were those of the old *cacique* named Unbaguya, who was not a Christian and whose remains were kept for veneration. When it was untied no gold was found, and there were only a few small, worthless emeralds and five or six moldy and torn cotton blankets. The Indian then revealed a small gold clasp hidden beneath a stone and that seemed to be worth about two pesos. Despite a search of all the caves and under all the stones around the cave referred to, nothing else was found.

Immediately thereafter, I as notary, and accompanied by those mentioned above, left the cave where the corpse of the old *cacique* was found and departed in the company of an elderly Indian named Pirama, to whom the *capitán* don Alvaro had referred. The Indian led us along the road that runs from this *repartimiento* to Villa de Leiva, and as the road he took us on was rough, I [the notary] stayed behind. The *alguacil* Bartolomé de Ospino and Alonso de Molina went with the Indian and later explained that Pirama had led them high into the hills where he showed them a chest and six cotton *tunjos* which they brought before me. They stated that

no gold had been found, and we thereupon returned to the *repartimiento* at approximately three o'clock in the afternoon.

When we arrived back at Iguaque we exhibited to the judge the body and bones of the *cacique* and the six small cloth *tunjos* referred to, as well as a few blankets in which the bones of the old *cacique* were wrapped and the little gold clasp. The six small *tunjos* were cut open with a knife and within were found some tiny emeralds of no value, rotten corn, cotton seeds, beans, and other rubbish. The judge ordered that all of this be burned along with the bones and blankets in the small square in front of the church, and in accord with his orders fires were lit and these things were burned. The witnesses to this act and to the opening of the *tunjos* were señor Arroyo de Guevara, don Andres Patiño, and many others, to which I as notary hereby attest.

In this *repartimiento,* at approximately seven o'clock in the evening of the same day, further proceedings were undertaken with the *capitán* Ventura to make him declare whether he possessed any shrines either of gold or of cloth. He stated that he had two figurines of unrefined gold, both of which he then exhibited and handed over to the officials.

Thereafter, at the same hour of seven o'clock in the evening, interrogations were begun involving the Indian woman Francisca Fusgay. Her arms were tied with a rope and she was ordered to speak the truth. Just before being hoisted off the floor with the rope, she begged that this not be done and said that she would deliver the two gold figurines that she used in her shrine. The *corregidor* Pedro de Arellano went in the company of the Indian woman and returned with the two figurines, which were of unrefined gold.

Further questioning was then undertaken with the Indian named Pirama, and he was commanded to state and declare what sort of shrine he possessed and its whereabouts. Having been warned that he would be tied with the rope and raised off the floor, he said that he had four gold figurines at his shrine and pleaded not to be bound. The Indian said that he would fetch them immediately, and the *alguacil* Bartolomé de Ospino went with him and returned with the four figurines of unrefined gold and handed them in.

The proceedings then continued with Juan Pirasuca, who of his own free will and without being pressed, declared that he had in a clay pot in his house two gold figurines that comprised his shrine, and that they should go with him and he would hand in the figurines. Bartolomé de Ospino went with the Indian and brought back the two figurines of unrefined gold and delivered them over.

Following the above, on October 29 of the same year, there appeared before the judge the aforementioned Cristóbal de Sanabria and Luis Sasmia, an Indian from the *pueblo* of Iguaque. The former said that Luis Sasmia came to his house the night before and gave him four figurines of very poor quality gold and a few worthless emeralds, all of which were then handed over to the judge.

Following the above, in the *pueblo* of Iguaque on October 30, 1595, the judge and *visitador* said that as he had been given word that an elderly Indian man and woman of this *repartimiento* possessed the bones of an Indian *cacique* that they keep hidden and worship as a shrine according to their pagan customs, he ordered them to appear before him in order to discover the truth. Speaking through Cristóbal de Sanabria, the Indian man stated that his name was Pedro Unbarique and that the name of the Indian woman was Elena Pine. Judging by their appearance, the man appeared to be about ninety years old and the woman looked more than fifty-five years old. As both were *chontales* and of such advanced age they were not made to swear an oath, giving their testimony in the spirit of the proceedings and in the presence of Leandro Sanchez, the defender appointed for these Indians and for the others mentioned in these proceedings.

They stated that some seven years ago an Indian named Domingo—now very ill—removed from the church in this *repartimiento* the bones of don Juan, former *capitán* of this *repartimiento*. To remove them. Domingo had been given the key to the church by a young Indian *sacristán,* a native of Santa Fe and an assistant to Father Alonso, who was then the local priest. The bones were buried in a field near the pueblo, but the two Indians testified that they did not know why the bones were removed from the church and added that they knew nothing more about this matter. Asked if they worshipped the bones of the dead man like a shrine, they responded that they did not bury them for that purpose nor did the bones serve as a shrine. The Indian woman said that Unbagoche, who is now deceased, showed her the location of this Indian's bones,

but that she knew nothing about them nor had she seen them until today, when by order of the judge she went with three Christian men, showed them the place where they lay, and they were then dug up and brought back to this *repartimiento*. Those who went on the orders of the judge to remove the bones of this Indian were the *alguacil* Bartolomé de Ospino, Alonso de Molina, and Alonso López. They declared that only the bones of the old *capitán* were found and that no gold was discovered with the bones or in the vicinity, and that this is the truth of what took place.

Following the above, in the *pueblo* of Iguaque on October 30, the *alguacil* Bartolomé de Ospino addressed the judge and produced the two small figurines of fine gold that he said Elena Pine had given him and that she had had in her shrine. The Indian woman had freely declared this fact and handed over the figurines.

Thereafter, on the same day, the *alguacil* Bartolomé de Ospino came before the judge and *visitador-general* and brought with him an Indian from this *pueblo* who calls himself Pedro. The Indian showed the *visitador* two figurines of unrefined gold that he said he had as a shrine left to him by his forebears and that he handed over voluntarily.

The same day there came before the judge an Indian named Lucas Cuyteque, who of his own will handed over a burned figurine of unrefined gold that he said was left to him by his forebears. The judge, in order to make [Lucas] reveal the whereabouts of his shrine and to identify other persons who have them, ordered him bound. To this end and to frighten him, for a brief moment the Indian was hoisted off the floor with his arms tied behind him. He stated that he had no other shrine nor did he know of anyone else who had.

In the *pueblo* of Iguaque on this same day, of October 30, the judge and *visitador-general* called before him Luis Aguaquen, an Indian from this *pueblo*, having received word that the latter had a shrine inherited from his forebears. Through the interpreter Cristóbal de Sanabria, he was commanded to speak and declare the truth and was warned that he would be tied and raised off the floor with the rope, which he was shown. He said that he knew nothing, and the judge then ordered his hands tied behind his back and that he be hoisted off the floor. He was bound and hoisted about one *palmo*, and being thus suspended, Luis Aguaquen declared that they should untie him and he would tell them the truth. On the orders of the judge he was lowered to the floor and still bound as described stated that it was true that an uncle had left him a shrine in which there were two gold figurines and two *tejuelos* of fine gold. He said he had been told to make a shrine with these but had not done so, and these objects were being kept by an Indian named Pirateque. In light of this testimony, the judge ordered the Indian brought before him. The Indian was brought and produced the two figurines of unrefined gold. Luis Aguaquen said that if they set him free he would fetch the *tejuelos*. On the orders of the judge he was freed and then brought the two *tejuelos* of fine gold and handed them over to the judge.

In the *pueblo* of Iguaque on the same day, the judge and *visitador-general* stated that in order for this case to proceed in accordance with legal and juridical form—and due to the absence of Francisco García de Frutos, defender-general of the natives—he was appointing and appointed Leandro Sánchez, resident of this *pueblo*, as defender of all the Indian men and women implicated and held in custody in these proceedings. The judge ordered the latter to accept and to swear the obligatory solemn oath.

Leandro Sánchez was immediately notified of this act and accepted the post of defender of the Indians. He then took the oath on the sign of the cross, according to the forms of law, and swore to carry out his duty well and faithfully, to gather their statements and protect them, and that he would do all that was required of a good defender. In view of this acceptance and oath, the judge granted him formal powers to defend the Indians and to undertake whatever measures might assist in their defense.

### 5.3   The Guilty Are Charged

Following the above, in the *pueblo* of Iguaque on October 31, 1595, the judge and *visitador-general,* having approved these acts, stated that he intended and hereby did charge the Indians now in custody: the *cacique* don Juan, don Fernando, don Diego Unbayan, Juan Riba, Ventura, Sebastián, Juan Pitasique, don Diego Sipaguancha, Juan Neaquenchia, Juan Cacaria, Diego Raga, Piramaca, Francisca Fusgay, Juan Pirasuca, Luis Sasmia, Antonico, who provided the key [to the church], Domingo, who is not present, Elena Pine, Pedro Pacacura, and Luis Aguaquen as guilty as a result

of these proceedings and their own confessions. The judge ordered them brought to face the charges and respond as they see fit and stated that, without regard to what they might say, in the light of the evidence in this case the charges shall stand for two years from the conclusion and publication of these proceedings. In this *repartimiento* at the close of the month of October at approximately seven o'clock in the morning, I as notary read the above charges and evidence to Leandro Sánchez, defender of the Indians.

In the *pueblo* of Iguaque on October 31, 1595, Pedro Ganbasicha, a native of this *pueblo*, came before the judge and showed his grace two figurines of unrefined gold that he had kept as a shrine and that he then handed in.

In the *pueblo* of Iguaque on the same day, there came before the judge an Indian who stated his name as Gonzalo Conbaria who produced the corpses of two Indians he said were from the old times before the arrival of the Spaniards and that had been buried in some nearby fields. The Indian said that in the *pueblo* the bodies were treated as a shrine, and he exhibited them before the judge along with a belt sheathed in gold leaf that he said had belonged to the dead men. Having seen the above, the judge ordered the two bodies brought by this Conbaria the bones of pagan Indians as Conbaria had stated, burned in the square of the *pueblo*. The judge thereupon ordered that measures be used upon Conbaria to force him to reveal the location of the gold contained in this shrine, and to this effect he was bound with the rope and raised two *palmos* off the floor. Thus suspended he was commanded to speak the truth, and said that he possessed nothing more than two gold figurines that serve as his shrine and that he will hand over. As he would not declare anything more, he was ordered set loose and was freed from the rope.

### 5.4   Statement by Defender of the Indians

I, Leandro Sánchez, appointed by your grace to respond on behalf of all the Indians involved in these proceedings and implicated and imprisoned on the charges made against them as idolators and for having kept small figurines and other idols, say that the aforementioned Indians should be absolved of the guilt attributed to them. Although it is true that they have kept certain figurines, they have not used them for

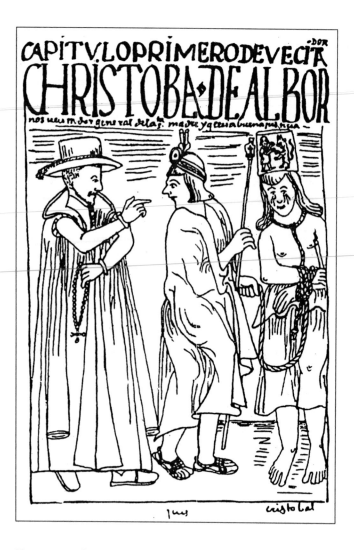

**Figure 3** Campaigns against idolatry also occurred in the central Andean region in the sixteenth century. This drawing depicts the *visitador-general* Cristóbal de Albornoz, his Andean assistant, and a person accused of worshipping local shrines (Guaman Poma de Ayala [1615] 1980, f. 675).

idolatrous worship and for this reason have so readily shown them to your grace. And if these Indians have also surrendered a number of other idols, *tunjos,* and bones found outside this *pueblo,* they do not bear the guilt. Rather it is the old Indians, their ancestors, who are to blame, since they were not Christians and it was they who left these things. It is because the Indians I represent are not idolators as they are imputed to be, but rather baptized Christians that they have revealed the location of such things. If they have had some few figurines in their possession, these they inherited from their forebears and they have kept them until now

without paying them much attention. And if the Indians do bear some small guilt for having kept these things in their possession, the eight days that they have already spent in custody is a more than adequate punishment.

I thus ask and plead that your grace dismiss the charges made against these Indians. For the reasons stated and argued on their behalf, and since the imprisonment and trouble they have been given and suffered has taught them their lesson and is a sufficient penalty for these wretched Indians, I ask for justice.

### 5.5 *The Judgment of* Visitador-General *Guzmán*

In the *pueblo* and *repartimiento* of Iguaque, on the final day of the month of October of 1595, his honor señor Egas de Guzmán—counsel to our lord the king, his senior judge on the royal *audiencia* of this kingdom and *visitador-general* of the province of Tunja—said that from the proceedings on the shrines in this *repartimiento* it is evident that the remains of the *capitán* don Juan were removed from the church where they were buried and reinterred in a field. On the order of his grace they were exhumed, and because this Indian was a Christian and had been buried in the church the judge intended and did order that his body be reburied in the Church, both because it was befitting for a Christian and because it would serve as a good example to the natives. Friar Juan Gutiérrez, the priest of this *pueblo* and member of the Order of Saint Francis, was respectfully requested to see to the interment of the Indian's remains in the church.

I the notary notified the priest Father fray Juan Gutiérrez of this act, in order that he bury the bones of the aforementioned *capitán* and I, in compliance with the wishes of the judge, certify that the bones that had been brought, and that were said to be those of the *capitán* don Juan, were buried in the church by the priest, Father fray Juan Gutiérrez.

In the *pueblo* of Iguaque in the aforementioned *encomienda* on November 1, his honor Egas de Guzmán made note of the statements made by the *gobernador* don Pedro Conba, the *cacique* don Juan, don Fernando, don Diego Unbayan, Juan Ruiz, Ventura and Sebastián Cipaquen, in which they voluntarily confessed that each had a *cuca* which in the Indian tongue means temple of adoration left to each by their respective forebears. Although it is recorded in these proceedings that his grace the judge inspected these houses and found no idols, there is reason to believe that since these Indians kept them that they retain some memory of the old rites and ceremonies and that it is right in the service of the Lord our God to extirpate all idolatrous abuses and to see that no trace or memory of them remains among the Indians. To make an example the judge intended and did order that the seven houses and temples of idolatry in which the Indians used to perform their ceremonies and idolatrous rites, be immediately burned and demolished, reserving as his grace does the right to impose upon these Indians whatever punishment he sees fit.

In compliance with the above act, immediately thereafter on the same day, month and year, the houses and huts known as *cucas,* which in the Indian tongue means temple of idolatry, were burned.

On the same day there were also burned three other huts known as *cucas,* and the Indians who testified that these were *cucas* did so of their own free will.

In the *repartimiento* of Iguaque in the *encomienda* of Juan de Otalora on November 1, 1595, Juan de Otalora came before his honor señor Egas de Guzmán, and before me, the notary. Without swearing an oath, he stated and declared that he had heard and it was public knowledge in this *repartimiento* that when the old local *capitán* and *principal* don Martín died, he left a shrine that was inherited by his nephew, the *capitán* and *principal* don Fernando, who at present lives in this *repartimiento* and who it is presumed has and possesses this shrine. Juan de Otalora has also heard and been informed that another Indian *principal* from this *repartimiento*—who died many years ago and likewise served as *capitán*—left another shrine, in which he practiced idolatry, which they say contained a quantity of gold, and that was inherited by the *capitán* don Alonso, nephew of a dead Indian. According to what Otalora states, he has been informed that these Indians have and possess these shrines, and the judge ordered him to make this same testimony under oath and to sign it. The latter said that he did not dare to do so because

the Indians, on knowing that he testified against them, might then rise up or flee his *encomienda.*

In the *repartimiento* of Iguaque in the *encomienda* of Juan de Otalora on November 2, 1595, his honor señor Egas de Guzmán, speaking through the interpreter Cristóbal de Sanabria and in the light of the last statement made by Otalora (to the effect that don Fernando, *capitán* of this *repartimiento,* possesses the shrine left by his uncle don Martín), ordered don Fernando, who was present, to state and declare the true location of the shrine left by don Martín. He was warned that if he did not, he would be tortured. Don Fernando said that he knew nothing about this shrine since he is neither a relative nor an heir of don Martín, and that the person who will know and be able to reveal this is an Indian woman named Leonor China, daughter of don Martín. The judge immediately called the Indian woman to come before him and through the interpreter ordered her to state and declare the truth regarding the whereabouts of the shrine belonging to her father don Martín, as she admitted to being his daughter. She said that she knew nothing of this shrine or its location, or whether her father possessed any such shrine. Neither don Fernando nor the Indian woman declared anything further.

Faced with the denials of don Fernando and Leonor China, and in order to discover the truth as this case requires, the judge immediately ordered the Indian man and woman subjected to a form of torture with a rope and, according to his instructions, prepared cords and bonds he keeps for this purpose, as well as the water that would be used on them in this torture.

The judge then immediately ordered that don Fernando be stripped of his clothing, and once the Indian was naked, his arms were bound and tied to another rope so that he could be hoisted into the air. On the direction of the judge, the interpreter Cristóbal de Sanabria told him to state and declare the true whereabouts of the shrine, and that if he did not he would be raised off the floor and that this torture would be inflicted and if he died or if his arms broke it would be his own fault and responsibility. The Indian said that he knows nothing about the questions they ask, and on the instructions of the judge they hoisted him off the floor where he was suspended for the length of time it takes to recite two *credos.*[6] Since he denied all knowledge of this matter and declared nothing, the judge ordered the ropes untied and the man set loose.

Immediately thereafter, the judge ordered that Leonor China have her arms tied behind her back and that she be commanded to state and declare the truth. This was done, but she said that she knew nothing. The judge then ordered the rope pulled and she was hoisted about a yard off the floor,[7] where she remained suspended for the time it takes to recite one Hail Mary. She denied any knowledge regarding the questions put to her, and the judge therefore ordered that she be let down and untied.

The judge then ordered the interrogation of the *capitán* don Ventura against whom evidence of guilt had been given in previous declarations and gave instructions for his arms to be bound behind him and that he be hoisted off the floor with the rope slung over the beam. Through the interpreter the Indian was warned that he should speak the truth, but he said he knew nothing. On the signal of the judge, Ventura was hoisted some two *palmos* into the air, where he remained for the time it takes to recite one *credo*. Seeing that the Indian denied everything and refused to make any declaration, the judge ordered him freed and he was immediately let down and untied.

### 5.6  Final Determinations

In the light of this trial and of the evidence rendered here in the name of the royal high court with regard to the absent Pedro Conba, the *cacique* don Juan, don Fernando, don Diego Unbayan, Juan Riba, don Ventura and Sebastián, all of whom are *capitanes* and *principales* of this *repartimiento* of Iguaque, and against Juan Pitasique, don Diego Sipaquencha, Juan Neaquenchia, Juan Cacaria, Diego Raga, Piramaca, Francisca Fusgay, Juan Pirasuca, Luis Sasmia, Antonio Aguaquen, and Gonzalo Conbaria for being idolators and for keeping shrines for the practice of their old pagan customs as is evident from these proceedings:

There is guilt established in this trial against the aforementioned don Pedro Conba, the *cacique* don Juan, don Fernando, don Diego Unbayan, Juan Riba, don Ventura and Sebastián, all of them *capitanes* and *principales* of this *repartimiento,* and against Juan Pitasaque, don Diego Sipaquencha, Juan Neaquenchia, Juan Cacaria, Diego Raga, Piramaca, Francisca Fusgay, Juan Pirasuca, Luis Sasmia, Antonio Aguaquen, and

Gonzalo Conbaria for keeping old temples, idols, figurines, and Indian bones.

Therefore I the judge must and hereby do find the above guilty and sentence them to the following: I must and do order the absent Pedro Conba arrested wherever he is found and brought before me in order to deal with him as is fit and necessary. The *cacique* don Juan shall have his hair cut off and be exiled from this *repartimiento* for six months.[8] The *capitán* don Fernando is hereby fined twelve pesos in gold—one third of which shall be reserved for the court of our Lord the king and the other two thirds applied in equal parts to defray the expenses of this court and of the present visit of inspection—and if this fine is not paid immediately he shall serve four months' hard labor in the construction of the church of Chiquinquirá. Don Ventura shall serve four months' hard labor at Chiquinquirá under penalty that if he abandons this service he shall serve twice this sentence, receive fifty lashes, and have his hair cut off. Diego Raga is likewise sentenced to serve four months' uninterrupted hard labor in the same works on pain of the same punishment: that if he leaves he shall serve twice the sentence, receive fifty lashes, and have his hair cut off. Domingo, for having removed the bones of don Juan from the church where they were buried, I sentence to fifty lashes, order that his hair be cut off, and that he be exiled from this *repartimiento* for exactly one year, which time he shall serve laboring in the construction works at Chiquinquirá, and if he flees he shall serve twice this time; in regard to this Indian, who is ill, the sentence shall be carried out as soon as he recovers his health. In regard to the absent Indian Antonio from Santa Fe, for having provided the keys to the church in order to remove the bones of the Indian don Juan, I must and do order his arrest, and that he be taken from jail and in the name of justice given one hundred lashes, that he serve one year's labor in Chiquinquirá and two years' exile from this *repartimiento*; should he fail to serve either punishment fully, the sentence shall be doubled. I sentence each of don Diego Unbayan, Juan Riba, Sebastián, Juan Pitasaque, don Diego Sipaquencha, Juan Neaquenchia, Juan Cacaria, Piramaca, Francisca Fusgay, Juan Pirasuca, Luis Sasmia, Elena Pine, Pedro Patacuca, Luis Aguaquen, and Gonzalo Conbaria to have their hair cut off and to receive thirty lashes. As regards the lashes to be given to Piramaca, who is very ill, they are to be reserved until he recovers his health.

The Indians named above are hereby commanded that from this day forward they are to live as good Christians, not to be idolators nor to keep pagan shrines as they have in the past, and are warned that if they do not obey, they shall be punished with great rigor. Fray Father Juan Gutiérrez of the Order of Saint Francis and priest of this *pueblo* was entrusted with this task and was asked to endeavor with particular care to instruct the Indians in the matters of our Holy Catholic Faith. The *corregidor* was then ordered to carry out the sentences I have passed and set down herein.

## NOTES

*Acknowledgments* I would like to thank Edward M. Farmer, Trinity College, Cambridge, for co-translating the document.

1. Unfortunately, there is little published material in English on the Muisca Indians of Colombia. My dissertation, currently in preparation for publication, will help fill that gap (J. Michael Francis, "The Muisca Indians Under Spanish Rule, 1537–1636" (Unpublished Ph.D. dissertatation, Cambridge University, 1998). With the exception of the above work, the suggestions for further reading that follow this document therefore refer readers to material from other regions of Spanish America that will help to shed some light on the nature of the proceedings at Iguaque.

2. This would translate into perhaps six hundred people for in general, tribute was assessed against adult male heads of households.

3. For example, in 1580 it had been estimated that the illegal theft of native sanctuaries had cost the royal treasury more than 200,000 pesos in unpaid taxes.

4. The proceedings from Iguaque can be found in Archivo General de la Nación (Colombia), Caciques e Indios 58, no. 2, ff. 1–37 (1595). Editors' note: In this chapter the author has retained the original and often variant spelling of Muisca names (e.g., Diego Sipaguan-cha/Diego Sipaquencha).

5. This would be a reference to a *congregación* or forced resettlement having taken place at some earlier point.

6. The *credo*, of course, was a brief statement of the articles of Christian belief that every Christian would have memorized and repeated countless times. The phrase "en un credo" (in a creed) was a common expression meaning "in a short time." The sense here seems to be that don Fernando was suspended in the air for a brief period but for more than the proverbial "one creed."

7. Note that in this case the notary uses the *vara*, or yard, as a measure, rather than the *palmo*.

8. The decision to cut the hair of those individuals found guilty of idolatry was a deliberate attempt to humiliate and discredit the accused. Although we have no record of Muisca responses or attitudes to having their long hair cropped, colonial officials often remarked that Muisca men considered such a punishment more harsh than the physical torment of the lashes that followed. We do know that during Muisca rites of passage, which involved long periods of seclusion, fasting, and sexual abstention, men allowed their hair to grow long.

## DOCUMENT THEMES

Cultural Contact/Ethnogenesis/Resistance; Ethnicity; Governance, colonial; Indigenous Peoples; Religion; Rural Life.

## SUGGESTIONS FOR FURTHER READING

Arriaga 1968.
Clendinnen 1987.
Francis 1998.
Griffiths 1996.
Haliczer 1987.
Mills 1997.
Perry and Cruz, eds. 1991.
Reichel-Dolmatoff 1965.
Ricard 1966.

# CHAPTER 7

The Spiritual and Physical Ecstasies of a
Sixteenth-Century *Beata*: Marina de San
Miguel Confesses Before the Mexican
Inquisition
*(Mexico, 1598)*

Jacqueline Holler

## INTRODUCTION

By 1521, when Hernán Cortés conquered the Aztec Empire, the Inquisition was already well established in Spain. It was transferred to the newly colonized land as an ad hoc institution under the guidance of missionary friars and, later, Mexico's archbishop. This rather informal arrangement was replaced, in 1571, by an officially constituted Tribunal of the Holy Office of the Inquisition, based in Mexico City and with ostensible authority over the whole of New Spain.[1]

The document presented here is taken from one of the less common types of Mexican Inquisition trials, a major heresy case.[2] The Mexican tribunal spent much more time enforcing socioreligious norms than attacking heresy and crypto-Judaism. About 11 percent of trials dealt with heresy; the remainder investigated less serious crimes such as bigamy, witchcraft, superstition, and blasphemy. In 1598, however, the Holy Office of Mexico received information about an alleged group of *alumbrados,* heretics whose religious beliefs emphasized mental prayer and denigrated the authority of the Church. The Mexican group apparently believed that the Day of Judgment would soon come and that the group's members would be selected to found a New Jerusalem on earth. Among the group denounced was a religious woman called Marina de San Miguel, apparently of some importance within the group because of her mystical visions, which others believed to be revelations from God. Marina was imprisoned in November 1598. Her confessions, presented here, were taken between that date and January 1599.[3]

Although the Inquisition functioned as a sort of police force, the confessions were not taken in the same way that a modern statement might be taken from the

accused in a criminal case. A person was imprisoned and investigated in response to a denunciation. In contrast to modern police arrests, those arrested were not informed of the charges against them. Rather, the suspect was urged to confess whatever he or she might have done that was worthy of punishment by the Holy Office. The inquisitor's questions, the confessant's testimony, and any other events that transpired were recorded by a notary, who was instructed to record testimony in a complete and accurate manner.

Notaries were professionals who carried out their task carefully and, for the most part, conscientiously. Readers will note, however, that these are not verbatim transcripts as are modern court transcripts. Notaries transcribed testimony in the third person ("she said that … "). They very occasionally summarized rather than transcribed, particularly in the sections of the case that followed set formulas. For example, when a suspect was asked to recite the catechism, the notary did not record the words the suspect said, but simply said that the suspect had said it well, or poorly, or had said sections of it, or could not recite it. Within these limitations, however, the documents followed the suspect's testimony very closely, and are remarkably personal and reminiscent of speech. Moreover, such records are detailed. Every attempt was made to elicit a truthful, complete, and remorseful confession from the individual, for such a confession would "discharge the conscience" and bring the suspect to penitence, and thus to God's forgiveness. Questions were often open-ended, and suspects were usually allowed to speak without interruption and at great length. Only after the confession(s) of the suspect were judged complete was an actual accusation created. This would contain the charges alleged by those who denounced the suspect as well as any information the suspect had willingly confessed. At this point, the actual trial began, and the suspect responded to the particular charges contained in the accusation with the assistance of legal counsel appointed by the court.

Historians now use Inquisition documents as a way to access the experience of individuals who might otherwise be absent from documentation. In the case of Mexico, the Inquisition section of the National Archive offers one of the most complete bodies of documentation for the sixteenth century. The information contained in this case provides a very rare glimpse into the life of a sixteenth-century woman whose life deviated dramatically, in many ways, from the standard picture of Spanish American women in colonial times. I have rendered the original text of Marina's confessions into English as faithfully as possible. However, because the document is almost totally unpunctuated, I have added a certain amount of punctuation. In addition, I have removed the repetitive use of the term *said,* as in "the said witness said that the said man accompanied her to the said house." Though the literal translation conveys very well the legalistic character of this document, the accretion of so many *saids* impairs readability.

Marina de San Miguel confessed nine times. Because of the length and detail of her confessions, I have found it necessary to edit some material. The confessions still yield a great deal of information about Marina's life, particularly in regard to her spiritual and sexual activities. Readers will want to consider the circumstances of the document's production and how they affect its usefulness; the strategies used by both Marina and her interlocutor in their unequal encounter; the credibility of Marina's testimony; and how that testimony changes over time.

Readers will also no doubt want to know Marina's fate. In the auto de fe of March 25, 1601, a gagged and haltered Marina was paraded naked to the waist upon a mule. After abjuring her errors, Marina received one hundred lashes. She was also sentenced to a fine of 100 pesos and to ten years' reclusion in the plague hospital, where, evidently, she became very ill. The remainder of her story eludes us.

## THE DOCUMENT

### 7.1  *First Confession*

In the city of Mexico, Friday, November 20, 1598, The Lord Inquisitor *licenciado* don Alonso de Peralta in his morning audience ordered that a woman be brought before him from one of the secret prisons of this Holy Office. Being present, she swore an oath *en forma devida de derecho* under which she promised to tell the truth here in this audience and in all the others that might be held until the determination of her case, and to keep secret everything that she might see or believe or that might be talked about with her or that might happen concerning this her case.

She was asked what her name is, where she was born, how old she is, what her profession is,[4] and when she was arrested.

She answered that she is Marina de San Miguel, a *natural* of the city of Córdoba in the kingdoms of Castile; that she is fifty-three years old and is a *beata*[5] of the Order of Saint Dominic; and that she occupies herself in needlework[6] and in teaching girls to do the same. She was arrested last Saturday, which was the fourteenth of the present month, and placed in one of the secret prisons of this Holy Office. And she declared her genealogy in the following form:

### Parents

- **Gonzalo Abril,** *natural* of La Granja, next to Fuente Ovejuna in the diocese of Córdoba, blacksmith (*herrador*), who died in Puebla de los Ángeles.
- **María González de Escalorán,** from Córdoba, who died in this city of Mexico and who had no profession.

### Paternal Grandparents

- **Juan Abril,** resident and *natural* of La Granja, farmer (*labrador*), deceased.
- **Marina Atín,** his wife, resident of the said place, deceased.

### Maternal Grandparents

- **Hernán Gil,** resident and *natural* of Córdoba, saddler (*albardero*), deceased.
- **Catalina Rodríguez de Escalona,** his wife, resident and *natural* [of Córdoba], already dead, who had no profession, other than raising her children.

### Father's Siblings[7]

- **Sebastián Abril,** who was an army officer (*alférez*) in Italy and got married in Fuente Ovejuna to doña Mayor de Castillejos, and who has children; one is called Pedro Alonso Romero and the daughter doña Lucrecia Romero, and the others she doesn't remember, nor their ages, and they were rich farming people, and she doesn't know whether they are dead.

- **Bartolomé Abril,** resident of La Granja, farmer, married, and she doesn't know whom he married nor whether he has children, only that he lived in La Granja, and she does not know whether he might be dead.
- **Pedro Abril,** who went to Italy, and they said that he was a military field officer (*maese de campo*), and she does not know what became of him, nor whether he got married, and she has no other uncles or aunts on her father's side.

## Mother's Siblings

- **Doctor Hernándo de Escalona,** physician, resident of the city of Lerida in Catalonia, where he married dona Thomasia, and she knows that he had children, one of whom was called doña Catalina, and she does not know whether they are dead.
- **Martín de Córdoba,** merchant (*mercader*) in Medina del Campo, where he got married, and she does not know to whom; and she heard that he had a daughter, whose name she does not remember, nor does she know whether they're dead.
- **Victoria Gil,** married in Córdoba to Juan de Baratorno, and they have children, whose names she does not remember, nor [does she know] whether they are dead.
- **Ana de los Ángeles,** *doncella,* who went to Lerida with the said Doctor Hernando de Escalona.
- **Isabel de Escalona,** *doncella,* who left with the said, her sister. And she has no more uncles and aunts on her mother's side.

## Siblings

- **Juan Abril,** who died in Peru, single, blacksmith, who left no children.
- **Luisa de Los Angeles,** *doncella,* who died in Mexico in the house of this woman. And she had no more siblings.

## Husband and Children

This confessant has never been married nor had children and is a *doncella* and has taken a vow of chastity.

She was asked what caste and parentage are her parents and grandparents and the others, transverse and collateral, whom she has named, and if they or any one of them or this confessant have been imprisoned, given penitence, reconciled, or condemned by the Holy Office of the Inquisition.

She said that they are *cristianos viejos,* and that none of them has ever been imprisoned, given penitence, reconciled, or condemned by the Holy Office, and that this is the first time that she has been imprisoned by it.

She was asked whether she is a Christian, baptized and confirmed, and if she hears mass, confesses, and receives communion at the times ordered by the Holy Mother Church.[8]

She said that she is a Christian baptized and confirmed by the grace of God, and that she was confirmed in this city by a bishop, friar of the Order of Saint Dominic, called Diego de San Francisco. She said that she confesses and receives communion at all the times ordered by the Holy Mother Church, and that the last time she confessed was Sunday the eighth in the church of Saint Dominic with fray Honorato Navarro, and she received communion.

She made the sign of the cross and said the Our Father, Hail Mary, *Credo,* Salve Regina, the Ten Commandments, and Fourteen Articles well in Spanish.[9]

She was asked whether she knows how to read and write and whether she has studied any subjects.

She said that she knows how to read and write and she has not studied any subject, and that her brother taught her the alphabet and how to make letters; and she learned writing from a book that her brother gave her, and without more teaching, by her own work and industry, she learned to read and write.

She was asked for the story of her life.

She said that she was born in the city of Córdoba [in Spain] in the house of her parents, where she was raised until they died,[10] and she was left at nineteen years, and while they lived she occupied her time in working for and serving them. And at the age of three, she came with her parents to this land in a fleet whose commander she cannot remember, as she was so young. Once arrived in this city of Mexico, they lived in the street of San

Agustin for nine years. And having made some money[11] they returned to the city of Córdoba where her father spent lavishly, in such a way that they came to poverty, and [so] returned to this city of Mexico in the fleet of General Pedro Meléndez. When her mother died here, her father married again to a widow, Leonor Arías, and because her father wanted to get married the confessant went to the *colegio de las niñas* (girl's residential school), where she spent four years. After her father got married, he found his wife with a man and killed him, though his wife recovered from her wounds. For this reason her father went away to Peru.[12] And so she left the school and went to live at the school, "I mean at San Pablo,"[13] with Mariá de Acosta, wife of Diego Rodríguez, a tanner (*curtidor*). And she lived there two years, and after that she took her sister out of the said school and together they took a little house in the street of San Agustín. There they lived for seven or ten years on their sewing and from teaching girls. While they were living there their father came back and surrendered to the *cárcel de corte*. He was exiled and went to Puebla, where he died, leaving the confessant with her sister. And later the confessant went to the house of Juan Núñez, accountant, *vecino* of this city,[14] where she was for ten months. After that she rented a house across from his until she bought the house where she currently lives, which she bought from some Indians for 200 pesos. After that she spent 300 pesos on it, using 200 pesos she inherited from her father and what she earned by the needle and from teaching girls. And for thirteen years she has lived there, until she was brought before this Holy Office. And she has associated all this time with very honored, good-living people, both religious and secular.

She was asked what goods she has in order that they may be sequestered, so that she will not lose them.[15]

She said that the house is hers, and the white clothing that she has in it, and that she has no other treasures as can be seen in her strongboxes. And then she said that she remembered that she has a nephew in her house. He is Alonso Gutiérrez de Castro who is a tailor of jackets (*jubetero*) and son of her first cousin on her mother's side, who is a native of Córdoba where her nephew was born. He lives in her house, and anything he claims to be his is his, because she takes him for a man of good conscience. And she remembers that Alonso Gutiérrez de Castro made some repairs in the

house at his expense, making a gift of it as her nephew. Then she said that she did not spend 300 pesos repairing her house, but only 100. And she does not really know how much it was because money comes and goes. And her nephew made the other repairs, making her a gift of the money that he spent, as she has said. He has lived in her house for two years and four months.[16]

She was asked if she knows, presumes, or suspects the cause for her arrest and imprisonment in the prisons of this Holy Office.

She said that she presumes and suspects that the cause of her imprisonment must be that four years ago a secular youth called Luis de Zárate came to visit her. And she does not know where he lives, only that he was sent to her by Gregorio López,[17] who died in the Holy Faith, and who was her spiritual brother. ... She was with Luis, talking about spiritual things, and about hell, and he said that there was no hell and no devils, and that men[18] were the devils and hell. And she, feeling uncomfortable about this, said to him, "What are you saying, that there is no hell?" Luis de Zárate said that men through their sins were hell. Another day she fell ill in her bed, and lost her senses. This illness lasted three months, and then she came to her senses and, being well, sent to speak with the Lord Inquisitor Doctor Loboguerrero and with fray Gonzalo de Illescas of the Order of Saint Dominic, telling all that had passed with Luis de Zárate, and how she had been sick with this illness. The inquisitor said that with her illness she must have imagined it. And she says that she wants to go over her memory so that she can tell the truth about everything that she might remember.

With this the audience ceased, because it was past eleven. The above was read and she approved it and signed it. And she was ordered to return to her cell, very admonished to examine her memory as she has offered to do.

[signed] Marina de San Miguel
Pedro de Manozca, *escribano*

## 7.2 *Second Confession*

In the city of Mexico, Monday, November 23, 1598, the Lord Inquisitor *licenciado* don Alonso de Peralta in his afternoon audience ordered that Marina de San Miguel, *beata*, be brought before him. And when she was present, she was told to say anything she had remembered in her case, and the truth by the oath that she made [in her first audience].

She said that she has remembered that Juan López de Zárate, "I mean Luis de Zárate," said to her that on the day of justice the flesh will be renewed, and that there will be a New Jerusalem on earth, which was an opinion that Gregorio López held. And [Luis] wanted to know when the day [of justice] would be. And he asked the confessant to entrust it to God, so that [the date] would be revealed [to her]. And this is what she has remembered.

She was told that in this Holy Office it is not customary to seize any person without sufficient evidence of having done, said, or committed, or seen done, said, or committed by others, anything that may be or appear to be against our Holy Catholic Faith; against the evangelical law that the Holy Mother Roman Catholic Church holds, preaches, follows, and teaches; or against the lawful and free exercise of the Holy Office. Therefore, if she has been imprisoned, she must believe that evidence of a fault of this nature has been presented against her. So for reverence of God our Lord and of his blessed and glorious mother our Lady the Virgin Mary, she is admonished and charged to examine her memory and say and confess the whole truth of anything about which she feels guilty or knows of other people, whoever they are, without covering up things about herself or about others, and without giving false testimony about herself or about others. Because if she does this [tells the truth] she will discharge her conscience as a Catholic Christian, and she will save her soul, and her case will be dispatched with all the brevity and mercy possible, as the Holy Office is accustomed to use with good and truthful confessants.[19]

And being given to understand this admonition she said that she doesn't remember anything else about what she has said. And with that the audience ceased and this was read to her, which she approved and signed. And heavily admonished that she examine her memory she was ordered to return to her cell.

[signed] Marina de San Miguel
It passed before me Pedro de Manozca

In the city of Mexico, Tuesday, November 24, 1598. The Lord Inquisitor *licenciado* don Alonso de Peralta in his afternoon audience ordered Marina de San Miguel to be brought from her cell.

And when she was present she was told that if she has remembered anything in her case to say it, and the truth, under the oath she made.

She said that what she has remembered is that in the course of her life some spiritual things have happened to her, which she has talked about to some people. And she believes that they have been the cause of her imprisonment, because they were scandalized by what she told them. And the things that happened are these. Well, since her childhood she has had an exercise of mental prayer, in which she always felt great gifts from our Lord. And eight years ago on Palm Sunday, during the night, when she was sleeping (because she goes to bed with a desire to love and serve God) she was awakened and felt and then said she saw with her interior eyes[20] Christ crucified. And he came so close to her that it seemed to her that the body of Christ our Redeemer and her body were united, and appeared not two bodies but one. And at the same moment she felt in her hands and in her feet the burning of fire.[21] In her feet it began in the soles and moved to the other part, and in the hands, on the contrary, the fire began on top of the hand and then passed to the palm. And in her heart, in the same manner as happened with the said burning, she felt an intense interior pain that reached down into her bones. The pain lasted from midnight, when she saw (as she has said) the figure of our Redeemer Jesus Christ, until the dawn. And she could not sleep because the pain was so great that she wanted to cry out, but did not because she did not want to reveal the cause. And two whole years she had the pain from time to time, some days more than others. And the fire and pain in her heart have lasted until today, so that her heart seems wounded. Thus every time she remembers the vision her heart and her left arm tremble.

And thus while I was writing this she began to shake, and raised her hands and lifted her eyes to heaven and then lowered them, smiling and saying many loving words to our Lord Jesus Christ. ... She remained in a trance, hands down, inclining her head to the left side. ... And in the same trance she tried with great force to free her hands, and she could not, even though she used much force. Once her hands were untied she opened them and said, "My sweet Jesus, stretch out thy hand; because thou art so good everyone loves thee."[22] And she returned to being in a trance, with her arms open and raised and her eyes and face lifted to heaven, and her mouth a little open as though laughing, and her body inclined toward the right side. Later she put her hands together again with her fingers crossed and seemed as though sleeping.

And the Lord Inquisitor ordered that until the trance stopped no one speak nor say anything, and that I the secretary be on the lookout and write down whatever might succeed.

And then she opened her eyes and began to shake and get up from the bench on which she was seated, saying, "My love, help me God, how strongly you have given me this."[23] And among these words she said to the Lord Inquisitor that when she is given these trances, she should be shaken vigorously to awaken her from her deep dream. Then she returned to being as though sleeping. The inquisitor called her by her name and she did not respond, nor the second time. And the third time she opened her eyes and made faces, and made signs with her hands to her mouth. And then she returned again to being as though asleep. And with a tremble she moaned to herself, without saying anything other than seeming to mumble.[24] And the Lord Inquisitor ordered me, the secretary, to call her, because she was next to me, but she did not respond. The trance lasted for near a half hour, and having called her and pulled her right arm two or three times, she woke up with much happiness, saying that we should pull hard so that she could stretch her senses and pull them away from God. Then she asked God license, to permit that, "this little body return to earth," and that her imagination not be so uplifted. And then, beginning to say, "Sweet Jesus, love of my soul," she returned to being transported, and then asked again that we pull on her arm. She said she would try to pay attention but that she wanted to show the gifts that our Lord has given her even after she was imprisoned.

And returning to full presence in herself, she said that on Palm Saturday shortly after dark she lay down on her bed. Being awake adoring God, she heard an interior voice that said, "Make the betrothals." And then she saw, internally, our Redeemer Jesus Christ in the form of a youth dressed in white. He grasped her hand, and then the vision disappeared. And she understood that this had been a betrothal, which the wisdom of God had given her to understand. And she was left with an interior rapture, and did not return to herself until the morning of Easter Sunday. ...

And with this it appeared that she might go into another trance, and the Lord Inquisitor ordered her to be attentive. ... And because it was already close to six, the audience ceased, and having been read the above, she approved it and signed it.

And heavily admonished that she go and reexamine her memory, she was ordered to be taken to her cell. ...

[signatures]

### 7.4  *Fourth Confession*

In the city of Mexico, Wednesday, November 25, 1598, the Lord Inquisitor *licenciado* don Alonso de Peralta in his morning audience ordered that Marina de San Miguel be brought before him from her cell. And when she was present she was told that if she had remembered anything, she should say it, and the truth, under the oath that she swore. ...

She said that four years ago her interior body was enraptured another time, and she found herself in a place which was purgatory, which was told to her by the youth to whom she was betrothed. ... In that place she saw many people walking, like human bodies, because God shows things in accordance with the understanding of man. And some of the bodies were in the middle of fires, and others were in holes like wells, which were full of something black which seemed to be boiling tar. Some of them were in it up to their waists, others up to their chests, and others so far that only the tops of their heads could be seen. And others she saw in a lake of bubbling, boiling water, in the same way, and they were quiet and peaceful. And what astonished her most was that they did not take up space, which she didn't understand. And in the same place she saw streets, and in them some priests in vestments, and others with their dalmatics (*dalmáticas*), and these were the priests who say masses for souls. And the holy water that they throw in churches reaches the souls. And the youth dressed in white, whom she takes for Christ our Redeemer, told her that the souls feel very refreshed by masses and holy water. And he wanted to give her some grace, allowing her to bless the souls; and so she did it, and the souls that were already ready to be freed from their pains went to heaven. And there were many saved, because she was carried through all the streets three times, and afterward she found herself very tired. And she heard, internally, that in very clear voices the souls said these words: "Maiden of God, have mercy,"[25] asking her to hurry and bless them, and at the same time they cried out to her, "Our Redemptress." This gave her pain, because she did not like that they called her by the name that belongs to our Redeemer Jesus Christ. And she told this to Friar Andrés de la Cruz, a discalced brother of the Order of Lord Saint Francis, who went to *la China*. He told her that this could be understood as God's using her as the means for removing souls from the pains of purgatory. ...

She said that about a week before she saw purgatory, she was enraptured by our Redeemer Jesus Christ in the form of the youth, except that instead of being dressed in white he was dressed in purple. And he took her "interior man" to a place in which she saw three large jars, all the same, made out of white and gold metal. And Christ our Redeemer said to her, daughter, this is the inn where they say the bride was taken and made drunk with the wine of love. ... And she remembers that the drink left her so drunk with the love of God, and the strength of her "interior man" was so great that it seemed he flew to heaven.

She says that after she was imprisoned in this Inquisition God gave her many mercies, and gave her in her cell so much company that she sees internally in her presence many circles of angels and saints, who appear as if in a sketch, in such a way that in one moment she sees them clearly and resplendently; and then they cover themselves, so that she sees only some things, as if they are in shadow. ...

She said that yesterday she was very afflicted because she could not discover what to say, nor how to begin.[26] Between eleven and twelve in the morning our Redeemer Jesus Christ appeared to her in her cell, glorious as they paint him in the resurrection, and seated on the sun with much brilliance. ...

She was told that she already knows how she was admonished in the last audience. ... Therefore now for the second time she is admonished in the same way. ...

She said that with all her heart and her will, if she knew what was against her she would say it; and she said that she will reexamine her memory.

And with this, because it was close to twelve, the audience ceased. And having been read it, she approved it and signed it. And admonished to reexamine her memory she was ordered to returned to her cell.

[signatures]

### 7.5   Fifth Confession

In the city of Mexico, Friday, November 27, 1598, the Lord Inquisitor *licenciado* don Alonso de Peralta in his morning audience ordered that Marina de San Miguel be brought from her cell. And when she was present she was told that the *alcaide* said that she was asking for an audience; and that she should say why she asked for it, and tell the truth under the oath that she has already sworn.

She said that she asked for the audience to tell and declare something of which it seems the Mother of God has reminded her. That is that for nine years she has eaten meat on all prohibited days, with license of a physician and of the *provisor*. And she has reexamined her memory about the things she was told to reexamine, and the Lord did not enlighten her about them.

She was told that she already knows how she was admonished ... and with this she was admonished for the third and final time.

She said that she asks for the love of God that the accusation be delayed so that she may reexamine her memory.

With this the audience ceased and having been read it she approved and signed. And admonished to reexamine her memory as she has offered to do, she was ordered to return to her cell.

[signatures]

### 7.6a   Sixth Confession

In the city of Mexico, Monday, January 25, 1599, the Lord Inquisitor *licenciado* don Alonso de Peralta in his morning audience ordered that Marina de San Miguel be brought from her cell. And when she was present she was told that the *alcaide* said that she asks for an audience, and that she should declare why she wanted it, and tell the truth under the oath she has made.

She said that it's like this. ... She has been condemned to hell, because for fifteen years she has had a sensual temptation of the flesh, which makes her perform dishonest acts with her own hands on her shameful parts. She came to pollution[27] saying dishonest words that provoke lust, calling by their dishonest names many dirty and lascivious things. She was tempted to this by the devil, who appeared to her internally in the form of an Angel of Light, who told her that she should do these things, because they were no sin. This was to make her abandon her scruples. And the devil appeared to her in the form of Christ our Redeemer, in such a way that she might uncover her breasts and have carnal union with him. And thus, for fifteen years, she has had carnal union occasionally from month to month, or every two months. And if it had been more she would accuse herself of that too, because she is only trying to save her soul, with no regard to honor or the world. And the carnal act that the devil as Angel of Light and in the form of Christ had with her was the same as if she had had it with a man. And he kissed her, and she enjoyed it, and she felt a great ardor in her whole body, with particular delight and pleasure. And the contact with herself, and the pollutions, were more frequent than what she had with the devil. And the devil told her when she resisted him, "This will make you abandon your scruples" ... and he wouldn't let her confess. And thus for fifteen years she received communion twice each week and sometimes three times, on Wednesdays, Fridays, and Sundays, and on Easter. And she felt a great hunger for the holy sacrament, and wanted to receive it, though she had not confessed the said sins. And she did not confess them because the demon told her not to have scruples, and that she should not confess because of them. And also, because sometimes she imagined that this was the work of the devil and did not want her confessor to know that she treated with the devil.

She said that for about twenty years she had a relationship with Juan Núñez, accountant (*balanzario*), as a spiritual brother. And this relationship lasted until about six years ago. And he talked to her about God, and about loving him, and about resignation to his will. And while they were talking like this he kissed and hugged her, and put his tongue in her mouth, and felt her breasts and shameful parts, saying, "All of this is earth." And once he put his finger in her shameful parts, and he said it was just to see whether she was a *doncella*. And now she remembers that this happened twice. And three times Juan Núñez showed her his shameful parts and made her touch them, and she touching them came to pollution. And she doesn't know whether he did. And he told her that all of these things were earth, and could be done if they were not done with an evil intention or will. And about twelve or thirteen years ago, she was dressed and lying on her bed when Juan Núñez arrived and hugged her. And after hugging her he threw himself upon her. She resisted and got up from the bed and said to him, "Brother, what you did makes me afraid." And he said, "Sister, you resisted strongly. I did it only to tempt you." And he never again made this demonstration. And in the twenty years that she knew Juan Núñez she saw him once each week. Kissing her and putting his tongue in her mouth, and hugging her and touching her breasts he did commonly; but touching her shameful parts was not ordinary. And about ten years ago Juan Núñez asked her to show him her shameful parts, and she consented, believing that he wanted to see whether she was a *doncella*. And thus she took a candle in her hands and raised her chemise, being seated on a cushion. And he saw her shameful parts, and did nothing but smile. And later, they talked about spiritual things, talking about the love of God, with the will to always love him and one's neighbour. And she had a bad suspicion about Juan Núñez, because he told her that he did not esteem penances, like fasts, disciplines, and hair shirts. Because he esteemed loving God more; and thus he told her not to believe in penances, but only in love, because penance without love is worth nothing, and for now this is what she remembers happened with Juan Núñez.

She said that from her relationship with Juan Núñez she learned the custom of kissing and hugging, and thus she kissed and hugged Alonso Gutiérrez whom she has said is her nephew. She has no family relation with him, other than that he is her spiritual son. And he hugged and kissed her with purity of conscience as when two children kiss. And he said to her, "Mother, I love you very much in the Lord." And she responded to him, "God make you holy and pure of heart." And she never had any sensual delight with him; and she does not know whether Alonso Gutiérrez had with her.

And because the hour was over, the audience ceased, and having been read this, she approved it and signed it. And admonished to go on reexamining her memory for the afternoon audience, she was taken to her cell.

[signatures]

### 7.6b  Sixth Confession (continued)

In the city of Mexico, Monday, January 25, 1599, the Lord Inquisitor *licenciado* don Alonso de Peralta in his afternoon audience ordered that Marina de San Miguel be brought from her cell. And when she was present she was told to continue with whatever else she had to say, and to tell the truth under the oath that she had already sworn.

She said that as a weak and miserable woman, she allowed herself to be tricked by the devil for the whole time that she had the dishonest relationship with him. And thus from shame she did not confess. And she received communion in a state of sin. And she has nothing else to say.

And later she asked that the interview end until tomorrow, as she wishes to reexamine her memory to say what she knows and to discharge her conscience. With this the audience ceased and having been read this she approved it and signed. And admonished to reexamine her memory, as she has offered, in order to proceed with all purity and truth, she was ordered to return to her cell.

[signatures]

### 7.7a Seventh Confession

In the city of Mexico, Tuesday, January 26, 1599, the Lord Inquisitor *licenciado* don Alonso de Peralta in his morning audience ordered that Marina de San Miguel be brought before him. And when she was present she was told that if she has remembered anything in her case she should declare it, and the truth, under the oath she has sworn.

She said that she believed that the devil was our Redeemer Jesus Christ when he appeared to her in that form, and he offered her his heart and soul, saying that they should trade hearts and souls so that she could become more perfect in her heart. And afterward it became clear that this offering had been made to the devil. And she saw this clearly fifteen days ago, because he showed himself to her in his demonic figure. She saw him with her bodily eyes, and with him many demons with snouts and ugly bodies and *guirnaldas*[28] with silver and brilliance, sticking out their tongues and breathing fire, though only a little. And they lifted her with her bed three or four times each day, and she was very afflicted and asked the *alcaide* to send her a confessor because the demons were taking her. And being lifted by these evil spirits, she heard a proclamation that said, "This is the justice that is ordered to be given to Marina de San Miguel, *beata*: That she be taken to hell for hiding her sins from her confessor and treating with the devil and receiving the holy sacrament so many times as she has said in such a bad state." And wanting to defend herself she said that she was not sure that it was the devil, nor that she was receiving communion in mortal sin; and that as an evil one he had tricked her. And they [the demons] responded that they had won her in fair battle and that there was no remedy for it, because the sentence had been handed down in the tribunal of God. And that even should she confess in the Holy Office, it was already too late and the confession would not be valid. And she did not confess these things when she first came before this tribunal because she did not know as she does now that they were all illusions of the devil, and she has nothing more to say.

She was asked who was the demon with whom she had a relationship for fifteen years, and of what legion.

She said that he was called Satan, and that he was of the legion of seraphim. … The other two they called Barrabus and Beelzebub pursued and tricked her. But the one with whom she had carnal contact was Satan.

She was asked how—having said in yesterday's afternoon audience that as a weak and miserable woman she allowed herself to be tricked by the devil for the whole time that she has said she had the dishonest relationship with him, and having said that out of shame she didn't confess it, and received communion in a state of sin—now she says that she did not know for certain that it was the devil, nor that she was receiving communion with any fear of mortal sin. See the contradiction there and assent in the truth.

She said that she neither wanted to lie in discharging her conscience nor to avoid telling the truth. And thus she asks and begs our Lady the Virgin Mary to light up her understanding. And the truth is, that she, as a bad woman, wanted to appear holy without being so, and she received communion to appear so. And she has no more to say.

She was told to satisfy the question, and if she knew for fifteen years that the love and relationship she had was with the devil, and whether she knew that she received communion in a bad state.

She said that she did not know until she came to the Holy Office, as she has said, but that she felt certain scruples and suspicions about whether it was the devil or not, and shame made her too uncomfortable to confess it, and also [she avoided confessing] so her confessor would not know that she treated with the devil. … And she spoke badly in saying that she clearly knew that she had been tricked by the devil and that she had received communion in a bad state.

She was asked how she could ignore that the things she has declared, being so dirty, obscene, and dishonest, could be anything but from the devil. And thus it can be clearly seen that she is hiding from the path of truth, and that after she determined to confess these things, later she regretted it, and this gives birth to her contradictions. Such that when she lived with the intent of appearing holy, without being so, and having a suspicion that these things were demonic, and not confessing them out of shame, she could not possibly fail to believe that she was receiving communion in mortal sin. Nor can one presume that she did not clearly know that her own acts and dishonest touchings, which brought her so many times to pollution, were very grave sins, which must be confessed if one is to avoid knowingly receiving communion in a bad state.

She said that it is true that she knew that all the carnal and obscene things she has confessed, the union with the devil and having carnal copulation with him as well as her own dishonest acts with which she came to pollution, were bad and grave sins. But as a weak and miserable woman she fell into them, and for discomfort and shame she did not confess them. Because as she was held holy, she wanted to hide her weaknesses. And thus she received communion knowing that she was in mortal sin. And she ratifies this now, and it is the truth, and the devil made her wander into these contradictions.

She was asked what other things happened with Juan Núñez, *balanzario*, and Alonso Gutiérrez. And that as

she has decided to proceed with purity, she should tell the whole truth, because as she had no shame in offending our Redeemer Jesus Christ, she should not have it in confessing her sins, which is the principal remedy for the salvation of her soul. And moreover, from today on she should abandon raptures and illusions, as the devil cannot counsel any good thing. And thus in no way should she give him credit, nor should she despair of the mercy of God, because as grave and enormous as her sins are, his mercy is much greater. And thus if he is served to not take her in such a bad state, and to bring her before this holy tribunal, she should have great confidence that it is so she might come to know her misery and misfortunes and beg him with a true heart to use with her his accustomed mercy, giving her strength to defend herself from the snares of the enemy in whose trap[29] she was for so long.

She said that she has said what happened with Juan Núñez and Alonso Gutiérrez, and that if any other thing had happened she would say it, because she must give account to God.

She was asked if she knew that the kisses and hugs that she gave to Juan Núñez and Alonso Gutiérrez could not be given without sinning mortally, because she gave them delighting in them, and because with her contacts with Juan Núñez she came to pollution the times that she has declared.

She said that she didn't believe that she sinned mortally in these things, because she had no intention of doing them to enjoy them, but rather did them because she was melancholy. She did them with pure love and clean intention, because as Saint Augustine says, the sin is in the bad intention and will. And once Juan Núñez told her this, and that the things that he did were earth, and that he did not do them with the intention of sinning with her, but for mortification; and she took this to heart and believed it until now … and he embraced her and gave her so many kisses and hugs with a fire so spiritual that he seemed like an angel. And when he came to her shameful parts and to her breasts and legs he said, "Unless you become as children you shall not enter the kingdom of heaven," and, "To the pure all things are pure." He said this to mean that as children with purity of heart and sincerity kiss each other and touch their shameful parts, he with the same sincerity did these things without dirty or obscene words. And later he returned to talking about very beautiful affairs of God, like a man drunk with his love, so inflamed that his ears and face were the color of *grana*.

She was asked how she could have good intentions when she enjoyed the touching, hugging, and kissing and came to pollution. Because even if the first time she thought it good, it cannot be excused because of the danger it put her in. And her own touchings of her shameful parts are sin; and seeing that she came to an act so abominable, one must punish it severely and believe that even the first time she sinned mortally, because of what followed, when she returned to the pollutions and enjoyed them, not only with the kisses which under some pretext can be reduced to good intention without attributing them to evil; but with an act as lascivious as putting the tongue in the mouth, which cannot appear anything but carnality. And even more, having contacts so dishonest in the shameful parts, and having so little shame, born of the greatest misery that has ever been seen or heard or come to human understanding, as to take a candle to look at them [her genitals]. From which it is clearly seen that things went farther and that she went along with similar things, acts, and occasions. It is impossible that things went no farther than what she has declared, and thus she is admonished to tell the truth so that it may be seen that she is telling the truth and repents her past life.

She said that she has told the truth and that nothing more happened with Juan Núñez, and that she did not know at the time that it was a sin, because the relationship[30] was holy and good. And she never had the goal of offending God with her will and intention. Neither did anything more happen with Alonso Gutiérrez, and she remembers now that twice when she kissed Alonso Gutiérrez it gave her the desire to have him touch her breasts, but she did not tell him, nor did he do it. And last night the demons told her that she is condemned for having spoken against Juan Núñez and defaming him; because the things that she told about him here in the tribunal of the Inquisition should have been [told] in a confessional.

And because it was very close to twelve the audience ceased, and having been read she approved it and signed. And admonished to go reexamining her memory, she was taken to her cell.

[signatures]

## 7.7b  *Seventh Confession (continued)*

In the city of Mexico, Tuesday, January 26, 1599, the Lord Inquisitor *licenciado* don Alonso de Peralta in his afternoon audience ordered that Marina de San Miguel be brought from her cell. And when she was present she was told that the *alcaide* said she had asked for an audience, and that she should declare the reason, and the truth, under the oath she swore.

She said that she asked for [the audience] to say that at the age of sixteen she took a vow of chastity in the Mercedarian monastery in the city of Seville, on our Lady's day in September;[31] and thus she has broken her vow with all her obscene, carnal, and dishonest acts, and at the same time she has concealed the existence of the vow in her sacramental confessions. And she doesn't remember anything else, and for this reason she asked for this audience.

She was asked if she has felt bad about anything related to our Holy Catholic Faith or if she has had any doubts about it.

She said that she has never felt bad about the faith, although she has had certain temptations about it, wondering if there is a heaven, and if it is true that there was a Mother of God and Jesus Christ her son; but she never consented with her deliberate reason in thinking that they did not exist, although she had some lukewarmness in believing it, which she attributed to the devil and confessed to her confessor. And what she [also] thought was that God could remove those condemned to hell from there, and lift them to glory; and she received much comfort in not seeing souls condemned. This lasted until she learned that the church holds the contrary, because in hell there is no redemption, and with this she was sure. But from time to time temptations came to her about whether or not condemned souls could be saved, even though she did not allow herself to believe the contrary of what the Holy Mother Roman Catholic Church holds.

She was asked what she felt about the sacraments of penance and communion.

She said that she felt very good about them.

She was asked if she knew that to receive the sacrament of penance, one must feel pain for and repent one's sins, and have a firm purpose of not returning to them; and that confession must be complete, without hiding any sin or circumstance which might aggravate or change their substance and kind.

She said that she knew this and she knows that all the requisites contained in the question are necessary to achieve the sacrament of penance.

She was asked if she knew that the consecrated host was the true body of our Redeemer Jesus Christ; and that to receive such a high sacrament great purity and cleanness of conscience are necessary.

She said that she knew this and she knows very clearly the contents of the question.

She was asked if she knew all the above-said, how has she used the sacraments so poorly, using them when she was in mortal sin, and adding sin to sin, hiding them so as not to lose her reputation with her confessors; coming to eat the bread of the angels so many and diverse times that it seems she could not commit sins so entrenched[32] if she had the beliefs that she says she has and had about the sacraments.

She said that she firmly believed and believes that the body of our Redeemer Jesus Christ is in the consecrated Host, but as a sinner and a weak woman she dared to take the sacraments with a bad conscience, and not because she doubted them.

She was asked if she has believed that our redeemer and saviour Jesus Christ could do anything that might be evil or imperfect.

She said no.

She was asked what moved her to say that when she had carnal copulation with the devil who appeared as an angel of light and as our Redeemer, she believed that it was with His Divine Majesty, a thing which shocks and offends the ears even to think about it.

She said that when the devil had carnal copulation with her in the form of Christ, later she imagined that it was Christ, and then when she came to her senses she realized that as such a friend of virgins and of purity, Christ our Redeemer would find impossible a dishonest act or any imperfect thing, and thus she believes that it was the devil. And from shame she did not confess it to her confessors (as she has said) so they would not know that she had been involved with the devil, and every time that the devil came to her, evilly putting himself in the form of Christ, she had doubts about whether it was Christ or the devil. But considering that Christ could not sin, she saw clearly that it was the devil, from which she received much pain and affliction; and when the said vision took a long time to come and have carnal copulation with her, she was happy and said to herself, "It is not coming," and gave thanks to God.

She was asked if she saw the devil with her bodily eyes the times that he appeared to her in the form that she has declared, and what they talked about, aside from having copulation.

She said that she did not see him with her exterior eyes, but rather that she was enraptured in such a way that she saw him in the form that she has declared, stuck to and united with her performing the carnal act, in such a way that she felt it in the way she has said, as if she were with a man. And she came to pollution as she could come with him [a man], without feeling on top of her any corporeal thing, other than that without being [corporeal] he [the devil] used force to have carnal copulation with her. And thus she had it, without being able to resist it. And at the same time she remembers that when (as she has said) she touched herself dishonestly, the same devil forced her to do it; and thus she did it many times against her will.

She said she has not lied in all that she has said about lights that she has seen and things that have happened to her, but that the devil made them appear to her to trick her, even though he never told her he was Christ our Redeemer, other than that she saw his figure and the other lights that she has declared. And she only stretched her story in saying that when she woke up with Christ she saw his form, because she did not see it, but rather, enraptured, internally heard an interior speech which said, "Make the betrothal," without seeing who spoke. And at the same time she stretched the truth when she said that when she saw purgatory she saw the figure of Christ, because she did not, only a body in the form of a youth, without being able to make out his face perfectly. And the trances that she has had have been with the aid of the devil. And she faked much of what happened, and thus she faked here in the tribunal, and made a demonstration of how she was enraptured, doing the same thing that she is accustomed to do in her house. For this she begs mercy, and subjects herself to the correction of this Holy Office.

She was asked which things in particular concerning the love of God Juan Núñez talked about with her, and who was the person who taught him these things, and which persons other than Juan Núñez and Alonso Gutierrez have spoken with her about prayer and the love of God.

She said that Juan Núñez talked to her about mystical theology and God's Union,[33] and gave her a book. … And because Juan Núñez is so well read, he knows many things about prayer and contemplation, and he gave her account of them, which in particular she does not remember. And Juan Núñez was the first who taught her the road of love of God and his union. And she has talked about these things, about devotion to the love of God and his union, with friars of all orders except the Mercedarian. And with Alonso Gutiérrez she has not spoken anything other than what she has declared.

She was asked if, with any of the persons with whom she talked of the union and love of God, she had hugs, kisses, dishonest touches, and pollutions, of the type that she has declared having with Juan Núñez, saying that because he had no intent and will to offend God, it was no sin.

She said that the contents of the question never happened with anyone but Juan Núñez.

She was asked to say whether she truly saw the things she has declared, lights and visions, because it appears to be her fabrication, especially because she said that she was enraptured and taken to purgatory where she was taken through many streets, and that when she returned to herself she was very tired from so much walking, but she did not walk corporeally, but only in spirit, as she has said and declared.

She said that she felt much fatigue when she returned to herself, and she does not know what occasioned it, only that God must have permitted it. With this the audience ceased and having read it she approved and signed.

[signatures]

### 7.8  *Eighth Confession*

In the city of Mexico, Wednesday, January 27, 1599, the Lord Inquisitor in his afternoon audience ordered Marina de San Miguel to be brought from her cell. And when she was present she was told that if she has remembered anything she should say it, and the truth, under the oath she made.

She said that what she has remembered is that when she was talking about devotion to the love and union of God with a friar of the Order of the blessed Saint Dominic called fray Juan Baptista Gazete, who is now in *la China,* they hugged and kissed the times that he came to her house, for the two years that they knew each other. She does not remember the times, other than that it wasn't ordinary but only every fifteen days, about eight years ago. And although he brought a companion, he didn't see the kisses, because they gave them cautiously. And she does not remember if there were any alterations,[34] but she remembers well that there were no dishonest words, only the hugs and kisses. And if the said friar had alterations, they were not apparent.

She was asked whether fray Juan Baptista Gazete told her that they could kiss and hug in the manner that she was taught by Juan Núñez, having good intentions.

She said he did not tell her whether it was good or bad.

She was asked if when she thought about whether heaven existed, and whether it was true that the Mother of God and her precious son existed, if she ever came to the point of doubting it, or whether she believed it, even in a lukewarm fashion.

She said that she did not doubt the said things, other than that it was a temptation she had, and some lukewarmness in belief, until she came to her senses, and afterward she believed it firmly.

She was asked how many times she had the lukewarmness in believing, and how she could avoid having doubts.

She said that it befell her only once, and that if she had any doubt, [it was when] she was enraptured by this temptation without being in her senses, but coming back to her senses she believed firmly in all the said things.

She was asked to say and declare if she believed that it was Christ our Redeemer the times that she had carnal copulation with the devil appearing in the form of Christ, because—aside from having said that she believed it (although later she said no)—considering that our Redeemer is the highest good and such a friend of cleanness and of virgins, she must have known clearly that it was the devil. But all the times she had the copulation with the devil in the form of Christ she doubted whether it was the devil or not, from which doubts one can infer that she did not believe as firmly as she ought to have that such things could not possibly be from Christ. In this she should urgently discharge her conscience.

She said that the thought whether it was Christ or the devil came to her memory without her wanting it; and thus she was tempted in this by the devil, but when she returned to her senses she firmly believed that it was his work, and not Christ's, because he is the highest good and a friend of cleanliness and chastity.

She was asked whether when she believed that God could take someone out of hell, she thought it was with his absolute potency, or his ordinary.

She said that she thought that he could do it with his absolute potency, because for God nothing is impossible. And afterward she learned that the Church says that in hell there is no redemption; and thus for this reason she stopped believing that God would take anyone out [of hell], not because he could not, but because of what the Church says, and the Catholic faith, and because she knows that if a seraph comes and says things against what the Church says, one must not believe it but rather throw him out as a bad spirit.

She was told that she answers very well. …

And with this the audience ended, and having been read it she approved and signed. And admonished to reexamine her memory she was ordered taken to her cell.

*do they doubt her sincerity?*

[signatures]

### 7.9   *Ninth Confession*

In the city of Mexico, Friday, January 28, 1599, the Lord Inquisitor *licenciado* don Alonso de Peralta in his morning audience ordered Marina de San Miguel to be brought before him. And when she was present she was told that the *alcaide* said she had asked for an audience, and that she should declare why she wanted it, and the truth, under the oath that she swore.

She said that she asked for it to say and manifest that the other day for shame she did not say that she had a friendship with a certain *beata*, who died two years ago, who also had made a vow of chastity. And commonly when they would see one another they would kiss and hug, and put their hands on their breasts. And she remembers that with the kisses, hugs, and touching on the breasts she came to pollution ten or twelve times. And she doesn't know whether the *beata* felt it, nor what effect these things had on her. And she [Marina] knowing these things were sins, determined to confess

them, although later she did not confess them to her confessors because it seemed to her that she had not sinned mortally because she had no intention of doing so. And although sometimes she had a scruple, shame made her not confess [the sins], and at the same time receive the Holy Sacrament.

She was asked if in the hugs, kisses, and touches any amorous or dishonest words were said.

She said that amorous words were said, and that she said to the other woman, "Mother of my soul and of my life," but no dishonest ones.

She was asked, if she didn't take these things for sins, as she had no desire and will to come to pollution, why she had a scruple.

She said that because she felt that this was a weakness, it gave her a scruple about whether it was a sin or not. And afterward she looked on the bright side[35] and decided to believe that it was no sin; and this removed all her scruples, and she lived in great peace with herself.

She was asked how she could quiet her conscience, not having talked about her scruples with anyone who might enlighten her, especially as she had formed them, and knowing clearly that what obliged her not to confess them was shame; and not confessing them was not looking on the bright side, but rather on the dark side, because in doubt one must incline to the more secure side. From which one infers that she did not sin out of ignorance, but out of malice. And thus she is admonished on behalf of God our Lord to discharge her conscience, making a clear and pure confession so that one sees that she proceeds with purity and procures the remedy of her soul.

She said that she refers to what she has confessed, and that she remembers that the devil, about fifteen or sixteen years ago, incited her to take a mirror, being alone, and to look at her shameful parts, which she did eight or ten times, six with interior touchings, and two times she had pollution, and the other times there was no touching. And she did not confess these things because she did not do them with the motive of offending God, but rather before she gave thanks for having created the said things, and putting them in order for the increase of creatures. And thus the lewd things she sees in little animals serve to remind her of God and to give him thanks for having put everything in such order.

She was asked how she could ignore sinning in the said things when she says she did them incited by the devil, *by the devil*,[36] aside from which she knows that in such things one sins mortally by seeing them; even without touches so lewd and dishonest, with which she came to pollution voluntarily. Because at the point when she determined to have the said touches, she decided also to have the pollutions which followed from them.

She said that she says clearly that she believed she did not offend God in these things, although she knew that she sinned with her sight and with all the other things that she did (as she has confessed), but as she had no intention of offending God nor did she consent to it, and she spoke poorly in saying that the devil tempted her, because she didn't know whether it was he, or nature itself.

She was asked if she knew that she offended God in the said things, that she say and declare how she could have good intentions and not give consent; when she delighted in her shameful parts she put it in execution, taking a mirror to look at them, from which came the temptation of the flesh and the putting into execution. Things, so abominable and lewd, that even the devil himself would be offended by them. ...

She said that it is true that she consented in these things and put them into execution, but she did not believe that she offended God because she did not have the intention of offending him.

She was asked if these things of hers are evil and offend God, and she put them in execution, how could she believe that she did not offend him because she had no will to offend him. Well, it is an impossible case. On one hand she consents in a sin and put it into action, offending our Lord gravely; and on the other hand she had no intention of offending him.

She said that she always based herself on the interior will, with which she determined not to consent to the said things even though she put them into play.

She was asked, if she were to go to bed with a man and have carnal union with him, if she would sin mortally, even though she might not consent with her interior will.

She said that she would sin, because she clearly sees the danger in something declared to be against God.

She was asked, if thus she would sin, what difference is there in the case between the proposed case, and what she has done, which one cannot deny is a thing against what God has ordered; rather the sin she has committed is worse, because it is against nature, and the danger [in it] can be seen clearly as with the touches, kisses, and hugs [with which] she came so many times to pollution.

She said that then she was in bestiality, and now through the questions that have been put to her it is clear how blind she has been.

And admonished that she still go reexamining her memory and discharge her conscience, she was ordered taken to her cell.

[signatures]

In the city of Mexico, Tuesday, Day of the Purification of our Lady, February 2, 1599, the Lord Inquisitor in his afternoon audience ordered Marina de San Miguel brought before him. And once present she was told that if she has remembered anything in her case she should say it, and the truth, under the oath that she has made.

She said no.

She was told that she should understand that the *promotor fiscal* of this Holy Office wants to pose the accusation, and that before it is posed she would be best off to say and confess the whole truth as she has been admonished, because thus there will be more room to use with her mercy. ...

She said she had no more to say.

## NOTES

*Acknowledgments* The research for and translation of this document were completed with the generous support of the Social Sciences and Humanities Research Council of Canada.

1. New Spain included modern-day Mexico, large parts of Central America, parts of what is now the southwestern United States, and the Philippines. I say "ostensible" authority because it was virtually impossible to police such a large and diverse area.

2. This document can be found in Mexico City in the. Archivo General de la Nación, Ramo Inquisition, Vol. 210, Exp. 3, ff. 307–430. The

confessions translated here are found in folios 347r–72v.

3. There are few studies in English of colonial Spanish American women's encounters with the Inquisition. The suggestions for further reading I have listed at the end of the document will provide an introduction to the Inquisition in colonial Mexico and to inquisitorial investigations of religious women in Europe for those interested in pursuing this subject further.

4. Literally, "que oficio tiene," or "what office she holds" the standard formulation, in the sixteenth century, for the question "What does she do?"

5. A *beata* was a semireligious woman who devoted her life to God. *Beatas* generally wore habits and lived chastely, either in communities or in private homes. Unlike nuns, *beatas* were not obliged to take solemn vows of poverty, chastity, and obedience; nor were they obliged to follow a rule. Many did take simple vows, allying themselves with one of the religious orders. Marina allied herself with the Order of Saint Dominic, an important order in Spanish America.

6. Literally, in "working" (*labrar*), which when used by women refers to work with the needle.

7. Literally, uncles and aunts, siblings of father.

8. In the sixteenth century, Catholics were to attend mass on Sundays and holy days. Though holy days varied from region to region, there generally were about fifty. Confession and communion were obligatory only at Easter; but many people, particularly women, received communion much more frequently than that.

9. Literally, in "romance," as opposed to Latin.

10. That is, in the house of her parents, not in Córdoba. As we will see, they changed their house several times.

11. Literally, having gained something to eat (*ganado de comer*).

12. Marina's testimony does not make clear whether her father and his wife remained together after the adultery and murder.

13. Here the notary has transcribed the testimony verbatim as Marina corrected herself.

14. Juan Núñez de León was accountant of the Royal Treasury, a wealthy and important man. He too was tried and disciplined by the Inquisition (AGN 210, Exp. 2).

15. A suspect's goods were often sequestered for the duration of the trial; any fines levied could be taken from the sale of the sequestered goods.

16. 16. This apparently rambling and irrelevant information shows that Marina was clearly thinking forward to what might occur when bailiffs went to her home to seize her property. She was anticipating that Gutiérrez would be able to keep his property—and perhaps some of hers, if he claimed it—out of the hands of the Holy Office. By detailing his spending on her house, she was presumably attempting to cast it as an encumbered asset that the bailiffs could not with impunity seize.

17. Gregorio López was arguably sixteenth-century Mexico's most famous mystic and was regarded by many contemporaries as a saint.

18. Literally men (*hombres*), but here used in its "universal" sense to include all people.

19. This was a standard admonition given to overcome confessants' reticence.

20. That is, not physically, but in a vision.

21. Literally, "cauterios de fuego", or "cauterization."

22. Here Marina was using the familiar form of address, expressing intimacy.

23. "Que fuertemente me ha dado esto."

24. Literally, to speak through her teeth (*hablar entre dientes*).

25. Literally, give alms (*hazed limosna*).

26. Literally, to have light where to begin (*tener lumbre por donde empeçar*).

27. That is, experienced orgasm.

28. *Guirnaldas* were flowers and fragrant herbs woven into a garland to adorn the head. The sense here is that "with silver and brilliance" they dramatize the grotesqueness of the demons.

29. Literally, lasso (*lazo*).

30. "Trato", which could mean either the relationship or the discussion.

31. The Catholic Church classified vows as either solemn or simple. The former was public and made with formal clerical intervention and ceremony, the latter was private and sometimes unwitnessed and unrecorded. Marina's vow of chastity would have been a "simple" vow but nevertheless seems

to have been publicly made. She claimed that she made the vow in the convent of La Merced in Sevilla, which suggests that it was witnessed and "accepted" by a superior. This vow, therefore, went beyond a personal promise; it was a binding obligation to God that she had clearly breached.

32. Literally, so germinated (*tan germinados*).

33. Presumably Marina and Juan were discussing the union of God in the Trinity, a favorite theme of mystical devotion, rather than their own mystical union with God, also a topic of interest to mystics.

34. That is, arousal.

35. Literally, at the better part (*a la mayor parte*).

36. Emphasis and repetition in original.

# The Notebooks of Nehemiah Wallington

―――――――――――○※○―――――――――――

## [1598–1658]

Historians of the pre-modern period face a challenge in that we lack source materials for understanding the lives and habits of ordinary people. This is why the diaries of Nehemiah Wallington, a London artisan of the seventeenth century, are so precious. Wellington, who lived his entire life within a single neighborhood in the eastern portion of the city of London, was a wood turner, that is, a maker of rough furniture and other finished wooden goods. Turners were neither particularly wealthy nor distinguished; but as skilled, often independent, artisans, they were also not, generally, among the poorest of Londoners. What made Wallington so special was the fact that he was an assiduous diarist. During his lifetime, he filled at least fifty notebooks with observations, meditations, news reports, prayers, and material copied from books and sermons. All of this was very much a part of Wallington's identity as a Puritan. Committed to a rigorous Calvinist faith, which valued intense self-examination, Wallington saw it as a religious duty to scrutinize every aspect of his life, and to inscribe his devotion to God in ink and paper on a daily basis. Although only seven of his fifty notebooks have survived, they provide invaluable insight into the thought world of a Londoner who was at once ordinary (in his vocation and his circumstances) and completely extraordinary (in the extent of his religiosity and his commitment to the written word). Although many English Puritans left behind testimonies, this is by far the most extensive and personal set of meditations on the godly life that we now possess. It is also the only such ongoing memoir of ordinary life surviving for this period and place; there are few equivalents elsewhere in Europe. What follows are some very brief extracts, touching on themes of wealth and religiosity that are raised in Weber's *Protestant Ethic*.

### Undated:

The chief care of a child of God is and must be still to glorify God in the place and calling wherein God hath set him.

### Undated:

Poverty is no token of God's displeasure … for, as it is no argument that the Lord loves a wicked man because he is rich, so it is no argument that God rejects the godly because they are poor.

### 1630:

Another sorrow and affliction that I had, is this: I had a journeyman[1] which was with me two years: whom I and divers others took to be a very honest simple man: but we were all deceived in him: for he was false unto me and stole from me: as near as I and other can judge near a hundred pound or more. But the chief thing I note here, is the great mercy of God in bringing this unto light. For I found my estate to decay, and to run in debt very much: and I and divers others could not

―――――――――――

1  *Journeyman:* someone who had learned his trade as an apprentice, and now worked for wages.

tell how, and we did wonder at it being I had very good trading and great helps:

1 but I and my wife had many reproaches and hard words: and we were judged to consume our estate ourselves but oh the goodness of God in the hearing of our prayers in bringing this unto light in the clearing of the innocent: and in the shaming of the guilty. My journeyman had served me two years and then in May 1630 he took a shop and then asked me for his wages: for he had scarcely asked me before neither did I offer him any till now: Wherefore my Father and Master Cole[1] asked him how he kept house all this while having a charge and never asked nor received wages and he said one while he had ten pounds a year for land: and that he had threescore pounds nay fourscore pounds lay by him when he came to his master: and many more such tales he told which afterward proved lies: and he did so falter and shuffle in his speech that they did lay it to his charge that he had been false unto me and I laid some money that I missed to his charge, but he denied all very stiffly. They told him that a time would come that he must confess whether he would or no: and many more excellent words they spoke to him: and telling him of many examples of others how well it had gone with some that did confess their sin: and how heavily it had gone with others that did not confess this sin and many more words they spoke urging him to confess his fault: but he would not and said he would take his oath and sacrament that he never wronged me of one penny nor farthing so then they let him depart. And I let him have some ware for his wages to furnish his shop for I was bare of money.

After all this with other examinations, neither promises nor threatening would make him confess anything but at least a maid told me that he took money off a customer and put it in his purse and said she would take her oath of it. Then I went to my man Robert's house: and called him and his wife together and I said to him very patiently that whereas before we dealt on suspicion now I come on more certainty. …

Then his wife said to him good husband confess deal plainly for if we confess and forsake we shall find mercy but if we hide our sin we shall not prosper.[2] Tell us therefore how much you have taken. Then he said eighteen pounds. How much said Master Cole. Then he said eighteen pounds. Then Master Cole gave thanks to God for moving his heart at least to confess and he prayed earnestly to God to forgive him this his heinous sin. …

Then Robert made suit to my Father that I might give him some money: for he said he had none at all: Then my father asked him saying prithee Robert tell me true what have you done with the fourscore pounds that you said that you had when you came to your Master? Then he did protest if there were any truth in him, he had none at all when he came unto his Master. Then I replied again upon his own words and said then by your own reason and confession you have lived these two years on my charge all this while. Now let anyone count what they will board him: his wife, his wife's sister for two years, and another sister, for half a year, besides his wife's lying in childbed, and a great fit of sickness, and house rent with paying of duties: and furnishing his house after he came to me, buying a very good rug, sheets, curtains, and valance,[3] and cushions, a great kettle, and porridge pot, pewter and other good household stuff: besides very good apparel for them both. Moreover he lent abundance of money forth to others as he himself told me, as six pounds to one four pounds to another forty shillings to another with divers other dribbling debts. Now let anyone count all this, and they may perceive that he could not wrong me less than a hundred pounds and if not more and this he did under ten pounds land a year. And surely if he had tarried a little longer with me he would have quite undone me. And now that there is a dead time of trading come on this my great loss, and housekeeping very chargeable it has almost broken my back: But God can, and will raise me up again and restore it to me double and if it be for his glory and my good and if not I humbly entreat him of his infinite mercy to bless and sanctify this my poverty to me for his Christ's sake Amen.

---

1 A family friend and neighbor.

2 Echoing 1 John 1:9–10.

3 *Valence:* a piece of drapery hanging around the canopy of a bed.

## 1631:

Again I have often thought within myself why the Lord should restrain or keep back these outward things from me: he being a loving kind and merciful Father and also a rich and bountiful God even the king of heaven and earth. But only to conform me to my Savior Christ Jesus and his Apostles which were not rich here in this world: but poor men. Again when I walked in the fields and saw sheep feed on the bare commons for if we had ranker grass or had abundance of these outward things: it would rot us and do us much hurt and surely it is so. For at that very time I did see the deceitfulness for my heart: for I began to delight in pleasure. Then began I to lift up my heart to God saying within myself I thank thee O Lord that I have no more for if I had thou seest how my heart would be more drawn from thee to voluptuous pleasures and the nearer to earth the further from heaven: and therefore thou sayest how hard a thing is it for a rich man to enter into the kingdom of heaven?[1]

Whatsoever we may propound to ourselves and think we could serve God more cheerfully and we could do so much good with riches: but O we know not the snares that lie in riches nor we know not the deceitfulness of our own hearts. Ay remember Hazael when the prophet wept and told him the evil that he would do when he is king of Aram. Saith he is thy servant a dog, he little thought he had such a dog's nature as he had (2 Kings 8:11–13). A child thinks a knife is a splendid thing to play with: but the father takes it away from him: for he knows it will hurt him or kill himself.

Remember Demas: under this read 1 Timothy 6:6–11.[2]

Therefore I account this none of the least favors of God. That the world goes no better forward with me: for I fear if my estate were better to the world, it might be worse to God: as it is a happy necessity that enforces to good: so it is that next happy, that hinders from evil.

Again in the midst of the greatest of all my sorrows and wants I have considered what I have deserved, and I have been stirred up to much thankfulness that things have been no worse with me. And although sorrows and miseries have come on me like waves of the sea that follow one upon the neck of another: even so have I found the Lord follow me with his so many more mercies for his compassions fail not.

## 1631–2:

It is best putting our trust in the Lord and not on outward things. For once I thought those other things did fail, yet I did comfort myself in this that this small benefit of lead nails which brings me six pounds a year would not fail but would be a benefit to me and my children after me, but I was deceived for there was another that offered at the doors for twopence halfpenny a pound which I had five pence a pound which was a great hindrance to me: but I did see the great goodness of God to me in this which was to unbutton and to unloose me of the world and to settle my heart on the riches which cannot be taken away and herein I had greater gain inward than my loss outward. And now the Lord has restored me this benefit to me again his Name be praised.

## 1641:

The first of August 1641 being the Lord's day when I and all my family was gone to church (in the forenoon) and when I was come home I did find my keys were taken out of my study door and when I had inquired for them I did hear that the street door was picked open. So I made a shift to open my study door and did see my child Sarah's desk opened and all her work tumbled and scattered out and then I opened my desk and they had taken out as I think about three pounds[3] and a box (written on this is the poor's box[4]) with as I think about twenty shillings[5] in it (and my keys were taken

---

1   Matthew 19:23–4; Mark 10:25; Luke 18:25

2   *Demas:* was a companion of St. Paul but deserted him and "embraced this present world" (2 Timothy 4:10). 1 6:6–11 is relevant to Demas' shortcoming.

3   It is difficult to convert this into a modern dollar equivalent, but it was not an insubstantial sum. A very poor country laborer during this period could subsist on £5–10 per year; £3 would thus be equivalent to several months of subsistence wages for an impoverished family.

4   Wallington was at the time an officer within his parish church. He appears to have been keeping the "poor box" for charitable donations in his own home. Perhaps this was known in the community.

5   There were twenty shillings to a pound.

away) but four days I found my keys again amongst my wooden sieves.

The loss of this my money did somewhat trouble me. But yet I was cheerful and could not but be very thankful to God that I lost no more. Neither did I shed one tear for my loss. But

I did shed tears in thoughts of God's goodness that I lost no more. For they might have broken into my chamber and have taken that little plate[1] and some other money that was there with some other things even to my undoing. But God did restrain them (and said to them as he did to the raging sea hither shalt thou go and no further[2]) and preserve me. The Lord's name has the praise now and for ever. But by the way let me ask a question or two. First why does the Lord permit this thief to steal from me his poor child that has had some care to get it honestly? Answer. Because the Lord does see the world is ready to steal away my heart therefore he does it in love to wean me from the world and to cause me to set my heart on that which no thief can steal away and that the Lord might have all my love himself: as likewise that I should examine myself how I have gained this money whether I have not robbed others by lying and deceit or else to make me call to mind my former sins of old how I have wronged others or else because thou was not thankful for that which was honestly gotten.

---

1   *Plate:* probably used as a collective noun here, referring to high quality household utensils made of metal.

2   11 Psalms 89:9.

# Galileo's Sidereus Nuncius
# or a Sidereal Message

Translated by William R. Shea

Translated by William R. Shea

## DEDICATION

*To the Most Serene Cosimo de' Medici II,
Fourth Granduke of Tuscany.*[11]

Noble and truly public-spirited was the intention of those who determined to protect from envy the great achievements of men of outstanding virtue and to rescue their names, which deserve immortality, from neglect and oblivion. Hence, as a memorial to future ages, likenesses sculptured in marble or cast in bronze; hence, statues on foot or on horseback; hence, columns and pyramids whose cost is sky high, as the poet says;[12] hence also, the building of cities to bear the names of those whom posterity deemed worthy of being remembered throughout the ages. For recollection all too easily slips away from the human mind unless it is constantly reminded by outside stimuli.

There were others, however, who looked for more stable and enduring memorials. These did not entrust the eternal praise of great men to building blocks or strips of metal but to the custody of the Muses and the imperishable monuments of literature.[13] But why mention this? Could it be that human ingenuity, satisfied with what happens here below, dared proceed no further? No, on the contrary, looking beyond and realizing that warfare, the weather, or the passing of time eventually raise all human monuments to the ground, less corruptible signs were sought over which devouring time and envious age could claim no rights. So betaking itself to the heavens, human ingenuity inscribed on the well-known and eternal orbs[14] of the brightest stars the names of those who for their eminent and godlike deeds were deemed worthy of enjoying all eternity in company of the stars. Wherefore, the fame of Jupiter, Mars, Mercury, Hercules, and the other heroes by whose names the stars are called, will not fade until the splendour of the stars themselves is extinguished. But noble and admirable custom went out of fashion ages ago when those glorious seats were occupied by the ancient heroes who now hold them, as it were, in their own right. In vain did the affection of Augustus try to introduce Julius Caesar into their company.[15] The star that appeared in his day and that he wanted to name "Julian" belonged to those that the Greeks call comets and we "hair-like,"[16] and it vanished in a short time and mocked his too eager hope.

But, Most Serene Prince, we can augur far more genuine and happy things for your Highness, for no sooner had the immortal greatness of your mind begun to shine on Earth than bright stars presented themselves in the heavens like tongues to tell and celebrate your surpassing virtues for all time. Behold, therefore, four stars reserved for your famous name. They do not belong to the common and less distinguished multitude of fixed stars but to the illustrious rank of the planets. Moving at different rates around Jupiter, the noblest of the planets,[17] as if they were his own children, they trace out their orbits with marvellous speed while, at the same time, with one harmonious accord, they go round the centre of the world, namely the Sun itself,[18] and complete their great revolutions in twelve years.[19]

The Creator of the stars seems to have himself[20] provided me with clear reasons for dedicating these new planets to Your Highness' famous name in preference to all others.[21] For just as these stars, like worthy children, never leave the side of Jupiter by any appreciable distance, so everyone knows that clemency, kindness of heart, gentleness of manners, splendour of royal blood, majesty in deportment, wide extent of influence and authority over others have all fixed their abode and seat in your Highness. Who, I say, ignores that all these qualities emanate from the most benign planet Jupiter,[22] according to the will of God from Whom all good things flow? Jupiter, Jupiter I say, that at the moment of your Highness' birth had already risen above the misty vapour on the horizon and occupied the midheaven.[23] Illuminating the eastern angle[24] from its royal house, it looked down from its exalted throne upon your blessed birth, and poured out the brightness of its majesty in the pure air in order that your tender body and your mind, already adorned by God with the most noble ornaments, might imbibe with its first breath the whole of that strength and power.

But why should I use merely plausible arguments when I can demonstrate my conclusion with practically absolute certainty? It pleased God Almighty that I should be considered worthy by your Most Serene Parents[25] to teach your Highness mathematics during the last four years[26] at that time of year when it is customary to rest from more exacting studies. It was clearly God's will that I should serve your Highness and be exposed at close quarters to the rays of your incredible kindness and gentleness. What wonder is it, therefore, if you have so warmed my heart that I, who am your subject not only by choice but by birth and lineage, should night and day scarcely think of anything else but how to make known how grateful I am to you, and how desirous to promote your glory. And so, since it was under your auspices, Most Serene Cosimo, that I discovered those stars that were unknown to all astronomers before me, I have the right to call them by the most august name of your family.[27] Since I was the first to discover them, who can rightly reproach me if I also give them a name and call them MEDICEAN STARS, hoping that perhaps as much honour may accrue to the stars from this title, as other stars have brought the other heroes? For to say nothing of your most serene ancestors whose everlasting glory is attested by the historical record, your virtue alone, Great Hero, can confer on those stars a name that is immortal.[28] For who can doubt that you will not only maintain and preserve the high expectations that you have aroused at the beginning of your reign, but far surpass them? So when you have conquered your equals, you will nonetheless still vie with yourself and become greater day by day.

Receive then, most clement Prince, this honour that was reserved for you by the stars, and may you enjoy for many years those blessings that descended upon you not so much from the stars, as from God, their Creator and Governor.

Padua, on the fourth day before the Ides of March MDCX.[29]
Your Highness' most devoted servant,

*Galileo Galilei*

### PERMISSION TO PRINT

The undersigned, their Excellencies the Heads of the Council of Ten,[30] having been informed by the Overseers of the University of Padua[31] that the two persons appointed for this task, namely the Reverend Father Inquisitor and the circumspect Secretary of the Senate, Giovanni Maraviglia,[33] declared under oath that in the book entitled *Sidereal Message etc.* of Galileo Galilei[33] there is nothing that is contrary to the Holy Catholic Faith, principles or good customs, and that it is worthy of being printed, authorize its publication in this city.

Dated 1 March 1610.
Heads of the Council of Ten

D. M(arco) Ant(onio) Valaresso
D. Nicolò Bon
D. Lunardo Marcello[34]

Bartolomeo Comino
Secretary of the Illustrious Council of Ten

1610, on 8 March. Registered in the book on page 39.

Giovanni Battista Breatto
Coadjutor of the Office against Blasphemy[35]

## AN ASTRONOMICAL MESSAGE

that contains and explains
*recent observations*
made with the aid of a new spyglass of the face of
the moon, the Milky Way, the nebulous stars, and an
innumerable number of fixed ones, as well as in
four planets,
*called cosmic stars*[36]
that have never been seen before.

Great indeed are the things that this small book offers to the consideration and study of anyone interested in nature. I call them great because of the excellence of the subject matter[37] and their absolute and unheard of novelty, but also on account of the instrument whereby they became known to our senses.

It is surely a great thing to add countless stars to the large number that have already been observed with the naked eye, and to render them clearly visible when they had never been seen before, and are more than ten times as numerous as the old with which we are familiar.[38]

It is a most beautiful and a very pleasing sight to look at the body of the Moon, which is removed from us by almost sixty terrestrial diameters,[39] and to see it as if it were only two diameters away[40] This means that the diameter of the Moon looks almost thirty times larger, its surface nine hundred times bigger, and its whole body close to twenty-seven thousand times more voluminous than when seen with the naked eye.[41] The observational evidence is so compelling that anyone can grasp for himself that the Moon's surface is not smooth and polished but rough and uneven. Like the face of the Earth,[42] it is covered all over with huge bumps, deep holes, and chasms.

Furthermore, it is no small matter to have put an end to disputes about the Galaxy, namely the Milky Way, and to have made its nature clear to the senses, let alone the understanding. It is also a fine and a pleasant thing to be able to point out, as with one's finger, the nature of those stars that all astronomers have hitherto called nebulous, and to show that it is very different from what was believed until now.

But what is even more admirable, and what we mainly want to let astronomers and philosophers know, is that we have found four wandering stars[43] that no one before us had heard about or observed, and that these revolve around one of the conspicuous planets. Like Venus and Mercury, which go around the Sun, they have their own periods of revolution so that they sometimes precede, sometimes follow their planet but in such a way that they never stray beyond certain limits.[44] All this was found and observed a few days ago with a spyglass that I devised after having been enlightened by divine grace.

Other and perhaps greater things will be discovered in the days to come by me or by others with the aid of a similar instrument, so before giving an account of my observations I will briefly say something about its shape and its construction, as well as how I came to think of it.

About ten months ago the rumour[45] reached us that a Dutchman[46] had made a spyglass by the aid of which visible objects, although at a great distance from the eye of the observer, were seen distinctly as if near. News of this truly wonderful result spread, and if it was believed by some, it was denied by others. But confirmation arrived a few days later in a letter written from Paris by a noble Frenchman, Jacques Badouere,[47] and this is what made me concentrate all my energy on finding how this was achieved and by what means I could make a similar instrument.[48] Basing myself on the theory of refraction,[49] I achieved my goal in little time. I first got a tube of lead, and fitted the ends with two lenses that were both plane on one side but, on the other side, convex in one case, and concave in the other. I then applied my eye to the concave lens, and saw objects as fairly large and near at hand. They appeared to be three times closer and nine times larger than when seen with the naked eye alone. I then constructed a better instrument that made objects appear sixty times bigger.[50] Sparing neither time nor expense,[51] I managed to construct an instrument that was so good that objects seen through it appeared a thousand times bigger, and more that thirty times closer than when viewed by the natural power of sight alone. It would be superfluous to list the number and the importance of the advantages of this instrument on land and at sea.[52]

But leaving terrestrial observation, I turned to the study of the heavens and saw, first of all, the Moon as near as if it were hardly two terrestrial diameters away[53] Next I repeatedly observed, with the greatest pleasure, the fixed and the wandering stars.[54] When I realized their huge number, I began to ponder how to measure the intervals between them, and I eventually discovered a way of doing so. It is fitting to warn those who may want to undertake this kind of observation that they must, in the first place, acquire an excellent spyglass that shows objects clearly, distinctly, and free from any haziness. It should magnify at least four hundred times so that the objects appear twenty times closer. Without such an instrument, everything we saw in the heavens and that we list below will be sought for in vain.

In order to determine without great trouble the magnifying power of the instrument, trace on paper the outline of two circles or two squares such that one is four hundred times as large as the other, as will be the case when its diameter is twenty times that of the other. Then, having attached these two figures to the same wall, observe them both simultaneously from a distance, looking at the smaller one through the spyglass, and at the larger with the other, naked eye. This can easily be done by keeping both eyes opened at the same time. The two figures will appear to be of the same size if the instrument magnifies the objects in the said ratio. With such an instrument, we can determine distances, and we proceed in the following way. In the interest of clarity, let ABCD be the tube, and E the eye of the observer. When there are no lenses in the tube, the rays are carried to the object FG along the straight lines ECF and EDG,[55] but when the lenses are inserted they are carried along the refracted lines ECH and EDI. The rays, which before were directed without constraint towards FG, are now squeezed together and only include the part HI.

Next we determine the ratio of the distance EH to the line HI and, with the help of a table of sines, we find that the size of the angle subtended at the eye by object HI is only a few minutes of an arc.[56] Now if we perforate thin sheets of metal, some with larger and others with smaller holes, and place over the lens CD one size or another, as need may be, we can obtain any number of angles subtending a few minutes of an arc. By this means we shall be able to conveniently measure the intervals between stars a few minutes apart within an error of one or two minutes.[57]

Let it suffice for the present, however, to have touched upon this rapidly and to have given a foretaste of what is to come for, on some further occasion, we shall provide a complete theory of this instrument.[58] But let us now review the observations that we made over the last two months,[59] and here I call upon all those who are eager for true philosophy to witness the beginnings of important considerations.[60]

Let us first consider the face that the Moon turns towards us and, to make things easier, I distinguish two parts, the brighter and the darker one.[61] The brighter seems to surround and illuminate the whole hemisphere of the Moon whereas the darker one, like a cloud, spreads over the face of the Moon and makes it appear covered with spots that are somewhat dark and of considerable size. These have always been observed and are obvious to everyone. We shall call them *great* or *ancient* spots to distinguish them from others of smaller size that are so thickly scattered that they cover the whole surface of the Moon but mainly the brighter part. These were never observed by anyone before us. After examining them repeatedly we were led to a conclusion about which we are certain. The surface of the Moon is not even, smooth and perfectly spherical, as the majority of philosophers have conjectured that it and the other celestial bodies are but, on the contrary, rough and uneven, and covered with cavities and protuberances just like the face of the Earth, which is rendered diverse by lofty mountains and deep valleys. The appearances that enabled me to reach this conclusion are the following.

On the fourth or the fifth day after New Moon,[62] when the Moon presents itself with bright horns, the boundary line that separates the darker from the brighter side does not follow a regular oval line, as would be the case on a perfectly spherical solid, but traces out an uneven, rough and altogether sinuous line, as the figure below shows. Several bright excrescences, as it were, extend beyond the boundary of light and darkness and penetrate into the darker part while, on the other hand, patches from the dark side enter the brighter one. Indeed, a great number of small black-ish spots, completely separated from the dark part, are scattered over most of the area that is already flooded by sunlight, with the exception of the part occupied by the *great* and *ancient* spots. We note furthermore that the small spots just mentioned always have this feature in common that their darker side faces the Sun while on the side opposite the Sun their contours are brighter, as if they were crowned with shining peaks. We see exactly the same thing on Earth at sunrise when the sunlight has not yet spread over the valleys although the mountains surrounding them on the side away from the Sun are already shining brightly. And just as shadows in hollows on Earth decrease in size as the Sun rises higher, so these lunar spots shed their darkness as their illuminated parts grow larger.

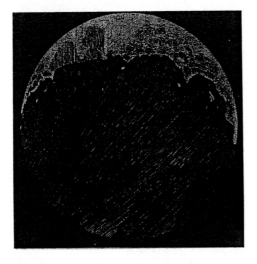

But not only is the boundary of light and shadow on the Moon seen to be uneven and sinuous, what causes even greater astonishment is that very bright points appear inside the darker portion of the Moon. They are divided and separated from the illuminated part, and removed from it by a considerable distance. After some time, they gradually increase in size and brightness until, after two or three hours, they become joined with the rest of the bright portion, which has now increased in size. In the meantime, more and more bright points light up inside the dark portion, swell in size and eventually embrace the brighter surface that has extended still further. This is illustrated in the same figure.

On Earth, before sunrise, are not the peaks of the highest mountains illuminated by the Sun's rays while the plains are still in shadow? In a little while, does not

the light spread further until the middle and larger parts of these mountains become illuminated and, in the end, when the Sun has risen, the illuminated parts of the plains and the hills are joined? On the Moon, however, the difference between high peaks and depressions appears to be much greater than the one caused by ruggedness on the surface of the Earth, as we shall show below. In the meantime, I cannot pass over in silence something worthy of consideration that I observed when the Moon was hasting towards first-quarter, as can be seen in the same figure above. Near the lower cusp, a great dark gulf extends into the illuminated side. I observed it for a while and saw that it was dark throughout, but after a couple of hours a bright peak began to emerge a little below the centre of the depression. It gradually grew in size and assumed a triangular shape that was still completely detached and separated from the illuminated area. Around it three other small points soon began to shine until, when the Moon was just about to set, this triangular shape, which had become more extended and larger, joined the rest of the illuminated part and penetrated into the dark gulf like a vast promontory, still surrounded by the three bright peaks that we have just mentioned. At the ends of the top and bottom cusps, some bright points emerged, completely separated from the rest of the illuminated part, as can be seen in the same figure.

There was also a great number of dark spots in both cusps, but mainly in the lower one. Those nearer the boundary of light and shadow appeared larger and darker while those further removed were fainter and not so dark. But as we mentioned above, the dark portion of each spot was always turned towards the incoming rays of the Sun while the bright rim that surrounded it on the other side always faced the dark region of the Moon. This part of the lunar surface, which is spotted like a peacock's tail is decked with azure eyes, resembles glass vases that are plunged while still hot into cold water and acquire that crackled and wavy surface from which they receive the common name of frosted glass. But the *great* spots on the Moon do not appear to be cracked or crowded with depressions and prominences in this manner, but rather to be even and uniform, for only here and there do some bright patches emerge.

So if someone wanted to revive the ancient Pythagorean theory, namely that the Moon is like an-other Earth,[63] its land surface would be more fittingly represented by the brighter region, and the expanse of water by the darker one. I have never doubted that if the terrestrial globe were observed from afar, bathed in sunlight, the land surface would appear brighter and the expanse of water darker.[64] Furthermore, whether the Moon is waxing or waning, the *great* spots on the Moon appear to be more depressed than the brighter tracts that appear here and there in the vicinity of the *great* spots, and always along the boundary of light and shadow, as we noticed when drawing the figures. The edges of the large spots are not only lower but more even, and free from creases and ruggedness. The bright part stands out particularly near the spots and, before first quarter and approaching last quarter, huge stretches arise above and below a certain spot in the higher and northerly region of the Moon,[65] as can be seen in the figures reproduced here below:

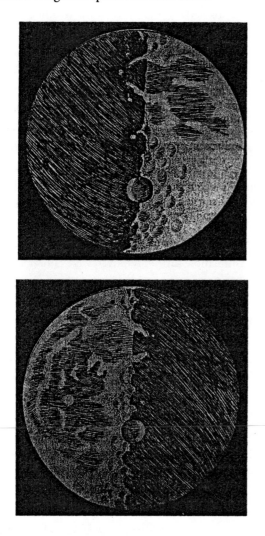

Before the last quarter this same spot is seen to be surrounded by darker contours that, like the highest

ridges of mountains, appear darker on the side that is facing away from the Sun, and brighter on the side that is turned towards the Sun. Now just the opposite happens in the case of the cavities where the side that is facing away from the Sun appears brilliant, while the side that is turned towards the Sun appears dark and shadowy. When the illuminated portion of the Moon has decreased in size, and the spot we have mentioned is nearly all covered in darkness, the brighter mountain ridges climb above these shadows. This twofold appearance of the spot is illustrated in the following figures:

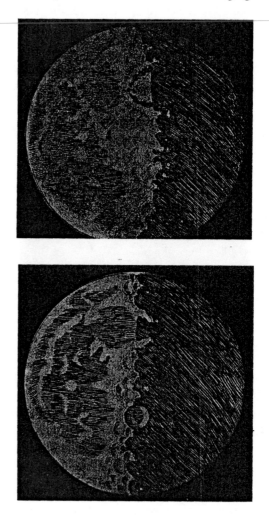

There is another thing that I must not omit, because I found it very striking: near the centre of the Moon there is a cavity that is larger than all the other ones and perfectly round in shape. I observed it near both the first and the last quarter, and I have portrayed it as well as possible in the second of the two figures above. As to light and shade, this cavity offers the same appearance as would a region like Bohemia,[66] if it were enclosed on all sides by very high mountains arranged along the circumference of a perfect circle. For on the Moon this area is walled in by such high peaks that the side adjacent to the dark portion of the Moon is seen to be bathed in sunlight before the boundary between light and shadow reaches halfway across the cavity. Just like other spots, its shaded portion faces the Sun while its lighted part faces the dark region of the Moon. It gives me pleasure, for the third time, to draw attention to this very cogent argument that ruggedness and unevenness are spread over the entire brighter region of the Moon. Of these spots, moreover, the darker ones are always next to the boundary between light and shadow, and those further away appear smaller in size and less dark, so that when the Moon, at its opposition to the Sun, becomes full there remains only a slight and faint difference between the darkness of the cavities and the brightness of the peaks.

The things we have enumerated were observed in the brighter parts of the Moon. In the *great* spots we see no such differences of depressions and heights as those that we are compelled to recognize in the brighter regions on account of the changes in their shape that result from the different ways they are illuminated by rays of the Sun that arrive from a variety of angles. Inside the *great* spots we also find small zones that are less dark, as we have indicated in the illustrations, but they always have the same appearance, and their darkness neither increases nor decreases, although they sometimes appear a little darker or a little brighter according as the rays of the Sun fall upon them more or less obliquely. Furthermore, they are joined to their neighbouring parts by a very gradual connection so that their boundaries run together and blend. But matters are quite different in the case of the spots that occupy the brighter part of the Moon's surface.

The sharp contrast of light and shadow gives them well defined boundaries as if they were steep walls covered with jagged and projecting rocks. Moreover inside these *great spots* certain small zones are observed to be brighter than the surrounding region, and some are very bright indeed. But their appearance, as well as that of the darker parts, is always the same because there is never any change in their shape, brightness or darkness. Hence, it is …

* * *

I have briefly recounted what I observed in the Moon, the fixed stars, and the Milky Way. There remains what deserves to be considered the most important of all, namely the disclosure of four planets[105] that were never seen from the creation of the world up to our own times,[106] and to declare how they were found and observed, what are their positions, and what observations I made during almost two months[107] concerning their motion and their changes. I call upon all astronomers to devote themselves to the study and the determination of their periods,[108] which so far I have not been able to ascertain because of lack of time. I warn them again, however, in order that they may not undertake such an inquiry in vain, that they will need a very sharp spyglass of the kind I described at the beginning of this account.[109]

On the 7th of January of the present year 1610, at the first hour of night,[110] when I was observing the celestial bodies with the spyglass, Jupiter came forward. As I had just made an excellent instrument for myself, I saw (what I had not done before because of the weakness of the former instrument)[111] three little stars,[112] small but very bright. Although I assumed that they belonged to the number of fixed stars, they caused me no little surprise because they appeared to lie exactly on a straight line, parallel to the ecliptic,[113] and brighter than other stars of the same magnitude. Their arrangement with respect to Jupiter and among themselves was as follows:

**Ori.**    *   *   **O**   *    **Occ.**

There were two stars on the eastern side, but just one on the western. The furthest to the east and the western one seemed slightly larger than the third. I paid no attention to the distance between them and Jupiter for, as I have said, I thought at first that they were fixed stars. When on the 8th of January, led by I know not what Fate, I turned to look at them again, I found a very different arrangement. There were now three small stars to the west of Jupiter, closer to each other than the night before, and separated by equal intervals as shown in the diagram below. At the time I gave no thought as to how these small stars could have come together, but I began to wonder how Jupiter could be found to the east of all those fixed stars when it had been to the west of two of them the day before.

**Ori.**    **O**   *   *   *    **Occ.**

I therefore asked myself whether, contrary to the computations of astronomers, Jupiter might not be moving eastward at this time and had passed in front of the stars by its own proper motion. I eagerly awaited the next night, but my hopes were dashed: the sky was everywhere covered with clouds.

On the 10th of January, the stars appeared in the following position with regard to Jupiter: there were only two and both were to the east:

**Ori.**    *   *   **O**    **Occ.**

The third one, I conjectured, was hiding behind Jupiter. They were, as before, in the same straight line with Jupiter, and located exactly along the line of the Zodiac. When I saw this, and knowing that such changes of position could in no way be ascribed to Jupiter and moreover, having had to recognize that the stars that I saw had always been the same (there were no other stars within a great distance before or after on the line of the Zodiac), I realized that the changes of position were not due to Jupiter but to the stars that had been observed. My perplexity gave way to amazement, and I therefore resolved to observe them with greater care and attention from then on.

# English Parish Registers and Wills

I n the 1530s, King Henry VIII of England ordered every parish in his realm to begin recording all baptisms, burials, and marriages performed within their boundaries. These records often survive, and have been used by researchers to help reconstruct the social and demographic history of the period. Transcribed below are baptismal records for the parish of St. Dunstan, Stepney, for May 1602 and May 1640. St. Dunstan was a sizeable parish that stretched along the Thames river to the east of the city walls of London. Originally, it had been largely rural, encompassing a number of separate settlements (Ratcliff, Mileend, Limehouse, Shadwell, Knockfergus, etc.). But as London grew and spilled beyond the old city walls, the area became more heavily developed, until by the eighteenth and nineteenth centuries it had become a central part of the zone described as "the East End" of London. By examining these documents as closely as possible, what sorts of conclusions can we draw about the area and its inhabitants? How it might have changed over time?

**Baptisms for the month of May, in the year 1602:**

| | | |
|---|---|---|
| Matthew son of John Grant of Ratcliff baptized | (10) 9 boys | first of May |
| Thomas son of Thomas Coroy of Mileend baptized | (14) 13 girls | the first day |
| John son of Richard Rollins of Tenters baptized | | the first day |
| Ann daughter of Edward Smyth of Knockfergus baptized | | the iiii day |
| Ann daughter of Humfrey Lowefield of Mileend vintner | | the vi day |
| Samuell | | |
| Jane   / Children of James Symson of Limehouse baptized | | the viii day |
| Nicholas son of Thomas Pett of Shadwell baptized | | the viii day |
| Herle son of Gregory Reignolds of Bishops Hall baptized | | viii day |
| Catherine daughter of Robert Doughty of Shadwell, smith, baptized | | viii day |
| Edward son of Master Edward Mumies vicar of Stepney bapt | | x day |
| Elizabeth daughter of Robert Dage of Ratcliff baptized | | the xv day |
| Elizabeth daughter of Peter Waters of Ratcliff bapt | | xxii day |
| Elizabeth daughter of Thomas Hunte of Limehouse bapt | | xxii day |
| Elizabeth daughter of Orem Huffe of Ratcliff baptized | | the xxii day |
| Marian daughter of Thomas Browne of Poplar baptized | | the xxii day |
| Abraham son of Robert Dawes of Limehouse baptized | | the xxv day |
| Ann daughter of George Ely of Limehouse baptized | | the xxv day |
| Elizabeth daughter of Jarvis Bood of Limehouse baptized | | the xxv day |
| James son of ~~Ekas~~ Erasmus Michell of Whitehorsestreet bapt | | the xxvi day |

| | |
|---|---|
| Wlm son of John Pierce of Ratcliff baptized | the xxviii day |
| Mary daughter of William Lauglys of Ratcliff baptized | the xxix day |
| Elin daughter of Thomas Faulton of Poplar baptized | the xxix day |
| Mary daughter of Humfry Milton of Poplar baptized | the xxix day |

### Baptisms for the month of May, in the year 1640:

| | | |
|---|---|---|
| 1 | Jane daughter of Francis Ball of Whitehorse street Ropemaker & Jane uxor[is][1] | |
| 1 | Anthony son of Anthony Watts of Mileend Silkweaver & Susanna uxor[is] | |
| 1 | Joane daughter of John Bargen of King street in Wapping Marin[er] & Elizabeth up | |
| 1 | Hannah daughter of John Lake of Greene banke in Wapping Gent & Mary uxor[is] | |
| 1 | Richard son of John Jeffreys of Blackwall Merchant & Rachell uxor[is] | |
| 1 | Elizabeth daughter of Phillip Doer of Wappingwall Mariner & Elizabeth uxor[is] | |
| 3 | Robert son of Edmond Goldner of Prusons I[s]land Shipwright & Anne uxor[is] | |
| 3 | Edmond son of James Gurney of Ratcliff Glassmaker and Mary uxor[is] | |
| 3 | Elizabeth daughter of Thomas Carvell of Ratcliff Marin[er] & Elizabeth uxor[is] | |
| 3 | Francis son of Richard Bush of Limehouse Shipwright & Grace uxor[is] | |
| 3 | Elias son of Thomas Clarke of Wappingwall Marin[er] & Phillida uxor[is] | |
| 3 | Anthony son of Anthony Pike of new Gravellane Marin[er] & Barbara uxor[is] | |
| 3 | Regnold son of Leonard Besar of Foxes lane Smith & Elizabeth uxor[is] | |
| 3 | Elizabeth daughter of William Corbet of Spittlefeilds Tailor & Margery up | |
| 3 | Katherine daughter of Thomas Pharaoh of Wentworthstreet Needlemaker and Anne his wife | |
| 5 | Isaack son of John Worlocke of Ratcliff Mariner and Mary uxor[is] | |
| 5 | Humfery son of Humphery Felstead of Ratcliff Mariner & Alice uxor[is] | |
| 6 | Robert son of William White of Shadwell Marin[er] & Elizabeth uxor[is] | |
| 7 | Rachel daughter of Peter Broyer of Ratcliff Marin[er] & Rachell uxor[is] | 10[2] |
| 7 | Elizabeth daughter of John Orsby of Greenestreet Cittizen & Girdler of London and Mary his wife | 8 |
| 8 | Richard son of John Waller of Blackwall Merchant and Ursula uxor[is] | 10 |
| 10 | James son of John Carmien of Ratcliff Mariner and Mary uxor[is] | 7 |
| 10 | Andrew son of Edward Ferris of Prusons I[s]land Tallow Chandler and Mary his wife | 7 |
| 10 | John son of Daniell Jones of Wappingwall Shipwright & Anne uxor[is] | 8 |
| 10 | Mary daughter of Cornelius Tugeson of Wappingwall Marin[er] & Alice uxor[is] | 4 |
| 10 | Mary daughter of Thomas Petchey of the lie of Doggs Husbandman and Anne his wife | 7 |
| 10 | Anne daughter of Rowland Noble of Wapping Marin[er] & Anne uxor[is] | 14 |
| 10 | George son of John Mould of Spittlefeilds Silkweaver and Anne uxor[is] | 8 |
| 10 | William son of John Heughes of Poplar Miller & Francis uxor[is] | 3 |
| 10 | George son of George Terry of Common Stair alley in Ratcliff Tailor and Alice his wife | 10 |

Twinnes

| | | |
|---|---|---|
| 10 | George son  \ of George Knowles of Bethnel Green Yeoman and | |
| 10 | Alice daughter  / Alice his wife | 3 |
| 13 | Anne daughter of John Dobbison of Limehouse Shipwright & Rebeccah uxor[is] | 10 |

---

1   "uxoris" is Latin for "of [his] wife"; so the first entry here amounts to "on the first of May 1640, was baptized Jane Ball, daughter Francis Ball of Whitehorse Street, ropemaker, and of his wife Jane."

2   The numbers in the right-hand column refer to age of the child, in days, when it was baptized. For entries on even-numbered pages, these entries are not legible, which is why they are given only for some of the children.

| | | |
|---|---|---|
| 13 Elizabeth daughter of John Styton of upper Shadwell Marin[er] & Katherine up | | 7 |
| 13 John son of John Morden of Ratcliff highway Grocer & Sarah uxor[is] | | 6 |

Twinnes

| | | |
|---|---|---|
| 13 James  \ sons of James Hodge of Mileend Silkweaver & Margaret uxor[is] | | 4 |
| 13 John   / | | |

Twinnes

| | | |
|---|---|---|
| 13 Joseph    \ sons of Michaell Yates of Limehouse Marin[er] and Mary uxor[is] | | 4 |
| 13 Benjamin  / | | |
| 14 Mary daughter of James Story of Ratcliff Marinfer] and Mary uxor[is] | | 6 |
| 14 Abraham son of Thomas Heughes of Pettycoat lane Silkweaver & Dorothy his wife | | 5 |
| 14 John son of John Funnell of Wentworthstreet Packthred spinner and Elizabeth his wife | | 11 |
| 15 Sarah daughter of George Clarke of Limehouse Mariner & Blanch uxor [is] | | 8 |
| 15 Alice daughter of Thomas Chamberlayne of Wentworthstreet Husbandman and Jane uxor[is] | | 7 |
| 15 Abimelech son of Abimelech Hackett of Ratcliff Highway Smith and Margurit his wife | | 12 |
| ,17 John Angola a Negro at Mans estate servant to Captain Philip Bell[1] | | |
| Planter out of a Shipp called the South Hampton, | | |
| lying in the River of Thames near Ratcliff Crosse | | — |
| 17 Richard son of Thomas Willis of Three Jolt street Marin[er] & Elizabeth ux | | 7 |
| 17 Mary daughter of Thomas Cooke of upper Shadwell Statoner & Mary ux | | 5 |
| 17 William son of William Mathewes of Foxes lane Marin[er] & Anne uxor [is] | | 5 |
| 17 Diana daughter of John Nutting of Prusons I[s]land Shipwright and Sarah uxor[is] | | 9 |
| 17 John son of William Smith of Ratcliff Crosse Tailor & Joane uxor[is] | | 7 |
| 17 Elizabeth daughter of Thomas Chapman of Foxes lane Marin[er] & Maud uxor[is] | | 6 |
| 17 Anne daughter of Thomas Ravens of Greenebank Marin[er] and Elizabeth uxor[is] | | 8 |
| 17 Thomas son of Richard Bullard of Ratcliff highway Marin[er] and Anne uxor[is] | | 5 |
| 17 Francis daughter of George Irwin of Limehouse Barber & Elizabeth his wife | | 7 |
| 17 Richard son of Walter Feare of Spittlefields Tailor and Anne uxor[is] | | 11 |
| 17 Robert son of William Alvin of Kingstreet Marin[er] and Sarah uxor[is] | | |
| 19 Elizabeth daughter of John Watson of Ratcliff Mariner and Sarah uxor[is] | | |
| 20 Mary daughter of Isaack Hearsby of Blackwall Shipwright & Dorothy uxor[is] | | |
| 22 John son of Thomas Jarrett of Limehouse Mariner and Damaris uxor[is] | | |
| 22 Elizabeth daughter of Edward Cox of upper Shadwell Gunsmith & Elizabeth his wife | | |
| 22 Anne daughter of Abell Earle of Foxes lane Tailor and Dorcas uxor[is] | | |
| 22 Mary daughter of Thomas Harris of Ratcliff Mariner and Rebeccah uxor[is] | | |
| 24 Clement son of William Ling of Shadwell Mariner and Phillys uxor[is] | | |
| 24 Robert son of John Audley of Wappingwall Carpenter and Elizabeth uxor[is] | | |
| 24 Anne daughter of John Hannover of Limehouse Mariner & Joane uxor[is] | | |
| 24 Joane daughter of Thomas Bramton of Ratcliff highway Butcher & Margaret uxor[is] | | |
| 25 Richard son of John Fawkener of Prusons I[s]land Tayler and Dowsabell uxor[is] | | |

Bast

25 Richard son of Elizabeth Chambers the wife of William Chambers of lower Shadwell Mariner begotten as shee affirmed by Richard Leaver alias Cleaver of Ipswich in the county of Suffolk Mariner

25 Silvester daughter of John Barnard of Whitehorsestreet Yeoman & Sarah his wife

26 Martha daughter of Joseph Spundance of Wapping Tailor & Rebeccah uxor[is]

26 Emmanuell son of Samuell Gampin of New gravellane Tailor & Katherine uxor[is]

---

1  Possibly the same Philip Bell who would appointed governor of Barbados colony the next year.

27 John son of Anthony Dixon of Prusons I[s]land Tailor and Sarah uxor[is]

27 Elizabeth daughter of Thomas Dunning of Limehouse Mariner & Elizabeth uxor[is]

27 Edward son of John Otter of Limehouse Mariner and Alice uxor[is]

27 Katherine daughter of John Chapman of Wapping Shipwright and Jane uxor[is]

Bast

27 Elizabeth daughter of Mary Dyer late of Blackwall Singlewoman begotten as she affirmed by Richard Lucy (late keeping the Pigeon) at Stepney a Tapster[1], borne in the feilds & now in the house of George Jelley of Whitehorsestreet Bricklayer

28 Susanna daughter of John Bradanke of Ratcliff Mariner and Ursula uxor[is]

29 John son of John Sniftus of Ratcliff Mariner and Alice his wife

29 Thomas son of Daniell Clarke of Limehouse Mariner and Abigail uxor[is]

29 Luke son of Richard Harris of Limehouse Mariner & Margaret uxor[is]

29 John son of John Smith of Wapping Shipwright & Anne his wife

29 Mary daughter of John Hearne of Poplar Mariner and Elizabeth his wife

29 Anne daughter of John Symon of Whitehorsestreet Mariner and Luce uxor[is]

29 William son of Henry Raven of Wappingwall Mariner and Anne uxor[is]

29 John son of Edmond Gouder of Mileend Vintner and Francis uxor[is]

31 Katherine daughter of John Showers of Ratcliff Baker & Sicely uxor[is]

31 John son of Thomas Williams of Blackwall Laborer and Sarah uxor[is]

31 William son of Morris Power of Wappingwall Mariner and Mary uxor[is]

31 Charles son of John Reed of Foxes lane Mariner and Anne uxor[is]

31 Katherine daughter of William Smith of Bethnel Green Silkweaver & Katherine uxor[is]

31 Isaack son of Isaack Todd of Wappingwall Mariner and Mary uxor[is]

31 Robert son of Thomas Birch of Poplar Laborer and Anne uxor[is]

31 Anne daughter of Richard Ellis of King street Mariner and Mary uxor[is]

The following passages are drawn from the wills of Londoners who died in 1658, 1676, and 1681. The first two men lived in Wapping, one of the suburbs along the Thames, just east of the walls of the city of London, and adjacent to the riverside parish of St. Dunstan Stepney. The third man, Thomas Chapman, also lived in East London, just outside the city walls in the parish of St. Botolph Aldgate.

During this period, most people, even in towns and cities, did not leave wills, either because they possessed no substantive property, or because they did not regard the disposition of that property as demanding a formal, legal will. Nevertheless, those wills that have survived can often provide an interesting window into people's everyday lives and into the legal and social customs that governed economic existence. In addition, as part of the probate process, it was necessary to draw up inventories of the moveable goods belonging to the deceased. Most London inventories have not survived for this period, but included below is a transcript of a rare extant example from the East End. Again, try to examine these documents from multiple angles so as to extract as much information as possible.

---

1 i.e., one who taps beer, or in this case, a tavern-master

## 1) Will of Thomas Taylor, written Dec. 15, 1658, and formally proved (after his death) on Jan. 10, 1659.

"...I Thomas Taylor of Wapping in the County of Middlesex, Shipwright, sick and weak in body, Doe make my last Will and Testament Commending my Soule unto Almighty God my Creator assuredly trusting and believing to be saved only by the precious death and passion of my Savior and Redeemer Jesus Christ and my body to the Earth to be buried at the discretion of my loving Wife. And for that Worldly Estate wherewith Almighty God in great mercy hath blessed me, I give order and dispose thereof as followeth: First if my son Jonathan Taylor shall live and Come home from the East Indies whither he is gone on a voyage and shall come to and live in his own house and continue in health and be of sound mind for a year, then after, I charge my said son Jonathan as he shall expect a blessing from the Lord, That he surrender all those Copyhold[1] Lands and Tenements with the appurtenances which I have in the County of Essex[2] according to the Custom of that Manor whereof the said Lands are holden, to the use of my son Caleb Taylor and his heirs for ever, which said Copyhold Lands and tenements I give and devise to my said son Caleb and his heirs. And if my said son Jonathan, Coming home and living, shall accordingly surrender the said Copyhold Lands and Tenements, Then and not otherwise I give and bequeath unto my said son Jonathan Taylor and to his heirs and Assignees for ever All those my fee-farm Rents[3] arising or in any wise Coming out of or from the Manor of Wighton in the County of Norfolk[4] or elsewhere soever in the County. And in Case of such his surrendering, Then and not otherwise I also give and devise unto my said son Jonathan Taylor and unto his heirs for ever All those my Lands, Tenements, and hereditaments in or about Hanworth in the said County of Middlesex.[5] And if my said son Jonathan shall come home and doe and surrender the said Copyhold Lands, accordingly, Then and not otherwise I give and bequeath unto my said son Jonathan Taylor the sum of five hundred pounds to be paid him in and by and out of my parts in shipping to be indifferently and reasonably valued, And all my part also in the ship or vessel wherein he went forth on the said voyage, Together with all the Adventure which I had in the said ship upon her setting forth to sea and I also give unto him the one hundred pounds which he oweth me on account. And if my said son Jonathan shall come home and surrender the said Copyhold Lands accordingly, Then also I give unto his daughter Elizabeth Two hundred pounds, To be paid unto her at her age of one and twenty years or on the day of her marriage first happening, with the profits and increase thereof in the meantime towards her education and bringing up. And if my said son Jonathan coming home and living at his house qualified as aforesaid shall not surrender the said Copyhold Lands according to my very mind before declared in this my Testament, Then I give and devise all the said Fee-Farm rents in Norfolk unto my said son Caleb Taylor and to his heirs and Assignees for ever. But if my said son Jonathan shall be dead and not Come home and that either his Wife shall by Custom of the said Manor have any Estate or Interest in my said Copyhold Lands or in any part thereof or that if the said Lands shall descend or Come to my said son Jonathan's Child and its heirs, Then I give no Legacy by this my Testament either to my said son's Wife or to his Daughter. But if my said son shall not come home but die and that neither his Wife nor Child shall have any right or interest by Custom in or to the said Copyhold Lands, Then And not otherwise I give my said son Jonathan's Wife One hundred pounds. Item: I give and devise unto my loving wife Sarah the Rents and profits as well of my said Copyhold Lands and Tenements as also of my Freehold[6] Lands, Tenements and hereditaments in the said County of Essex during such time only as she shall remain sole

---

1   *Copyhold: A* form of land tenure common in England at the time, whereby the precise conditions of tenure were based on longstanding manorial custom. The exact details of Taylor's property holdings are not entirely clear here, but he appears to be worried that Jonathan, as his eldest son, will according to the custom of the manor be able to stake a claim on these lands in Essex, which Thomas hoped to set aside as an estate for his younger son Caleb.

2   County near London, to the east.

3   Fee-Farm Rent: another technical category common in English land-law during this period. The details need not concern you. Taylor owns the rights to perpetual rents from these properties.

4   County north and east of London. Farther away than Essex.

5   Middlesex: County immediately surrounding London. Taylor's Wapping home was in Middlesex.

6   Freehold: another medieval form of land tenure (closer to our contemporary notions of absolute property ownership).

and unmarried and from and after her marriage if so it happeneth. Then only the half of those rents of the said Free and Copyhold Lands for and towards the education and bringing up of my said son Caleb, until he shall attain the age of one and twenty years, and when the said Caleb shall have attained that age, Then I will and devise unto my said son Caleb and to his heirs for ever all my said Freehold and Copyhold Lands and Tenements in Essex. And if by the purport of this my Testament in the Cases aforesaid the same Fee-farm Rents in Norfolk shall descend or come to my son Caleb and his heirs, Then I give the same Fee-farm Rents To hold to my said Wife during her Widowhood, and after her marriage the half thereof until my said son Caleb's [majority is] attained and from and after his [adult] age attained, Then I give all the said Fee-farm Rents unto the said Caleb Taylor and to his heirs and assignees for ever … Item: if the Father of the intended husband of my daughter Hannah Taylor shall (as hath been propounded) settle for my said Daughter's Jointure[1] Thirty pounds a year in Lands or Tenements and the Reversion or remainder of those Lands and Tenements upon the heirs of her son begotten on my said daughters body, Then I give to my said Daughter Hannah for her marriage portion[2] four hundred pounds. Otherwise, I give to my said Daughter Hannah no more than three hundred pounds unless my Overseers hereafter named shall see cause and agree to pay the rest. Item: to my Daughter, Ruth Taylor, I give five hundred pounds to be paid unto her for her portion at her age of one and Twenty years or on the day of her Marriage, first having provided she marry with the approbation and Consent of my Wife and Overseers. Item: I give and bequeath unto my Daughter Wilmer One hundred pounds, and to her daughter lately borne fifty pounds, to be paid unto her at her age of one and Twenty years or on the day of her marriage first happening. And if she live not to that age or be married, Then I give that Fifty pounds to be divided among other the Children which my said daughter shall have. Item: to my daughter Wilson I give one hundred pounds and to her Child Fifty pounds, to be paid at one and Twenty years of age or marriage first happening, and if it live not so long then that Legacy to be divided among such other Children as my said Daughter Wilson shall have. Item: I give to each of my brothers' and sisters' Children and my Wife's sister's Children Twenty shillings apiece. Item: to Master Mathew Chafey I give five pounds and to Master Robert Lambe Four pounds. Item: to the Church of Christ in Wapping aforesaid whereof I am a member, I give five pounds to be disposed of at the discretion of the said Master Chafey and Mr Lambe. Item: to my Apprentice Nathaniel Prestland I give Forty shillings and all his term of Apprenticehood, and to Richard Goffe, my other apprentice, Forty shillings and the last year of his Term. Item: to Master Hanserd Knowles,[3] my son Caleb's schoolmaster, for his care and pains to be taken in his education, I give five pounds. The rest and residue of all my Goods, Chattels and personal Estate whatsoever my debts Legacies and funerals first paid and discharged and this my Testament in all things performed, I give and bequeath to my said loving Wife Sarah, whom I make, name and appoint to be sole Executrix of this my last Will and Testament, desiring her to see the same duly and truly performed as my trust is in her, willing and Charging all my Children to be ruled by my said Executrix and Overseers hereafter named. And I entreat my good friends my brother Master John Taylor and my Cousin Richard Arnold to be Overseers of my … Testament and to aiding and assisting to my said Executrix in such businesses touching this my Testament as wherein she may have occasion to use them, and for their pains therein to be taken, I give each of them Three pounds apiece. And I hereby revoke" all former wills.

[signed] Thomas Taylor

---

1   *Jointure (from OED):* A sole estate limited to the wife, being "a competent livelihood of freehold for the wife of lands and tenements, to take effect upon the death of the husband for the life of the wife at least."

2   Dowry, or monies earmarked for a dowry.

3   Hanserd Knowles (or Knollys) was a famous Anabaptist preacher in London. He had tried to emigrate to Massachusetts in the 1630s, but was kicked out because of suspicions about his radical religious views. He then moved to New Hampshire, but was kicked out after coming into conflict with a puritan minister. He then returned to England in the early 1640s. He would be repeatedly arrested and imprisoned during subsequent years.

## 2) Will of Dennis Liddell, written on Dec. 27, 1675, and formally proved (after his death) on Jan. 22, 1676

"In the Name of God Amen I, Dennis Liddell of Wapping Compass maker" do bequeath that "after my just debts are paid and satisfied I doe will and bequeath to my daughter Sarah Harrison All the Estates Goods and Chattels that her late husband[1] died possessed of (that is) All Plate and household stuff and his house and Land at Jamaica and likewise those Debts lately due to him, That is to say Eighty Pounds due from his Majesty more or less, Seventy Pounds due from Thomas Beckford more or less, to receive and enjoy the same money to her own proper use. Notwithstanding also I give to her Four Children (Mary, Submit, Mark, Sarah) each of them Twelve Pence.[2] Item: I give to my daughter Mary and to her son Peter each of them the like sum of Twelve Pence. Item: I will and bequeath the rest of my Estate real and personal Goods, Chattels, moneys, Debts, my Two Tenements built lately upon a piece of Ground formerly called the 'Saw Pit Yard,' all the interest of the house I now live in with the next adjoining, and all the rest of my worldly Estate wherewith God hath bin pleased to bless me to my loving wife Frances Liddell, to my son Dennis Liddell, and to my son James Liddell to be equally divided among them as soon as they shall come to age. Lastly I doe ordain and appoint my dear wife Frances Liddell my sole Executrix of this my last Will and Testament"

[signed]Dennis Liddell

## 3) Will of Thomas Chapman, formally proved, Nov. 29, 1681:

"In the name of God Amen, I, Thomas Chapman, Citizen and Blacksmith of London[3], being Sick and weake of body but of Sound and perfect mind and memory praise be to God, Doe make and declare this my last will and Testament, as followeth, That is to say, first and principally I Commit my soul to God, who gave it, and my body I Commit to the earth from whence it came, in Sure and certain hope of the pardon of all my Sins, through the merits, death and passion of my blessed Lord and Savior Jesus Christ, and a glorious resurrection at the last day, And as to such worldly goods and Estate as it hath pleased God to bless me with in this life I give and dispose thereof as followeth: Item: I give and bequeath to my Son Christopher Chapman the sum of Five pounds, All the rest and residue of my Estate personal and real, ready moneys, debts, goods and Chattels, of what kind or quality and in whose hands or possession, soever the same Shall be found, at the time of my decease, I wholly give leave and bequeath to my very loving wife Sarah Chapman, whom I doe hereby make and ordain full and sole Executrix of this my last will and doe hereby revoke all former wills by me made, and these presents only I ordain to be my last Will and Testament."

[signed: with the mark of
Thomas Chapman]

---

1 Sarah Liddell had married Mark Harrison in 1651. He was undoubtedly the "Captain Mark Harrison" who commanded ships on behalf of the English Republic in the 1650s, and who took part in English conquest of Jamaica from the Spanish in 1656– 7.

2 There were twelve pence to a shilling, and twenty shillings to a pound. So he is leaving them each 1/20 of a pound.

3 *Citizen and Blacksmith of London:* Chapman was a member of the London guild of blacksmiths, having served a standard apprenticeship, and was therefore entitled to the privileges of London citizenship. The blacksmiths' company was not one of the wealthy or prestigious guilds, and its members were traditionally among the poorer of artisans.

An Inventory of the goods and Chattles of Thomas Chapman late of the parish of St. Botolph Aldgate Citizen and Blacksmith of London deceased, taken and appraised by John Anderson Citizen and Sadler of London, and Stephen Slade Citizen and Haberdasher of London the Twenty Eighth day of November in the year of our Lord one thousand Six hundred Eighty one, as followeth

| **In the Kitchen or Lower Room** | £ | sh. | p.[1] |
|---|---|---|---|
| One Silver Tankard | 5 | 0 | 0 |
| One feather bed, one flock bed, one rug, one leather bolster, one flock bolster, four feather pillows, one quilt, two Blankets, and one press bedstead | 4 | 0 | 0 |
| One paire of grates, fire shovel, Tongs, forks and spits | 1 | 2 | 0 |
| One Jack | 0 | 2 | 0 |
| One great Kettle, three brass candlesticks, one warming pan, one little brass Kettle and one ladle | 0 | 18 | 0 |
| Chairs, stools, and an old Cupboard and other lumber | 0 | 10 | 0 |
| Sixteen pewter dishes, four Candlesticks, one Salt and other | 2 | 9 | 6 |

| **In the Chamber up one pair of stairs** | | | |
|---|---|---|---|
| One Clock | 3 | 0 | 0 |
| One Chest of Drawers | 1 | 0 | 0 |
| One flock bed, bedstead, Curtains and valance[2], two blankets, one Coverlet and one feather bolster | 2 | 5 | 0 |
| Five pairs of sheets, one dozen of napkins, two Table Cloths, one dozen of Towels and other old Linen | 1 | 10 | 0 |
| His wearing apparel | 4 | 0 | 0 |
| One pair of brass and irons and fire Irons | 0 | 16 | 0 |
| One Table, one Chest, two settles, other lumber | 0 | 8 | 0 |

| **In the Chamber up two pair of stairs** | | | |
|---|---|---|---|
| One musket, two pair of swords and one Collar of bandoliers | 0 | 15 | 0 |
| One flock bed, three Coverlets and three Curtains | 1 | 0 | 0 |
| In the Garret | | | |
| Item one old settle bed, one old Chest and other lumber | 0 | 3 | 0 |
| One Close stool | 0 | 5 | 0 |
| In the Shop | | | |
| Item two Anvils ... five Vices, two pair of Bellows and other working tools with Benches, Blocks and old Iron and other lumber | 10 | 0 | 0 |
| Sum | 39 | 17 | 17 |
| Item Debts good and bad owing to the said deceased by several persons | 34 | 3 | 11 |

---

1   Pounds, shillings, pence.

2   either a curtain hanging from a bed frame, or the fringing designed to cover the space between the bed frame and floor.

For purposes of comparison, contrast the London wills against this somewhat earlier will and probate inventory from the county of Lancashire in northwestern England. The area was at the time rugged and rural, and it was dominated by pastoral agriculture, although as you will see below, farming was not the only economic activity in the region.

This part of Lancashire would eventually become the center of the nascent "industrial revolution" that would transform Britain (and ultimately, this rest of the world).

## Will of Thomas Brearley, formally proved November 11, 1617:

In the name of God Amen the Second day of September In the yeares of the Reign of our Sovereign Lord James by the grace of god of England France and Ireland king defender of the faith the Fifteenth and of Scotland the one and Fiftieth—I Thomas Brearley of Marland in the county of Lancaster husbandman sick in body but of sound and perfect memory do ordain and make my Testament containing my last will in manner and forme following. First I commend my soul into the hands of Almighty god trusting by the death of Jesus Christ to obtain free pardon and remission of All my sinnes and by no other way or meanes and my body to be comitted to Christian Burial in the parish Church yard of Rochdale or where it shall please god to appoint it. And as touching such temporall goods as god hath blessed mee withal. It is my will and mind that after my debts paid and funeral expenses and forthbringing being discharged. All the rest and Residue of my goods Chattels and debts whatsoever shall be divided into three equal parts, whereof one third part I give and bequeath unto Alice Brearley my wife, as to her the same of Right belongeth. One other third part I give and bequeath unto all my Children equally to be divided amongst them And the Third and last part I bestow as followeth First I give unto Mary Brearley my youngest daughter one Cow. And the residue of the said third part I give unto five of my youngest Children to be equally divided amongst them. Item: I appoint and make Alice Brearley my wife and Roger Brearley my Eldest son Executors of this my Testament Containing my last will to perform and execute the same according to the true intent and meaning of the same as my trust is the[y] will. And I desire my wellbeloved in Christ Richard Brearley of Marland aforesaid and Robert Maden my brother in Law supervisors and overseers of this my last will to aid and assist my said Executors and to see the same executed and performed according to the true Intent and meaning hereof

[signed] Thomas Brearley

These being witnesses

Richard Brearley
Robert Maden

A true Inventory of all the goods, Catt;es and Chattels that were or did belong unto Thomas Brearley late of Marland within the parish of Rochdale yeoman deceased, priced the first day of November [1617] by James Tayler, Richard Brearley, Edmund Duerden and Robert Maden as followeth:

| Goods | Value (£-shillings-pence) |
| --- | --- |
| 2 oxen: | 10 pounds-13 shillings-4 pence |
| Eight kyne: | 25-0-0 |
| One fat cow: | 3-13-4 |
| Two twinters: | 5-13-4 |
| Four stirks: | 8-0-4 |
| Three mares and a foal: | 16-0-0 |
| Four calves: | 4-13-4 |
| In corn: | 23-6-8 |
| In Hay: | 7-0-0 |
| In meale and malt: | 9-0-0 |
| In indico Cloth: | 31-10-0 |
| In wool and yarn: | 13-0-0 |
| Two swine: | 4-0-0 |
| In pewter: | 1-17-0 |
| In brass: | 4-12-0 |
| In arks and chests: | 5-10-0 |
| In bedding: | 20-17-0 |
| In bed stands: | 2-8-0 |
| In cushions: | 0-14-0 |
| In butter and cheese: | 5-18-0 |
| 3 stone troughs: | 0-6-0 |
| One cupboard: | 0-6-0 |
| In wooden vessel: | 2-4-10 |
| In muck: | 1-0-0 |

In Carts wheels and other husbandry stuffe: 10-10-8
In Chairs stools tables forms sucks Combs Cards fire upon spit and other huslement of the house: 4-17-8

His apparel: 3-0-0
In money: 10-4-6.

[Note: in early modern England, one pound was equivalent to twenty shillings, one shilling was equivalent to twelve pence. In 1649, one observer estimated that the poorest wage labors supported themselves and their families on five to six pounds in wages per year]

# Selections from
# Testaments of Toluca

❧❧

## Edited by Caterina Pizzigoni

## 16.
## ESTEBAN DE SAN JUAN, SAN MIGUEL TOTOCUITLAPILCO, 1652

### (AGN, Civil 1207, exp. II)[1]

Like the first testament in this collection, that of Andrés Nicolás of 1671, this one of 1652 gives us a glimpse of the condition of things and the manner of expressing them in a time well before the bulk of the corpus, which dates from after 1700, and indeed it takes us an additional twenty years back. As in the other case, much is familiar, yet some differences are also to be observed. In the 1671 will, it seemed that the dominant term in the Toluca subarea for the primary residential building in the household complex after 1700, *ichantzinco Dios,* "the home of God," had not yet jelled, other formulations being used. Here, in 1652, the term is used once, but it means a church, not a household building, reinforcing our impression that the standard post-1700 meaning of the expression is a relatively late development. In the 1671 will, it was noteworthy that in an older pattern, ordinary citizens including women were the witnesses rather than officials, but here, though the date is even earlier, the witnesses are male officials, as so often in the later time.

A major characteristic of eighteenth-century Toluca Valley Nahuatl is that a man's wife is referred

to normally as his *-cihuahuatzin,* "his woman," and the term *-namic,* originally meaning one's spouse of either gender, is reserved for the husband of a woman. Here in 1652 the testator refers to his wife exclusively as *-namic,* in the older pattern, using the word a total of three times. For this circle of Nahuatl speakers the post-1700 pattern of use of spousal terms had clearly not yet been established.

The testament included here is only the most intelligible part of a larger body of obscure papers which represent two or three separate attempts to write Esteban de San Juan's will. That explains perhaps why it does not open with a traditional formula, the identification of the entity in which the will is issued, and the self-introduction of the testator, which is known only from the Spanish translation and from some of the other papers.

Apart from that, Esteban de San Juan follows a familiar pattern in bequeathing his property, giving most of it to Nicolás de los Santos, in all probability his son. His wife, who gets much less, is to raise a little daughter who gets nothing, but her mother is probably expected to pass her bequest on to her once she grows up. The wife clearly remains in the household complex even though it formally goes to the son, and she may even be in charge there. The testator gives her the responsibility of paying some of his debts, making it seem that she may have been active in his business.

Esteban shows a special devotion to Santa Maria and San Nicolás, leaving a field for their worship. Note that his son's name may derive from this devotion. The

---

1 The testament is accompanied by a contemporary Spanish translation in very bad condition.

funeral ceremony and offerings are described in detail, giving the impression that the testator is of relatively high status. There is even some money for the church cantors, which is generally uncommon in the corpus; perhaps their mention is mainly a trait of an earlier time. Esteban seems to request a burial by charity, but this may be a mere formula; the statement is immediately followed by a small offering anyway. A larger offering is given for his vigil, and in addition there is a crossed-out line in which a cow and its calf, very valuable property, are to be sold to pay for the vigil.

The numerous sums of money that are owed to Esteban de San Juan and are owed by him to others imply that he was in some sort of business. Many different communities are mentioned in this connection.

His business associate and executor Juan de Vicuña has a name like a Spaniard, and there are some other Spanish surnames, though more ambiguous, among those with whom he has dealings. It seems likely that Esteban was involved in low-level cross-community trade of the kind that often involved both Spaniards and indigenous people.

Francisco Matías, the notary as emerges from the Spanish translation, writes in a relatively conservative style, just as we would expect from the early period compared to the rest of the corpus (note the retention of ç before vowels, as well as final *z*, *uh*, and *tl*). He also includes a series of typical letter substitutions in loanwords betraying Nahuatl-style pronunciation, to a greater extent than we usually see in later documents.

[f. 5]

Axca biernes ypa meztli de março a i 1652 años

v[1] yhua niquitohua ytla Dios quimonequiltia
nopa tzimliniz capana mocahuatiuh huentli me⁰
ayaqui-tlacoz—

v yhua niquitohua nosepoltura ynahuac Sata yclesia
mocahuatiuh huetztli ayaquitlacoz— i to—

v yhua niquitohua noquimiliuhca ca ça yca notilma
yez ayaquitlacoz—

v yhua niquitohua vca mocehuiz notlalnacayo par
amol te tios nicchihua mocahuatiuh huetli me⁰
ayaquitlacoz

v yhua nitohu[. . .] Sa miguel yhua totlagonatzin Sata
mana mocahuatiuh huetzin[. . .] i to

v yhua nitohu[. . .] [tl?]a onaci ychatzinco y Dios nopa
mitoz bixilia mocahuatiuh huetzintli ayaquitlacoz—4
to

v yhua niquitohua macozque Cuicanime—2
ayaquitlacoz

v yhua nitohua cocoxcatzintzinti macozque i to me⁰
ayaquitlacoz

v yhua nitohua baca yhua yconeuh monamacazque
notech monequi [? . . . ] nobixilia yez ayaquitlacoz[2]

v yhua niquitohua nictechtia cali ytoca nicolas de lo
Satos yhua ynatzin quihuapahuaz ytoca marcarita
ayaquitlacoz

v yhua niquitohua mili monamaca[c?] cepohua ytla
monamacac notech monequi

v yhua niquitohua nictechtia y nonamic çano opa
cepohuali yc mani ayaquitlacoz

v yhua niquitohua çanopa ce tlapatl oteco cepohuali
ypa macquahuitl nictechtia ytoca Nicolas de lo Satos
ayaquitlacoz

[f. 5]

Today Friday the lst of the month of March of the
year 1652

v[1] And I say that, if God desires it, the bells are to
be rung for me; an offering of half a real is to be
delivered. No one is to go against it.—

v And I say that my grave [is to be] close to the holy
church; an offering of 1 real is to be delivered. No one
is to go against it.—

v And I say that my shroud will just be with my cloak.
No one is to go against it.—

v And I say that my earthly body is to rest there; I
do it by charity. An offering of half a real is to be
delivered. No one is to go against it.

v And I say that to San Miguel and to our precious
mother Santa María an offering of 1 real is to be
delivered.

v And I say that when [my body] reaches the home
of God [the church], a vigil is to be said for me; an
offering of 4 reales is to be delivered. No one is to go
against it.

v And I say that the singers are to be given 2 [reales].
No one is to go against it.

v And I say that the sick will be given 1 real and a half.
No one is to go against it.

v And I say that a cow and its calf are to be sold; [the
proceeds] will be used for me for my future vigil. No
one is to go against it.[2]

v And I say that I assign the house to Nicolás de los
Santos, and his mother is to raise the one named
Margarita. No one is to go against it.

v And I say that a cultivated field of 20 [quahuitl] is to
be sold; when it has been sold it will be used for me.

v And I say that I assign [a field or piece of land] to
my spouse, also there; it is 20 [quahuiti]. No one is to
go against it.

v And I say that also there is a piece at the side of the
road, 30 quahuiti; I assign it to the one named Nicolás
de los Santos. No one is to go against it.

---

1 The first eight entries have the word *oneltic,* "it was carried
out," in the left margin; the notations seem to have been added
afterwards.

2 This entry was marked out.

v yhua niquitohua p⁰ hernadez quipie¹ mili cepohuali
oteco tlatzintla nictechtia totlasonatzin Sata maᵃ yhua
Sato Sa nicolas cocahuia ayaquitlacoz

v yhua niquitohua otictlane tomi capoltitla nonamic
quixtlahuaz ce i ps⁰ 4 to yhua p⁰ lopiz ytech ca i ps⁰ 4
to ayaquitlacoz

v yhua niquitohua Sa peliphe nichuiquilia 2 b⁰s [n?]
ytoca Ana yhua xporal Rafael quixtlahuaz—2 ps⁰
ayaquitlacoz

v yhua niquitohua tlacotepec nichuilia ytomi
Cobernatol 2 ps⁰ quixtl[ … ]huaz non[. . .]c² ayaquitlacoz [f. 5v]

v yhua niquitohua nechhuiquilia i ce ps⁰ ytoca Grabiel
[a ?] sa loreço quixtlahu[ … ] Ayaquitlacoz

v yhua niquitohua Sa Sebastia mili colaltitla
Dios—oquimotlapopolli do Juah? [ … ]do oquimona-
maquilitia yehuatl oquicouh Jua te bicoya matlactli
p⁰s 4 to ca nicno[ … ]tiz ayaquitlacoz

v yhua niquitohua ytla onechmopolhui y notlaço-
mahuiztatzin y Dios At⁰ Feliciano yhua Jua de bicoya
y noalhuaciales yehuatl quimocuitlahuizque y tley
nictecpanaz yn itoca textameto auh ytla [y? …]qui
quimochihuilique Dios quimo[tla?]tlaxtlahuiliz-que
yhua nehuatl nixpa miguel de stiago fiscal

|      †       |      †       |       †       |
| diego juárez | franᶜᵒ matias | miguel garᵃ  |
| tifotatos    |             | tifotatos     |

---

v And I say that Pedro Hernández holds¹ a cultivated
field of 20 [quahuitl] at the edge of the road, below. I
give it to our precious mother Santa María and holy
San Nicolás; they share it. No one is to go against it.

v And I say that we borrowed money at Capultitlan;
my spouse is to pay 1 peso and 4 reales; and Pedro
López owes 1 peso. No one is to go against it.

v And I say that at San Felipe I owe 2 pesos to one
named Ana; and Cristóbal Rafael is to pay 2 pesos. No
one is to go against it.

v And I say that in Tlacotepec I owe money to the
governor, 2 pesos; my spouse² is to pay it. No one is to
go against it. [f. 5v]

v And I say that one named Gabriel [in] San Lorenzo
owes me 1 peso; he is to pay it. No one is to go against
it.

v. And I say that don Juan ? [ … ], whom God
removed, at death sold a cultivated field in San
Sebastián, next to a corral [or at Corraltitlan]; Juan de
Vicuña bought it [for] 10 pesos and 4 reales. I will [
… ] it. No one is to go against it.

v And I say that, when my precious revered father
God has destroyed me [when I die], Antonio Feliciano
and Juan de Vicuña are my executors; they are to take
care of what I will order in what is named the testament. If they do so, God will reward them. Before me,
Miguel de Santiago, fiscal.

Diego Juárez, diputado; Francisco Matías; Miguel
García, diputado.

---

1    Here the verb *pia* seems to have its older meaning to hold, have
custody of.
2    The original was no doubt "nonamic."

# 42.
# MARÍA SALOMÉ, SAN PABLO TEPEMAXALCO, PASIONTITLAN, 1654

## (AGN, Tierras 2300, exp. 18)[1]

One of the earliest testaments in the present volume, this document was written half a century before the bulk of the Toluca Valley corpus begins, and some of its many interesting traits were not to be retained in later times. It is included here among the wills of the tlaxilacalli Pasiontitlan in Tepemaxalco, for although the notary writes San Pedro Tepemaxalco, we can be pretty sure that he meant San Pablo. In the Calimaya/Tepemaxalco jurisdiction, San Pedro was the patron saint of Calimaya and San Pablo of Tepemaxalco, but here the connection with the latter is evident through the names of prominent witnesses.[2] It appears that there must have been a little confusion with the saint's name; maybe it even represents evidence that the distinction between the two conjoined altepetl was beginning to break down by this time.

María Salomé is in all probability a widow, since the only reference to her husband appears at the end of the testament, in a sort of afterthought and merely in an effort to cement her children's rights to some distant landed property. She divides her possessions mainly among her four children, who all seem to be grown up and possibly already married.

The two sons who play the part of the principal heirs, Josef and Francisco, bear a second name well known in Tepemaxalco, de la Cruz. They are to share two pieces of land, one with magueyes and the other a large piece apparently devoted to maize agriculture. They are also to share some more magueyes that María had bought or cultivated on lots belonging to five different individuals, among them her father, don Pedro

Jacobo, and a possible relative who shares the same second name, Sebastián Jacobo. Some furniture and tools also appear, whether because of the fact that such things were mentioned more frequently in wills of earlier times, or because these items are particularly valuable. The sons get a chest each, while Josef receives a lot with magueyes, a plow, and a chisel for himself alone; most likely he is the eldest, followed by Francisco, whose first name is the second name of his father.

Some of the names here are difficult to judge; in post-1700 terms, Salomé and Jacobo are rare second names and might imply distinction, but both had been common in the sixteenth century and possibly still were at the time this will was issued. At least we can be sure that the title don borne by María's father marks high status.

At the end of the testament, María seems to remember that there is more property she wishes to leave to the two sons, in Tenango del Valle at the southern end of the Toluca Valley. The note is a bit confused because this part of the original is badly deteriorated and many words are partly illegible; however, it seems that this property was accumulated by her husband and she is now passing it on to the two sons, or whichever one of them should survive. The outstanding feature is that the holdings are outside the Calimaya/Tepemaxalco area, located in another altepetl altogether and at some distance. Either María's husband Juan Francisco, whose name is not distinguished, was originally from there, or he had important interests there.

The testator also has another son, Gabriel de Santiago, who gets nothing more than a wooden corncrib and is reminded to pay back a quite substantial debt, and a daughter, Luisa María, who receives another wooden corncrib and a metate, as well as some land to share. These children would seem either to be in disfavor or already to have received much of their inheritance. A grandchild of the testator, Leonor, is luckier in the will, since she gets two houses and a piece of land planted in magueyes to be shared with Luisa María, probably because she is still too young to take care of everything by herself. Leonor must be Luisa's daughter, and it is significant here that some important property is passed on to the second generation of heirs through females, with no reference at all to Luisa's husband, who could easily have been entrusted with taking care of the houses and land. At the same time, note that María

---

1  The testament is accompanied by a contemporary Spanish translation.

2  The first three witnesses are prominent figures of San Pablo Tepemaxalco around the time the will was issued. Don Matías de San Francisco was to be governor there in 1656; don Baltasar de los Reyes, present governor, had been governor before in 1647; don Diego de la Cruz, past alcalde, was to be governor in 1655 (Lockhart 1992, p. 137; see also pp. 128–29). Note that both Calimaya and Tepemaxalco seem to have had a tlaxilacalli Pasiontitlan.

Salomé follows the same policy as many male testators in favoring males in the central part of the inheritance.

Due to the frequent mention of magueyes and the number of plants involved, at least 32 plus various rows (the standard row included eight plants), we have every reason to assume that the testator's principal activity was the cultivation of the plant and the production of beverages. It is very interesting to notice that María seems to have bought some of the magueyes from other people who still own the land, so that she and her heirs would exploit the plants independently of the land itself. Yet she also had more land of her own than most women who specialized in maguey production.

Thus putting together magueyes, lands and houses, María appears to be a relatively wealthy woman, and she probably was even more so earlier, since at the end of the testament she reports that property of hers was lost when thieves entered her home. All was listed in a document, but unfortunately it is not attached to the testament, so we will never know the nature of what was stolen, but clearly she considered it valuable.

The testator's high status is also evident through the complete and elaborate opening formula and the funeral arrangements. She requests the shroud and rope of San Francisco, burial inside the church, and as many as three high masses with at least two responsory prayers. But what is even more striking is the fact that she names a high-ranking woman as her executor, doña María de Guzmán, thereby indirectly showing her own prominent status. The appointment of women as executors is extremely rare in the Toluca Valley corpus, but it may have been a more common practice earlier in time, during the seventeenth century.

Along the same lines, María has four women in the list of her witnesses, one being another doña, which is practically not seen anywhere else in the Toluca Valley testaments. Female witnesses were present in early testaments such as those of Culhua-can (sixteenth century), but did not correspond to Spanish custom, and the Toluca corpus in general shows that by the eighteenth century indigenous communities of the valley, like those elsewhere, had adopted the Spanish practice. María Salomé might be seen as an exception, but it is more likely that in the seventeenth century the older way still survived in the Toluca region. As for the other witnesses, the three dons who head the list all at some time held the governorship of Tepemaxalco and are powerful evidence of María Salomé's connections.[1]

The notary is a don Juan de la Cruz.[2] His style is much more conservative and standard than that of most later notaries, and his formulas are usually longer and more complete; the whole long preamble (including its lack of Jesus, Mary, and Joseph as a heading) could virtually have been written in the sixteenth century, except for its tendency to use *s* instead of final *z*. We see here the reverential *ma-huiz-*, "revered," instead of the doubled *tlaçomahuiz-*, "precious revered" that is so common later. Late in the document the testator addresses the witnesses directly, using the second person plural, also a very archaic trait. It is striking, too, that a person so well endowed mentions no saints; since they are lacking in the preamble as well, the absence may be due to an older style. Nevertheless, the text already contains the loan particle *hasta*, here meaning "as far as."

---

1 A witness is listed as fiscal, but he lacks the don. It is hard to know whether this person is fiscal in a minor church, or whether at this time the important fiscal for the altepetl at the main church does not yet ordinarily bear the title.

2 It would be tempting to think that this person is the same who would later become governor of San Pablo Tepemaxalco and who left us his testament in 1691 (No. 39). But not only is the stretch of years very considerable and the name in its way common, it is not likely that the governor don Juan de la Cruz would have borne the don until he attained high office; he was not governor to our knowledge until the 1680s, and even the founder of the de la Cruz governors was plain Pedro de la Cruz until 1657 (Lockhart 1992, p. 136). In any ease, it is quite unusual for a notary to bear the don even after 1700, and even less so earlier. Perhaps this don Juan has already held some higher office.

yca yn imahuistoCatzin yn dios tetatzin yhuan yn
dios tepiltzin yhuan yn dios espiritu santo Ma y
mo-chihua nican nicpehualtia yn notestamento
nehuatl notoCa maᵃ salomen nican nochan San
pedro te-pemaxalco notlaxilaCalpan paxioti[ … ] ma
qui-matican yn yxquichtin quitazque ynin amatl Auh
maçhuin mococohua yn notlalnaCayo yec y noyolo y
noçalis y notlalnamiquilis y notlacaquia aquin ca san
pactica Auh nicchixtiCa yn miquistli yn [ … ]yac huel
yxpanpa yehuis yn huel quitlalcahuia ynic niCtlalia y
notestamento yc çan tla[ … ]ca yn çan tlatzonco not-
lanequilis y ye mochipa mopi[ … ] ynic ayac quitlacoz
ca yehuatl i yn ys Catqu[ … ] nicpehualtia huel achto
yehuatl y[ … ] naniman ymac-tzinCo noContlalia yn
tt.º dios Ca o[ … ]imochihuili yhuan ninotlatlauhtilia
yn ne[ … ]motlaoColilis nechmopopolhuililis y
notlatla[ … ] nechmohuiquilis yn ichantzinCo yn
ilhuiCatl [ … ] yn iquac naniman quitlalCahuis y
nonacayo Ca [ … ]tech nicpohua yn tlalli ca ytech
oquis ca tlalli ca [ … ]quitli yhuan notlanequilistica
y noquimiliuhca yes san fransᶜᵒ yabitotzin yhuan
yCordontzin yc quimiliuhtias y notlalnacayo auh y
nose[ … ]ltura onCan toctos y notlalnaCayo te[ … ]
ncalitic axCan mani metztli a 19 de no[ … ]bre ypan
xihuitl de 1654 Años =

v ynic sentlamantli niquitohua yey missa huehuey
yn nopanpa mitos au[ … ]n Responsos ome ypale-
huiloca yn naman = 3 misas = [?] Responsos—
v ynic ontlamantli niquitohua y notelpoch Jose de la
Cruz yhuan fransᶜᵒ de la crus niquinmaCa tlalli mani
Coyohuaca meyot[ … ]auhpantli metl coca-huisque
quiCuisque yhuā yC o[ … ] mani tlali paxiotitlan ome
yota Ca no Concahuisque notelpochhuan Juseph de
la Cruz yhuan [15v] fransᶜᵒ de la Crus yhuan [ … ]¹
ynemac Juseph de la Cruz yhuan se escoplo—

v ynic yetlamantli yn niquitohua y notelpoch gabriel
de Santiago se quauhcuescomatl ynemac yhuan
y-panpa onitlaxtlauh matlactli omome pesos yn
qui-huiquilia yehuatl [ … ]imatia ça nechtlaixtlahuilis
no[ … ] amo [?] =
v ynic nauhtlamantli yn niquitohua y Juseph de la
Cruz nicmaCa se solar mani san simon senpantli metl

---

1 The Nahuatl is not legible; the meaning is taken from the
Spanish translation.

In the revered name of God the father, God the son,
and God the Holy Spirit, may it be done. Here I
named María Salomé begin my testament; my home is
here in San Pedro Tepemaxalco, and my tlaxilacalli is
in Pasiontitlan; may all who see this document know
it. Although my earthly body is ill, yet there is nothing
wrong with my heart, will, memory, and understanding, but they are sound. I am awaiting death, which
no one can flee from or avoid, so that I issue my
testament, my last and final will, that is always to be
observed, so that no one will violate it. Here it is,
as follows; I begin. First of all I place my soul in the
hands of our lord God, for he made it, and I pray to
him that he deign to pardon me my sins and take me
to his home in heaven when my soul abandons my
body. I assign [my body] to the earth, for from there
it came, and it is earth and clay. And by my will my
shroud is to be the habit of San Francisco, and my
earthly body is to be wrapped with his rope. My grave
where my earthly body is to lie buried is inside the
church building. Today, in the month of November in
the year of 1654. =

v First I say that three high masses are to be said for
me, with two responsory prayers, as the help of my
soul. = 3 masses. = [?] responsory prayers.—
v Second I say that I give to my son Josef de la
Cruz and to Francisco de la Cruz a piece of land at
Coyoacan with magueyes on it, four rows; they are to
share it. They are also to take another piece of land
in Pasiontitlan, [of a size to be cultivated by] two
yokes [of oxen]; my sons Josef de la Cruz and [15v]
Francisco de la Cruz are to share it also. And [a plow]¹
is the inheritance of Josef de la Cruz, and a chisel.—
v Third I say that a wooden corncrib is the inheritance
of my son Gabriel de Santiago. And I paid 12 pesos
back on his behalf; [he knew to whom he owed it?]; he
is to pay me back without fail [ … ]. =

v Fourth I say that I give to Josef de la Cruz a lot in
San Simón that has a row of magueyes, and outside
[the house] the lot is all planted with magueyes that
are also his inheritance. Then I bought 15 magueyes
from Melchor Leonardo, on his lot; Josef de la Cruz

quipia yhuan quiyahuac mani solar mochi meyotoc
no ynemac [ … ]man melchior leonardo ysolarpa
onicCohuili caxtonli metl no ConCahuiya Juseph de
la crus yhuan frans^co de la Cruz niman çe tlapal solar
onp[ … ]ntli metl no ConCahuia niman ysolarpa
notatzin [ … ]on pe^oxacobo chicome metl ynnemac
no ConCahuia niman Sebastian xacobo onicohuili
nahui metl ysolarpa no ynemac niman maria mag^na
biuda oniccohuili nahui metl ysolarpa no ynnemac
niman pe.° joachin oniccohuili ome metl ysolarpa no
ynemac notelpuchhuan—

v_ ynic macuiltlamantli y niquitohua y nochpoch luysa
maria ynnemac çe CuauhCuescomatl yhuan se metlatl
auh y nocihuamo Angelina ana se metlatl ynemac
niman noxhuiuh leonor nicmaca ome cali yhuan c[ … ]
]huaca^1 mani tlalli concahuisque luyssa maria yhuān
leonor no meyotoc maculip[ … ]tli metl

— 

v_ ynic chiquçentlamantli y niquitohua yn Joseph de
la crus yhuan frans^co de la crus ome Caxa ynnemac çe
huey se tepiton ynemac—

niCan nictzonquis[ … ]a yn notzonquiscatlanahuatil
yxpan noalbasea doña ma^a de gusman ynic quimo-
Cuitlahui[ … ]axcan yn notlatqui yhuan mochtin y
nopil[ … ]n yn oniquinteneuh yhuan naniman [ … ]
palehuiloca yntla yuhqui mochi[f. 16]huas yn notla-
nahuatil ca ylhuicatl itic quimotlaxtlahuilma-quilis yn
tt° dioz^2

yhuan ymixpan testigoshuan don matias de san frans^co
testigo Don Baltasar de los Reyes g.^or Don diego de la
Cms alld. pasado Doña maria bea-tris testigo Clara
beatris biuda testigo Maria magdalena testigo Catalina
bernardina testigo frans^co [mg^1?] fiscal Juan lucaz
teopan top[ … ]

Nehuatl [ … ] Don Juan de la Cruz onitlaCuilo
yhuan yn oniqui[ … ]uh^3 yn oquic amixpantzinco yn
anotestigohuan [ … ] se amatl mopixtica ynic oni-
tlapolo yni[ … ]laque ychteque nochan yn mochtin
nopilhuan [ … ]me yehuantin yn aquin quichicahua
yx[ … ]a ametetzacualo[ … ]que [?]—Auh ynin

and Francisco de la Cruz are to share them also. Then
on one side [of the same?] lot they also share two rows
of magueyes. Then on the lot of my father don Pedro
Jacobo 7 magueyes are their inheritance; they are
to share them too. Then I bought 4 magueyes from
Sebastián Jacobo on his lot; they are their inheritance
too. Then I bought 4 magueyes on her lot from María
Magdalena, widow; they are also their inheritance.
Then I bought two magueyes from Pedro Joaquín on
his lot; they are also the inheritance of my sons.—

v_ Fifth I say that a wooden corncrib and a metate
are the inheritance of my daughter Luisa María, and
a metate is the inheritance of my daughter-in-law
Angelina Ana. Then to my grandchild Leonor I give
two houses and a piece of land in [Coyoacan];[1] Luisa
María and Leonor are to share it. It is also planted in
magueyes, 5 rows of magueyes.—

v_ Sixth I say that two chests, one large and one small,
are the inheritance of Josef de la Cruz and Francisco
de la Cruz.—

Here I conclude my final commands in the presence
of my executor doña María de Guzmán, who is to
look after my property and all my children whom I
have mentioned, and the help of my soul. If my orders
are carried out well [f. 16], our lord God will give her
her reward in heaven. [It was done on the 9th day of
November of the year 1654.][2]

And it is in the presence of [my] witnesses don Matías
de San Francisco; don Baltasar de los Reyes, governor;
don Diego de la Cruz, past alcalde; doña María
Beatriz, witness; Clara Beatriz, widow, witness; María
Magdalena, witness; Catalina Bernardina, witness;
Francisco [Miguel], fiscal; Juan Lucas, church topile.

I, don Juan de la Cruz, did the writing.
And since I [forgot],[3] [I say] while it is still in the presence of you my witnesses that a document is preserved
about what I lost when thieves [entered] my home.
All my children [ … ] punished.—And as to another
thing that I say, my children here, Josef de la Cruz and
Francisco de la Cruz, whichever one of them should
live, to them you are to distribute [the following] in
Tenango del Valle, the home of our precious revered
mother Santa María Nativitas, and he is to take the
house[s?] along with however many [lots] there are; he
is to take all the fruit and all the [?] until where [the

---

1  The Spanish translation has "coyoaca."
2  The passage is now missing in the original and is taken from
the Spanish translation.
3  The Spanish translation has "que se me olvido." The Nahuatl
must have been "oniquilcauh."

oc centlamantli y niquitohua y nican [ … ]pilhua
Joseph de la crus yhuan frans<sup>co</sup> de la crus saso [ … ]
quin quimochicahuilis yn dioz a[?]quinmoxelihuis [?]
Tengo en el baye yn ichantzin[ … ] totlaçomahuisna[
… ] Santa ma<sup>a</sup> nativitas conanas y [ … ]cali mochi
quexquich [ … ]ares onCa moch quiCuis xoco[ … ]
li yhuan mochintin [ … ]sta Canin tlantiCac ca ysia-[
… ]miquilistzin [?] y nona[ … ]mictzin Ju° frans.<sup>co</sup>
ayac mostla [*16v*] huiptla quinquixtilis Ca ymaxca yes
y nopilhuan Ca tel oncan Catqui yn [ … ]-amatzintli
yn tlaneltilis ynic ayac quenmanian quinmaxcatis
ynon [ … ] anmetztzinoticate ? [ … ]-notestigohuan
yn oquic amixpantzinco noCon[ … ]lli y notlatol Ca
nestiCa ast[ … ] Canin tlantiCa [ … ] calli Ca tel
onca quaxochtl[ … ] yehuatl tlaneltili yhu n Canin [
…]tica ca se[ … ] tlacuilonlo ca tel amoixpantzinco
macamo mostla hui[ … ] ayac quenmania qu[ … ]
maxcatis Ca ynmaxca yes y[ …] nopilhuan Ca ye [ …
]notzonquis yn [ … ]tlatol

property] ends, for it is the result of the work of my
husband Juan Francisco. In future, no one [*16v*] is to
take it from them, for it is to be the property of my
children, for here are the papers to verify it so that no
one will ever appropriate it; you my witnesses [who
are here?], since I have [made?] my declaration before
you, and it appears how far the [land and ?] house
reach, for there are boundaries establishing to where it
goes, it is written, so before you [I say], let no one in
the future ever appropriate it, for it is to belong to my
children. Now I have concluded my statement.

# The Forgotten Trade

By Nigel Tattersfield

## COMPRISING THE LOG OF THE *DANIEL AND HENRY* OF 1700 AND ACCOUNTS OF THE SLAVE TRADE FROM THE MINOR PORTS OF ENGLAND, 1698–1725

### The Voyage of the *Daniel and Henry*

In the year 1699, the west-country English tobacco merchants Daniel Ivy and Henry Arthur decided to try their hand at a new trade. Taking advantage of recent legal changes that had opened up the Africa trade to merchants outside the Royal Africa Company, the two men prepared their ship, the *Daniel and Henry*, for a voyage down the west coast of Africa, with the intent to purchase and transport slaves to the Americas. They hired a captain, Roger Mathew, who had knowledge of African waters, and a young merchant, Walter Prideaux, to manage the enterprise aboard the ship; and they outfitted their boat with the various accoutrements necessary for this grim trade—chains, a cauldron, new maps and charts, and of course, all of the cargo that would be traded in Africa for slaves. The ship set out in early 1700. By April, the *Daniel and Henry* was actively moving down the African coast, as Mathew and Prideaux sought slaves for purchase. It took several months plying the coast of modern Ivory Coast and Ghana to fill their ship with some 452 slaves. In September, after stopping at the Portuguese island colony São Tomé in order to re-provision the ship, Mathew began the long journey across the Atlantic, to Jamaica, where the slaves would be sold; the final leg of the journey involved using the proceeds from the slave sales to purchase sugar for the return trip to Britain.

The documents reproduced here are portions of the ship's logs: Document (1) provides the details of the goods traded for slaves. Some of these items will be unfamiliar, but most of them can be quickly identified online via the Oxford English Dictionary (available through Stanford Libraries Database page; sometimes you need to play with the spelling or look for near matches on the left hand side of the page). Document (2) provides details from the log chronicling the trip from Africa to Jamaica. As you read the documents, try to strain every piece of information you can from them about the slave trade and its connections to other parts of early modern Atlantic life and economy.

ACCOUNT of what goods were put off for slaves on the coast of Guinea for account of Messrs Ivey, Arthur & Gould, merchants in Exon and London, on board their ship *Daniel and Henry* for their account and risk and bound for Jamaica.[3]

| 1700 | | | Men | Women | Boys | Girls |
|---|---|---|---|---|---|---|
| April 11 | To: | 3 pieces perpetuannas, 4 sheets & 2 small knives | 1 | | | |
| Dicky Cove | | (Gave 32 Ackeys of Gold, 28A of Gold & 32A of Gold for)* | 3 | | | |
| 18 | To: | 2 half barrels of powder & one small looking glass | | 1 | | |
| May 1 | To: | 2 whole cases of spirits (& paid 24AGold)* | 1 | | | |
| Commenda 6 | To: | 48 dozen large knives, 39 sheets & 8 half cases of spirits | | 3 | | 1 |
| | To: | 64 sheets, 1 firkin of tallow, 2 perpetuannas (& 1A of Gold)*    ↘ 40.9148 liters | | 3 | 1 | 1 |
| | To: | 33 sheets, 3 perpetuannas, 6 large knives (& 43A Gold)* | 2 | | | |
| Annamabo 9 | To: | 1 sea, 1 perpetuanna, 1 firkin of tallow, 4 X 3lb basins & 2 tankards | 1 | | | |
| 10 | To: | 2 seas & 4 X 3lb basins | 1 | | | |
| 11 | To: | 1 sea & 2 perpetuana | 1 | | | |
| 12 | To: | 1 sea & 3 firkins of tallow    Silver coin | | 1 | | |
| 13 | | (Gave 22 Ackeys of Gold for)*    minted in England | | | 1 | |
| 14 | To: | 2 firkins of tallow (& 16 Ackeys of gold)* | | 1 | | |
| | To: | 6 half cases of spirits, 6 perpetuannas & 6 looking glasses | 2 | | | |
| 15 | To: | 2 firkins of tallow (& 38 Ackeys of gold)* | | 2 | | |
| Aponferra | To: | 7 darnicks | | | | 1 |
| 16 | To: | 3 firkins of tallow & 36 sheets | 1 | | 1 | |
| T:C:Querry | | | | | | |
| 17 | To: | 16 sheets, 4 seas, 1 half case of spirits, 2 tankards, 1 firkin of powder[4] | 1 | 2 | | |
| | | The sum carried to the other side is | 14 | 13 | 3 | 3 |

| | | | Men | Women | Boys | Girls |
|---|---|---|---|---|---|---|
| | | To the sum brought over | 14 | 13 | 3 | 3 |
| | To: | 1 half barrel of powder, 1 firkin of tallow (& 8 Ackeys of gold)* | | 1 | | |
| | To: | 5 whole cases of spirits, 3 half ditto (& 48 Ackeys of gold)* | 1 | 1 | 1 | |
| | To: | 24 sheets for | | 1 | | |
| 18 | To: | 2 whole & 3 half cases of spirits (& 1 Ackey of gold)* | | | | 1 |
| 20 | To: | 1 firkin of tallow, 2 whole barrels of powder, 4 firkins ditto [powder] & 6 sheets | 2 | | | |
| | To: | 2 sheets (& 24 Ackeys of Gold)* | 1 | | | |
| | To: | 1 fuzee, 6 large knives, I firkin of tallow, 1 whole case of spirits, (& 12 Ackeys of gold)* | 1 | | | |
| | To: | 1 barrel of powder & 6 dozen large knives | 1 | | | |
| | To: | 7 firkins of tallow & 1 darnick | 1 | | | |
| 22 | To: | 1 nehallaware (& 1 Ackey of gold)* | | 1 | | |
| Winnabey | To: | 1 barrel of powder (& 4 Ackeys of gold)* | 1 | | | |
| 23 | To: | 32 sheets, 7 firkins of tallow & 28 dozen large knives | 2 | 1 | | |
| 24 | To: | 1 firkin of tallow, 1 barrel of powder & 1 X 3lb basins | 1 | | | |
| 25 | To: | 1 darnick (& 32 Ackeys of gold)* | 1 | | 1 | |
| 26 | To: | 2 dozen large knives (& 17 Ackeys of gold)* | | | 1 | |
| | To: | 2 dozen ditto (& 24 Ackeys of gold)* | | 1 | | |
| | To: | 5 nehallawares & 3 dozen large knives (Gave 26 Ackeys for a young man)* | | 2 | 1 | |
| | To: | 12 dozen small knives, 2 tankards, 2 dozen great knives & 2 firkins of tallow (and 25 Ackeys of gold)* | 1 | | | |
| | | The sum carried to the other side is | 27 | 21 | 7 | 4 |

*handwritten annotation next to "1 fuzee" row:* → old-fashioned clock.

| | | | Men | Women | Boys | Girls |
|---|---|---|---|---|---|---|
| | | To the sum brought over | 27 | 21 | 7 | 4 |
| | To: | 3 barrels of powder & 1 dozen great knives | 3 | | | |
| 27 | To: | 2 darnicks, 2 firkins of tallow, 32 dozen great knives | | 2 | | |
| | To: | 5 firkins of tallow, 2 X 3lb basins & 2 tankards | | 1 | | |
| 28 | To: | 1 barrel of powder & 2 tankards for | 1 | | | |
| 29 | To: | 2 firkins of tallow, 1 perpetuanna & 8 dozen great knives & 1 tankard | | 1 | | |
| | To: | 13 dozen great knives & 4 firkins of tallow for | | 1 | | |
| | To: | 1 barrel of powder for | 1 | | | |
| 30 | To: | 1 barrel of powder & 2 dozen great knives for | | 1 | | |
| 31 | To: | 2 barrels of powder for | | | 2 | |
| June 1 | To: | 1 barrel of powder & 1 firkin of tallow for | 1 | | | |
| | To: | 18 iron bars & 1 dozen great knives for | 1 | | | |
| 4 | To: | 26 dozen great knives & 1 barrel of powder for | 1 | 1 | | |
| | To: | 2 pieces of Nehallawares & 4 dozen great knives | | 1 | | |
| | To: | 21 iron bars & 2 firkins of tallow for | 1 | | | 1 |
| 6 | To: | 3 fuzees, 4 sheets, 1 perpetuana & 6 iron bars | 1 | 1 | | |
| | To: | 1 firkin of tallow, 15 sheets, 6 dozen small knives & 1 tankard | | 1 | | |
| Accra 10 | To: | 1 barrel of powder | | 1 | | |
| | To: | 2 pieces of nehallawares & 8 looking glasses | | 1 | | |
| | To: | 3 perpetuannas, 10 looking glasses & 3 X 1lb basins | 1 | | | |
| 11 | To: | 2 fuzees, 1 X 3lb basin, 1 tankard & 8 looking glasses | | 1 | | |
| | | The sum carried to the other side is | 38 | 34 | 9 | 5 |

| | | | | Men | Women | Boys | Girls |
|---|---|---|---|---|---|---|---|
| | | | To the sum brought over | 38 | 34 | 9 | 5 |
| Alampo 13 | To: | 4 tapseils, 1 blue sea, 9 x 2lb basins & 1 hanger | | 1 | 1 | | |
| | To: | 1 sea & 8 X 3lb basins, 1 tapseil & 6 darnicks | | | 1 | | 1 |
| | To: | 2 perpetuannas & 16 sheets, 1 perpetuanna, 8 sheets, 1 tapseil & 9 darnicks | | | 2 | | 2 |
| 14 | To: | 2 tapseils & 12 sheets | | 1 | | | |
| 15 | To: | 24 X 1lb & 7 X 3lb basins & 1 nickanee | | | 1 | | |
| | To: | 1 sea & 1 piece Nehallawares, 14 carpets, 8 tankards & 16 sheets | | 1 | 2 | | |
| | To: | 22 sheets, 11 darnicks or carpets for | | | 1 | | 1 |
| 16 | To: | 9 X 1lb, 1 X 3lb basins, 2 perpetuannas, 21 tankards & 1 tapseil | | 1 | 1 | | |
| | To: | 1 nehallaware, 2 X 3lb & 12 x 2lb basins & 3 perpetuanna | | | 2 | | |
| 17 | To: | 8 tankards, 3 iron bars, 2 perpetuannas, 8 sheets & 1 darnick | | 1 | | | 1 |
| | To: | 11 darnicks, 2 tapseils, 2 tankards & 1 nickanee | | | 1 | 1 | |
| 18 | To: | 4 pieces of nehallaware, 4 X 3lb basins, 11 sheets, 4 darnicks & 3 looking glasses | | | 2 | | 1 |
| | To: | 2 seas, 2 tapseils & 7 sheets | | 1 | 1 | | |
| | To: | 1 half barrel of powder, 2 x 3lb basins & 3 looking glasses . | | | | | 1 |
| 19 | To: | 1 sea & 19 tankards & 1 case of spirits, 1 sea & 6 tankards | | | 2 | | 1 |
| | To: | 12 looking glasses, 6 tankards, 4 darnicks, 8 x 3lb & 3 x 2lb basins, 1 case spirits | | | 1 | | 1 |
| June 20 | To: | 6 carbines, 1 hanger, 28 sheets, 2 brass pans, 1 sea & 8 tankards | | 2 | 1 | | |
| | | | The sum carried to the other side is | 46 | 53 | 10 | 14 |

| | | | Men | Women | Boys | Girls |
|---|---|---|---|---|---|---|
| | | To the sum brought over | 46 | 53 | 10 | 14 |
| | To: | 16 X 3lb basins, 8 tankards, 4 darnicks, 1 case of spirits & ½ barrel of powder | | 2 | | |
| | To: | 3 salem powers, 11 X 3lb basins, 2 tapseils, 2 darnicks & 1 tankard . | 1 | 1 | | |
| | To: | 4 firkins of powder, 1 tankard, 1 sea & 9 X 3lb basins | | 1 | | 1 |
| | To: | 9 X 2lb basins, 2 tankards, 1/2 barrel of powder, 2 half cases of spirits | | 1 | | |
| 21 | To: | 4 perpetuannas, 12 X 2lb basins, 2 tankards & 1 half case of spirits | 1 | | 1 | |
| | To: | 1 barrel of powder, 3 X 3lb basins, 1 tankard, 2 brass pans, 1 sea & 1 tapseil | 1 | 1 | | |
| 22 | To: | 1 sea, 8 tankards, 2 perpetuannas, 3 X 2lb basins, & 3 looking glasses | | 2 | | |
| | To: | 12 iron bars, 7 X 3lb basins, 4 tapseils, 1 perpetuanna, 1 darnick, a brawle, 8 tankards | 2 | 1 | | |
| | To: | 1 tapseil, 1 double brawle, 1 salem power & 5 tankards | 1 | | | |
| | To: | 1 darnick, 3 firkins of powder, 10 X 3lb basins & 1 tankard | | | 1 | 1 |
| 23 | To: | 7 whole cases of spirits & 1 tankard for pte a man & 1 sea | 1 | | | 1 |
| 27 | To: | 6 perpetuannas, of the owner's servants for 2 women at 8A per piece | | 2 | | |
| | To: | 1 barrel of powder, 1 sea, 9 X 2lb basins & 2 tankards | | 2 | | |
| | To: | 1 sea, 1 whole case of spirits, 1 X 3lb basin & 2 tankards | | 1 | | |
| 28 | To: | 2 brass pans, 3 X 2lb & 2 X 3lb basins, 60 rangoes & 1 tankard per pte | | 1 | | |
| | To: | 1 sea, 17 X 3lb basins, 60 rangoes, 6 X 2lb basins & 2 tankards | | 1 | | 1 |
| | | The sum carried to the other side is | 53 | 69 | 12 | 18 |

| | | | Men | Women | Boys | Girls |
|---|---|---|---|---|---|---|
| | | To the sum brought over | 53 | 69 | 12 | 18 |
| 29 | To: | 2 seas, 2 darnicks, 15 X 2lb basins, 1 tankard, 30 rangoes | | 2 | | |
| | To: | 16 darnicks, 1 X 3lb basin, 30 rangoes, 1 perpetuanna, & 1 case of spirits | | 1 | 1 | |
| 30 | To: | 3 tankards, 210 rangoes for pte | 1 | 1 | | |
| | To: | 5 firkins of powder | | | 1 | |
| July 1 | To: | 2 seas, 6 tankards & a nest of trunks – 8 | | | 1 | 2 |
| | To: | 24 brass pans, 6 carbines & 4 nickanees | 1 | 2 | | |
| 2 | To: | 1 perpetuanna, 13 brass pans, 1/2 barrel of powder & 60 rangoes | | | | 2 |
| | To: | 1 sea, 32 tankards, 5 cases of spirits, 1 darnick & 3 firkins of powder | | 3 | | 1 |
| 3 | To: | 3 perpetuannas, 1 darnick, 6 X 2lb basins & 8 tankards | | 1 | | 1 |
| 5 | To: | 24 brass pans, 8 tankards, 1 sea, 4 X 4lb & 2 X 3lb basins | 1 | 1 | | |
| | To: | 4 firkins of powder, 4 darnicks, 2 tankards & 3 X 2lb basins | | 1 | | |
| | To: | 2 perpetuannas 60 rangoes, & 4 darnicks | 1 | | | |
| | To: | 4 darnicks, 2 tankards, 3 X 2lb basins, 2 brass pans & 60 rangoes | | | | 1 |
| 6 | To: | 3 perpetuannas, 8A per piece | | 1 | | |
| 9 | To: | no papar'd slesia, 18 brass pans, 2 ounces of currell, 2 darnicks, 30 rangoes & 2lb beads | | 2 | | |
| 10 | To: | 1 sea, 3 tankards, 1 darnick, & 3lb of beads | | 1 | | |
| 11 | To: | 2 seas, 1 tankard, 9 carbines, & 12 brass pans | 1 | 2 | | |
| | To: | I barrel of powder, 3 darnicks, 4lb beads & 3 perpetuannas | 1 | 1 | | |
| 12 | To: | 4 darnicks, 12 iron bars, 120 rangoes & 20 brass pans | 1 | 1 | | 1 |
| | | The sum carried to the other side is | 60 | 89 | 15 | 26 |

| Date | | Item | Men | Women | Boys | Girls |
|---|---|---|---|---|---|---|
| | | To the sum brought over | 60 | 89 | 15 | 26 |
| | To: | 2 perpetuannas, 4 single brawles, 1 brass pan, 2 seas, 3 darnicks & 1 carbine | | 3 | | |
| July 14 | To: | 3 darnicks | | | | 1 |
| 15 | To: | 1 sea, 1 carbine, 1 darnick, 8 firkins of powder | | 1 | 1 | |
| | To: | 4 carbines, 1 carpet & 1 single brawle | | | | 1 |
| 16 | To: | 1 sea, 1 carbine, 2 papar'd slessia, 1 barrel of powder | 1 | 1 | | |
| | To: | 27 brass pans, 1 ounce currell, 600 flints | 1 | | | |
| | To: | 60 rangoes, 1 single brawle, 1 papar'd slessia, & 12 iron bars | | 1 | | 1 |
| 17 | To: | 8 brass pans, 6 carbines, 26 X 4lb basins, 30 rangoes | 1 | 3 | | |
| 19 | To: | 26 X 4lb basins, 2 seas, 1 barrel of powder & 30 rangoes | 1 | 3 | | |
| | To: | 21 X 4lb basins, 1lb beads, 25 brass pans | 1 | 1 | | |
| | To: | 2 barrels of powder, 1 sea & 2 firkins of powder | 1 | | | 2 |
| 20 | To: | 3 barrels of powder, 17 brass pans, 2 carbines, & 1 sea | 1 | 4 | | |
| 21 | To: | 1 sea, 3 iron bars, 30 rangoes, 2 fuzees & 3 barrels of powder | 1 | 4 | | |
| | To: | 5X4 basins 1lb beads, & a nest of trunks – 8 | | 2 | | |
| 22 | To: | 1 barrel of powder, 1 ounce currell, 60 rangoes, 2 X 4lb basins, 31 brass pans & 1lb beads | 1 | 1 | | |
| 24 | To: | 24 X 4lb basins, 12lb beads, 180 rangoes | | 2 | | |
| | To: | 1 sea, 3 Guinea stuffs, 4 brass pans & 12 fuzees | 3 | 1 | | |
| | To: | 9 papar'd slessia, 3 Guinea stuffs, 2 seas, 14 brass pans & 2 X 4lb basins | | 1 | | 2 |
| | | The sum carried to the other side is | 72 | 117 | 16 | 33 |

| | | | Men | Women | Boys | Girls |
|---|---|---|---|---|---|---|
| | | To the sum brought over | 72 | 117 | 16 | 33 |
| 25 | To: | 2 fuzees, 9 brass pans, 4 firkins of powder, 3 papar'd slessia | | 2 | | |
| | To: | 2 barrels of powder, 3 fuzees, 2 salem powers, 1 brass pan, 1 piece of ticking & 21 single brawles | 1 | 4 | | |
| 27 | To: | 11 fuzees, 1 barrel of powder, 8 X 4lb basins, 4 papar'd slessia & 4lb beads | 2 | 3 | | |
| | To: | 4 Guinea stuffs, 13 single brawles, 25lb beads | | 1 | 1 | |
| 28 | To: | 6 fuzees, 960 rangoes, 2 sea, 4 single brawles & 60 rangoes | | 5 | | |
| | To: | 11 papar'd slessia, 60 rangoes & 4 perpetuannas | | 2 | | |
| 29 | To: | 16 single brawles, 20 firkins of powder, 1 sea & 4 perpetuannas . | 1 | 3 | | |
| | To: | 1 sea, 16 papar'd slessia & 25 ounces of currell | 1 | 2 | 1 | |
| 30 | To: | 27 brass pans, 22 firkins of powder, 3 fuzees, 2 single brawles & 30 rangoes | | 4 | | |
| 31 | To: | 4 seas, 22 papar'd slessia, 4 single brawles & 60 rangoes | 1 | 4 | | |
| August 2 | To: | 28 Guinea stuffs | 1 | 1 | | |
| | To: | 12 brass pans, 1 fuzee & 3 Guinea stuffs | | 1 | | |
| | To: | 1 sea, 12 firkins of powder, 1 Guinea stuff & 60 rangoes | | 2 | | |
| | To: | 2 seas, 8 firkins of powder & 1 Guinea stuff | 1 | 1 | | |
| 3 | To: | 12 Guinea stuffs & 360 rangoes | | 1 | | 1 |
| | | The sum carried to the other side | 80 | 153 | 18 | 34 |

Here the existing details of goods exchanged from the ship come to a premature end. To this date, 3 August 1700, the *Daniel and Henry* had taken on board a total of 387 slaves: 102 of these had come from Walter Prideaux's endeavours in trading from the long-boat, and this account is detailed in the following pages.

* * *

"Accompt of shipp's way from St. Thomee to the Isle Jamaico, the former being in the N° latt^d 10° 10' ye latter in the N°· Latt^d 17° 50' the dist. between them is 81° 40' I say Merridianall the course is nearist W. by N. ¼ N. Wee satt sayle from St. Thomee Roade the 6 day of Septemb. being ffryday in the yeare 1700 God send us saffe to desired port Amen.

15 Sept. Att 6 a.m. saw a shipp which bore S. b.W. about 6 Lea. We suppose it to be Society Cap^ne Edw. Monck who sayled from St. Thomee 4 days before us.

16 Sept. Att 4 p.m. we tacked when Capne Moncke bore down to us and att 8 a.m. hee came on bord us and saith he makes but 1° 5' S° Equinoctiall and that he saw St. Thomee Thursday last.

17 Sept. We being still in company of Cap^ne Monck who sayles mutch worse then wee.

Mr. Chapman [1st mate] being sick and affraid of ye small pox.

20 Sept. See Cap^ne Monck, but at topmast head.

21 Sept. Att 9 p.m. Humph. Handcock departed this life having been sick in the small pox which struck in again after having been out three dayes have not seen Cap^ne Moncke this 24 hourrs.

27 Sept. Last night at about 9 a'clock Mr. John Chapman departed this life he being before very bad in a cold.

*Inventory of Mr. John Chapman Goods Deceased.* [Some goods for private trading.]
- 19 small ellophant teeth—mark'd J. C.
- 1 man slave—marked J. C.
- 1 girl ditto—marked J. C. [A list of personal clothing.]
- 2 old jackcoats.
- 1 hatt brush 1caane with joorry head cristil. *Books and Instruments.*
- 1 fforestaffe with 4 vaanes.
- 1 quadrant with 4 vaanes.
- 1 nocturnal 1gunter scale
- 1 playne and 1 gunner scale.
- 1 old epittome
- 1 old callender.

- 1 Practicall Navigation.
- 1 Seaman Practice.
- 2 old journal booke I pr. dividers 1 pr. compasses
- 1 Bible, 1 Whole Duty man 1 Comon prayer.
- 1 Q^rter Waggoner 1 booke call'd Heaven Opened.
- 1 paper pockett booke I old attless all torne.
- 1 old papard booke.

These things are put into two chest which are marked J. C. and this inventry is attested by us—ffrancis Snelling—Walt. Prideaux.

28 Sept. Moderate gale and this day att 9 a.m. we satt our fore and fore topmast studing sayle. Now 142 slaves dead and many Yerrey [yearning ?]

6 Oct. We have now throwne overbord 153 slaves.

14 Oct. Wee saw a shipp which stood away N.E.b.E. wee suppos'd shee was bound for ye Coaste of Guinia a Portugeese.

Cannot judge of any currant only bad steereadge which makes the diff. betweene the logg and obser^n however we suppose thers 4° 30' variation.

Eserly. Cannot gett an amplitude.

22 Oct. Last night at 9 oclock was seen a flameing sword in the Elam. Saw a starr shoott which continued like a flaming sword for 3 minnuetts.

23 Oct. Wee have had dyed 173 slaves which taken out of 452 remains on bord 279 for owners account.

25 Oct. The currant is as uncertayne as can bee in these pts. wee cannot hoyze our boate out soe cannot try which way it setts only by Esteemation.

27 Oct. A currant which setts to the westw^d and a great swell which comes out of the Eastward God send us a good landfall.

29 Oct. Sometymes our topgallant sayles out sometymes in haveing mutch wind in the showers, the wind at East and a great sea.

4 Nov. Att a 1/4 after 4 p.m. wee saw Barbadoes [sketch] and at 10 a.m. wee saw St. Vincent [sketch].

5 Nov. Wee have now att this day noone 183 slaves dead and many more very bad I wish may

escape with 200 dead the doct^r not knowing what to doe with them.

9 Nov. Wee have trimd'our long boate and are doing ye same to ye yoale; have 206 slaves dead and many more still sicke.

12 Nov. from the topm^t head I saw a barkalong: going to ye E.ward.

13 Nov. Off Hispaniola we saw a shipp who fired a gunn presently weighd and stood to windward but the wind favouring hee hald off S.W.

14 Nov. Att 6 p.m. the shipp we saw yesterday came in upon us when wee made our shipp ready supposing her a pirott but at 12.30 att night shee alterd her course and hal'd in for the land in the morning shee was within a mile of the shore when Cape Tiburoon bore W.N.W.½W. Dist. 7 to 8 Lea. We steared away with the wind att E.S.E. fresh gale. God send us a good sight of Jamaico.

16 Nov. In sight of Jamaico ye morning saw the Margrett, man warr and a small sloop with him turning to the E^tward who wee saluted with 5 gunns.

17 Nov. Att 4 a.m. were off Yellow Poynt being a low poynt full of trees about 3 Lea. to the W^tward off Poynt Morant when wee brought our ship two till 6 a.m. when made sayle for Port Royall harbour haleing in with plum poynt when saluted the Solldathas Prize wh. lay there Comadore bound home att Noone wee came to an ankor in Port royall harbour after saluting the fort with 9 gunns in 9 ffa. water soft ground where we found Capt. Mackfor.

You must be sure when you come from the East keep the shore close on bord by reason of several riffs wh. lye about 2 mils off shore You will have in going along shore 11 to 15 ffathom water sandy ground I say after you come off Plum Poynt, wh. poynt lyes on the low land being to the E^tward of Kingston, from 8 p.m. to 4 a.m. we went along shore and our fore sayle fresh gale at E.N.E. a strong windward currant ye must bring the Castle about S.S.E. or as the draught water the shipp shall draw comonly morre S.E. and N.W. haveing your best anchor for the S.E. sea breese for which Above Preservation God alone bee Blessed and Praised now an for ever more.

Amen.
Wee sold 246 slaves and six dyed in Port.

# In Miserable Slavery:
# Thomas Thistlewood in Jamaica, 1750–86

## Edited by Douglas Hall

*Excerpts of the diary of Thomas Thistlewood. Thistlewood was the overseer of Egypt, a sugar plantation in western Jamaica.*

In 1755 and 1756 ground provisions were scarce and dear and Thistlewood noted the usual heavier incidence in such circumstances of slaves moving beyond their grounds to find subsistence. The vicious responses of their masters were also noted by Thistlewood who in 1756 would calmly record his own disgraceful excesses.

'Tuesday, 25th February 1755: At dinner-time rode over the plantation to see who would be eating canes. Found Hector & Beck. Had them whipped.
Sunday, 2nd March 1755: Bought plantains for the new Negroes, house Negroes, &c. &c. at nine hundred for 27 bits.'

The plantocracy, as distinct from their white employees, differed from the latter only in their greater possession of resources and authority and, therefore, of responsibilities which Mr Cope at any rate seemed unable to bear. He was always in financial distress, and frequently in other predicaments, often of his own making.

'Monday, 17th March 1755: This morning Mr Cope took all Mrs Cope's china, glasses, &c she brought here when he was last at Town, and smashed them with all his force against the floor, and broke them in pieces; believe they were given her by an old sweetheart, J. Thorns". Then he went out and stayed the night, &c. &c.
Friday, 11th April 1755: Our Negroes have this week had but 3 plantains each per *diem*, and none on holy days or Negro days (New Negroes).
Sunday, 13th April 1755: Rode over the estate. The canes mostly destroyed by the cattle. Mr Cope talks of renting it out, or throwing it up.'

This was in the height of food scarcity and in the dry weather the cattle, even more than the slaves, were moving into the canefields in search of sustenance.

'Tuesday, 15th April 1755: Sent Port Royal with a mule and bags to Dr Frazier's at Negril, for corn. [He got a bag full]. Monday, 19th May 1755: Although Whitsun-Monday, Mr Cope made the Negroes work as a punishment (he says) for eating canes so much.
Sunday, 8th June 1755: In the morning rode into the Savanna to the Negro market. Plantains 5 bits per hundred; Corn 4 ditto. Bought none. William Crookshanks with me.'

Three days later London was sent with two mules to Paradise to buy plantains. He got only a few and the price there was the same. On the Sunday, Thistlewood tried the Negro Market at Hatfield gate. Again, he 'bought some' at the same high prices. In the next few days:

'I give our New Negroes a pint of Norward [from the American mainland] Corn each for a meal, three times per day, & a herring each day. Quaw, Cubbenna, Moll, Melia &c have but three plantains or a pint of corn each per day.'

On Sunday 22nd, at Hatfield, prices were down 1 bitt per 100 on each item; but on the 29th plantains were up to 5 again, and 'scarce'. Not until the end of July did prices begin to decline. On the first Sunday in August plantains were still at 4, but corn was being offered variously at 2, 2½, and 3 bitts per 100. Thistlewood planted corn at Egypt.

By this time, Mr Cope had changed his mind and re-employed Mrs Mould's slaves; but Mr Mould still seemed to carry some resentment, and perhaps with good reason for John Cope seemed never to be in good financial standing. When, in early April, Mr Cope offered to pay him for the slaves' hire with an order upon Mr Gardiner in Savanna la Mar, Mr Mould refused to accept it. It might even have come to blows.

'Wednesday, 23rd April 1755: Being St George's Day, Mr Cope dined out, and at night came home seemingly in liquor, and bloody, his lips seem bruised, &c. W[illiam] C[rookshanks] sent to Mr Mould's to enquire.'

No more was recorded, but time apparently mended differences.

'Sunday, 15th June 1755: Mr Cope dined out. Mrs Cope told me how much Mr Cope wants her to cut the entail off and settle upon him for life. Or, as it is going to be a war, he must go home and try to make his fortune that way, if she don't.
Wednesday, 13th August 1755: At night Mr Cope come home in liquor; wanted Silvia very much and was like a madman almost.

Had my supper sent into my house to me.
Monday, 6th October 1755: Mr Cope and Mr Christopher Senior went and took possession of Salt River and Paradise estates last Saturday p.m. and have agreed to pay the debts off if possible before they make any dividend.
Wednesday, 15th October 1755: Mirtilla has been at home all this week, ails little or nothing, only resolved to put William to a needless charge through spite.
Sunday, 28th December 1755: Mason Quashe had a feast here tonight'.

And in January, 1756, Thistlewood recorded a striking co-incidence:

'It is remarkable that one of the last New Negroes, named Achilles, is he who took Doll and sold her; and that having some clothes, some tobacco, dram & a gun, &c. was robbed going home, &c.'

And now, as a consequence of an increase in assault on the canefields by slaves who were by his own account on very short rations, Thistlewood inflicted punishments which seem to have gone even beyond the accepted bestiality of the time. One of the chief consumers of young canes was Derby.

Wednesday, 28th Jan 1756: Had Derby well whipped, and made Egypt shit in his mouth.
Tuesday, 24th February 1756: Mirtilla went away into the Savanna. It seems her time is up. Hear her neck is to be put in the yoke. She has worked 244 days in her year and earned William Crookshanks £15 15s. At night William Crookshanks abused Mr and Mrs Mould in an extraordinary manner in the Savanna, at their own house; afterwards crazed went down [on] his knees & begged their pardons, &c ... Mirtilla the cause.'

Mirtilla was now pregnant, near childbirth. In mid-March she was sent to Paradise where Crookshanks went to see her.

'Saturday, 13th March 1756: Hazat catched Derby last night stealing cane. Derby wanting this morning.'

Two days later he was caught, escaped, and a short while after recaptured and put in the bilboes. For days, said Thistlewood, he remained sullen, not eating or drinking, and not seeming to care when he was whipped.

'Monday, 15th March 1756: In the morning W.C. went to Paradise, Mirtilla in labour all day. At night Dr Robinson sent to her, who delivered her of a girl (a mulatto) after supper. Mr and Mrs Mould also came over to see her, and returned again in the night. W.C. came home & cried. She is in Egypt Lucy's house.' [At Paradise]

On the 19th Thistlewood went to visit Mirtilla and her daughter. About a week later Crookshanks was transferred to Paradise, Mirtilla was to remain there and Sancho would be sent to Egypt in her stead. At Paradise, William Crookshanks (according to Thistlewood) continued to pamper Mirtilla.

On Monday, 5th April 1756, the Moulds left Jamaica for England. For a while, before their departure, they had stayed at Egypt. It was also cropover time.

'Mr and Mrs Mould went away into the Savanna this morning. Wrote a letter to Mr Henry Hewitt, by Mr Wm. Mould … p.m. Mr and Mrs Cope went into the Savanna to take their leave of Mr and Mrs Mould. Egypt now seems very dull. However, I had a bottle of good ale at my supper, which I mixed with sugar & water & grated some nutmeg over it. Roast beef, roast turkey, cold tongue, cheese, &c. to my supper.
At night *Cum* Phibbah.
Sunday, 2nd May 1756: Sometime in the middle of last night Mr Cope come home and Mr McDonald with him. They sat drinking for sometime, then went to bed; Mr McDonald had Eve to whom he gave 6 bitts, and Mr Cope made Tom fetch Beck from the Negro houses for himself, with whom she was till morning.

Wednesday, 5th May 1756: p.m. Egypt Susanah & Mazerine whipped for refusal last Saturday night, by Mr Cope's order.[2] Little Phibbah told Mrs Cope last Saturday night's affair. Mrs Cope also examined the sheets and found them amiss.'

Mrs Cope had been away on the Saturday night spending a few days with Dr and Mrs Gorse. She had returned to Egypt on the morning of the 5th.

On Wednesday, 26th May, the Egypt slaves planted rice in the morass behind the mill house; but that, like much of the corn planted, would be eaten by the birds rather than them. And Derby was again:

'… catched by Port Royal eating canes. Had him well flogged and pickled, then made Hector shit in his mouth.'

This sadistic and degrading punishment seemed to appeal to Thistlewood.

In June, 1756, came an interesting instance of an unusual domestic event. Nancy, Phibbah's sister, was then a house slave at Egypt and she had an infant son. Rose, an Egypt field slave who had been sent to Salt River at the end of February '… to be salivated for the bone-ache' now returned to Egypt.

'… and is to live with Nancy who is to give Mr Cope five pounds per ann. for her.'

Unfortunately, Thistlewood made no further comment on the arrangement by which one slave was hiring another from the owner of both, but the reason for it seems clear—little Davie was ill. About noon on 18th July he died.

'Saturday, 24th July 1756: Nancy's play tonight.[3]
Sunday, 25th July 1756: Nancy's play ended, much music & dancing all day, &c.'

In July, Port Royal, who had run away, was taken and brought home.

'Gave him a moderate whipping, pickled him well, made Hector shit in his mouth, immediately put in a gag whilst his mouth was full & made him wear it 4 or 5 hours.'

Next day, the 24th, a woman slave, Phillis, caught breaking canes, was similarly treated, but spared the gag. On the 31st her punishment was repeated. The reason was not stated, but perhaps she had run away after the 24th; for on the 30th two other runaways had been apprehended and punished.

'Friday, 30th July 1756: Punch catched at Salt River and brought home. Flogged him and Quacoo well, and then washed and rubbed in salt pickle, lime juice & bird pepper; also whipped Hector for losing his hoe, made New Negro Joe piss in his eyes & mouth &c.'

On 1st August, another runaway, Hazat, who had absconded in early April was caught.

'Put him in the bilboes both feet; gagged him; locked his hands together; rubbed him with molasses & exposed him naked to the flies all day, and to the mosquitoes all night, without fire.'

On the 4th, Derby was again caught, this time by the watchman as he attempted to take corn out of Col Barclay's Long Pond corn-piece. He was severely chopped with a machete, his right ear, cheek, and jaw almost cut off. On the 27th of the same month, Egypt was whipped and given 'Derby's 'dose' [that is Derby was made to shit in his mouth] for eating cane. On Thursday, 5th October, Hector and Joe and Mr Watt's Pomona were similarly punished for the same misdemeanour. Thereafter, for unmentioned reason, Mr Thistlewood shed his depravity of 1756 and resorted to the usual whippings and chainings.

# Two Biographical Fragments on the Life of Olaudah Equiano (a.k.a. Gustavus Vasa)

In recent years, scholars interested in the biography and writings of Equiano have searched archives and records for further details about his life and career. Many of the details of his *Interesting Narrative* have been confirmed and further elaborated using independent archival evidence—his service on several of the ships he mentions in Chapter 3, for instance, has been corroborated by mining the records of the Royal Navy for the period. Two of the very early documents relating to his life have puzzled researchers and occasioned some debate:

### 1. From the Parish Records of St. Margaret's Church, Westminster (England)

In Chapter 4 of his narrative, Equiano tells readers that he was baptized at St. Margaret's Church, Westminster, in February 1759, shortly after returning to England from the battle of Louisburg. The registers of the parish survive, and provide the following information:

Baptism, listed for 9 Feb 1759: "Gustavus Vassa a Black born in Carolina, 12 years old"

### 2. From the records of *The Racehorse*

In a later chapter of his narrative, Equiano claims to have served on a ship called *The Racehorse*. Records concerning *The Racehorse* survive in the National Archives of the UK. These include a muster list (a list of the seamen and officers assigned to the ship), dated 1773, which gives one of the seamen as "Gustavus Weston,"[1] aged 28, born in "South Carolina."

Think about these passages in the light of the chapters you read from Equiano's *Interesting Narrative*.

---

1   Remember that names and spelling during this period were often rendered with casual imprecision: elsewhere in naval records, Equiano is listed as "Gustavus Vassor," "Gustavus Vasser" and "Gustavus Vassan."

# The Interesting Narrative of the Life of Olaudah Equiano

## CHAP. II.

*The author's birth and parentage—His being kidnapped with his sister—Their separation—Surprise at meeting again—Are finally separated—Account of the different places and incidents the author met with till his arrival on the coast—The effect the sight of a slave ship had on him—He sails for the West Indies—Horrors of a slave ship—Arrives at Barbadoes, where the cargo is sold and dispersed.*

I hope the reader will not think I have trespassed on his patience in introducing myself to him with some account of the manners and customs of my country. They had been implanted in me with great care, and made an impression on my mind, which time could not erase, and which all the adversity and variety of fortune I have since experienced served only to rivet and record; for, whether the love of one's country be real or imaginary, or a lesson of reason, or an instinct of nature, I still look back with pleasure on the first scenes of my life, though that pleasure has been for the most part mingled with sorrow.

I have already acquainted the reader with the time and place of my birth. My father, besides many slaves, had a numerous family, of which seven lived to grow up, including myself and a sister, who was the only daughter. As I was the youngest of the sons, I became, of course, the greatest favourite with my mother, and was always with her; and she used to take particular pains to form my mind. I was trained up from my earliest years in the art of war; my daily exercise was shooting and throwing javelins; and my mother adorned me with emblems, after the manner of our greatest warriors. In this way I grew up till I was turned the age of eleven, when an end was put to my happiness in the following manner:—Generally when the grown people in the neighbourhood were gone far in the fields to labour, the children assembled together in some of the neighbours' premises to play; and commonly some of us used to get up a tree to look out for any assailant, or kidnapper, that might come upon us; for they sometimes took those opportunities of our parents' absence to attack and carry off as many as they could seize. One day, as I was watching at the top of a tree in our yard, I saw one of those people come into the yard of our next neighbour but one, to kidnap, there being many stout young people in it. Immediately on this I gave the alarm of the rogue, and he was surrounded by the stoutest of them, who entangled him with cords, so that he could not escape till some of the grown people came and secured him. But alas! ere long it was my fate to be thus attacked, and to be carried off, when none of the grown people were nigh. One day, when all our people were gone out to their works as usual, and only I and my dear sister were left to mind the house, two men and a woman got over our walls, and in a moment seized us both, and, without giving us time to cry out, or make resistance, they stopped our mouths, and ran off with us into the nearest wood. Here they tied our hands, and continued to carry us as far as they could, till night came on, when we reached a small house, where the robbers halted for refreshment, and spent the night. We were then unbound, but were unable to take any food; and, being quite overpowered by fatigue and grief, our only relief was some sleep, which allayed our misfortune for a short time. The next morning we left the house, and continued travelling all the day. For a long time we had kept the woods, but at last we came into a road which I believed I knew. I had now some hopes of being delivered; for we had advanced but a little way before I discovered some people at a distance, on which I began to cry out for their assistance: but my cries had no other effect than to make them tie me faster and stop my mouth, and then they put me into a large sack. They also stopped my sister's mouth, and tied her hands; and in this manner we proceeded till we were out of the sight of these people. When we went to rest the following night they offered us some victuals; but we refused it; and the only comfort we had was in being in one another's arms all that night, and bathing each other with our tears. But alas! we were soon deprived of even the small comfort of weeping together. The next day proved a day of greater sorrow than I had yet experienced; for my sister and I were then separated, while we lay clasped in each other's arms. It was in vain that we besought them not to part us; she was torn from me, and immediately carried away, while I was left in a state of distraction not to be described. I cried and grieved continually; and for several days I did not eat any thing but what they forced into my mouth. At length, after many days travelling, during which I had often changed masters, I got into the hands of a chieftain, in a very pleasant country. This man had two wives and some children, and they all used me extremely well, and did all they could to comfort me; particularly the first wife, who was something like my mother. Although I was a great many days journey from my father's house, yet these people spoke exactly the same language with us. This first master of mine, as I may call him, was a smith, and my principal employment was working his bellows, which were the same kind as I had seen in my vicinity. They were in some respects not unlike the stoves here in gentleman's kitchens; and were covered over with leather; and in the middle of that leather a stick was fixed, and a person stood up, and worked it, in the same manner as is done to pump water out of a cask with a hand pump. I believe it was gold he worked, for it was of a lovely bright yellow colour, and was worn by the women on their wrists and ancles. I was there I suppose about a month, and they at last used to trust me some little distance from the house. This liberty I used in embracing every opportunity to inquire the way to my own home: and I also sometimes, for the same purpose, went with the maidens, in the cool of the evenings, to bring pitchers of water from the springs for the use of the house. I had also remarked where the sun rose in the morning, and set in the evening, as I had travelled along; and I had observed that my father's house was towards the rising of the sun. I therefore determined to seize the first opportunity of making my escape, and to shape my course for that quarter; for I was quite oppressed and weighed down by grief after my mother and friends; and my love of liberty, ever great, was strengthened by the mortifying circumstance of not daring to eat with the free-born children, although I was mostly their companion. While I was projecting my escape, one day an unlucky event happened, which quite disconcerted my plan, and put an end to my hopes. I used to be sometimes employed in assisting an elderly woman slave to cook and take care of the poultry; and one morning, while I was feeding some chickens, I happened to toss a small pebble at one of them, which hit it on the middle and directly killed it. The old slave, having soon after missed the chicken, inquired after it; and on my relating the accident (for I told her the truth, because my mother would never suffer me to tell a lie) she flew into a violent passion, threatened that I should suffer for it; and, my master being out, she immediately went and told her mistress what I had done. This alarmed me very much, and I expected an instant flogging, which to me was uncommonly dreadful; for I had seldom been beaten at home. I therefore resolved to fly; and accordingly I ran into a thicket that was hard by, and hid myself in the bushes. Soon afterwards my mistress and the slave returned, and, not seeing me, they searched all the house, but not finding me, and I not making answer when they called to me, they thought I had run away, and the whole neighbourhood was raised in the pursuit of me. In that part of the country (as in ours) the houses and villages were skirted with woods, or shrubberies, and the bushes were so thick that a man could readily conceal himself in them, so as to elude the strictest search. The neighbours continued the whole day looking for me, and several times many of them came within a few yards of the place where I lay hid. I then gave myself up for lost entirely, and expected every moment, when I heard a rustling among the trees, to be found out, and punished by my master: but they never discovered me, though they were often so near that I even heard their conjectures as they were looking about for me; and I now learned from them, that any attempt to return home would be hopeless. Most of them supposed I had fled towards home; but the distance was so great, and the way so intricate, that they thought I could never reach it, and that I should be lost in the woods. When I heard this I was seized with a violent panic, and abandoned myself to despair. Night too began to approach, and aggravated all my fears. I had before entertained hopes of getting home, and I had determined when it should be dark to make the attempt; but I was now convinced it was fruitless, and I began to consider that, if possibly I could escape all other animals, I could not those of the human kind; and that, not knowing the way, I must perish in the woods. Thus was I like the hunted deer:

—Ev'ry leaf and ev'ry whisp'ring breath
Convey'd a foe, and ev'ry foe a death.[1]

I heard frequent rustlings among the leaves; and being pretty sure they were snakes I expected every instant to be stung by them. This increased my anguish, and the horror of my situation became now quite insupportable. I at length quitted the thicket, very faint and hungry, for I had not eaten or drank any thing all the day; and crept to my master's kitchen, from whence I set out at first, and which was an open shed, and laid myself down in the ashes with an anxious wish for death to relieve me from all my pains. I was scarcely awake in the morning when the old woman slave, who was the first up, came to light the fire, and saw me in the fire place. She was very much surprised to see me, and could scarcely believe her own eyes. She now promised to intercede for me, and went for her master, who soon after came, and, having slightly reprimanded me, ordered me to be taken care of, and not to be ill-treated.

Soon after this my master's only daughter, and child by his first wife, sickened and died, which affected him so much that for some time he was almost frantic, and really would have killed himself, had he not been watched and prevented. However, in a small time afterwards he recovered, and I was again sold. I was

now carried to the left of the sun's rising, through many different countries, and a number of large woods. The people I was sold to used to carry me very often, when I was tired, either on their shoulders or on their backs. I saw many convenient well-built sheds along the roads, at proper distances, to accommodate the merchants and travellers, who lay in those buildings along with their wives, who often accompany them; and they always go well armed.

From the time I left my own nation I always found somebody that understood me till I came to the sea coast. The languages of different nations did not totally differ, nor were they so copious as those of the Europeans, particularly the English. They were therefore easily learned; and, while I was journeying thus through Africa, I acquired two or three different tongues. In this manner I had been travelling for a considerable time, when one evening, to my great surprise, whom should I see brought to the house where I was but my dear sister! As soon as she saw me she gave a loud shriek, and ran into my arms—I was quite overpowered: neither of us could speak; but, for a considerable time, clung to each other in mutual embraces, unable to do any thing but weep. Our meeting affected all who saw us; and indeed I must acknowledge, in honour of those sable destroyers of human rights, that I never met with any ill treatment, or saw any offered to their slaves, except tying them, when necessary, to keep them from running away. When these people knew we were brother and sister they indulged us together; and the man, to whom I supposed we belonged, lay with us, he in the middle, while she and I held one another by the hands across his breast all night; and thus for a while we forgot our misfortunes in the joy of being together: but even this small comfort was soon to have an end; for scarcely had the fatal morning appeared, when she was again torn from me for ever! I was now more miserable, if possible, than before. The small relief which her presence gave me from pain was gone, and the wretchedness of my situation was redoubled by my anxiety after her fate, and my apprehensions lest her sufferings should be greater than mine, when I could not be with her to alleviate them. Yes, thou dear partner of all my childish sports! thou sharer of my joys and sorrows! happy should I have ever esteemed myself to encounter every misery for you, and to procure your freedom by the sacrifice of my own. Though you were early forced

---

1  These slightly altered lines are from *Cooper's Hill* (1642) by John Denham (1615–69), lines 287–88.

from my arms, your image has been always rivetted in my heart, from which neither *time nor fortune* have been able to remove it; so that, while the thoughts of your sufferings have damped my prosperity, they have mingled with adversity and increased its bitterness. To that Heaven which protects the weak from the strong, I commit the care of your innocence and virtues, if they have not already received their full reward, and if your youth and delicacy have not long since fallen victims to the violence of the African trader, the pestilential stench of a Guinea ship, the seasoning in the European colonies, or the lash and lust of a brutal and unrelenting overseer.

I did not long remain after my sister. I was again sold, and carried through a number of places, till, after travelling a considerable time, I came to a town called Tinmah, in the most beautiful country I had yet seen in Africa. It was extremely rich, and there were many rivulets which flowed through it, and supplied a large pond in the centre of the town, where the people washed. Here I first saw and tasted cocoa-nuts, which I thought superior to any nuts I had ever tasted before; and the trees, which were loaded, were also interspersed amongst the houses, which had commodious shades adjoining, and were in the same manner as ours, the insides being neatly plastered and whitewashed. Here I also saw and tasted for the first time sugar-cane. Their money consisted of little white shells, the size of the finger nail. I was sold here for one hundred and seventy-two of them by a merchant who lived and brought me there. I had been about two or three days at his house, when a wealthy widow, a neighbour of his, came there one evening, and brought with her an only son, a young gentleman about my own age and size. Here they saw me; and, having taken a fancy to me, I was bought of the merchant, and went home with them. Her house and premises were situated close to one of those rivulets I have mentioned, and were the finest I ever saw in Africa: they were very extensive, and she had a number of slaves to attend her. The next day I was washed and perfumed, and when meal-time came I was led into the presence of my mistress, and ate and drank before her with her son. This filled me with astonishment; and I could scarce help expressing my surprise that the young gentleman should suffer me, who was bound, to eat with him who was free; and not only so, but that he would not at any time either eat

or drink till I had taken first, because I was the eldest, which was agreeable to our custom. Indeed every thing here, and all their treatment of me, made me forget that I was a slave. The language of these people resembled ours so nearly, that we understood each other perfectly. They had also the very same customs as we. There were likewise slaves daily to attend us, while my young master and I with other boys sported with our darts and bows and arrows, as I had been used to do at home. In this resemblance to my former happy state I passed about two months; and I now began to think I was to be adopted into the family, and was beginning to be reconciled to my situation, and to forget by degrees my misfortunes, when all at once the delusion vanished; for, without the least previous knowledge, one morning early, while my dear master and companion was still asleep, I was wakened out of my reverie to fresh sorrow, and hurried away even amongst the uncircumcised.

Thus, at the very moment I dreamed of the greatest happiness, I found myself most miserable; and it seemed as if fortune wished to give me this taste of joy, only to render the reverse more poignant. The change I now experienced was as painful as it was sudden and unexpected. It was a change indeed from a state of bliss to a scene which is inexpressible by me, as it discovered to me an element I had never before beheld, and till then had no idea of, and wherein such instances of hardship and cruelty continually occurred as I can never reflect on but with horror.

All the nations and people I had hitherto passed through resembled our own in their manners, customs, and language: but I came at length to a country, the inhabitants of which differed from us in all those particulars. I was very much struck with this difference, especially when I came among a people who did not circumcise, and ate without washing their hands. They cooked also in iron pots, and had European cutlasses and cross bows, which were unknown to us, and fought with their fists amongst themselves. Their women were not so modest as ours, for they ate, and drank, and slept, with their men. But, above all, I was amazed to see no sacrifices or offerings among them. In some of those places the people ornamented themselves with scars, and likewise filed their teeth very sharp. They wanted sometimes to ornament me in the same manner, but I would not suffer them; hoping that I might some time be among a people who did not thus disfigure themselves, as I thought they did. At last I came to the banks of a large river, which was covered with canoes, in which the people appeared to live with their household utensils and provisions of all kinds. I was beyond measure astonished at this, as I had never before seen any water larger than a pond or a rivulet: and my surprise was mingled with no small fear when I was put into one of these canoes, and we began to paddle and move along the river. We continued going on thus till night; and when we came to land, and made fires on the banks, each family by themselves, some dragged their canoes on shore, others stayed and cooked in theirs, and laid in them all night. Those on the land had mats, of which they made tents, some in the shape of little houses: in these we slept; and after the morning meal we embarked again and proceeded as before. I was often very much astonished to see some of the women, as well as the men, jump into the water, dive to the bottom, come up again, and swim about. Thus I continued to travel, sometimes by land, sometimes by water, through different countries and various nations, till, at the end of six or seven months after I had been kidnapped, I arrived at the sea coast. It would be tedious and uninteresting to relate all the incidents which befell me during this journey, and which I have not yet forgotten; of the various hands I passed through, and the manners and customs of all the different people among whom I lived: I shall therefore only observe, that in all the places where I was the soil was exceedingly rich; the pomkins, eadas, plantains, yams, &c. &c. were in great abundance, and of incredible size. There were also vast quantities of different gums, though not used for any purpose; and every where a great deal of tobacco. The cotton even grew quite wild; and there was plenty of red-wood. I saw no mechanics whatever in all the way, except such as I have mentioned. The chief employment in all these countries was agriculture, and both the males and females, as with us, were brought up to it, and trained in the arts of war.

The first object which saluted my eyes when I arrived on the coast was the sea, and a slave ship, which was then riding at anchor, and waiting for its cargo. These filled me with astonishment, which was soon converted into terror when I was carried on board. I was immediately handled and tossed up to see if I were sound by some of the crew; and I was not persuaded that I had gotten into a world of bad spirits, and that they were going to kill me. Their complexions too differing so much from ours, their long hair, and the language they spoke, (which was very different from any I had ever heard) united to confirm me in this belief. Indeed such were the horrors of my views and fears at the moment, that, if ten thousand worlds had been my own, I would have freely parted with them all to have exchanged my condition with that of the meanest slave in my own country. When I looked round the ship too and saw a large furnace of copper boiling, and a multitude of black people of every description chained together, every one of their countenances expressing dejection and sorrow, I no longer doubted of my fate; and, quite overpowered with horror and anguish, I fell motionless on the deck and fainted. When I recovered a little I found some black people about me, who I believed were some of those who brought me on board, and had been receiving their pay; they talked to me in order to cheer me, but all in vain. I asked them if we were not to be eaten by those white men with horrible looks, red faces, and long hair. They told me I was not; and one of the crew brought me a small portion of spirituous liquor in a wine glass; but, being afraid of him, I would not take it out of his hand. One of the blacks therefore took it from him and gave it to me, and I took a little down my palate, which, instead of reviving me, as they thought it would, threw me into the greatest consternation at the strange feeling it produced, having never tasted any such liquor before. Soon after this the blacks who brought me on board went off, and left me abandoned to despair. I now saw myself deprived of all chance of returning to my native country, or even the least glimpse of hope of gaining the shore, which I now considered as friendly; and I even wished for my former slavery in preference to my present situation, which was filled with horrors of every kind, still heightened by my ignorance of what I was to undergo. I was not long suffered to indulge my grief; I was soon put down under the decks, and there I received such a salutation in my nostrils as I had never experienced in my life: so that, with the loathsomeness of the stench, and crying together, I became so sick and low that I was not able to eat, nor had I the least desire to taste any thing. I now wished for the last friend, death, to relieve me; but soon, to my grief, two of the white men offered me eatables; and, on my refusing to eat, one of them held me fast by the hands, and laid me across I think the windlass, and tied my feet, while the other flogged me severely. I had never experienced any thing of this kind before; and although, not being used to the water, I naturally feared that element the first time I saw it, yet nevertheless, could I have got over the nettings, I would have jumped over the side, but I could not; and, besides, the crew used to watch us very closely who were not chained down to the decks, lest we should leap into the water: and I have seen some of these poor African prisoners most severely cut for attempting to do so, and hourly whipped for not eating. This indeed was often the case with myself. In a little time after, amongst the poor chained men, I found some of my own nation, which in a small degree gave ease to my mind. I inquired of these what was to be done with us; they gave me to understand we were to be carried to these white people's country to work for them. I then was a little revived, and thought, if it were no worse than working, my situation was not so desperate: but still I feared I should be put to death, the white people looked and acted, as I thought, in so savage a manner; for I had never seen among any people such instances of brutal cruelty; and this not only shewn towards us blacks, but also to some of the whites themselves. One white man in particular I saw, when we were permitted to be on deck, flogged so unmercifully with a large rope near the foremast, that he died in consequence of it; and they tossed him over the side as they would have done a brute. This made me fear these people the more; and I expected nothing less than to be treated in the same manner. I could not help expressing my fears and apprehensions to some of my countrymen: I asked them if these people had no country, but lived in this hollow place (the ship): they told me they did not, but came from a distant one. "Then," said I, "how comes it in all our country we never heard of them?" They told me because they lived so very far off. I then asked where were their women? had they any like themselves? I was told they had: "and why" said I, "do we not see them?" they answered, because they were left behind. I asked how the vessel could go? they told me they could not tell; but that there were cloths put upon the masts by the help of the ropes I saw, and then the vessel went on; and the white men had some spell or magic they put in the water when they liked in order to stop the vessel. I was exceedingly amazed at this account, and really thought they were spirits. I therefore wished much to

be from amongst them, for I expected they would sacrifice me: but my wishes were vain; for we were so quartered that it was impossible for any of us to make our escape. While we stayed on the coast I was mostly on deck; and one day, to my great astonishment, I saw one of these vessels coming in with the sails up. As soon as the whites saw it, they gave a great shout, at which we were amazed; and the more so as the vessel appeared larger by approaching nearer. At last she came to an anchor in my sight, and when the anchor was let go I and my countrymen who saw it were lost in astonishment to observe the vessel stop; and were now convinced it was done by magic. Soon after this the other ship got her boats out, and they came on board of us, and the people of both ships seemed very glad to see each other. Several of the strangers also shook hands with us black people, and made motions with their hands, signifying I suppose we were to go to their country; but we did not understand them. At last, when the ship we were in had got in all her cargo, they made ready with many fearful noises, and we were all put under deck, so that we could not see how they managed the vessel. But this disappointment was the least of my sorrow. The stench of the hold while we were on the coast was so intolerably loathsome, that it was dangerous to remain there for any time, and some of us had been permitted to stay on the deck for the fresh air; but now that the whole ship's cargo were confined together, it became absolutely pestilential. The closeness of the place, and the heat of the climate, added to the number in the ship, which was so crowded that each had scarcely room to turn himself, almost suffocated us. This produced copious perspirations, so that the air soon became unfit for respiration, from a variety of loathsome smells, and brought on a sickness among the slaves, of which many died, thus falling victims to the improvident avarice, as I may call it, of their purchasers. This wretched situation was again aggravated by the galling of the chains, now become insupportable; and the filth of the necessary tubs, into which the children often fell, and were almost suffocated. The shrieks of the women, and the groans of the dying, rendered the whole a scene of horror almost inconceivable. Happily perhaps for myself I was soon reduced so low here that it was thought necessary to keep me almost always on deck; and from my extreme youth I was not put in fetters. In this situation I expected every hour to share the fate of my companions, some of whom were almost daily brought upon deck at the point of death, which I began to hope would soon put an end to my miseries. Often did I think many of the inhabitants of the deep much more happy than myself. I envied them the freedom they enjoyed, and as often wished I could change my condition for theirs. Every circumstance I met with served only to render my state more painful, and heighten my apprehensions, and my opinion of the cruelty of the whites. One day they had taken a number of fishes; and when they had killed and satisfied themselves with as many as they thought fit, to our astonishment who were on the deck, rather than give any of them to us to eat as we expected, they tossed the remaining fish into the sea again, although we begged and prayed for some as well as we could, but in vain; and some of my countrymen, being pressed by hunger, took an opportunity, when they thought no one saw them, of trying to get a little privately; but they were discovered, and the attempt procured them some very severe floggings. One day, when we had a smooth sea and moderate wind, two of my wearied countrymen who were chained together (I was near them at the time), preferring death to such a life of misery, some-how made through the nettings and jumped into the sea: immediately another quite dejected fellow, who, on account of his illness, was suffered to be out of irons, also followed their example; and I believe many more would very soon have done the same if they had not been prevented by the ship's crew, who were instantly alarmed. Those of us that were the most active were in a moment put down under the deck, and there was such a noise and confusion amongst the people of the ship as I never heard before, to stop her, and get the boat out to go after the slaves. However two of the wretches were drowned, but they got the other, and af-terwards flogged him unmercifully for thus attempting to prefer death to slavery. In this manner we continued to undergo more hardships than I can now relate, hard-ships which are inseparable from this accursed trade. Many a time we were near suffocation from the want of fresh air, which we were often without for whole days together. This, and the stench of the necessary tubs, carried off many. During our passage I first saw flying fishes, which surprised me very much: they used fre-quently to fly across the ship, and many of them fell on the deck. I also now first saw the use of the quadrant; I

had often with astonishment seen the mariners make observations with it, and I could not think what it meant. They at last took notice of my surprise; and one of them, willing to increase it, as well as to gratify my curiosity, made me one day look through it. The clouds appeared to me to be land, which disappeared as they passed along. This heightened my wonder; and I was now more persuaded than ever that I was in another world, and that every thing about me was magic. At last we came in sight of the island of Barbadoes, at which the whites on board gave a great shout, and made many signs of joy to us. We did not know what to think of this; but as the vessel drew nearer we plainly saw the harbour, and other ships of different kinds and sizes; and we soon anchored amongst them off Bridge Town. Many merchants and planters now came on board, though it was in the evening. They put us in separate parcels, and examined us attentively. They also made us jump, and pointed to the land, signifying we were to go there. We thought by this we should be eaten by these ugly men, as they appeared to us; and, when soon after we were all put down under the deck again, there was much dread and trembling among us, and nothing but bitter cries to be heard all the night from these appre-hensions, insomuch that at last the white people got some old slaves from the land to pacify us. They told us we were not to be eaten, but to work, and were soon to go on land, where we should see many of our country people. This report eased us much; and sure enough, soon after we were landed, there came to us Africans of all languages. We were conducted immediately to the merchant's yard, where we were all pent up together like so many sheep in a fold, without regard to sex or age. As every object was new to me every thing I saw filled me with surprise. What struck me first was that the houses were built with stories, and in every other respect different from those in Africa: but I was still more astonished on seeing people on horseback. I did not know what this could mean; and indeed I thought these people were full of nothing but magical arts. While I was in this astonishment one of my fellow prisoners spoke to a countryman of his about the horses, who said they were the same kind they had in their country. I understood them though they were from a distant part of Africa, and I thought it odd I had not seen any horses there; but afterwards, when I came to converse with different Africans, I found they had many horses amongst them, and much larger than those I then saw. We were not many days in the merchant's custody before we were sold after their usual manner, which is this:—On a signal given, (as the beat of a drum) the buyers rush at once into the yard where the slaves are confined, and make choice of that parcel they like best. The noise and clamour with which this is attended, and the eagerness visible in the countenances of the buyers, serve not a little to increase the apprehensions of the terrified Africans, who may well be supposed to consider them as the ministers of that destruction to which they think themselves devoted. In this manner, without scruple, are relations and friends separated, most of them never to see each other again. I remember in the vessel in which I was brought over, in the men's apartment, there were several brothers, who, in the sale, were sold in different lots; and it was very moving on this occasion to see and hear their cries at parting. O, ye nominal Christians! might not an African ask you, learned you this from your God, who says unto you, Do unto all men as you would men should do unto you? Is it not enough that we are torn from our country and friends to toil for your luxury and lust of gain? Must every tender feeling be likewise sacrificed to your avarice? Are the dearest friends and relations, now rendered more dear by their separation from their kindred, still to be parted from each other, and thus prevented from cheering the gloom of slavery with the small comfort of being together and mingling their sufferings and sorrows? Why are parents to lose their children, brothers their sisters, or husbands their wives? Surely this is a new refinement in cruelty, which, while it has no advantage to atone for it, thus aggravates distress, and adds fresh horrors even to the wretchedness of slavery.

## CHAP. III.

*The author is carried to Virginia—His distress—Surprise at seeing a picture and a watch—Is bought by Captain Pascal, and sets out for England—His terror during the voyage—Arrives in England—His wonder at a fall of snow—Is sent to Guernsey, and in some time goes on board a ship of war with his master—Some account of the expedition against Louisbourg under the command of Admiral Boscawen, in 1758.*

I now totally lost the small remains of comfort I had enjoyed in conversing with my countrymen; the women too, who used to wash and take care of me, were all gone different ways, and I never saw one of them afterwards.

I stayed in this island for a few days; I believe it could not be above a fortnight; when I and some few more slaves, that were not saleable amongst the rest, from very much fretting, were shipped off in a sloop for North America. On the passage we were better treated than when we were coming from Africa, and we had plenty of rice and fat pork. We were landed up a river a good way from the sea, about Virginia county, where we saw few or none of our native Africans, and not one soul who could talk to me. I was a few weeks weeding grass, and gathering stones in a plantation; and at last all my companions were distributed different ways, and only myself was left. I was now exceedingly miserable, and thought myself worse off than any of the rest of my companions; for they could talk to each other, but I had no person to speak to that I could understand. In this state I was constantly grieving and pining, and wishing for death rather than any thing else. While I was in this plantation the gentleman, to whom I suppose the estate belonged, being unwell, I was one day sent for to his dwelling house to fan him; when I came into the room where he was I was very much affrighted at some things I saw, and the more so as I had seen a black woman slave as I came through the house, who was cooking the dinner, and the poor creature was cruelly loaded with various kinds of iron machines; she had one particularly on her head, which locked her mouth so fast that she could scarcely speak; and could not eat nor drink. I was much astonished and shocked at this contrivance, which I afterwards learned was called the iron muzzle. Soon after I had a fan put into my hand, to fan the gentleman while he slept; and so I did indeed with great fear. While he was fast asleep I indulged myself a great deal in looking about the room, which to me appeared very fine and curious. The first object that engaged my attention was a watch which hung on the chimney, and was going. I was quite surprised at the noise it made, and was afraid it would tell the gentleman any thing I might do amiss: and when I immediately after observed a picture hanging in the room, which appeared constantly to look at me, I was still more affrighted, having never seen such things as these before. At one time I thought it was something relative to magic; and not seeing it move I thought it might be some way the whites had to keep their great men when they died, and offer them libation as we used to do to our friendly spirits. In this state of anxiety I remained till my master awoke, when I was dismissed out of the room, to my no small satisfaction and relief; for I thought that these people were all made up of wonders. In this place I was called Jacob; but on board the African snow I was called Michael. I had been some time in this miserable, forlorn, and much dejected state, without having any one to talk to, which made my life a burden, when the kind and unknown hand of the Creator (who in very deed leads the blind in a way they know not) now began to appear, to my comfort; for one day the captain of a merchant ship, called the Industrious Bee, came on some business to my master's house. This gentleman, whose name was Michael Henry Pascal, was a lieutenant in the royal navy, but now commanded this trading ship, which was somewhere in the confines of the county many miles off. While he was at my master's house it happened that he saw me, and liked me so well that he made a purchase of me. I think I have often heard him say he gave thirty or forty pounds sterling for me; but I do not now remember which. However, he meant me for a present to some of his friends in England: and I was sent accordingly from the house of my then master, one Mr. Campbell, to the place where the ship lay; I was conducted on horseback by an elderly black man, (a mode of travelling which appeared very odd to me). When I arrived I was carried on board a fine large ship, loaded with tobacco, &c. and just ready to sail for England. I now thought my condition much mended; I had sails to lie on, and plenty of good victuals to eat; and every body on board used me very kindly, quite contrary to what I had seen of any white people before; I therefore began to think that they were not all of the same disposition. A few days after I was on board we sailed for England. I was still at a loss to conjecture my destiny. By this time, however, I could smatter a little imperfect English; and I wanted to know as well as I could where we were going. Some of the people of the ship used to

tell me they were going to carry me back to my own country, and this made me very happy. I was quite rejoiced at the sound of going back; and thought if I should get home what wonders I should have to tell. But I was reserved for another fate, and was soon undeceived when we came within sight of the English coast. While I was on board this ship, my captain and master named me *Gustavus Vasa*. I at that time began to understand him a little, and refused to be called so, and told him as well as I could that I would be called Jacob; but he said I should not, and still called me Gustavus; and when I refused to answer to my new name, which at first I did, it gained me many a cuff; so at length I submitted, and was obliged to bear the present name, by which I have been known ever since. The ship had a very long passage; and on that account we had very short allowance of provisions. Towards the last we had only one pound and a half of bread per week, and about the same quantity of meat, and one quart of water a-day. We spoke with only one vessel the whole time we were at sea, and but once we caught a few fishes. In our extremities the captain and people told me in jest they would kill and eat me; but I thought them in earnest, and was depressed beyond measure, expecting every moment to be my last. While I was in this situation one evening they caught, with a good deal of trouble, a large shark, and got it on board. This gladdened my poor heart exceedingly, as I thought it would serve the people to eat instead of their eating me; but very soon, to my astonishment, they cut off a small part of the tail, and tossed the rest over the side. This renewed my consternation; and I did not know what to think of these white people, though I very much feared they would kill and eat me. There was on board the ship a young lad who had never been at sea before, about four or five years older than myself: his name was Richard Baker. He was a native of America, had received an excellent education, and was of a most amiable temper. Soon after I went on board he shewed me a great deal of partiality and attention, and in return I grew extremely fond of him. We at length became inseparable; and, for the space of two years, he was of very great use to me, and was my constant companion and instructor. Although this dear youth had many slaves of his own, yet he and I have gone through many sufferings together on shipboard; and we have many nights lain in each other's bosoms when we were in great distress. Thus such a friendship was cemented between us as we cherished till his death, which, to my very great sorrow, happened in the year 1759, when he was up the Archipelago, on board his majesty's ship the Preston: an event which I have never ceased to regret, as I lost at once a kind interpreter, an agreeable companion, and a faithful friend; who, at the age of fifteen, discovered a mind superior to prejudice; and who was not ashamed to notice, to associate with, and to be the friend and instructor of one who was ignorant, a stranger, of a different complexion, and a slave! My master had lodged in his mother's house in America: he respected him very much, and made him always eat with him in the cabin. He used often to tell him jocularly that he would kill me to eat. Sometimes he would say to me— the black people were not good to eat, and would ask me if we did not eat people in my country. I said, No: then he said he would kill Dick (as he always called him) first, and afterwards me. Though this hearing relieved my mind a little as to myself, I was alarmed for Dick and whenever he was called I used to be very much afraid he was to be killed; and I would peep and watch to see if they were going to kill him: nor was I free from this consternation till we made the land. One night we lost a man overboard; and the cries and noise were so great and confused, in stopping the ship, that I, who did not know what was the matter, began, as usual, to be very much afraid, and to think they were going to make an offering with me, and perform some magic; which I still believed they dealt in. As the waves were very high I thought the Ruler of the seas was angry, and I expected to be offered up to appease him. They filled my mind with agony, and I could not any more that night close my eyes again to rest. However, when daylight appeared I was a little eased in my mind; but still every time I was called I used to think it was to be killed. Some time after this we saw some very large fish, which I afterwards found were called grampusses.[1] They looked to me extremely terrible, and made their appearance just at dusk; and were so near as to blow the water on the ship's deck. I believed them to be the rulers of the sea; and, as the white people did not make any offerings at any time, I thought they were angry with them: and, at last, what confirmed my belief was, the wind just then died away, and a calm ensued, and in

consequence of it the ship stopped going. I supposed that the fish had performed this, and I hid myself in the fore part of the ship, through fear of being offered up to appease them, every minute peeping and quaking: but my good friend Dick came shortly towards me, and I took an opportunity to ask him, as well as I could, what these fish were. Not being able to talk much English, I could but just make him understand my question; and not at all, when I asked him if any offerings were to be made to them: however, he told me these fish would swallow any body; which sufficiently alarmed me. Here he was called away by the captain, who was leaning over the quarter-deck railing and looking at the fish; and most of the people were busied in getting a barrel of pitch to light, for them to play with. The captain now called me to him, having learned some of my apprehensions from Dick; and having diverted himself and others for some time with my fears, which appeared ludicrous enough in my crying and trembling, he dismissed me. The barrel of pitch was now lighted and put over the side into the water: by this time it was just dark, and the fish went after it; and, to my great joy, I saw them no more.

However, all my alarms began to subside when we got sight of land; and at last the ship arrived at Falmouth, after a passage of thirteen weeks. Every heart on board seemed gladdened on our reaching the shore, and none more than mine. The captain immediately went on shore, and sent on board some fresh provisions, which we wanted very much: we made good use of them, and our famine was soon turned into feasting, almost without ending. It was about the beginning of the spring 1757 when I arrived in England, and I was near twelve years of age at that time. I was very much struck with the buildings and the pavement of the streets in Falmouth; and, indeed, any object I saw filled me with new surprise. One morning, when I got upon deck, I saw it covered all over with the snow that fell over-night: as I had never seen any thing of the kind before, I thought it was salt; so I immediately ran down to the mate and desired him, as well as I could, to come and see how somebody in the night had thrown salt all over the deck. He, knowing what it was, desired me to bring some of it down to him: accordingly I took up a handful of it, which I found very cold indeed; and when I brought it to him he desired me to taste it. I did so, and I was surprised beyond measure. I then

---

1  Grampusses are a fierce variety of toothed whales.

asked him what it was; he told me it was snow: but I could not in anywise understand him. He asked me if we had no such thing in my country; and I told him, No. I then asked him the use of it, and who made it; he told me a great man in the heavens, called God: but here again I was to all intents and purposes at a loss to understand him; and the more so, when a little after I saw the air filled with it, in a heavy shower, which fell down on the same day. After this I went to church; and having never been at such a place before, I was again amazed at seeing and hearing the service. I asked all I could about it; and they gave me to understand it was worshipping God, who made us and all things. I was still at a great loss, and soon got into an endless field of inquiries, as well as I was able to speak and ask about things. However, my little friend Dick used to be my best interpreter; for I could make free with him, and he always instructed me with pleasure: and from what I could understand by him of this God, and in seeing these white people did not sell one another, as we did, I was much pleased; and in this I thought they were much happier than we Africans. I was astonished at the wisdom of the white people in all things I saw; but was amazed at their not sacrificing, or making any offerings, and eating with unwashed hands, and touching the dead. I likewise could not help remarking the particular slenderness of their women, which I did not at first like; and I thought they were not so modest and shamefaced as the African women.

I had often seen my master and Dick employed in reading; and I had a great curiosity to talk to the books, as I thought they did; and so to learn how all things had a beginning: for that purpose I have often taken up a book, and have talked to it, and then put my ears to it, when alone, in hopes it would answer me; and I have been very much concerned when I found it remained silent.

My master lodged at the house of a gentleman in Falmouth, who had a fine little daughter about six or seven years of age, and she grew prodigiously fond of me; insomuch that we used to eat together, and had servants to wait on us. I was so much caressed by this family that it often reminded me of the treatment I had received from my little noble African master. After I had been here a few days, I was sent on board of the ship; but the child cried so much after me that nothing could pacify her till I was sent for again. It is ludicrous enough, that I began to fear I should be betrothed to this young lady; and when my master asked me if I would stay there with her behind him, as he was going away with the ship, which had taken in the tobacco again, I cried immediately, and said I would not leave him. At last, by stealth, one night I was sent on board the ship again; and in a little time we sailed for Guernsey, where she was in part owned by a merchant, one Nicholas Doberry. As I was now amongst a people who had not their faces scarred, like some of the African nations where I had been, I was very glad I did not let them ornament me in that manner when I was with them. When we arrived at Guernsey, my master placed me to board and lodge with one of his mates, who had a wife and family there; and some months afterwards he went to England, and left me in care of this mate, together with my friend Dick. This mate had a little daughter, aged about five or six years, with whom I used to be much delighted. I had often observed that when her mother washed her face it looked very rosy; but when she washed mine it did not look so: I therefore tried oftentimes myself if I could not by washing make my face of the same colour as my little play-mate (Mary), but it was all in vain; and I now began to be mortified at the difference in our complexions. This woman behaved to me with great kindness and attention; and taught me every thing in the same manner as she did her own child, and indeed in every respect treated me as such. I remained here till the summer of the year 1757; when my master, being appointed first lieutenant of his majesty's ship the Roebuck, sent for Dick and me, and his old mate: on this we all left Guernsey, and set out for England in a sloop bound for London. As we were coming up towards the Nore, where the Roebuck lay, a man of war's boat came alongside to press our people; on which each man ran to hide himself. I was very much frightened at this, though I did not know what it meant, or what to think or do. However I went and hid myself also under a hencoop. Immediately afterwards the press gang came on board with their swords drawn, and searched all about, pulled the people out by force, and put them into the boat. At last I was found out also: the man that found me held me up by the heels while they all made their sport of me, I roaring and crying out all the time most lustily: but at last the mate, who was my conductor, seeing this, came to my assistance, and did all he could to pacify me; but all to very little purpose, till I had seen the boat go off. Soon afterwards we came to the Nore, where the Roebuck lay; and, to our great joy, my master came on board to us, and brought us to the ship. When I went on board this large ship, I was amazed indeed to see the quantity of men and the guns. However my surprise began to diminish as my knowledge increased; and I ceased to feel those apprehensions and alarms which had taken such strong possession of me when I first came among the Europeans, and for some time after. I began now to pass to an opposite extreme; I was so far from being afraid of any thing new which I saw, that, after I had been some time in this ship, I even began to long for a battle. My griefs too, which in young minds are not perpetual, were now wearing away; and I soon enjoyed myself pretty well, and felt tolerably easy in my present situation. There was a number of boys on board, which still made it more agreeable; for we were always together, and a great part of our time was spent in play. I remained in this ship a considerable time, during which we made several cruises, and visited a variety of places: among others we were twice in Holland, and brought over several persons of distinction from it, whose names I do not now remember. On the passage, one day, for the diversion of those gentlemen, all the boys were called on the quarter-deck, and were paired proportionably, and then made to fight; after which the gentleman gave the combatants from five to nine shillings each. This was the first time I ever fought with a white boy; and I never knew what it was to have a bloody nose before. This made me fight most desperately; I suppose considerably more than an hour: and at last, both of us being weary, we were parted. I had a great deal of this kind of sport afterwards, in which the captain and the ship's company used very much to encourage me. Sometime afterwards the ship went to Leith in Scotland, and from thence to the Orkneys, where I was surprised in seeing scarcely any night: and from thence we sailed with a great fleet, full of soldiers, for England. All this time we had never come to an engagement, though we were frequently cruising off the coast of France: during which we chased many vessels, and took in all seventeen prizes. I had been learning many of the manoeuvres of the ship during our cruise; and I was several times made to fire the guns. One evening, off Havre de Grace, just as it was growing dark, we were standing off shore, and met with a fine large French-built frigate. We got all things immediately ready for fighting; and I now expected I should be gratified in seeing an engagement, which I had so long wished for in vain. But the very moment the word of command was given to fire we heard those on board the other ship cry "Haul down the jib;" and in that instant she hoisted English colours. There was instantly with us an amazing cry of—Avast! or stop firing; and I think one or two guns had been let off, but happily they did no mischief. We had hailed them several times; but they not hearing, we received no answer, which was the cause of our firing. The boat was then sent on board of her, and she proved to be the Ambuscade man of war, to my no small disappointment. We returned to Portsmouth, without having been in any action, just at the trial of Admiral Byng[1] (whom I saw several times during it): and my master having left the ship, and gone to London for promotion, Dick and I were put on board the Savage sloop of war, and we went in her to assist in bringing off the St. George man of war, that had ran ashore somewhere on the coast. After staying a few weeks on board the Savage, Dick and I were sent on shore at Deal, where we remained some short time, till my master sent for us to London, the place I had long desired exceedingly to see. We therefore both with great pleasure got into a waggon, and came to London, where we were received by a Mr. Guerin, a relation of my master. This gentleman had two sisters, very amiable ladies, who took much notice and great care of me. Though I had desired so much to see London, when I arrived in it I was unfortunately unable to gratify my curiosity; for I had at this time the chilblains to such a degree that I could not stand for several months, and I was obliged to be sent to St. George's Hospital. There I grew so ill, that the doctors wanted to cut my left leg off at different times, apprehending a mortification; but I always said I would rather die than suffer it; and happily (I thank God) I recovered without the operation. After being there several weeks, and just as I had recovered, the small-pox broke out on me, so that I was again confined; and I thought myself now particularly

---

1 Admiral John Byng (1704–57) was tried for cowardice and negligence after failing to relieve the British garrison on Minorca, which subsequently surrendered to the French. He was convicted and sentenced to death by a firing squad on March 14, 1757

unfortunate. However I soon recovered again; and by this time my master having been promoted to be first lieutenant of the Preston man of war of fifty guns, then new at Deptford, Dick and I

were sent on board her, and soon after we went to Holland to bring over the late Duke of Cumberland][1] to England.—While I was in this ship an incident happened, which, though trifling, I beg leave to relate, as I could not help taking particular notice of it, and considering it then as a judgment of God. One morning a young man was looking up to the fore-top, and in a wicked tone, common on shipboard, d—d his eyes about something. Just at the moment some small particles of dirt fell into his left eye, and by the evening it was very much inflamed. The next day it grew worse; and within six or seven days he lost it. From this ship my master was appointed a lieutenant on board the Royal George. When he was going he wished me to stay on board the Preston, to learn the French horn; but the ship being ordered for Turkey I could not think of leaving my master, to whom I was very warmly attached; and I told him if he left me behind it would break my heart. This prevailed on him to take me with him; but he left Dick on board the Preston, whom I embraced at parting for the last time. The Royal George was the largest ship I had ever seen; so that when I came on board of her I was surprised at the number of people, men, women, and children, of every denomination; and the largeness of the guns, many of them also of brass, which I had never seen before. Here were also shops or stalls of every kind of goods, and people crying their different commodities about the ship as in a town. To me it appeared a little world, into which I was again cast without a friend, for I had no longer my dear companion Dick. We did not stay long here. My master was not many weeks on board before he got an appointment to be sixth lieutenant of the Namur, which was then at Spithead, fitting up for Vice-admiral Boscawen,[2] who was going with a large

fleet on an expedition against Louisburgh.[3] The crew of the Royal George were turned over to her, and the flag of that gallant admiral was hoisted on board, the blue at the maintop-gallant mast head. There was a very great fleet of men of war of every description assembled together for this expedition, and I was in hopes soon to have an opportunity of being gratified with a sea-fight. All things being now in readiness, this mighty fleet (for there was also Admiral Cornish's fleet in company, destined for the East Indies) at last weighed anchor, and sailed. The two fleets continued in company for several days, and then parted; Admiral Cornish, in the Lenox, having first saluted our admiral in the Namur, which he returned. We then steered for America; but, by contrary winds, we were driven to Teneriffe, where I was struck with its noted peak. Its prodigious height, and its form, resembling a sugar-loaf, filled me with wonder. We remained in sight of this island some days, and then proceeded for America, which we soon made, and got into a very commodious harbour called St. George, in Halifax, where we had fish in great plenty, and all other fresh provisions. We were here joined by different men of war and transport ships with soldiers; after which, our fleet being increased to a prodigious number of ships of all kinds, we sailed for Cape Breton in Nova Scotia. We had the good and gallant General Wolfe[4] on board our ship, whose affability made him highly esteemed and beloved by all the men. He often honoured me, as well as other boys, with marks of his notice; and saved me once a flogging for fighting with a young gentleman. We arrived at Cape Breton in the summer of 1758: and here the soldiers were to be landed, in order to make an attack upon Louisbourgh. My master had some part in superintending the landing; and here I was in a small measure gratified in seeing an encounter between our men and the enemy. The French were posted on the shore to receive us, and disputed our landing for a long time; but at last they were driven from their trenches, and a complete land-

---

1   Duke of Cumberland, William Augustus (1721–65) had triumphed over the Jacobite rebels in 1746, but resigned from army service in 1757 after experiencing severe military losses.

2   Vice-Admiral Edward Boscawen (1711–61) was a distinguished naval leader.

3   Louisburg was situated at the entrance to the St. Lawrence River. Its capture was essential for gaining access to the interior parts of Canada and the Great Lakes regions of North America.

4   Colonel James Wolfe (1727–59) became the major general of the attack on the French-Canadian city of Quebec in 1759. His courageous action and death on the battlefield made him an heroic figure to the British.

ing was effected. Our troops pursued them as far as the town of Louisbourgh. In this action many were killed on both sides. One thing remarkable I saw this day:—A lieutenant of the Princess Amelia, who, as well as any master, superintended the landing, was giving the word of command, and while his mouth was open a musquet ball went through it, and passed out at his cheek. I had that day in my hand the scalp of an indian king, who was killed in the engagement: the scalp had been taken off by an Highlander. I saw this king's ornaments too, which were very curious, and made of feathers.

Our land forces laid siege to the town of Louisbourgh, while the French men of war were blocked up in the harbour by the fleet, the batteries at the same time playing upon them from the land. This they did with such effect, that one day I saw some of the ships set on fire by the shells from the batteries, and I believe two or three of them were quite burnt. At another time, about fifty boats belonging to the English men of war, commanded by Captain George Balfour of the Aetna fire-ship, and another junior captain, Laforey, attacked and boarded the only two remaining French men of war in the harbour. They also set fire to a seventy-gun ship, but a sixty-four, called the Bienfaisant, they brought off. During my stay here I had often an opportunity of being near Captain Balfour, who was pleased to notice me, and liked me so much that he often asked my master to let him have me, but he would not part with me; and no consideration could have induced me to leave him. At last Louisbourgh was taken, and the English men of war came into the harbour before it, to my very great joy; for I had now more liberty of indulging myself, and I went often on shore. When the ships were in the harbour we had the most beautiful procession on the water I ever saw. All the admirals and captains of the men of war, full dressed, and in their barges, well ornamented with pendants, came alongside of the Namur. The vice-admiral then went on shore in his barge, followed by the other officers in order of seniority, to take possession, as I suppose, of the town and fort. Some time after this the French governor and his lady, and other persons of note, came on board our ship to dine. On this occasion our ships were dressed with colours of all kinds, from the topgallant-mast head to the deck; and this, with the firing of guns, formed a most grand and magnificent spectacle.

As soon as every thing here was settled Admiral Boscawen sailed with part of the fleet for England, leaving some ships behind with Rear-admirals Sir Charles Hardy and Durell. It was now winter; and one evening, during our passage home, about dusk, when we were in the channel, or near soundings, and were beginning to look for land, we descried seven sail of large men of war, which stood off shore. Several people on board of our ship said, as the two fleets were (in forty minutes from the first sight) within hail of each other, that they were English men of war; and some of our people even began to name some of the ships. By this time both fleets began to mingle, and our admiral ordered his flag to be hoisted. At that instant the other fleet, which were French, hoisted their ensigns, and gave us a broadside as they passed by. Nothing could create greater surprise and confusion among us than this: the wind was high, the sea rough, and we had our lower and middle deck guns housed in, so that not a single gun on board was ready to be fired at any of the French ships. However, the Royal William and the Somerset being our sternmost ships, became a little prepared, and each gave the French ships a broadside as they passed by. I afterwards heard this was a French squadron, commanded by Mons. Conflans; and certainly had the Frenchmen known our condition, and had a mind to fight us, they might have done us great mischief. But we were not long before we were prepared for an engagement. Immediately many things were tossed overboard; the ships were made ready for fighting as soon as possible; and about ten at night we had bent a new main sail, the old one being split. Being now in readiness for fighting, we wore ship, and stood after the French fleet, who were one or two ships in number more than we. However we gave them chase, and continued pursuing them all night; and at day-light we saw six of them, all large ships of the line, and an English East Indiaman, a prize they had taken. We chased them all day till between three and four o'clock in the evening, when we came up with, and passed within a musquet shot of, one seventy-four gun ship, and the Indiaman also, who now hoisted her colours, but immediately hauled them down again. On this we made a signal for the other ships to take possession of her; and, supposing the man of war would likewise strike, we cheered, but she did not; though if we had fired into her, from being so near, we must have taken her. To my utter surprise the

Somerset, who was the next ship a-stern of the Namur, made way likewise; and, thinking they were sure of this French ship, they cheered in the same manner, but still continued to follow us. The French Commodore was about a gunshot ahead of all, running from us with all speed; and about four o'clock he carried his foretopmast overboard. This caused another loud cheer with us; and a little after the topmast came close by us; but, to our great surprise, instead of coming up with her, we found she went as fast as ever, if not faster. The sea grew now much smoother; and the wind lulling, the seventy-four gun ship we had passed came again by us in the very same direction, and so near, that we heard her people talk as she went by; yet not a shot was fired on either side; and about five or six o'clock, just as it grew dark, she joined her commodore. We chased all night; but the next day they were out of sight, so that we saw no more of them; and we only had the old Indiaman (called Carnarvon I think) for our trouble. After this we stood in for the channel, and soon made the land; and, about the close of the year 1758–9, we got safe to St. Helen's. Here the Namur ran aground; and also another large ship astern of us; but, by starting our water, and tossing many things overboard to lighten her, we got the ships off without any damage. We stayed for a short time at Spithead, and then went into Portsmouth harbour to refit; from whence the admiral went to London; and my master and I soon followed, with a press-gang, as we wanted some hands to complete our complement.

# Colonial Spanish America: A Documentary History

## Edited by K. Mills and W. B. Taylor

### JOSÉ DE GÁLVEZ'S DECREES FOR THE KING'S SUBJECTS IN MEXICO (1769, 1778)

#### Regulations on Wages and Peonage, Sonora, 1769

José de Gálvez was a chief architect of Bourbon reforms in the American colonies, especially for New Spain. As *visitador* for New Spain and then Minister of the Indies, he oversaw the creation of a vast military district for the northern frontier (the Comandancia de Provincias Internas), intendancies for the entire viceroyalty south of the Provincias Internas, and other new administrative offices. He established the first Academy of Fine Arts (La Academia de San Carlos in Mexico City), which promoted neoclassical restraint; tripled the public rents; corrected various abuses; reduced restrictions on trade; and moved to give practical, strictly regulated meanings to "freedom" and "equality," two watchwords of eighteenth-century Europe that, conceived more broadly, became closely associated with revolution in France and the United States.

Wage labor came within his restless regulatory gaze. As Charles Gibson writes in his introduction to this document,

> Wages for repartimiento [corvée] workers had been fixed by viceregal order from the beginning, but wages for free labor had not ordinarily been adjusted to any regular schedule. It was entirely characteristic of Gálvez, and of his eighteenth-century frame

of mind, that efforts were now made to systematize wages. Everyone should have a job, and equivalent jobs should be paid equally. Many jobs in the Spanish colonies involved payment of food as well as financial payments, and these also were to be specified. With respect to peonage or debt labor, a type of employment that had begun in the sixteenth century and had become general in many forms of labor, Gálvez sought to establish a typical compromise: that workers in debt to their employers could not renege on their contracts, but that employers could not advance workers' wages more than the equivalent of two months' pay.

Mexican novelist Carlos Fuentes's pithy remark that Spanish Bourbons of the eighteenth century were "modernizing busybodies" may be one of those exaggerations in the direction of the truth. Gálvez's decrees seem more concerned with efficiency, productivity, order, and minute regulation than with freedom, equality, and justice for all.

Don Joséph de Gálvez of the Supreme Council and Chamber of the Indies, intendant of the army of America, general visitor of all the tribunals of justice and royal finance and the treasuries and branches of it in these kingdoms of New Spain, and with His Majesty's approval commissioned with the fullest powers by the very excellent viceroy Señor

Marques de Croix, viceroy, governor, and captain general of the same kingdoms:

In order to make sure that workers needed for the cultivation of lands and the grazing of cattle are not lacking, through agreement with the mine owners and hacienda owners, I have resolved upon a measure that will benefit the poor and promote the public welfare, namely, to set a quota upon salaries and rations of goods that will prevail in the future in the provinces of this jurisdiction, for workers, wage earners, and servants, of the following classifications:

1. The leaders, captains, and heads of mining labors; majordomos of haciendas and ranches, whether for agriculture or for grazing; mule-train shippers; and the overseers of other kinds of occupations equivalent to these, are to receive from their masters the wages and rations so that they may negotiate with them in accordance with the skill and circumstances of each one, with the indispensable requirement that wages must be paid in reales or in silver.

2. Workers in mines and others laboring at equivalent tasks should receive at least seven pesos per month in money, and each week they should receive two almudes [about one-fourth of a bushel] of maize and one-half arroba [a 12-pound measure] of fresh meat or one-quarter arroba [a 6-pound measure] of dried meat, whether they be married or single, and with no innovation for the present in the arrangement commonly granted to mine workers by the owners of mines.

3. The same salary and rations are to be paid to the principal cowboys, farm hands, muleteers, horse guards, and others of similar work in other tasks and occupations, except that carriers are to receive six pesos with the same ration.

4. Subordinate shepherds and cowboys who are aides in mule trains or have other equivalent work are to receive the same weekly ration and are to receive as salary five pesos per month in reales, or in silver if reales are lacking. But if they are Indians under the age of eighteen, they are to receive only four pesos in money, with the same rations.

5. In accordance with the laws, I prohibit vagabonds in these provinces and order that everyone is to have a precise job or office, under penalty of one month in jail for the first offense, whether he be Spaniard or Indian or other non-Indian; and a fine of twenty pesos against anyone who protects him under pretext of refuge and

fails to report him to the judge, so that he may be punished and set to work. And with any repetition of the offense, the vagabonds will be assigned to the public or royal works, with rations but without wages for two months.

6. Servants have a natural freedom to leave one master in order to make arrangements with another, but this freedom is used by some with such impudence and to such excess that the matter requires some effective correction; there is also the opposite extreme, wherein servants are forced to work for masters who do not treat them well or do not pay them the wages agreed upon. To remedy both abuses, I declare and order that the worker who is in debt to his master cannot leave him without first fulfilling the terms of the contract, and no other employer may accept him without having assurance that this is the case, in the form of a written statement by the former employer. And no master may advance the wages of his workers or servants more than the amount of two months' wages; nor may he stand in the way of those who have paid up their debt and who want to look for better employment, at least so long as they are not repartimiento workers.

And so that no one may contravene this regulation, which is useful for all, and so that the masters, servants, and workers may ensure from the government its observance, it is to be published and posted in all the reales [licensed mining settlements] and towns of these provinces, with the corresponding testimonies placed in their archives.

Done in the Real de los Alamos [Sonora], June 2, 1769. Don Joseph de Gálvez, by order of His Most Illustrious Highness.

## ROYAL CÉDULA THAT AMERICAN AND EUROPEAN VASSALS ARE TO BE EQUAL, MADRID, JANUARY 2, 1778

On the surface, the royal decree that elicited a complaint by the Mexico City municipal council and the following somewhat testy reply by Gálvez (now the king's Minister of the Indies in Madrid), seemed to strike a blow for equality of opportunity between peninsular Spaniards and people born and raised in the American colonies, inspired by the king's abiding love for all his subjects. But Creole Spaniards in New Spain's viceregal capital took it as a move to insinuate more peninsulares into high offices of American cathedral chapters. Invoking Enlightenment rationality, Gálvez replied that the new decree merely made Americans and peninsular Spaniards equally eligible for these offices; it did not mean to favor one group over another. Past experience, at least, would have suggested the opposite to ambitious Creole Americans, for few of their ancestors had ever received preferment for important offices in Spain, whereas many *peninsulares* were selected for prestigious offices in the American colonies, especially in the second half of the eighteenth century. They also might well remember Gálvez's retort as the king's *visitador* to New Spain in 1767 to those who questioned the expulsion of the Jesuits: "Vassals of the throne of Spain were born to be silent and obey, not to debate or discuss the affairs of Government."

Joséf de Gálvez to the municipal council and judicial and military branches of the city of Mexico. I have advised the king of your communication of last July 24 in which you complain of His Majesty's order of February 21, 1776, reserving one-third of the places in American cathedral chapters for American Spaniards [Creoles], and another order of September 17 of the same year providing for the nomination of European Spaniards for the vacant post of deacon in the cathedral chapter of the Archdiocese of Mexico and cathedral dignitaries elsewhere in the Indies. Naturally, His Majesty noticed the imprecision with which you refer to the two royal orders and that you either do not understand, or pretend not to understand, the spirit that motivated them and their purpose. It is clearer than light that the spirit of the two royal orders is His Majesty's religious ardor, the motivation is his paternal love for his American vassals, and the purpose is the wellbeing and happiness of these same vassals. In the first order, His Majesty stipulated that for the purpose of maintaining the splendor of the divine cult in the cathedrals of the Indies and the greatest exactitude in administration of justice in the secular tribunals, and also to strengthen the union of those Kingdoms with these and reward equally the merit and services of his vassals, it was his will that the Council of Castile consider Americans for prebends and dignitaries in the churches and tribunals of Spain,

and that the Council of the Indies do the same for the churches and tribunals of those dominions, with the proviso that one-third of the cathedral chapter posts there be filled by American Spaniards. This wording makes it perfectly clear that at least one-third of the prebends must be from the Indies. It does not exclude the possible appointment of many more, as there have always been, are now, and will be.

In the second order, His Majesty directed that for the deaconate of the cathedral chapter of the Archdiocese of Mexico, which was then vacant, European Spaniards be considered and that the same be done for the dignitaries of other American cathedrals. But it did not order the exclusion of Americans for consideration; rather, for that post and for others in the cathedral of Mexico that have been filled lately, Americans as well as Europeans have been considered, and His Majesty appointed the American Don Luis de Torres Tuñón.

Therefore, it is evident in these two orders that His Majesty opened the doors of the churches and the tribunals of Spain to his vassals from the Indies, demonstrating his paternal desire that they and his European vassals be considered equals. It is well known that since the two royal orders were issued, Americans have been considered and appointed as dignitaries. And lately the few Europeans in the Mexican cathedral chapter and other cathedrals of both Americas are conspicuous. So there is no rational or just reason for your communication, especially not for the complaints that figure in it. His Majesty orders me to make this known to you, and advise you that the efforts and care with which his generosity seeks the well-being, happiness, and security of his beloved American vassals deserve justice from the municipal council of Mexico City, not unfounded complaints. They deserve that recognition, love, and gratitude which has always been its [the council's] most glorious keynote and character.

## THE FOUNDATION OF NUESTRA SEÑORA DE GUADALUPE DE LOS MORENOS DE AMAPA, MEXICO (1769)

In the following prologue to a parish register of baptisms (now among the manuscripts of the Zimmerman Library, University of New Mexico), part of the complex history of slavery and freedom for Americans of African descent in this colonial history can be glimpsed. Here, Licenciado Joseph Antonio Navarro, the priest of Nuestra Señora de Guadalupe de los Morenos de Amapa in northeastern Oaxaca, near the southern tip of Veracruz, Mexico, traces events that led to the recent founding of his town and parish. Amapa's residents were descended from *cimarrones*, runaway black slaves, who had taken refuge in the mountainous district of Teutila from the early seventeenth century. These cimarrones reputedly robbed travelers on the road to Córdoba, terrorized nearby valley settlements and sugar mills, and sowed rebellion among settled slaves.

The early colonial history of the Teutila district and this account of the establishment of Amapa in the late eighteenth century reveal a paradoxical combination of motives and responses to the cimarrón problem by Spanish authorities, which contributed to a growing free black population but not an egalitarian view of society. Colonial authorities' treatment of slaves and cimarrones in Mexico varied from exceedingly cruel punishment (including execution, castration, and amputation of hands and feet) to offers of freedom, property, and spiritual care in exchange for loyalty to the Crown and colonial laws. During the early seventeenth century, after punitive expeditions had failed, a policy of conciliation was favored. In 1630 the town of San Lorenzo Cerralvo near the Villa de Córdoba was established as a settlement for peaceable runaways, but few agreed to reside there, and sporadic raids and counterattacks followed. An intensification of unrest among slaves and cimarrones in the vicinity during the mid-eighteenth century led to more repression by colonial authorities. Abortive punitive expeditions by the Córdoba militia were launched in 1748 and 1750 to root out the cimarrones. Shortly thereafter, Teutila's *alcalde mayor*, or district governor appointed by the Crown, also failed in his attempt to negotiate a settlement in his district.

Although their guerrilla activities continued during the 1750s, the runaway slaves of the Teutila area apparently split into two factions: one willing to accept the Spanish offer of freedom and rights to a separate town; and the other preferring to oppose the Spaniards and continue a fugitive life in the mountains. An armed clash between the two factions ended with the victory of the pro-settlement chief, Fernando Manuel, and his

followers. Eighteen of the opponents were turned over to their former masters and their leader was imprisoned. In 1762 a group of cimarrones from the Amapa area formally obtained their freedom after serving in the defense of the port of Veracruz against British attack. Finally, in 1767 an agreement was reached between the *alcalde mayor* of Teutila and the cimarrones for the establishment of a town and church services, and a declaration of freedom for its inhabitants. Some of the original settlers of the town of Amapa had been fugitives for as long as fifty years, but most had lived in mountain refuges of the Teutila district for less than eight years, having escaped masters from the Villa de Córdoba who operated sugar mills and plantations. By December 1767 land titles had been secured, boundary markers laid out, and houses and a church were under construction. With this new town the colonial authorities had succeeded in incorporating a group of fugitives from colonial rule who had proven that they could not be subdued by force. (At least this was the idea. As the story behind and beyond that arresting portrait of the black dons of Esmeraldas, Ecuador, in 1599 suggests, fairytale endings were unlikely for anyone in these circumstances.)

That a preoccupation with security underlay the colonial officials' willingness to grant privileges of freedom, municipal life, and spiritual salvation to the cimarrones is suggested by the duties and obligations to the Crown assumed by the *morenos* (dark ones) of Amapa. The townsmen of Amapa were obliged to take up arms in defense of the king of Spain and to undertake expeditions into the mountains every two months to capture runaway slaves and prevent the formation of new cimarrón colonies. The parish priest, identified as a peninsular Spaniard of pious intentions, admitted that "the principal motive" for the establishment of a parish at Amapa was the government's desire to form a *reducción*, or settlement, for more effective administration and law enforcement.

Here, Spanish officialdom found security and control to be compatible with more disinterested motives in dealing with runaway slaves. In 1750 the alcalde mayor saw two potential benefits from the foundation of a town; "The salvation of their souls would be facilitated by instruction in Christian doctrine, which they sorely lack; also the roads they used to terrorize would be safe to travel." In the priest's mind the impossible had been achieved at Amapa: "The Negroes are extremely happy in their town; the countryside is free from the outrages they perpetrated as vagabonds; sugar mill slaves are more secure in their servitude; the king has more soldiers in his service; and the salvation of these souls is more certain." The legal freedom obtained by Amapa's residents was not without strings, nor was it simply an act of Christian conscience. Practical, paternalistic, and religious considerations appear all at once, under the mutually celebrated protection of the Virgin Mary as Our Lady of Guadalupe, New Spain's official patroness since 1754.

Although Black slaves near the end of the colonial period were comparatively few in Mexico—reportedly fewer than 10,000, while Venezuela and Cuba each had more than 60,000, and Peru still had 90,000—the legacy of forced African immigration there since the sixteenth century was substantial. In the 1790s, 381,941 free Blacks and Mulattoes were counted (about 6 percent of the viceroyalty's population), most of them residing in highland mining and ranching districts of the north center and west, as did Miguel Hernandez and Beatriz de Padilia over a century earlier (see Selections 19 and 28).

I n order to trace the beginnings of runaway Negro slaves in the high mountains of Mazateopam whose consolidation into a town was the principal reason for the founding of this new parish of Nuestra Señora de Guadalupe de Amapa, it is necessary to recall that Negro slaves were brought to this kingdom shortly after the Conquest. According to the post-Conquest histories, Negroes were introduced to work the fields, mines, and sugar mills and to perform other onerous labor considered too strenuous for the weaker Indians. Royal law enacted to preserve the Indian population even prohibited the relocation of Indians in different climates in order to prevent illness.

Thus entered the Negroes, seedbed of the various castes that perverted the purity of the Indians—a painful thought. Disaffected with life in the mines, haciendas, and sugar mills, many slaves deserted their masters, forming small settlements in the mountains of Totula, Palmilla, Tumbacarretas, and Totolinga, presently in the jurisdiction of the illustrious Villa de Córdoba and Veracruz. They assaulted travelers, robbing them of their belongings. Under existing conditions they could not be contained or captured. As a result, residents of the town of San Andres Huatuxco … in 1617 petitioned the viceroy, the Most Excellent Don Diego Fernández de Córdoba, Marques de Guadalcazar, for permission to found the Villa de Córdoba. The following year, 1618, the villa was established, bearing the viceroy's family name. The founding is described by the parish priest of the said villa, Doctor Don José Antonio Rodríguez Valero, in his sacred historical treatise published in Mexico in the year 1759.

Various measures were attempted to dislodge and subjugate the cimarrones. Since force alone proved inadequate, a policy of forbearance was applied with the thought that by winning the affection of the cimarrones the difficulties could be more easily overcome. … The cimarrones were offered their freedom on the condition that they come together in a permanent settlement and parish so as not to lack the spiritual nourishment of which they were deprived in such a licentious and dissolute life. The majority of the runaways accepted the offer. The town of San Lorenzo Cerralvo was founded a considerable distance from the said Villa between 1630 and 1635 during the viceregency of the Marques de Cerralvo, after whom it was named.

Suspicious of this settlement, a band of Negroes continued to roam the highlands of Mazateopam, venturing into the valleys and sugar mills from time to time to plunder travelers, arouse the slaves, and even carry off women from the small, isolated communities. Taking advantage of the cover afforded by the palenques [protected upland refuges], slaves frequently fled from their masters, continually venturing back in surprise attacks. After considerable expense and effort it was at last sadly realized that the cimarrones could not be subdued by force. On the contrary, armed sorties into the mountains in pursuit of the cimarrones only gave them more reason for revenge to the detriment of the sugar mills, travelers, and the inhabitants of the entire region.

In the years 1725 and 1735 there were slave revolts in the above-mentioned sugar mills of the Villa de Córdoba. In 1725 the greater part of the area in the direction of Xalitatuani to the banks of the Quetzalapa River in this jurisdiction of Teutila was involved. A large number of slaves fled; some were captured; others escaped deep into the mountains of Mazateopam where they joined the long-established cimarrones, as José de

Padilla, Marques de Guardiola, former alcalde mayor, told me and described in a written account. In 1735 the region was menaced by a nearly general uprising. If the dragoons from the plaza of Veracruz and the provincial militia had not arrived in time to subdue the runaways before they penetrated deep into the mountains and procured arms, the result would have been grievous. As it was, not all were returned to slavery. Many disappeared into the palenques where their comrades were hiding. With the ranks of the cimarrones thus expanded, vigilance had to be increased day by day. The available means were not sufficient to contain or diminish their forays, which resulted in widespread damage.

In 1748 two punitive expeditions into the mountains of Mazateopam were attempted by the militia. One was directed by Don Gabriel de Segura, Don Bernardo de Zeballos, Don Miguel de Leiba Esparragoza, and Don Vicente Tapia; the other in the direction of Xalitatuani was led by Captain Don Nicolás Carvaxal Castillo de Altra. Both efforts failed miserably. In 1750 two more expeditions were undertaken with the same result. Don Andres de Otañes, alcalde mayor of Teutila, realizing the futility of these attempts, decided to engage in talks with the said Negroes. He met with the captain and some of his comrades on the banks of the Quetzalapa River two leagues from the town of Zoyaltepec and persuaded them to establish a town to facilitate the salvation of their souls through instruction in Christian doctrine. ... The result would be that the cimarrones would no longer be persecuted and the roads would be free from their frequent attacks. The alcalde mayor offered his complete support for this Christian purpose. He stipulated only that the unanimous consent of the runaway slaves living in the highlands be secured. This seemed agreeable to the leaders, who returned to the mountains to tell their comrades of the proposal, promising to return with a reply. Viceroy Revilla Gigedo was informed of the talks, but for the moment nothing resulted.

In 1750 at this stage in the negotiations another punitive expedition by the militia was made on behalf of the sugar mill owners. The Negroes now became suspicious of the promises made by alcalde mayor Otañes, for they did not return with the reply. They undoubtedly believed that he intended to bait them with deception. From 1750 to 1760 the region experienced various incursions at the expense of the mill owners and travelers. Meanwhile the Negroes had divided into two groups. Some, who were less distrustful, joined the party seeking the formation of a town; others continued to oppose the Spanish proposal. The cimarrones' course of action was decided by formal combat. The part against a settlement was led by Captain Macute, longtime chief of the cimarrones. Fernando Manuel, Macute's lieutenant, headed the other group. Fernando Manuel acknowledged that before firing his guns he made a fervent plea to Nuestra Señora de Guadalupe, humbly seeking protection for the success of his Christian purpose. From that moment he designated her Patroness and Guardian of the town which would be founded by his followers, an admirable recognition for such uncivilized people, worthy of envy by the most enlightened and zealous [Christian]. God allowed that Fernando Manuel be rewarded with victory over his opponents. He gravely wounded Captain Macute; and after killing many others, he captured eighteen of those still living who were brought to the Villa de Córdoba, where they were turned over to their respective masters. Captain Macute today is still imprisoned in the Córdoba jail. ...

Having done this, the said Fernando Manuel went to the Hacienda de la Estanzuela where he encountered the owner, Don Fernando Carlos de Rivadeneyra, and Bachiller Don Apolinar de Cosio, his administrator and chaplain. Fernando Manuel sought their protection in establishing the town. Whether or not they agreed to do so cannot be determined because shortly thereafter both men died. The cimarrones settled at sites known as Palacios, Breva Corina, and Mandinga, belonging to the hacienda. These settlements were located near the summit of the mountain leading to the palenques as an escape route should they be pursued. In 1762, on advice given to them, the cimarrones went down to the plaza of Veracruz where they presented themselves to the Most Excellent Viceroy Marques de Cruillas. They offered to serve the viceroyalty in the current war with Great Britain and requested that he grant them their freedom in exchange. Undoubtedly he agreed, for they were incorporated into the corps of lancers, as we know from the document appointing Fernando Manuel sergeant, authorized by Don Santiago Cubillos, infantry captain. When peace was achieved they returned to their settlements to live with their customary distrust, for they could find no one to protect their communities and they had lost the decree signed by the Marques de Cruillas. At the same time a suit initiated by the mill owners was pending, which threatened the Negroes' freedom and their town. The mill owners lost the case for lack of a sound legal base. However, the records of this case were maliciously jumbled or abridged on behalf of the mill owners.

In 1767, when Andrés de Otañes was again serving as alcalde mayor of Teutila, the Negroes appeared before him in the town of Zoyaltepec. Remembering the proposal of 1750, he offered to support them in the declaration of freedom and founding of the town. The cimarrones readily agreed … and this became the fundamental basis for the good fortune they later experienced. The proposal for founding the town was formalized in a written document relating their former occupations and residence; designating the land where the town would be located …; and fervently imploring the protection of the most illustrious Senor Doctor Don Francisco Fabian y Fuero, most dignified bishop of this bishopric. The bishop, upon whom they depended for judgment and pastoral zeal, joyfully complied. The alcalde mayor ordered that various judicial formalities be carried out and informed the Most Excellent Viceroy Marques de Croix of the proceedings. An agent was appointed on behalf of the Negroes to expedite the petition. Reports were gathered by various ministers; and finally, on January 12, a decree signed by the señor fiscal [the high court's legal adviser] Don Juan Antonio Velarde C. and the señor asesor [special adviser to the court] Don Diego Cornide declared a list of cimarrones and others still living in the palenques liberated from servitude and perpetually exempt from paying the royal tribute. The decree further granted them the power to found a town in the appointed location and obligated them to destroy completely the runaway bands of Mazateopam; to take up arms in the service of king and country whenever called; to capture henceforth those Negro slaves who fled from their masters with a reward of twenty-five pesos each; to prevent the formation of other marauding bands; to go into the mountains every two months to verify that no bands had formed; to live in obedience to the Royal Justice of Teutila; and to name alcaldes and regidores to govern the community. …

On February 5 of the said year a dispatch was drawn up directing Don Andrés de Otañes to oversee the establishment of the town and apportionment of lands. I, Don José Antonio Navarro, native of the city of Valencia in the Spanish kingdoms, was selected for the spiritual guidance of the community. … On May 3, accompanied by the alcalde mayor and the Negroes, I went to survey this location known as Amapa. The site chosen is a gently sloping hill formerly occupied by a Mulatto Juan Gonzalez and his wife Manuela Rodríguez, both natives of the port town of Tamiagua in the jurisdiction of Guauchinango. González was employed in cultivating corn and cotton, carrying travelers across the Amapa River in his canoe, and defending the area against attack by cimarrones. This was a favorite spot for their ambushes. The hill was chosen for its supply of potable water, healthful winds, proximity to the highway, and access to the Amapa River.

On May 6 a town meeting was held at which alcaldes, regidores, and other community officials were elected and presented with the trappings of magistrates. Immediately thereafter the locations of the church and houses were designated. The alcalde mayor ordered that materials be secured for the buildings as soon as possible, to which the Negroes agreed. The alcalde mayor returned to the town of Zoyaltepec and I returned to the Hacienda de la Estanzuela.

On May 31, Don Miguel Rodriguez de la Vega, alcalde mayor of Córdoba, brought an order at the instance of the mill owners to suspect the establishment of the new town. For reasons totally unfounded in fact, it was asserted that the town should be established at Mata del Agua, located between the exposed areas of Totolinga and San Campuz. The order was promptly obeyed. A document opposing the settlement at Mata del Agua was then submitted on behalf of the Negroes, which the mill owners tried to refute with arguments of more bulk than substance. It should be noted here that alcalde mayor Otañes, realizing that further delays would revive the Negroes' distrust, resolved to begin construction at the townsite. At Amapa on August 30 he was joined by the Negroes who had come down from their huts at the edge of the mountains. With the help of more than 125 local Indians, who worked on a rotating basis for a week at a time, the church was begun. On September 17 the church was ready for celebration of the first Mass, which I performed with a happy throng of assistants and communicants. Construction of public offices and private dwellings for the Negroes was then begun along streets laid out in straight lines. As a whole it was a very pleasing sight and in time will be the most resplendent town in the lowlands. The viceroy approved the entire proceeding and extended his congratulations for the efficacy and devotion with which this important matter was carried out. On October 19 the matter of the mill owners' opposition was resolved. In a strongly worded order their petition was denied and the completion of the town approved. The mill owners subsequently failed in an appeal to the Audiencia. The Audiencia refused jurisdiction since the Negroes, as soldiers, were subject to the captaincy general.

On December 5 possession of the land was finalized and boundary markers were set out. The Negroes are extremely happy in their town; the countryside is free from the outrages they perpetrated as vagabonds; the plantation slaves are more secure in their servitude; the king has more soldiers in his service; and the salvation of these souls is more certain. In this, the impossible has been conquered without staining the endeavor with human blood; accomplished in the felicitous and just reign of Our Catholic Monarch Charles III (May God protect him many years!), being Viceroy the most excellent Señor Marqués de Croix, Knight and Comendador de Molinos y Laguna Rota of the Order of Calatrava and Lieutenant General of the Royal Armies, and being Bishop the Most Illustrious Señor Don Francisco Fabián de Fuero. The establishment of this town has not been carried out at the expense of Your Majesty or any other person. The undertaking was supervised and paid for by the said Don Andrés Fernández de Otañes. It seemed opportune to me to recount this as an introduction to this book [the baptismal record of Amapa] so it may serve as a monument to posterity. …

## PLAN OF AMAPA (1769–70)

*Alcalde mayor* Andrés Fernández de Otañes, sponsor of Amapa in its first years, had a plan of the town and surroundings prepared to commemorate its founding. His sense of himself in the project and his vision of its future are apparent in this image and his ebullient description of the place. Here the neatly ordered grid plan of the pueblo dwarfs the landscape; as it never would have done in fact. The little community of twenty-two adults centers on an ample plaza about 200 feet across, defined by the church and eight houses with modest arcades, two of them reserved for the priest and the town office. A road linking Amapa to the Villa de Córdoba and the Indian pueblo of Zoyaltepec enters on the open north side of the plaza and turns off to the west. The plan shows room for expansion of the settlement on a plain bounded by rivers, pasturelands, and woods arranged in orchard-like rows.

Writing in February 1770 of "this great work of settling the Blacks in their own pueblo," the alcalde mayor described the site is "agreeable, even delicious, in a hot climate well suited to this type of people, very healthful and good for raising maize, cotton, vanilla, and other crops—better than other places that do not enjoy these advantages—and with ready access to various towns, which will facilitate commerce." Fernández de Otañes wrote of the good order of the town and the civil life to which the once-naked residents were growing accustomed in their elections, new clothes, farms, and the "yoke" of Christianity. In the town itself he was especially proud of the church, with its freestanding bell-tower and two "beautiful" bells. This wooden structure with a fine thatched roof was more than 75 feet long and 25 feet wide. The high altar displayed painted images of Our Lady of Guadalupe (patroness of the new community and personal protectress of Fernando Manuel, who had led the struggle to make peace with the colonial government and settle at Amapa), Saint Joseph (the Virgin's husband), and Saint Carlos Borromeo (in honor of the reigning king of Spain, Charles III). Facing each other near the altar were a portrait of King Charles and his coat of arms, with inscriptions noting that the foundation of the town was accomplished under the protection and at the expense of Alcalde Mayor Fernández de Otañes. All of the paintings were housed in fine gold frames, he added.

Six years later, the original settlers were still in place, quite contented despite the difficulty of tilling land laced with tree roots, but a different alcalde mayor and interim priest took a dimmer view of the town and its citizens. The priest lamented their drunkenness and torpor, especially when it came to serving the church. The alcalde mayor wanted the town disbanded because the settlers showed little fear or respect for his authority (which he exercised from the distant head town of Teutila); they harbored Indians, castes (people of mixed racial ancestry), and military fugitives from Veracruz, usurped lands from a neighboring Indian community, and failed to pay tribute or personally submit their annual elections for his confirmation. They lived, he said, "in complete independence and the pueblo is nothing more that a Castle from which they sally forth to commit outrages."

The viceroy and his legal adviser rejected this 1776 proposal to disband the settlement. The likelihood that the residents of Amapa would return to their mountain refuge and raids weighed heavily in the decision, but the viceroy's adviser also noted that most of the alcalde mayor's complaints were without foundation. The people of Amapa, he noted, had been granted extended relief from the tribute tax and sacramental fees. Moreover, they were only required to submit their election results to the alcalde mayor's lieutenant who lived nearer to their town, and there was no prohibition on non-Blacks settling there if they wished. Nuestra Señora de Guadalupe de los Morenos de Amapa prevailed, at least for the time being.

# Tupac Amaru and Catarista Rebellions

Translated and edited by Ward Stavig and Ella Schmidt

## 31.
## ORDER ISSUED BY VICEROY VÉRTIZ IN VIEW OF THE APPEARANCE OF LAMPOONS IN BUENOS AIRES

*To control information and to limit the criticism and ridicule of individuals, government officials, and governmental policy, efforts were made to control the lampoons that appeared in public places. The anonymity allowed biting words and accusations to be made in public, often to the detriment of the persons or policies against which they were directed. In the following order, the viceroy makes it clear that such public declarations are not to be tolerated. By 1779, the situation was such that Viceroy Vértiz ordered a clampdown on lampoons in Buenos Aires that reflected a growing concern about this form of protest and condemnation.*

Buenos Aires, 23rd of August 1779

Being against the law the publication of lampoons, satires, verses, manifests, and other seditious or insulting papers of public Individuals, or anybody else in particular; in contravention of this general prohibition, and against the public tranquility that this City usually enjoys, we have been observing lately that some idle individuals with pernicious intentions have been composing, distributing and copying these seditious papers that are being unwarily read in circles and conversations without realizing the cunningness of their authors, as has been verified in the one addressed to Don Francisco Escalada concentrating on various expressions of mockery and ridicule against several individuals of this town, and among them are some serious and supposed insults. And this Government wanting to apply the required remedy to such a pernicious harm, separating this corrupting vice from the Republic ... to stop in time such malevolent writings. ... I order that a thorough investigation be made with the goal of finding out the author or authors of said writings, investigating in first place the aforementioned Don Francisco Escalada so that he can indicate how the mentioned paper attached at the beginning of this, got into his house, who was the individual who delivered, opened, and read it, who was present at the time, giving their first names and last names, as well as the author of said paper, or whether he knew or thought of who could be the one who, based on the writing or any other assumption, could have written it and this based on prior information, or anything that he legitimately knew or possessed. And let it be known to him that he needs to submit the original that was sent to his houses, as well as the cover or envelope in which it was guarded. And in the case he indicates that he does not have it, he should then indicate who he gave it to and whether the document attached here conforms to the said original: and that all individuals mentioned by said Escalante be searched as well as others that might be deemed necessary to get at the truth. And this is submitted to the First Assistant in Place, Don Josef Borras, Scribe of the Government.

Vértiz Don Manuel de Ortega Before Me
Joseph Zenzano
Royal public and government Scribe
[RTA, 778–79]

## 32.
## ACCOUNT OF WHAT HAPPENED IN THE CITY OF AREQUIPA WITH THE UPRISING OF THE INDIANS AND OTHER DISCONTENT INDIVIDUALS

*Spanish officials were often at odds with one another with regard to what course of action to take against the rebels in Arequipa as well as the wisdom of the customhouse existing at all, given the circumstances. The following document not only gives a clear account of the very real danger that many of the leading Spanish officials and others faced, it casts doubt on the wisdom of Areche in forcing people to register with the government. Many people thought that this was done so they would have to pay tribute. Those who had been exempt, such as* zambos *and* cholos, *were disturbed at the thought that they too might be subjected to tribute. Thus, in the following document one gets a sense of the growing levels of uncertainty expressed by various segments of society with regard to Spanish policy and to just what this policy actually meant or where it was headed.*

Ever since it was known that the Commission led by Dr. Don Juan Baptista Pando was to impose and administer the Customs: and of his diligence towards getting information from the valleys and coast to ascertain the goods produced by the Haciendas so that the tax-rolls could be made; the good will of people has dwindled and the omen of a fatal ending is looming large. ... [E]ver since the first of January when the Customs were opened, they have inverted the handling of things that the Royal Officials had instituted and have been charging duties without exempting food nor the goods produced by the Indians' own labor. Things were going in such a way that Pando himself announced publicly that custom duties will go from 80,000 to more than 150,000 pesos.

It is for this reason that on the same day [that the customhouse opened] you could find lampoons that threatened the Administrator and his staff; and even though *Corregidor* Semanat took measures to contain and punish such behavior, every day one could see posses of horsemen from various places, all in disguise. It was believed that they were peoples from the countryside [*chacras*] who without any doubt [felt they] were being harassed or were angry [learning] ... that they would need to pay taxes on their wheat, corn, potatoes, and fruits. For their part, the muleteers, of which there are plenty in this region, were groaning about having to unload at the customhouse, and then re-pack all their liquors [*aguardientes*] and the rest of their things that came from the valley. In addition to this regulation, they [were upset by the] fact that they could not enter the customs plaza wearing their spurs and hats.

Rumors about [possible action by] the masses in the city, and the peoples from their fields [*chacras*] were being heard. The *Corregidor*, suspicious of any movement, didn't cease sending official letters to the Administrator telling him to take it easy and proceed with fairness, and to not make changes in how the Royal Officials were dealing with things before everything calmed down. The aforementioned Pando, nevertheless, judged [it was] wise to govern everything with despotism. They [Customs Officials] responded shamelessly and with contempt to the latest official letter sent them by the *Corregidor*, which was quite deferential and civil, saying among other things: that they had come to augment the Royal Treasury by virtue of the orders that they possessed to that end, and that they would sacrifice their lives to do that. Ignoring the *Corregidor*, that same day Pando told the city council these formal words: The *Corregidor* is consumed with fear and is trying to make me believe there is a revolt. In my opinion he looks more like a visionary nun than a member of the military.

Thus ... were things happening when on the night of Thursday the thirteenth, a group of people forced themselves into the Customhouse. They remained there just as a probe, for it seemed they only went with the purpose and will to explore. This was confirmed the following night, when, being informed of the carelessness they had noted in the Customs officials (because the latter thought that nothing so depraved as a tumult could happen) 200 men charged into [the customhouse] with the firm resolution of killing Pando and all the other staff. ... Pando fled over the walls behind his house, like a frightened cat, when confronted with the possibility of [his death]. ... God thus allowed me to confirm the bad opinion I had formed about the *Corregidor*. The others, among them Torre, stopped awhile to make a fire. But witnessing the destruction of the gates, he got curious to see who was committing such action and when he stuck his head out of a window he was cut with a dagger, miraculously not losing his life right there and being able to escape with the help of his companions who pulled him to safety.

The doors [of the customhouse] being completely broken, the masses rushed into the building, burning some papers and stealing 2,032 pesos that were in the chest. They left everything else that they considered to be from legitimate charges. They left the premises after midnight of the fourteenth, causing some confusion by passing by houses ... belonging to some of the individuals who had been threatened in the lampoons, especially the Royal Officials who had been ... carefully searched for but who were able to slip away as best they could.

The *Corregidor* was now totally confused by the causes of the revolt that he could not by himself solve, be it because he felt in obvious danger of losing his life and wealth or for other reasons that are also easy to understand. Immediately he gave orders that such serious circumstances require. He went to the Customhouse on the morning of the fifteenth accompanied by the Town Council members and gathered up all the documents that had not burned and handed them to the Royal Officials who were present. Finishing this task, they left on their own to do whatever they deemed necessary in such circumstances.

Word spread on the fifteenth that Cosío, Goyeneche, and Alvizuri should be killed for having been friends of the *Corregidor* and Pando. With this warning, one could notice the consternation that their hearts were suffering. In fact, they locked themselves in their houses anxiously awaiting the throng. At ten at night of the same day a strange commotion and shouting was heard in the street of San Francisco and then some people threateningly attacked the house of Lastarria. From there they passed by Cosío's house and then went straight to the *Corregidor's* house who had been sentenced to die in the latest lampoons that were circulated. They found the house locked, and setting fire to the windows and doors, they found no living person, for all those who had been hidden there had fled. But, they ransacked it not leaving even a nail in the wall.

They finished their toil at two in the morning of the sixteenth, and after going through the street of Mercaderes, they robbed Candero's store. ... They then planned to go to the house of Cosío and they were yelling so loud that they could hear them say from the interior of the house: *Lets go to Cosío's house;* but this did not discourage him, although he did keep the door locked so that as soon as the first blow to the door was felt, the entire family could escape to the Bishop's Palace, which had been disposed to receive them: they had previously placed ladders to access that contiguous building. The riches that he kept in the house had already been safely hidden, even though he was not able to gather up things at their store. The mob, leaving this project, decided to continue down Mercaderes street. They went on to the jail, freed the prisoners and wanted to attack the Royal Treasury, but they could not do this due to lack of time for it was already after four-thirty in the morning.

Amidst this confusion and turmoil, the night of the fifteenth and the morning of the sixteenth passed. The *Corregidor* retired to the Municipality where all the noble citizens came to offer their skills and lives in defense of the King and the city. They prepared themselves quickly and organized the best defense possible at the time. Don Mateo Cosío, as Colonel of the Cavalry, gave the order to gather a regiment and ... most of them were in the plaza by four in the afternoon. It was then that it was learned that it was not the people from the countryside who had participated in last night's uprising, nor had they intervened in the looting. Those who had perpetrated this were the poorest of the city dwellers who were stirred up by the uprising in the Customhouse, even though nobody could tell who gave the order for the mutiny which had been very disorganized due to the numbers involved. The investigation is being conducted with great secrecy in order to punish those responsible.

Once this decision was made, it was ordered that the seven cavalry companies that were gathered on the sixteenth should protect the entrances to the city. The Infantry, which only had two companies armed and ready, stayed in the plaza with orders to go wherever they were needed. The fear was that the people from the *chacras*, especially those from Tiabaya, whose two companies did not want to obey or come, might attack the city. In consequence, they also suspected all the cavalry who were also *chacra* owners. To these concerns were added a rightful suspicion of an uprising by the Indians of the Pampa, so as to warrant a general surveillance from prayer time until nine at night of the area around the city by Cosío and a company of cavalry and accompanied by Pober and two of his friends. All was calm, and there was no movement on the Pampa, but once he came back to the Plaza he was informed at nine that the two companies from Tiabaya were in the outskirts of the city. He went there with his company and convinced them to come to the plaza and serve as good subjects of the King.

They willingly accepted and while they were being separated from the two companies their captains got to know the people, as they all had come together in one platoon, [Cosío] was advised that in the Pampa where Felan and his company were they had been attacked by more than 800 Indians. Cosío immediately left to assist them with the two companies from Tiabaya and the infantry of noblemen. He found them retreating to the small square of Santa Marta, all the street to the Pampa (more than two blocks long) being occupied by the Indians. Felan resisted the attack with courage and force. He killed two Indians and one of his men was wounded and a horse was dead.

With Cosío's reinforcements the Indians retreated, leaving several dead and wounded in the street. The company of Don Martín Solares of grenadiers .... arrived. With the help of two more companies that they took from less dangerous locations, the Indians of the Pampas were defeated and they fled to the mountains. That night six dead and four wounded were brought in. With the first sun rays, Cosío left for the Pampas with two of his companies. He caught several wounded Indians who couldn't flee, and found all the *chacras* deserted. He followed the trail of the Indians on the Pampa and captured many that were fleeing with their wives and children.

Dawn broke on the morning of the seventeenth with all those killed in the fighting stacked in the halls of the Municipality, and in the afternoon two cavalry companies with the infantry of the nobility went and burned all of the *ranchos* of the Pampa. At two in the afternoon

of the eighteenth another six wounded Indians were hanged, and all the rest are fleeing with their women and children, dead from hunger and need, according to muleteers who have arrived from the Sierra, who also said that there are many who are wounded and some have already died or who are dying in agony from their wounds. The jail is also full of Indians, both men and women, awaiting their fates after charges have been filed.

The defeat of the Indians of the Pampa seems to have mobilized the rest of them [Indians] in the surrounding region. This was supported by a lampoon that was intercepted that indicates that tomorrow, the twentieth, the city would be assaulted during the night. With this warning (that even though it is from the enemy it should not be dismissed) a state of readiness continues with a larger number of cavalry. For this reason the people from the countryside have come to the city, even though they are in the middle of their harvests. The threat has not become a reality so far—seven in the morning of the twenty first—and this is because they are aware that the city is defended by ... regiments of infantry and cavalry.

Today from nine to eleven in the morning ... a meeting ... was held that was attended by several lawyers, royal officials, and some army captains that are here in order to determine the protection that is needed tonight. Two Infantry companies and two more Cavalry companies remain under arms guarding all the entrances to the city. It is hoped that everything will remain quiet, even though it is good to live with precaution for we know the Indians' character which is treasonous.

One of the main ... concerns that disturbed the people of the countryside and the masses in the city and put them against the *Corregidor* was the order that came from the *Visitador* [Areche] to register as tax-payers not only the Indians—*naturales* and *forasteros*—but also the *Zambos* and *Cholos*. They believed that this was done in order to have them pay tribute. This procedure will need to be suspended for a long time or should not even be considered at all, or the problems that we have seen might be experienced again. Arequipa, January 21st, 1780. [*CDIP*, 40. 1780-I-21]

## 33.
## THREAT AGAINST BERNARDO GALLO, HEAD OF LA PAZ CUSTOMS

*In most cities in which a customhouse had been established, tensions built up between customs officials and those subject to the duties. La Paz was one of the cities in which* criollos, mestizos, *and Indians were raised. The La Paz* aduana *and its head, Bernardo Gallo, came under attack in March 1780. The following lampoon threatened Gallo with death and denounced his actions, claiming that they would surely lead to bloodshed. The author of the document plays with Gallo's name, which means "rooster" or "cock." Gallo was eventually hanged by the rebel leader Andrés Tupac Amaru for his role as the head of the* aduana *and because of the hatred that both* criollos *and Indians had for him.*

This is the third and final announcement, and we will cry with sorrow, because as a result of two or three unworthy thieves, many innocent people will die. And blood will flow in the streets and square on the 13th of March; it will run like water, if the Creoles are not defended. And this thieving old cock [Gallo] will be skinned alive, cut into pieces and thrown into the river. He is perfectly aware of what is happening here, and cannot claim that his misfortune is due to unforeseen circumstances, since this is the third announcement. It is only regrettable, that because of this villainous thief, many will pay with their lives. [*RR*, 188. Translated by Scarlett O'Phelan Godoy. This document is also included with the Tupac Catari materials, document 126.]

## 34.
## ACCOUNT OF THE MOST HORRIBLE CRIME COMMITTED BY JOSÉ GABRIEL TUPAC AMARU, *CACIQUE* OF PAMPAMARCA

*The following document is an account of the first stages of the rebellion, beginning with the dinner that Tupac Amaru and Corregidor Antonio de Arriaga shared with others on November 4, 1780. Subsequent to this social gathering, Tupac Amaru took Corregidor Arriaga prisoner. The corregidor was then sentenced to death, which was carried out on November 10, 1780—the executioner himself was a slave of Arriaga's. The rebel leader Tupac Amaru declared himself the new Inca. The author of the document also refers to Micaela Bastidas, the wife of Tupac Amaru, as no less cruel of a monster than her husband. In this way, the author indirectly attests to the important role Bastidas would have in the rebel leadership.*

*The document is most interesting in that so much has been made of the antagonisms between Tupac Amaru and Arriaga. Although this discord is obviously true, they were also united by the bond of fictive kinship. Perhaps this is the reason that the person working for Arriaga did not hesitate to put the* corregidor's *wealth in the hands of Tupac Amaru when he received a letter from the* corregidor *asking him to do this.*

*One of the first things Tupac Amaru did as the new Inca was to attack textile mills* (obrajes). *In doing this, he not only attacked a symbol of oppression, he distributed the cloth—just as the Incas had done to reward people. Thus, he most likely called on this ancient tradition to solidify his claim to the title of Inca.*

On Saturday November 4th of 1780, the day on which our Sovereign Monarch … Dn. Carlos the Third (God keep him) is celebrated, a dinner was held at the house of Dr. Carlos Rodriguez, priest of the Doctrine (Parish) of Yanaoca with Crl. Don Antonio Arriaga *Corregidor* of the Province of Tinta, the priest of the Doctrine of Pampamarca, and the *Cacique* of that town José Gabriel Tupac Amaru. Once the banquet was over, the *Corregidor* was pressed to leave early for Tinta where he had some unfinished businesses, but having offered to keep him company, the *Cacique* (who was like his *compadre*) would not hear of it. Instead, José Gabriel left before him so that he could meet with those who were waiting in a ravine ready to ambush the *Corregidor* who had to take that route. Once the *Corregidor* arrived to said site, Tupac Amaru came out and confronted him with all his men. The *Corregidor*, … trying to defend himself, grabbed a pistol but be was immediately caught with a rope around his neck and was forced down off his mule before having a chance to shoot. They also wounded the clerk who was accompanying him and captured the rest of his slaves who were following him at a distance. They were all taken to a hidden, secret site off the path and were left there tied up, guarded, and under threat of death if they shouted.

Having done this the traitor promptly went back to a house he owned in the annex [community of a parish] named Tungasuca. And having given his orders, he went back at midnight to bring the prisoners to this house. He put the *Corregidor*, burdened with chains and shackles, in one of the underground cells, and his clerk in another; as well as the other slaves. He made the clerk write several letters of convocation and forced the *corregidor* to sign them and address them to: his principal cashier Dn. Manuel San Roque; to all those who called themselves Spaniards in the region; and to other subjects, from whose persons and resources he desired to take advantage due to being who they were and because of their wealth. In fact, the letter addressed to the Cashier ordered him to come to Tungasuca without delay, bringing all the sealed and minted silver and firearms … as these were all necessary to serve the King and to which end he was sending his *compadre* with the necessary mules. In the letters of convocation he threatened, under penalty of death, all those who would not present themselves with their arms in Tungasuca. To Don Bernardo de la Madrid, and the Galician Dn. Juan de Figueroa, the first the overseer of Pomacanchi and the second of Quipococha, he wrote to them in the following manner:

*Esteemed friend: it is imperative that you put yourself on the road for this pueblo of Tungasuca as soon as you read this, for we have several matters that we need to discuss tonight. And from here I am planning to go to Cuzco where I intend to clear my name. I wish your Honor perfect health and that God keep you for years to come. Tungasuca, November 5th, 1780. Your dear friend—Arriaga.*

After sending these letters of convocation, Tupac Amaru got two strings of mules ready after one in the morning and left immediately carrying the letter to the Cashier himself. The Cashier, recognizing the handwriting and signature of the *Corregidor* and seeing that his *compadre* was in charge, did not hesitate. The traitor carried 22,000 pesos in cash, carved silver, ninety muskets, two boxes containing the sabers of the province, and all the various weapons of said *Corregidor*. And accompanied by the *Corregidor's* family—whom he convinced had also been summoned—he left without delay for Tungasuca. Once there, he put everybody in jail, doing the same thing with Dn. Bernardo de la Madrid and the Galician Dn. Juan de Figueroa.

Such silence was maintained that nobody knew the whereabouts of the *Corregidor*. Some were told that he had left to visit the higher villages of the Province. Others were told that he was attending to very important business in Tungasuca, which did not allow him to attend to anything else. He [Tupac Amaru] put spies in all entrances to Cuzco so that nobody in the Province could go and inform [people there] about what was going on in Tungasuca.

While the armed Indians and *Mestizos* of his faction were arriving, thanks to the Letters of Convocation, he [Tupac Amaru] had a gallows built in the Tungasuca plaza and he sentenced the *Corregidor*, his *compadre*, to die on it. Intimidated by his sentence, the *Corregidor* sent for the priest Dr. Dn. Antonio Lopez, who happened to be in the principal pueblo, a league and a half away, to come and hear the confession of an invalid. The priest walked there and discovered that he had to confess the … *Corregidor*. He asked why he was treated in such a way, and he answered that the *Cacique* Tupac Amaru was thinking of killing him. … [Tupac Amaru] told the Priest that he had orders from the *General Visitador*, authorized by the Royal *Audiencia* of Lima, and he had had it for twenty-six days. He was worried that he was guilty of taking too much time [to comply with the order]. …

The priest then proceeded to assist the unfortunate *Corregidor*, giving him confession and the last *viaticum* [communion] and supporting him during the six days he was given.

On the morning of Friday, November 10th, Tupac Amaru ordered that three columns … be organized from all the people from his Province that were already there. Two were composed of Spaniards and *Mestizos* armed with muskets, sabers, and sticks; and one of Indians with slings. In the middle of this, he brought out the *Corregidor* dressed in his military uniform, and publicly started taking his uniform off, stripping him of his rank following the rituals he had understood and seen in other occasions, until he was left in his shirt. He then put a shroud on him … that had the title of *La Caridad* on it. He then gave the order to take him to the gallows, accompanied by the Priest and two other clergymen, where he went with a resignation and patience worthy of somebody who was already touching the portals of eternity.

Once on the gallows the *Corregidor* was forced by the tyrant to publicly declare that he deserved to die in that way. A black slave of the *Corregidor* served as his executioner, but the ropes snapped and both fell to the ground. But they suspended them again with a lariat around their necks, and thus they completed the execution in clear sight and tolerance of all his Province. Not one voice was raised that would disturb the operation. And most surprising of all was that those same Collectors and those close to the *Corregidor* were the ones who (oh, what an awful spectacle of perfidy!) sped his way to the ignominious place of execution, and who pulled on his feet so he could die even more violently.

While all this was happening, the *Cacique* [Tupac Amaru] circled the village and its entrances on his horse. The troops were surprised at an action so unimaginably cruel as … that of a *Corregidor* being executed by one of his subjects. … They were all so intimidated by these events that nobody dared to complain or contradict what was being carried out. And everything was done with such secretiveness and care that even though the execution took place six days after his arrest, the news was not known in Cuzco until after the death of the *Corregidor* was confirmed by those closest to him. Two

days later the body was buried with the regular pomp in the church of the same town. The *Cacique* was not present at the function as he was occupied on other expeditions.

With this first coup the tyrant was getting ready for even more audacious deeds, showing himself capable and willing to do whatever it took. Several years before he had gone to Lima and appeared before the Royal *Audiencia* to determine the legitimate quality of his descendancy from Dn. Felipe Tupac Amaru, the last of the Incas. It is there where he gladly started down a path filled with contradictory judgment. … The papers that were approved through the recklessness of those who handled the documents of his lineage gave him the chance to form a high idea of his own lineage, a fact that took him where he should have never gone.

Returning from Lima with even more presumption than when he had left, he knew how to hide his intentions under a facade of moderation, general affability, and generosity … tricks used by those who try to command the affection of all only to despotically dominate them later on. Nothing of his plans was discovered until the very insolent act of publicly killing the *Corregidor*. More than six thousand men, Indians and *Mestizos* from surrounding villages, assisted him. And having called upon those in the surrounding area, he intimated in the tongue that the Incas used [Quechua]: *That the time had come when they must shake off the heavy burden under which they had been suffering for many long years at the hands of the Spaniards. … The* Corregidores *of the Kingdom would be punished in equal measure for all the taxes they had imposed. … They would exterminate all Europeans and terminate the* repartimientos, customs, *and other similar burdens that were only devastating the kingdom. He added that this in no way went against the obedience due to the King and … the Catholic Faith. The … [Catholic Church] had all his veneration, and … respect. Once all injustices were removed, his only goal was to bring the infidel Indians to the faith and retire to enjoy the fruits of his expeditions. They should not despair at the beginning and they would attain their freedom. They should rest assured that the love that he expressed through all this would probably cost him his life in a similar torment as they had just witnessed, but that he would do it with happiness if it meant giving his nation glory and restoring its ancient state. He then put a rope around his neck as used in the previous execution, so as to move* the Indians, who … cried out offering to follow him and to lose their lives before withdrawing their support.

He then proceeded to issue a proclamation with this beginning: Don José Gabriel Tupac Amaru, Inca, of royal blood and main lineage. In it, he called on all his beloved American *Criollos* of all classes, as well as Spaniards, *Mestizos*, and Indians … to follow him. He made it clear that he was a Christian Catholic and that he would never violate the Church's immunities. His only objective was to abolish the introduction of *Corregidores*, free the Kingdom of customs, monopolies and other taxes, and to do away with everything that was European and responsible for such institutions. Those who would oppose and resist his plans would suffer … the full weight of his anger. Copies of this proclamation and other edicts were distributed through people of trust so that they would be posted in public places in the Provinces and cities close to Cuzco and Arequipa. … He wrote … to the priests so that they would not influence the believers of their parishes and prevent their following his precepts. He did the same with other private individuals, even those who he did not know and whose trust he assumed, even though in reality he did not have it.

It was mentioned that the traitor Tupac Amaru did not attend the burial of the *Corregidor* for he was busy with other expeditions. These were reduced to him going personally to Tinta, to the said *Corregidor's* house, and ransacking it of what he had not had the chance to get when he went there with the Cashier. He took everything of taste and value that had been left, leaving not a mule nor food, of which he took plenty. Then he went to the *obrajes* of Parupuquio and Pomacanchi. He demolished the first and looted all the fine clothes he found and which he used as the first demonstrations of his generosity to all those who were helping him with the rebellion. In the second, we were assured, he took even more loot. … [H]e took over twenty mules loaded with clothes, lots of provisions, and 13,000 pesos in cash.

He then proceeded to go to the neighboring province of Quispicanchis to conquer it and surprise its *Corregidor* Dn. Fernando Cabrera, who … was in the town of Quiquijana some eight leagues from Tungasuca. He had arrived from Lima not even one month before but had the fortune of being able to flee to Cuzco, hidden by the dark of the night and riding bareback on a mule or mare that he managed to get. He was forced to leave 2,000 pesos in … silver and all his jewelry, which the rebel confiscated. This Province (Quispicanchis) declared itself in support of the rebel, and the Indians kissed his feet and hands as if he were their lord. He distributed the clothes that the *Corregidor* had for the *reparto* among the Indians and went back to his pueblo of Tungasuca where he established his royal throne with great ostentation and with guards who were named chiefs so as to better rule their people.

Then he went to hang those Europeans that he had taken prisoners when he arrested *Corregidor* Arriaga, but his wife, the *Cacica* Micaela Bastidas (she is as cruel a monster as he is), convinced him not to kill them for they could be of help in fixing arms, casting cannons and bullets, especially the Galician Figueroa whose skills in these matters were well known. And, in fact, after securing them with shackles and guards, he put them to work on those tasks. Tinta, November 10th, 1780. [*CDIP*, 60. 1780-XI-10]

## 35.
## DEATH CERTIFICATE OF *CORREGIDOR* ANTONIO DE ARRIAGA

*The priest Antonio Lopez de Sosa was almost like a father to Tupac Amaru. He was probably the person responsible for getting the future* kuraka *into the* kuraka *school in Cuzco after Tupac Amaru's father died. He also performed the marriage ceremony for the rebel leader to Micaela Bastidas. He was asked by Tupac Amaru to hear the confession of Corregidor Arriaga, and the priest was then present during Arriaga's execution. In the following document, Lopez de Sosa presents Arriaga's death certificate in a very matter-of-fact way, giving no indication of his personal relationship to the rebel leader nor the momentous implications of this death (one would not necessarily expect him to say such things), but briefly mentioning his role in the events surrounding the execution.*

Don Antonio de Arriaga, *Corregidor* of this Province.

In the Pueblo of San Felipe de Tungasuca, annex of the Doctrine (Parish) of Pampamarca, Province of

Tinta, on the thirteenth day of the month of November of 1780. I, Dr. Don Antonio Lopez de Sosa, Priest and Vicar of this Doctrine, buried the body of Don Antonio de Arriaga, *Corregidor* of this province, whom I assisted [with his confession] at his request and after seeing that all my efforts to save his life were in vain due to the resistance and disturbances of those [who were] accomplices in his imprisonment. And it was not registered then due to the rebellions, loss of the [register] book, and being late so that I forgot to register it, so I am doing it now, and signing it.

Doctor Don Antonio Lopez de Sosa
[*CDIP*, 64. 1780-XI-13]

## 36.
## TUPAC AMARU DECLARES HIMSELF INCA AND RULER

*Tupac Amaru most often argued that he was acting on behalf of the Spanish monarchs to create good government, but in the following selection he declares himself the Inca and ruler of his Andean territories and people. He also discusses how the Spanish rulers have usurped his legitimate position and exploited his people. The document was undated and unsigned. For this reason, and because other documents do not declare a break from the Spanish Crown, the possibility that it could be a forgery has been suggested.*

Don José I by the grace of God, Inca king of Peru, Santa Fe, Quito, Chile, Buenos Aires, and the continents of the seas of the south, highest duke and lord of the Césars and Amazonians, with dominion in the Gran Paititi, commissary and distributor of divine piety … decided in my council … on repeated and secret occasions, already made public, that the Kings of Castile usurped the throne and dominion of my people three centuries ago, making them vassals with unbearable services, tributes, money, custom dues, *alcabalas*, monopolies … tenths, and fifths. The viceroys, *audiencias*, *corregidores*, and other ministers [are] all equally tyrannous, selling justice at auction; and to him who bids most, most is given. Ecclesiastical and secular officials enter into

[administering justice] without fear of God, trample upon the natives of this kingdom as beasts, and take away the lives of all those who do not wish to rob. … In the name of God, all powerful, we order and command that none of the said pensions shall be paid to the intrusive European ministers of bad faith or shall they be obeyed in anything. Respect shall only be held for the priesthood. We shall pay the tenth and first fruits [*primicia*], which are given to God and the tribute and fifth [*quinto*] for the King as the natural Lord; and this with the moderation which shall be made known with other laws to be observed and kept. … I command … an oath to be taken to my royal crown in all the cities, towns, and places of my dominions; and [I wish] to be informed briefly of the ready and faithful vassals, for rewards, and those who rebel, for imposing fitting penalties. [*LIR*, 134–35. Translated by L. E. Fisher.]

## 37.
## TUPAC AMARU'S PROCLAMATION OF FREEDOM FOR SLAVES

*One of Tupac Amaru's first actions was to try to gain support for the rebellion and to undermine the strength of the Spanish. One of the ways he attempted to accomplish this was by stirring up the fears of the Spanish and by creating doubts about the loyalty of those around them, especially the people who worked in their households and served them. In the following proclamation, he asks all Peruvians to join him in the rebellion, and he calls not only for the freeing of the slaves but for the slaves to leave their masters. He offers the slaves their freedom if they comply with his orders, and he makes it clear that those who do not accept his offer will suffer his wrath for their disobedience.*

Don José Gabriel Tupac Amaru Indian of noble-blood of the Incas and royal family (*Tronco Principal*).

Proclamation of November 16, 1780 to the citizens of Cuzco so that they desert the Spaniards [*chapetones*] and free the slaves.

Through this proclamation let it be known to all Peruvians who live and inhabit the City of Cuzco who are friends of Spaniards and *Mestizos*, religious men that are in the city, priests and other distinguished persons who might have developed friendships with the Peruvian people and those who participate in my efforts to benefit this Kingdom: let it be perfectly understood: the hostilities and ill-treatment caused by all European people, who without fear of the Divine Majesty nor abiding by the Royal Orders of our natural Lord, have pushed to the limit the peace and tranquility of these lands by their ill-treatments and affronts, their taking advantage of the common good, even letting the natives die. And as everybody has experienced rough treatment from the Europeans they should all come, without exception, and support my position by totally deserting the Spaniards, even if they were slaves to their masters with the added benefit that they will be freed of the servitude and slavery to which they were subjected. And if they do not abide by this proclamation they will experience the most severe punishment that I can impose, regardless of whether they are Priests, Friars or of any other quality or character. And so that nobody can allege ignorance, I order that this proclamation be posted in all public places of the city. This was done in the Sanctuary of Tungasuca[1] Province of Tinta the 16th of November of 1780.

*Joph.* Gb. Thupa Amaro Inca [*sic*]
[*CDIP*, 69. 1780-XI-16]

# 38.
# REBEL VIEWS ON THE ILLEGITIMACY OF SPANISH RULE

*In the period leading up to the rebellion, and even after it began, rebels sent mixed messages concerning the role of the Spanish king, the Spaniards, and their right to govern. Some argued that the Spanish king was sovereign, and that the local government and Spaniards needed to be removed. This was often Tupac Amaru's position, but it was not always his sentiment. Others, however, argued that Spanish rule was illegitimate. The conquest by the Spanish did not give them a right to the territory or to rule.*

*The following are three brief passages that point to the illegitimacy of Spanish rule and, by implication, the legitimacy of indigenous actions. The first is from the province of Huarochirí, not far from Lima. The second is from Tupac Amaru. The third is from indigenous testimony in the region of La Paz. The prophecies referred to are unclear, but they could relate to the notion of Inkarrí, in which the Inca or the Inca Empire would be reborn and legitimate Andean rule reestablished.*

### 1. Huarochirí

The prophecies of Santa Rosa and Santo Toribio would be fulfilled, meaning that the territory would return to its former owners since the Spaniards had conquered it wrongfully [*la habían ganado mal*] and through a war brought unjustly against the natives who had lived in peace and quiet.

### 2. Tupac Amaru

The kings of Castile have usurped the crown and dominions of my people for close to three centuries.

### 3. La Paz

[The king of Spain] had conquered the kingdom wrongfully, and that the time had come for the fulfillment of the prophecies.
[*WAWR*, 164. Translated by Sinclair Thomson]

---

1  One of the four annexes of the parish of Pampamarca.

# An Inquiry into the Nature and Causes of the Wealth of Nations

*By Adam Smith*

*[handwritten margin notes: Gabe-talk / * should be "self critical" / do we agree w/ Adams?]*

*[handwritten margin notes: * expansion of the ability / of larger group? of people / to afford luxury goods]*

## BOOK I

OF THE CAUSES OF IMPROVEMENT IN THE PRODUCTIVE POWERS OF LABOUR, AND OF THE ORDER ACCORDING TO WHICH ITS PRODUCE IS NATURALLY DISTRIBUTED AMONG THE DIFFERENT RANKS OF THE PEOPLE

### CHAPTER I

OF THE DIVISION OF LABOUR

The greatest improvement in the productive powers of labour, and the greater part of the skill, dexterity, and judgment with which it is anywhere directed, or applied, seem to have been the effects of the division of labour.

The effects of the division of labour, in the general business of society, will be more easily understood by considering in what manner it operates in some particular manufactures. It is commonly supposed to be carried furthest in some very trifling ones; not perhaps that it really is carried further in them than in others of more importance: but in those trifling manufactures which are destined to supply the small wants of but a small number of people, the whole number of workmen must necessarily be small; and those employed in every different branch of the work can often be collected into the same workhouse, and placed at once under the view of the spectator. In those great manufactures, on the contrary, which are destined to supply the great wants of the great body of the people, every different branch of the work employs so great a number of workmen

that it is impossible to collect them all into the same workhouse. We can seldom see more, at one time, than those employed in one single branch. Though in such manufactures, therefore, the work may really be divided into a much greater number of parts than in those of a more trifling nature, the division is not near so obvious, and has accordingly been much less observed.

To take an example, therefore, from a very trifling manufacturer; but one in which the division of labour has been very often taken notice of, the trade of the pin-maker; a workman not educated to this business (which the division of labour has rendered a distinct trade), nor acquainted with the use of the machinery employed in it (to the invention of which the same division of labour has probably given occasion), could scarce, perhaps, with his utmost industry, make one pin in a day, and certainly could not make twenty. But in the way in which this business is now carried on, not only the whole work is a peculiar trade, but it is divided into a number of branches, of which the greater part are likewise peculiar trades. One man draws out the wire, another straights it, a third cuts it, a fourth points it, a fifth grinds it at the top for receiving the head; to make the head requires two or three distinct operations; to put it on is a peculiar business, to whiten the pins is another; it is even a trade by itself to put them into the paper; and the important business of making a pin is, in this manner, divided into about eighteen distinct operations, which, in some manufactories, are all performed by distinct hands, though in others the same man will sometimes perform two or three of them. I have seen

*[handwritten margin notes: - human nature / - role the individual plays]*

*[handwritten margin notes: - commenting on policy & public policy]*

a small manufactory of this kind where ten men only were employed, and where some of them consequently performed two or three distinct operations. But though they were very poor, and therefore but indifferently accommodated with the necessary machinery, they could, when they exerted themselves, make among them about twelve pounds of pins in a day. There are in a pound upwards of four thousand pins of a middling size. Those ten persons, therefore, could make among them upwards of forty-eight thousand pins in a day. Each person, therefore, making a tenth part of forty-eight thousand pins, might be considered as making four thousand eight hundred pins in a day. But if they had all wrought separately and independently, and without any of them having been educated to this peculiar business, they certainly could not each of them have made twenty, perhaps not one pin in a day; that is, certainly, not the two hundred and fortieth, perhaps not the four thousand eight hundredth part of what they are at present capable of performing, in consequence of a proper division and combination of their different operations.

In every other art and manufacture, the effects of the division of labour are similar to what they are in this very trifling one; though, in many of them, the labour can neither be so much subdivided, nor reduced to so great a simplicity of operation. The division of labour, however, so far as it can be introduced, occasions, in every art, a proportionable increase of the productive powers of labour. The separation of different trades and employments from one another seems to have taken place in consequence of this advantage. This separation, too, is generally carried furthest in those countries which enjoy the highest degree of industry and improvement; what is the work of one man in a rude state of society being generally that of several in an improved one. In every improved society, the farmer is generally nothing but a farmer; the manufacturer, nothing but a manufacturer. The labour, too, which is necessary to produce any one complete manufacture is almost always divided among a great number of hands. How many different trades are employed in each branch of the linen and woollen manufactures from the growers of the flax and the wool, to the bleachers and smoothers of the linen, or to the dyers and dressers of the cloth! The nature of agriculture, indeed, does not admit of so many subdivisions of labour, nor of so complete a separation of one business from another, as manufactures. It is impossible

to separate so entirely the business of the grazier from that of the corn-farmer as the trade of the carpenter is commonly separated from that of the smith. The spinner is almost always a distinct person from the weaver; but the ploughman, the harrower, the sower of the seed, and the reaper of the corn, are often the same. The occasions for those different sorts of labour returning with the different seasons of the year, it is impossible that one man should be constantly employed in any one of them. This impossibility of making so complete and entire a separation of all the different branches of labour employed in agriculture is perhaps the reason why the improvement of the productive powers of labour in this art does not always keep pace with their improvement in manufactures. The most opulent nations, indeed, generally excel all their neighbours in agriculture as well as in manufactures; but they are commonly more distinguished by their superiority in the latter than in the former. Their lands are in general better cultivated, and having more labour and expense bestowed upon them, produce more in proportion to the extent and natural fertility of the ground. But this superiority of produce is seldom much more than in proportion to the superiority of labour and expense. In agriculture, the labour of the rich country is not always much more productive than that of the poor; or, at least, it is never so much more productive as it commonly is in manufactures. The corn of the rich country, therefore, will not always, in the same degree of goodness, come cheaper to market than that of the poor. The corn of Poland, in the same degree of goodness, is as cheap as that of France, notwithstanding the superior opulence and improvement of the latter country. The corn of France is, in the corn provinces, fully as good, and in most years nearly about the same price with the corn of England, though, in opulence and improvement, France is perhaps inferior to England. The corn-lands of England, however, are better cultivated than those of France, and the corn-lands of France are said to be much better cultivated than those of Poland. But though the poor country, notwithstanding the inferiority of its cultivation, can, in some measure, rival the rich in the cheapness and goodness of its corn, it can pretend to no such competition in its manufactures; at least if those manufactures suit the soil, climate, and situation of the rich country. The silks of France are better and cheaper than those of England, because the silk manufacture, at least under the present high duties upon the importation of raw silk, does not so well suit the climate of England as that of France. But the hardware and the coarse woollens of England are beyond all comparison superior to those of France, and much cheaper too in the same degree of goodness. In Poland there are said to be scarce any manufactures of any kind, a few of those coarser household manufactures excepted, without which no country can well subsist.

This great increase of the quantity of work which, in consequence of the division of labour, the same number of people are capable of performing, is owing to three different circumstances; first, to the increase of dexterity in every particular workman; secondly, to the saving of the time which is commonly lost in passing from one species of work to another; and lastly, to the invention of a great number of machines which facilitate and abridge labour, and enable one man to do the work of many.

First, the improvement of the dexterity of the workman necessarily increases the quantity of the work he can perform; and the division of labour, by reducing every man's business to some one simple operation, and by making this operation the sole employment of his life, necessarily increases very much the dexterity of the workman. A common smith, who, though accustomed to handle the hammer, has never been used to make nails, if upon some particular occasion he is obliged to attempt it, will scarce, I am assured, be able to make above two or three hundred nails in a day, and those too very bad ones. A smith who has been accustomed to make nails, but whose sole or principal business has not been that of a nailer, can seldom with his utmost diligence make more than eight hundred or a thousand nails in a day. I have seen several boys under twenty years of age who had never exercised any other trade but that of making nails, and who, when they exerted themselves, could make, each of them, upwards of two thousand three hundred nails in a day. The making of a nail, however, is by no means one of the simplest operations. The same person blows the bellows, stirs or mends the fire as there is occasion, heats the iron, and forges every part of the nail: in forging the head too he is obliged to change his tools. The different operations into which the making of a pin, or of a metal button, is subdivided, are all of them much more simple, and the dexterity of the person, of whose life it has been the sole business to perform them, is usually much greater. The rapidity with which some of the operations of those manufactures are performed, exceeds what the human hand could, by those who had never seen them, be supposed capable of acquiring.

Secondly, the advantage which is gained by saving the time commonly lost in passing from one sort of work to another is much greater than we should at first view be apt to imagine it. It is impossible to pass very quickly from one kind of work to another that is carried on in a different place and with quite different tools. A country weaver, who cultivates a small farm, must lose a good deal of time in passing from his loom to the field, and from the field to his loom. When the two trades can be carried on in the same workhouse, the loss of time is no doubt much less. It is even in this case, however, very considerable. A man commonly saunters a little in turning his hand from one sort of employment to another. When he first begins the new work he is seldom very keen and hearty; his mind, as they say, does not go to it, and for some time he rather trifles than applies to good purpose. The habit of sauntering and of indolent careless application, which is naturally, or rather necessarily acquired by every country workman who is obliged to change his work and his tools every half hour, and to apply his hand in twenty different ways almost every day of his life, renders him almost always slothful and lazy, and incapable of any vigorous application even on the most pressing occasions. Independent, therefore, of his deficiency in point of dexterity, this cause alone must always reduce considerably the quantity of work which he is capable of performing.

Thirdly, and lastly, everybody must be sensible how much labour is facilitated and abridged by the application of proper machinery. It is unnecessary to give any example. I shall only observe, therefore, that the invention of all those machines by which labour is so much facilitated and abridged seems to have been originally owing to the division of labour. Men are much more likely to discover easier and readier methods of attaining any object when the whole attention of their minds is directed towards that single object than when it is dissipated among a great variety of things. But in consequence of the division of labour, the whole of every man's attention comes naturally to be directed towards some one very simple object. It is naturally to be expected, therefore, that some one or other of those who are employed in each particular branch of labour should soon find out easier and readier methods of performing their own particular work, wherever the nature of it admits of such improvement. A great part of the machines made use of in those manufactures in which labour is most subdivided, were originally the inventions of common workmen, who, being each of them employed in some very simple operation, naturally turned their thoughts towards finding out easier and readier methods of performing it. Whoever has been much accustomed to visit such manufactures must frequently have been shown very pretty machines, which were the inventions of such workmen in order to facilitate and quicken their own particular part of the work. In the first fire-engines, a boy was constantly employed to open and shut alternately the communication between the boiler and the cylinder, according as the piston either ascended or descended. One of those boys, who loved to play with his companions, observed that, by tying a string from the handle of the valve which opened this communication to another part of the machine, the valve would open and shut without his assistance, and leave him at liberty to divert himself with his play-fellows. One of the greatest improvements that has been made upon this machine, since it was first invented, was in this manner the discovery of a boy who wanted to save his own labour.

All the improvements in machinery, however, have by no means been the inventions of those who had occasion to use the machines. Many improvements have been made by the ingenuity of the makers of the machines, when to make them became the business of a peculiar trade; and some by that of those who are called philosophers or men of speculation, whose trade it is not to do anything, but to observe everything; and who, upon that account, are often capable of combining together the powers of the most distant and dissimilar objects. In the progress of society, philosophy or speculation becomes, like every other employment, the principal or sole trade and occupation of a particular class of citizens. Like every other employment too, it is subdivided into a great number of different branches, each of which affords occupation to a peculiar tribe or class of philosophers; and this subdivision of employment in philosophy, as well as in every other business, improves dexterity, and saves time. Each individual

becomes more expert in his own peculiar branch, more work is done upon the whole, and the quantity of science is considerably increased by it.

It is the great multiplication of the productions of all the different arts, in consequence of the division of labour, which occasions, in a well-governed society, that universal opulence which extends itself to the lowest ranks of the people. Every workman has a great quantity of his own work to dispose of beyond what he himself has occasion for; and every other workman being exactly in the same situation, he is enabled to exchange a great quantity of his own goods for a great quantity, or, what comes to the same thing, for the price of a great quantity of theirs. He supplies them abundantly with what they have occasion for, and they accommodate him as amply with what he has occasion for, and a general plenty diffuses itself through all the different ranks of the society.

Observe the accommodation of the most common artificer or day-labourer in a civilised and thriving country, and you will perceive that the number of people of whose industry a part, though but a small part, has been employed in procuring him this accommodation, exceeds all computation. The woollen coat, for example, which covers the day-labourer, as coarse and rough as it may appear, is the produce of the joint labour of a great multitude of workmen. The shepherd, the sorter of the wool, the wool-comber or carder, the dyer, the scribbler, the spinner, the weaver, the fuller, the dresser, with many others, must all join their different arts in order to complete even this homely production. How many merchants and carriers, besides, must have been employed in transporting the materials from some of those workmen to others who often live in a very distant part of the country! how much commerce and navigation in particular, how many ship-builders, sailors, sail-makers, rope-makers, must have been employed in order to bring together the different drugs made use of by the dyer, which often come from the remotest corners of the world! What a variety of labour, too, is necessary in order to produce the tools of the meanest of those workmen! To say nothing of such complicated machines as the ship of the sailor, the mill of the fuller, or even the loom of the weaver, let us consider only what a variety of labour is requisite in order to form that very simple machine, the shears with which the shepherd clips the wool. The miner, the builder of the furnace for smelting the ore, the seller of the timber, the burner of the charcoal to be made use of in the smelting-house, the brick-maker, the brick-layer, the workmen who attend the furnace, the mill-wright, the forger, the smith, must all of them join their different arts in order to produce them. Were we to examine, in the same manner, all the different parts of his dress and household furniture, the coarse linen shirt which he wears next his skin, the shoes which cover his feet, the bed which he lies on, and all the different parts which compose it, the kitchen-grate at which he prepares his victuals, the coals which he makes use of for that purpose, dug from the bowels of the earth, and brought to him perhaps by a long sea and a long land carriage, all the other utensils of his kitchen, all the furniture of his table, the knives and forks, the earthen or pewter plates upon which he serves up and divides his victuals, the different hands employed in preparing his bread and his beer, the glass window which lets in the heat and the light, and keeps out the wind and the rain, with all the knowledge and art requisite for preparing that beautiful and happy invention, without which these northern parts of the world could scarce have afforded a very comfortable habitation, together with the tools of all the different workmen employed in producing those different conveniences; if we examine, I say, all these things, and consider what a variety of labour is employed about each of them, we shall be sensible that, without the assistance and cooperation of many thousands, the very meanest person in a civilised country could not be provided, even according to what we very falsely imagine the easy and simple manner in which he is commonly accommodated. Compared, indeed, with the more extravagant luxury of the great, his accommodation must no doubt appear extremely simple and easy; and yet it may be true, perhaps, that the accommodation of a European prince does not always so much exceed that of an industrious and frugal peasant as the accommodation of the latter exceeds that of many an African king, the absolute master of the lives and liberties of ten thousand naked savages.

# CHAPTER II

## OF THE PRINCIPLE WHICH GIVES OCCASION TO THE DIVISION OF LABOUR

This division of labour, from which so many advantages are derived, is not originally the effect of any human wisdom, which foresees and intends that general opulence to which it gives occasion. It is the necessary, though very slow and gradual consequence of a certain propensity in human nature which has in view no such extensive utility; the propensity to truck, barter, and exchange one thing for another.

Whether this propensity be one of those original principles in human nature of which no further account can be given: or whether, as seems more probable, it be the necessary consequence of the faculties of reason and speech, it belongs not to our present subject to inquire. It is common to all men, and to be found in no other race of animals, which seem to know neither this nor any other species of contracts. Two greyhounds, in running down the same hare, have sometimes the appearance of acting in some sort of concert. Each turns her towards his companion, or endeavours to intercept her when his companion turns her towards himself. This, however, is not the effect of any contract, but of the accidental concurrence of their passions in the same object at that particular time. Nobody ever saw a dog make a fair and deliberate exchange of one bone for another with another dog. Nobody ever saw one animal by its gestures and natural cries signify to another, this is mine, that yours; I am willing to give this for that. When an animal wants to obtain something either of a man or of another animal, it has no other means of persuasion but to gain the favour of those whose service it requires. A puppy fawns upon its dam, and a spaniel endeavours by a thousand attractions to engage the attention of its master who is at dinner, when it wants to be fed by him. Man sometimes uses the same arts with his brethren, and when he has no other means of engaging them to act according to his inclinations, endeavours by every servile and fawning attention to obtain their good will. He has not time, however, to do this upon every occasion. In civilised society he stands at all times in need of the cooperation and assistance of great multitudes, while his whole life is scarce sufficient to gain the friendship of a few persons. In almost every other race of animals each individual, when it is grown up to maturity, is entirely independent, and in its natural state has occasion for the assistance of no other living creature. But man has almost constant occasion for the help of his brethren, and it is in vain for him to expect it from their benevolence only. He will be more likely to prevail if he can interest their self-love in his favour, and show them that it is for their own advantage to do for him what he requires of them. Whoever offers to another a bargain of any kind, proposes to do this. Give me that which I want, and you shall have this which you want, is the meaning of every such offer; and it is in this manner that we obtain from one another the far greater part of those good offices which we stand in need of. It is not from the benevolence of the butcher, the brewer, or the baker that we expect our dinner, but from their regard to their own interest. We address ourselves, not to their humanity but to their self-love, and never talk to them of our own necessities but of their advantages. Nobody but a beggar chooses to depend chiefly upon the benevolence of his fellow-citizens. Even a beggar does not depend upon it entirely. The charity of well-disposed people, indeed, supplies him with the whole fund of his subsistence. But though this principle ultimately provides him with all the necessaries of life which he has occasion for, it neither does nor can provide him with them as he has occasion for them. The greater part of his occasional wants are supplied in the same manner as those of other people, by treaty, by barter, and by purchase. With the money which one man gives him he purchases food. The old clothes which another bestows upon him he exchanges for other old clothes which suit him better, or for lodging, or for food, or for money, with which he can buy either food, clothes, or lodging, as he has occasion.

As it is by treaty, by barter, and by purchase that we obtain from one another the greater part of those mutual good offices which we stand in need of, so it is this same trucking disposition which originally gives occasion to the division of labour. In a tribe of hunters or shepherds a particular person makes bows and arrows, for example, with more readiness and dexterity than any other. He frequently exchanges them for cattle or for venison with his companions; and he finds at last that he can in this manner get more cattle and venison than if he himself went to the field to catch them. From a regard to his own interest, therefore, the making of bows and arrows grows to be his chief business, and he becomes a sort of armourer. Another excels in making the frames and covers of their little huts or movable houses. He is accustomed to be of use in this way to his neighbours, who reward him in the same manner with cattle and with venison, till at last he finds it his interest to dedicate himself entirely to this employment, and to become a sort of house-carpenter. In the same manner a third becomes a smith or a brazier, a fourth a tanner or dresser of hides or skins, the principal part of the clothing of savages. And thus the certainty of being able to exchange all that surplus part of the produce of his own labour, which is over and above his own consumption, for such parts of the produce of other men's labour as he may have occasion for, encourages every man to apply himself to a particular occupation, and to cultivate and bring to perfection whatever talent or genius he may possess for that particular species of business.

The difference of natural talents in different men is, in reality, much less than we are aware of; and the very different genius which appears to distinguish men of different professions, when grown up to maturity, is not upon many occasions so much the cause as the effect of the division of labour. The difference between the most dissimilar characters, between a philosopher and a common street porter, for example, seems to arise not so much from nature as from habit, custom, and education. When they came into the world, and for the first six or eight years of their existence, they were perhaps very much alike, and neither their parents nor play-fellows could perceive any remarkable difference. About that age, or soon after, they come to be employed in very different occupations. The difference of talents comes then to be taken notice of, and widens by degrees, till at last the vanity of the philosopher is willing to acknowledge scarce any resemblance. But without the disposition to truck, barter, and exchange, every man must have procured to himself every necessary and conveniency of life which he wanted. All must have had the same duties to perform, and the same work to do, and there could have been no such difference of employment as could alone give occasion to any great difference of talents.

As it is this disposition which forms that difference of talents, so remarkable among men of different professions, so it is this same disposition which renders that difference useful. Many tribes of animals acknowledged to be all of the same species derive from nature a much more remarkable distinction of genius, than what, antecedent to custom and education, appears to take place among men. By nature a philosopher is not in genius and disposition half so different from a street porter, as a mastiff is from a greyhound, or a greyhound from a spaniel, or this last from a shepherd's dog. Those different tribes of animals, however, though all of the same species, are of scarce any use to one another. The strength of the mastiff is not, in the least, supported either by the swiftness of the greyhound, or by the sagacity of the spaniel, or by the docility of the shepherd's dog. The effects of those different geniuses and talents, for want of the power or disposition to barter and exchange, cannot be brought into a common stock, and do not in the least contribute to the better accommodation and conveniency of the species. Each animal is still obliged to support and defend itself, separately and independently, and derives no sort of advantage from that variety of talents with which nature has distinguished its fellows. Among men, on the contrary, the most dissimilar geniuses are of use to one another; the different produces of their respective talents, by the general disposition to truck, barter, and exchange, being brought, as it were, into a common stock, where every man may purchase whatever part of the produce of other men's talents he has occasion for.

## CHAPTER III

### THAT THE DIVISION OF LABOUR IS LIMITED
### BY THE EXTENT OF THE MARKET

As it is the power of exchanging that gives occasion to the division of labour, so the extent of this division must always be limited by the extent of that power, or, in other words, by the extent of the market. When the market is very small, no person can have any encouragement to dedicate himself entirely to one employment, for want of the power to exchange all that surplus part of the produce of his own labour, which is over and above his own consumption, for such parts of the produce of other men's labour as he has occasion for.

There are some sorts of industry, even of the lowest kind, which can be carried on nowhere but in a great town. A porter, for example, can find employment and subsistence in no other place. A village is by much

too narrow a sphere for him; even an ordinary market town is scarce large enough to afford him constant occupation. In the lone houses and very small villages which are scattered about in so desert a country as the Highlands of Scotland, every farmer must be butcher, baker and brewer for his own family. In such situations we can scarce expect to find even a smith, a carpenter, or a mason, within less than twenty miles of another of the same trade. The scattered families that live at eight or ten miles distance from the nearest of them must learn to perform themselves a great number of little pieces of work, for which, in more populous countries, they would call in the assistance of those workmen. Country workmen are almost everywhere obliged to apply themselves to all the different branches of industry that have so much affinity to one another as to be employed about the same sort of materials. A country carpenter deals in every sort of work that is made of wood: a country smith in every sort of work that is made of iron. The former is not only a carpenter, but a joiner, a cabinet-maker, and even a carver in wood, as well as a wheelwright, a plough-wright, a cart and waggon maker. The employments of the latter are still more various. It is impossible there should be such a trade as even that of a nailer in the remote and inland parts of the Highlands of Scotland. Such a workman at the rate of a thousand nails a day, and three hundred working days in the year, will make three hundred thousand nails in the year. But in such a situation it would be impossible to dispose of one thousand, that is, of one day's work in the year.

As by means of water-carriage a more extensive market is opened to every sort of industry than what land-carriage alone can afford it, so it is upon the sea-coast, and along the banks of navigable rivers, that industry of every kind naturally begins to subdivide and improve itself, and it is frequently not till a long time after that those improvements extend themselves to the inland parts of the country. A broad-wheeled waggon, attended by two men, and drawn by eight horses, in about six weeks' time carries and brings back between London and Edinburgh near four ton weight of goods. In about the same time a ship navigated by six or eight men, and sailing between the ports of London and Leith, frequently carries and brings back two hundred ton weight of goods. Six or eight men, therefore, by the help of water-carriage, can carry and bring back in the same time the same quantity of goods between London and Edinburgh, as fifty broad-wheeled waggons, attended by a hundred men, and drawn by four hundred horses. Upon two hundred tons of goods, therefore, carried by the cheapest land-carriage from London to Edinburgh, there must be charged the maintenance of a hundred men for three weeks, and both the maintenance, and, what is nearly equal to the maintenance, the wear and tear of four hundred horses as well as of fifty great waggons. Whereas, upon the same quantity of goods carried by water, there is to be charged only the maintenance of six or eight men, and the wear and tear of a ship of two hundred tons burden, together with the value of the superior risk, or the difference of the insurance between land and water-carriage. Were there no other communication between those two places, therefore, but by land-carriage, as no goods could be transported from the one to the other, except such whose price was very considerable in proportion to their weight, they could carry on but a small part of that commerce which at present subsists between them, and consequently could give but a small part of that encouragement which they at present mutually afford to each other's industry. There could be little or no commerce of any kind between the distant parts of the world. What goods could bear the expense of land-carriage between London and Calcutta? Or if there were any so precious as to be able to support this expense, with what safety could they be transported through the territories of so many barbarous nations? Those two cities, however, at present carry on a very considerable commerce with each other, and by mutually affording a market, give a good deal of encouragement to each other's industry.

Since such, therefore, are the advantages of water-carriage, it is natural that the first improvements of art and industry should be made where this conveniency opens the whole world for a market to the produce of every sort of labour, and that they should always be much later in extending themselves into the inland parts of the country. The inland parts of the country can for a long time have no other market for the greater part of their goods, but the country which lies round about them, and separates them from the sea-coast, and the great navigable rivers. The extent of their market, therefore, must for a long time be in proportion to the riches and populousness of that country, and consequently their improvement must always be posterior to the improvement of that country. In our North American colonies the plantations have constantly followed either the sea-coast or the banks of the navigable rivers, and have scarce anywhere extended themselves to any considerable distance from both.

The nations that, according to the best authenticated history, appear to have been first civilised, were those that dwelt round the coast of the Mediterranean Sea. That sea, by far the greatest inlet that is known in the world, having no tides, nor consequently any waves except such as are caused by the wind only, was, by the smoothness of its surface, as well as by the multitude of its islands, and the proximity of its neighbouring shores, extremely favourable to the infant navigation of the world; when, rom their ignorance of the compass, men were afraid to quit the view of the coast, and from the imperfection of the art of ship-building, to abandon themselves to the boisterous waves of the ocean. To pass beyond the pillars of Hercules, that is, to sail out of the Straits of Gibraltar, was, in the ancient world, long considered as a most wonderful and dangerous exploit of navigation. It was late before even the Phoenicians and Carthaginians, the most skilful navigators and ship-builders of those old times, attempted it, and they were for a long time the only nations that did attempt it.

Of all the countries on the coast of the Mediterranean Sea, Egypt seems to have been the first in which either agriculture or manufactures were cultivated and improved to any considerable degree. Upper Egypt extends itself nowhere above a few miles from the Nile, and in Lower Egypt that great river breaks itself into many different canals, which, with the assistance of a little art, seem to have afforded a communication by water-carriage, not only between all the great towns, but between all the considerable villages, and even to many farm-houses in the country; nearly in the same manner as the Rhine and the Maese do in Holland at present. The extent and easiness of this inland navigation was probably one of the principal causes of the early improvement of Egypt.

The improvements in agriculture and manufactures seem likewise to have been of very great antiquity in the provinces of Bengal, in the East Indies, and in some of the eastern provinces of China; though the great extent of this antiquity is not authenticated by any histories of

would this, then, encourage peace? or would it inhibit peace?

whose authority we, in this part of the world, are well assured. In Bengal the Ganges and several other great rivers form a great number of navigable canals in the same manner as the Nile does in Egypt. In the Eastern provinces of China too, several great rivers form, by their different branches, a multitude of canals, and by communicating with one another afford an inland navigation much more extensive than that either of the Nile or the Ganges, or perhaps than both of them put together. It is remarkable that neither the ancient Egyptians, nor the Indians, nor the Chinese, encouraged foreign commerce, but seem all to have derived their great opulence from this inland navigation.

All the inland parts of Africa, and all that part of Asia which lies any considerable way north of the Euxine and Caspian seas, the ancient Scythia, the modern Tartary and Siberia, seem in all ages of the world to have been in the same barbarous and uncivilised state in which we find them at present. The Sea of Tartary is the frozen ocean which admits of no navigation, and though some of the greatest rivers in the world run through that country, they are at too great a distance from one another to carry commerce and communication through the greater part of it. There are in Africa none of those great inlets, such as the Baltic and Adriatic seas in Europe, the Mediterranean and Euxine seas in both Europe and Asia, and the gulfs of Arabia, Persia, India, Bengal, and Siam, in Asia, to carry maritime commerce into the interior parts of that great continent: and the great rivers of Africa are at too great a distance from one another to give occasion to any considerable inland navigation. The commerce besides which any nation can carry on by means of a river which does not break itself into any great number of branches or canals, and which runs into another territory before it reaches the sea, can never be very considerable; because it is always in the power of the nations who possess that other territory to obstruct the communication between the upper country and the sea. The navigation of the Danube is of very little use to the different states of Bavaria, Austria and Hungary, in comparison of what it would be if any of them possessed the whole of its course till it falls into the Black Sea.

*The economy would be better if you could politically negotiate sharing the waterways*

* * *

# BOOK II

## CHAPTER III

### OF THE ACCUMULATION OF CAPITAL, OR OF PRODUCTIVE AND UNPRODUCTIVE LABOUR

There is one sort of labour which adds to the value of the subject upon which it is bestowed: there is another which has no such effect. The former, as it produces a value, may be called productive; the latter, unproductive[1] labour. Thus the labour of a manufacturer adds, generally, to the value of the materials which he works upon, that of his own maintenance, and of his master's profit. The labour of a menial servant, on the contrary, adds to the value of nothing. Though the manufacturer has his wages advanced to him by his master, he, in reality, costs him no expense, the value of those wages being generally restored, together with a profit, in the improved value of the subject upon which his labour is bestowed. But the maintenance of a menial servant never is restored. A man grows rich by employing a multitude of manufacturers: he grows poor by maintaining a multitude of menial servants. The labour of the latter, however, has its value, and deserves its reward as well as that of the former. But the labour of the manufacturer fixes and realises itself in some particular subject or vendible commodity, which lasts for some time at least after that labour is past. It is, as it were, a certain quantity of labour stocked and stored up to be employed, if necessary, upon some other occasion. That subject, or what is the same thing, the price of that subject, can afterwards, if necessary, put into motion a quantity of labour equal to that which had originally produced it. The labour of the menial servant, on the contrary, does not fix or realise itself in any particular subject or vendible commodity. His services generally perish in the very instant of their performance, and seldom leave any trace or value behind them for which an equal quantity of service could afterwards be procured.

*"productive" labor produces objects that continue to be productive.*

---

1 Some French authors of great learning and ingenuity have used those, words in a different sense. In the last chapter of the fourth book I shall endeavour to show that their sense is an improper one.

The labour of some of the most respectable orders in the society is, like that of menial servants, unproductive of any value, and does not fix or realise itself in any permanent subject, or vendible commodity, which endures after that labour is past, and for which an equal quantity of labour could afterwards be procured. The sovereign, for example, with all the officers both of justice and war who serve under him, the whole army and navy, are unproductive labourers. They are the servants of the public, and are maintained by a part of the annual produce of the industry of other people. Their service, how honourable, how useful, or how necessary soever, produces nothing for which an equal quantity of service can afterwards be procured. The protection, security, and defence of the commonwealth, the effect of their labour this year will not purchase its protection, security, and defence for the year to come. In the same class must be ranked, some both of the gravest and most important, and some of the most frivolous professions: churchmen, lawyers, physicians, men of letters of all kinds; players, buffoons, musicians, opera-singers, opera-dancers, etc. The labour of the meanest of these has a certain value, regulated by the very same principles which regulate that of every other sort of labour; and that of the noblest and most useful, produces nothing which could afterwards purchase or procure an equal quantity of labour. Like the declamation of the actor, the harangue of the orator, or the tune of the musician, the work of all of them perishes in the very instant of its production.

Both productive and unproductive labourers, and those who do not labour at all, are all equally maintained by the annual produce of the land and labour of the country. This produce, how great soever, can never be infinite, but must have certain limits. According, therefore, as a smaller or greater proportion of it is in any one year employed in maintaining unproductive hands, the more in the one case and the less in the other will remain for the productive, and the next year's produce will be greater or smaller accordingly; the whole annual produce, if we except the spontaneous productions of the earth, being the effect of productive labour.

Though the whole annual produce of the land and labour of every country is, no doubt, ultimately destined for supplying the consumption of its inhabitants, and for procuring a revenue to them, yet when it first comes either from the ground, or from the hands of the productive labourers, it naturally divides itself into two parts. One of them, and frequently the largest, is, in the first place, destined for replacing a capital, or for renewing the provisions, materials, and finished work, which had been withdrawn from a capital; the other for constituting a revenue either to the owner of this capital, as the profit of his stock, or to some other person, as the rent of his land. Thus, of the produce of land, one part replaces the capital of the farmer; the other pays his profit and the rent of the landlord; and thus constitutes a revenue both to the owner of this capital as the profits of his stock; and to some other person, as the rent of his land. Of the produce of a great manufactory, in the same manner, one part, and that always the largest, replaces the capital of the undertaker of the work; the other pays his profit, and thus constitutes a revenue to the owner of this capital.

That part of the annual produce of the land and labour of any country which replaces a capital never is immediately employed to maintain any but productive hands. It pays the wages of productive labour only. That which is immediately destined for constituting a revenue, either as profit or as rent, may maintain indifferently either productive or unproductive hands.

Whatever part of his stock a man employs as a capital, he always expects is to be replaced to him with a profit. He employs it, therefore, in maintaining productive hands only; and after having served in the function of a capital to him, it constitutes a revenue to them. Whenever he employs any part of it in maintaining unproductive hands of any kind, that part is, from that moment, withdrawn from his capital, and placed in his stock reserved for immediate consumption.

Unproductive labourers, and those who do not labour at all, are all maintained by revenue; either, first, by that part of the annual produce which is originally destined for constituting a revenue to some particular persons, either as the rent of land or as the profits of stock; or, secondly, by that part which, though originally destined for replacing a capital and for maintaining productive labourers only, yet when it comes into their hands whatever part of it is over and above their necessary subsistence may be employed in maintaining indifferently either productive or unproductive hands. Thus, not only the great landlord or the rich merchant, but even the common workman, if his wages are considerable, may maintain a menial servant;

or he may sometimes go to a play or a puppet-show, and so contribute his share towards maintaining one set of unproductive labourers; or he may pay some taxes, and thus help to maintain another set, more honourable and useful, indeed, but equally unproductive. No part of the annual produce, however, which had been originally destined to replace a capital, is ever directed towards maintaining unproductive hands till after it has put into motion its full complement of productive labour, or all that it could put into motion in the way in which it was employed. The workman must have earned his wages by work done before he can employ any part of them in this manner. That part, too, is generally but a small one. It is his spare revenue only, of which productive labourers have seldom a great deal. They generally have some, however; and in the payment of taxes the greatness of their number may compensate, in some measure, the smallness of their contribution. The rent of land and the profits of stock are everywhere, therefore, the principal sources from which unproductive hands derive their subsistence. These are the two sorts of revenue of which the owners have generally most to spare. They might both maintain indifferently either productive or unproductive hands. They seem, however, to have some predilection for the latter. The expense of a great lord feeds generally more idle than industrious people. The rich merchant, though with his capital he maintains industrious people only, yet by his expense, that is, by the employment of his revenue, he feeds commonly the very same sort as the great lord.

The proportion, therefore, between the productive and unproductive hands, depends very much in every country upon the proportion between that part of the annual produce, which, as; soon as it comes either from the ground or from the hands of the productive labourers, is destined for replacing a capital, and that which is destined for constituting a revenue, either as rent or as profit. This proportion is very different in rich from what it is in poor countries.

Thus, at present, in the opulent countries of Europe, a very large, frequently the largest portion of the produce of the land is destined for replacing the capital of the rich and independent farmer; the other for paying his profits and the rent of the landlord. But anciently, during the prevalency of the feudal government, a very small portion of the produce was sufficient to replace the capital employed in cultivation. It consisted commonly in a few wretched cattle, maintained altogether by the spontaneous produce of uncultivated land, and which might, therefore, be considered as a part of that spontaneous producer it generally, too, belonged to the landlord, and was by him advanced to the occupiers of the land. All the rest of the produce; properly belonged to him too, either as rent for his land, or as profit upon this paltry capital. The occupiers of land were generally bondmen, whose persons and effects were equally his property. Those who were not bondmen were tenants at will and though the rent which they paid was often nominally little more than a quit-rent, it really amounted to the whole produce of the land. Their lord could at all times command their labour in peace and their service in war. Though they lived at a distance from his house, they were equally dependent upon him as his retainers who lived in it. But the whole produce of the land undoubtedly belongs to him who can dispose of the labour and service of all those whom it maintains. In the present state of Europe, the share of the landlord seldom exceeds a third, sometimes not a fourth part of the whole produce of the land. The rent of land, however, in all the improved parts of the country, has been tripled and quadrupled since those ancient times; and this third or fourth part of the annual produce is, it seems, three or four times greater than the whole had been, before. In the progress of improvement, rent, though it increases in proportion to the extent, diminishes in proportion to the produce of the land.

In the opulent countries of Europe, great capitals are at present employed in trade and manufactures. In the ancient state, the little trade that was stirring, and the few homely and coarse manufactures that were carried on, required but very small capitals. These, however, must have yielded very large profits. The rate of interest was nowhere less than ten per cent., and their profits must have been sufficient to afford this great interest. At present the rate of interest, in the improved parts of Europe, is nowhere higher than six per cent., and in some of the most improved it is so low as four, three, and two per cent. Though that part of the revenue of the inhabitants which is derived from the profits of stock is always much greater in rich than in poor countries, it is because the stock is much greater: in proportion to the stock the profits are generally much less.

That part of the annual produce, therefore, which, as soon as it comes either from the ground or from the hands of the productive labourers, is destined for replacing a capital, is not only much greater in rich than in poor countries, but bears a much greater proportion to that which is immediately destined for constituting a revenue either as rent or as profit. The funds destined for the maintenance of productive labour are not only much greater in the former than in the latter, but bear a much greater proportion to those which, though they may be employed to maintain either productive or unproductive hands, have generally a predilection for the latter.

The proportion between those different funds necessarily determines in every country the general character of the inhabitants as to industry or idleness. We are more industrious than our forefathers; because in the present times the funds destined for the maintenance of industry are much greater in proportion to those which are likely to be employed in the maintenance of idleness than they were two or three centuries ago. Our ancestors were idle for want of a sufficient encouragement to industry. It is better, says the proverb, to play for nothing than to work for nothing. In mercantile and manufacturing towns, where the inferior ranks of people are chiefly maintained by the employment of capital, they are in general industrious, sober, and thriving; as in many English, and in most Dutch towns. In those towns which are principally supported by the constant or occasional residence of a court, and in which the inferior ranks of people are chiefly maintained by the spending of revenue, they are in general idle, dissolute, and poor; as at Rome, Versailles, Compiegne, and Fontainebleau. If you except Rouen and Bordeaux, there is little trade or industry in any of the parliament towns of France; and the inferior ranks of people, being chiefly maintained by the expense of the members of the courts of justice, and of those who come to plead before them, are in general idle and poor. The great trade of Rouen and Bordeaux seems to be altogether the effect of their situation. Rouen is necessarily the entrepot of almost all the goods which are brought either from foreign countries, or from the maritime provinces of France, for the consumption of the great city of Paris. Bordeaux is in the same manner the entrepôt of the wines which grow upon the banks of the Garonne, and of the rivers which run into it, one of the richest wine countries in the world, and which seems to produce the wine fittest for exportation, or best suited to the taste of foreign nations. Such advantageous situations necessarily attract a great capital by the great employment which they afford it; and the employment of this capital is the cause of the industry of those two cities. In the other parliament towns of France, very little more capital seems to be employed than what is necessary for supplying their own consumption; that is, little more than the smallest capital which can be employed in them. The same thing may be said of Paris, Madrid, and Vienna. Of those three cities, Paris is by far the most industrious; but Paris itself is the principal market of all the manufactures established at Paris, and its own consumption is the principal object of all the trade which it carries on. London, Lisbon, and Copenhagen, are, perhaps, the only three cities in Europe which are both the constant residence of a court, and can at the same time be considered as trading cities, or as cities which trade not only for their own consumption but for that of other cities and countries. The situation of all the three is extremely advantageous, and naturally fits them to be them entrepôts of a great part of the goods destined for the consumption of distant places. In a city where a great revenue is spent, to employ with advantage a capital for any other purpose than for supplying the consumption of that city is probably more difficult than in one in which the inferior ranks of people have no other maintenance but what they derive from the employment of such a capital. The idleness of the greater part of the people who are maintained by the expense of revenue corrupts, it is probable, the industry of those who ought to be maintained by the employment of capital, and renders it less advantageous to employ a capital there than in other places. There was little trade or industry in Edinburgh before the union. When the Scotch parliament was no longer to be assembled in it, when it ceased to be the necessary residence of the principal nobility and gentry of Scotland, it became a city of some trade and industry. It still continues, however, to be the residence of the principal courts of justice in Scotland, of the boards of customs and excise, etc. A considerable revenue, therefore, still continues to be spent in it. In trade and industry it is much inferior to Glasgow, of which the inhabitants are chiefly maintained by the employment of capital. The inhabitants of a large village, it has sometimes been observed, after having made considerable progress in manufactures, have become idle and poor in consequence of a great lord having taken up his residence in their neighbourhood.

The proportion between capital and revenue, therefore, seems everywhere to regulate the proportion between industry and idleness. Wherever capital predominates, industry prevails: wherever revenue, idleness. Every increase or diminution of capital, therefore, naturally tends to increase or diminish the real quantity of industry, the number of productive hands, and consequently the exchangeable value of the annual produce of the land and labour of the country, the real wealth and revenue of all its inhabitants.

Capitals are increased by parsimony, and diminished by prodigality and misconduct.

Whatever a person saves from his revenue he adds to his capital, and either employs it himself in maintaining an additional number of productive hands, or enables some other person to do so, by landing it to him for an interest, that is, for a share of the profits. As the capital of an individual can be increased only by what he saves from his annual revenue or his annual gains, so the capital of a society, which is the same with that of all the individuals who compose it, can be increased only in the same manner.

Parsimony, and not industry, is the immediate cause of the increase of capital. Industry, indeed, provides the subject which parsimony accumulates. But whatever industry might acquire, if parsimony did not save and store up, the capital would never be the greater.

Parsimony, by increasing the fund which is destined for the maintenance of productive hands, tends to increase the number of those hands whose labour adds to the value of the subject upon which it is bestowed. It tends, therefore, to increase the exchangeable value of the annual produce of the land and labour of the country. It puts into motion an additional quantity of industry, which gives an additional value to the annual produce.

What is annually saved is as regularly consumed as what is annually spent, and nearly in the same time too; but it is consumed by a different set of people. That portion of his revenue which a rich man annually spends is in most cases consumed by idle guests and menial servants, who leave nothing behind them in return for their consumption. That portion which he annually saves, as for the sake of the profit it is immediately employed as a capital, is consumed in the same manner, and nearly in the same time too, but by a different set of people, by labourers, manufacturers, and artificers, who reproduce with a profit the value of their annual consumption. His revenue, we shall suppose, is paid him in money. Had he spent the whole, the food, clothing, and lodging, which the whole could have purchased, would have been distributed among the former set of people. By saving a part of it, as that part is for the sake of the profit immediately employed as a capital either by himself or by some other person, the food clothing, and lodging, which may be purchased with it, are necessarily reserved for the latter. The consumption is the same, but the consumers are different.

By what a frugal man annually saves, he not only affords maintenance to an additional number of productive hands, for that or the ensuing year, but, like the founder of a public work house, he establishes as it were a perpetual fund for the maintenance of an equal number in all times to come. The perpetual allotment and destination of this fund, indeed, is not always guarded by any positive law, by any trust-right or deed of mortmain. It is always guarded, however, by a very powerful principle, the plain and evident interest of every individual to whom any share of it shall ever belong. No part of it can ever afterwards be employed to maintain any but productive hands without an evident loss to the person who thus perverts it from its proper destination.

The prodigal perverts it in this manner. By not confining his expense within his income, he encroaches upon his capital. Like him who perverts the revenues of some pious foundation to profane purposes, he pays the wages of idleness with those funds which the frugality of his forefathers had, as it were, consecrated to the maintenance of industry. By diminishing the funds destined for the employment of productive labour, he necessarily diminishes, so far as it depends upon him, the quantity of that labour which adds a value to the subject upon which it is bestowed, and, consequently, the value of the annual produce of the land and labour of the whole country, the real wealth and revenue of its inhabitants. If the prodigality of some was not compensated by the frugality of others, the conduct of every prodigal, by feeding the idle with the bread of the industrious, tends not only to beggar himself, but to impoverish his country.

Though the expense of the prodigal should be altogether in home-made, and no part of it in foreign commodities, its effect upon the productive funds of the society would still be the same. Every year there would still be a certain quantity of food and clothing, which ought to have maintained productive, employed in maintaining unproductive hands. Every year, therefore, there would still be some diminution in what would otherwise have been the value of the annual produce of the land and labour of the country.

This expense, it may be said indeed, not being in foreign goods, and not occasioning any exportation of gold and silver, the same quantity of money would remain in the country as before. But if the quantity of food and clothing, which were thus consumed by unproductive, had been distributed among productive hands, they would have reproduced, together with a profit, the full value of their consumption. The same quantity of money would in this case equally have remained in the country, and there would besides have been a reproduction of an equal value of consumable goods. There would have been two values instead of one.

The same quantity of money, besides, cannot long remain in any country in which the value of the annual produce diminishes. The sole use of money is to circulate consumable goods. By means of it, provisions, materials, and finished work, are bought and sold, and distributed to their proper consumers. The quantity of money, therefore, which can be annually employed in any country must be determined by the value of the consumable goods annually circulated within it. These must consist either in the immediate produce of the land and labour of the country itself, or in something which had been purchased with some part of that produce. Their value, therefore, must diminish as the value of that produce diminishes, arid along with it the quantity of money which can be employed in circulating them. But the money which by this annual diminution of produce is annually thrown out of domestic circulation will not be allowed to lie idle. The interest of whoever possesses it requires that it should be employed. But having no employment at home, it will, in spite of all laws and prohibitions, be sent abroad, and employed in purchasing consumable goods which may be of some use at home. Its annual exportation will in this manner continue for some time to add something to the annual consumption of the country beyond the value of its own annual produce. What in the days of its prosperity had been saved from that annual produce, and employed in purchasing gold and silver, will contribute for some little time to support its consumption in adversity. The exportation of gold and silver is, in this case, not the cause, but the effect of its declension, and may even, for some little time, alleviate the misery of that declension.

The quantity of money, on the contrary, must in every country naturally increase as the value of the annual produce increases. The value of the consumable goods annually circulated within the society being greater will require a greater quantity of money to circulate them. A part of the increased produce, therefore, will naturally be employed in purchasing, wherever it is to be had, the additional quantity of gold and silver necessary for circulating the rest. The increase of those metals will in this case be the effect, not the cause, of the public prosperity, Gold and silver are purchased everywhere in the same manner. The food, clothing, and lodging, the revenue and maintenance of all those whose labour or stock is employed in bringing them from the mine to the market, is the price paid for them in Peru as well as in England. The country which has this price to pay will never be long without the quantity of those metals which it has occasion for; and no country will ever long retain a quantity which it has no occasion for.

Whatever, therefore, we may imagine the real wealth and revenue of a country to consist in, whether in the value of the annual produce of its land and labour, as plain reason seems to dictate; or in the quantity of the precious metals which circulate within it, as vulgar prejudices suppose; in either view of the matter, every prodigal appears to be a public enemy, and every frugal man a public benefactor.

The effects of misconduct are often the same as those of prodigality. Every injudicious and unsuccessful project in agriculture, mines, fisheries, trade, or manufactures, tends in the same manner to diminish the funds destined for the maintenance of productive labour. In every such project, though the capital is consumed by productive hands only, yet, as by the injudicious manner in which they are employed they do not reproduce the full value of their consumption, there must always be some diminution in what would otherwise have been the productive funds of the society.

It can seldom happen, indeed, that the circumstances of a great nation can be much affected either by the prodigality or misconduct of individuals; the profusion or imprudence of some being always more than compensated by the frugality and good conduct of others.

With regard to profusion, the principle which prompts to expense is the passion for present enjoyment; which, though sometimes violent and very difficult to be restrained, is in general only momentary and occasional. But the principle which prompts to save is the desire of bettering our condition, a desire which, though generally calm and dispassionate, comes with us from the womb, and never leaves us till we go into the grave. In the whole interval which separates those two moments, there is scarce perhaps a single instant in which any man is so perfectly and completely satisfied with his situation as to be without any wish of alteration or improvement of any kind. An augmentation of fortune is the means by which the greater part of men propose and wish to better their condition. It is the means the most vulgar and the most obvious; and the most likely way of augmenting their fortune is to save and accumulate some part of what they acquire, either regularly and annually, of upon some extraordinary occasions. Though the principle of expense, therefore, prevails in almost all men upon some occasions, and in some men upon almost all occasions, yet in the greater part of men, taking the whole course of their life at an average, the principle of frugality seems not only to predominate, but to predominate very greatly.

With regard to misconduct, the number of prudent and successful undertakings is everywhere much greater than that of injudicious and unsuccessful ones. After all our complaints of the frequency of bankruptcies, the unhappy men who fall into this misfortune make but a very small part of the whole number engaged in trade, and all other sorts of business; not much more perhaps than one in a thousand. Bankruptcy is perhaps the greatest and most humiliating calamity which can befall an innocent man. The greater part of men, therefore, are sufficiently careful to avoid it. Some, indeed, do not avoid it; as some do not avoid the gallows.

Great nations are never impoverished by private, though they sometimes are by public prodigality and misconduct. The whole, or almost the whole public revenue, is in most countries employed in maintaining unproductive hands. Such are the people who compose a numerous and splendid court, a great ecclesiastical establishment, great fleets and armies, who in time of peace produce nothing, and in time of war acquire nothing which can compensate the expense of maintaining them, even while the war lasts. Such people, as they themselves produce nothing, are all maintained by the produce of other men's labour. When multiplied, therefore, to an unnecessary number, they may in a particular year consume so great a share of this produce, as not to leave a sufficiency for maintaining the productive labourers, who should reproduce it next year. The next year's produce, therefore, will be less than that of the foregoing, and if the same disorder should continue, that of the third year will be still less than that of the second. Those unproductive hands, who should be maintained by a part only of the spare revenue of the people, may consume so great a share of their whole revenue, and thereby oblige so great a number to encroach upon their capitals, upon the funds destined for the maintenance of productive labour, that all the frugality and good conduct of individuals may not be able to compensate the waste and degradation of produce occasioned by this violent and forced encroachment.

This frugality and good conduct, however, is upon most occasions, it appears from experience, sufficient to compensate, not only the private prodigality and misconduct of individuals, but the public extravagance of government. The uniform, constant, and uninterrupted effort of every man to better his condition, the principle from which public and national, as well as private opulence is originally derived, is frequently powerful enough to maintain the natural progress of things toward improvement, in spite both of the extravagance of government and of the greatest errors of administration. Like the unknown principle of animal life, it frequently restores health and vigour to the constitution, in spite, not only of the disease, but of the absurd prescriptions of the doctor.

The annual produce of the land and labour of any nation can be increased in its value by no other means but by increasing either the number of its productive labourers, or the productive powers of those labourers who had before been employed. The number of its productive labourers, it is evident, can never be much increased, but in consequence of an increase of capital, or of the funds destined for maintaining them. The productive powers of the same number of labourers cannot be increased, but in consequence either of some addition and improvement to those machines and instruments which facilitate and abridge labour; or of a more proper division and distribution of employment. In either case an additional capital is almost always required. It is by means of an additional capital only that the undertaker of any work can either provide his workmen with better machinery or make a more proper distribution of employment among them. When the work to be done consists of a number of parts, to keep every man constantly employed in one way requires a much greater capital than where every man is occasionally employed in every different part of the work, when we compare, therefore, the state of a nation at two different periods, and find, that the annual produce of its land and labour is evidently greater at the latter than at the former, that its lands are better cultivated, its manufactures more numerous and more flourishing, and its trade more extensive, we may be assured that its capital must have increased during the interval between those two periods, and that more must have been added to it by the good conduct of some than had been taken from it either by the private misconduct of others or by the public extravagance of government. But we shall find this to have been the case of almost all nations, in all tolerably quiet and peaceable times, even of those who have not enjoyed the most prudent and parsimonious governments. To form a right judgment of it, indeed, we must compare the state of the country at periods somewhat distant from one another. The progress is frequently so gradual that, at near periods, the improvement is not only not sensible, but from the declension either of certain branches of industry, or of certain districts of the country, things which sometimes happen though the country in general be in great prosperity, there frequently arises a suspicion that the riches and industry of the whole are decaying.

The annual produce of the land and labour of England, for example, is certainly much greater than it was, a little more than a century ago, at the restoration of Charles II. Though, at present, few people, I believe, doubt of this, yet during this period, five years have seldom passed away in which some book or pamphlet has not been published, written, too, with such abilities as to gain some authority with the public, and pretending to demonstrate that the wealth of the nation was fast declining, that the country was depopulated, agriculture neglected, manufactures decaying, and trade undone. Nor have these publications been all party pamphlets, the wretched offspring of falsehood and venality. Many of them have been written by very candid and very intelligent people, who wrote nothing but what they believed, and for no other reason but because they believed it.

The annual produce of the land and labour of England, again, was certainly much greater at the restoration, than we can suppose it to have been about an hundred years before, at the accession of Elizabeth. At this period, too, we have all reason to believe, the country was much more advanced in improvement than it had been about a century before, towards the close of the dissensions between the houses of York and Lancaster. Even then it was, probably, in a better condition than it had been at the Norman conquest, and at the Norman conquest than during the confusion of the Saxon Heptarchy. Even at this early period, it was certainly a more improved country than at the invasion of Julius Caesar, when its inhabitants were nearly in the same state with the savages in North America.

In each of those periods, however, there was not only much private and public profusion, many expensive and unnecessary wars, great perversion of the annual produce from maintaining productive to maintain unproductive hands; but sometimes, in the confusion of civil discord, such absolute waste and destruction of stock, as might be supposed, not only to retard, as it certainly did, the natural accumulation of riches, but to have left the country, at the end of the period, poorer than at the beginning. Thus, in the happiest and most fortunate period of them all, that which has passed since the restoration, how many disorders and misfortunes have occurred, which, could they have been foreseen, not only the impoverishment, but the total ruin of the country would have been expected from them? The fire and the plague of London, the two Dutch wars, the disorders of the revolution, the war in Ireland, the four expensive French wars of 1688, 1702, 1742, and 1756, together with the two rebellions of 1715 and 1745. In the course of the four French wars, the nation has contracted more than a hundred and forty-five millions of debt, over and above all the other extraordinary annual expense which they occasioned, so that the whole cannot be computed at less than two hundred millions. So great a share of the annual produce of the land and labour of the country has, since the revolution, been employed upon different occasions in maintaining an extraordinary number of unproductive hands. But had not those wars given this particular direction to so large a capital, the greater part of it would naturally have been employed in maintaining productive hands, whose labour would have replaced, with a profit, the whole value of their consumption. The value of the annual produce of the land and labour of the country would have been considerably increased by it every year, and every year's increase would have augmented still more that of the following year. More houses would have been built, more lands would have been improved, and those which had been improved before would have been better cultivated, more manufactures would have been established, and those which had been established before would have been more extended; and to what height the real wealth and revenue of the country might, by this time, have been raised, it is not perhaps very easy even to imagine.

But though the profusion of government must, undoubtedly, have retarded the natural progress of England towards wealth and improvement, it has not been able to stop it. The annual produce of its land and labour is, undoubtedly, much greater at present man it was either at the restoration or at the revolution. The capital, therefore, annually employed in cultivating this land, and in maintaining this labour, must likewise be much greater. In the midst of all the exactions of government, this capital has been silently and gradually accumulated by the private frugality and good conduct of individuals, by their universal, continual, and un-interrupted effort to better their own condition. It is this effort, protected by law and allowed by liberty to exert itself in the manner that is most advantageous, which has maintained the progress of England towards opulence and improvement in almost all former times, and which, it is to be hoped, will do so in all future times. England, however, as it has never been blessed with a very parsimonious government, so parsimony has at no time been the characteristical virtue of its inhabitants. It is the highest impertinence and presumption, therefore, in kings and ministers, to pretend to watch over the economy of private people, and to restrain their expense, either by sumptuary laws, or by prohibiting the importation of foreign luxuries. They are themselves always, and without any exception, the greatest spendthrifts in the society. Let them look well after their own expense, and they may safely trust private people with theirs. If their own extravagance does not ruin the state, that of their subjects never will.

As frugality increases and prodigality diminishes the public capital, so the conduct of those whose expense just equals their revenue, without either accumulating or encroaching, neither increases nor diminishes it. Some modes of expense, however, seem to contribute more to the growth of public opulence than others.

The revenue of an individual may be spent either in things which are consumed immediately, and in which one day's expense can neither alleviate nor support that of another, or it may be spent in things more durable, which can therefore be accumulated, and in which every day's expense may, as he chooses, either alleviate or support and heighten the effect of that of the following day, A man of fortune, for example, may either spend his revenue in a profuse and sumptuous table, and in maintaining a great number of menial servants, and a multitude of dogs and horses; or contenting himself with a frugal table and few attendants, he may lay out the greater part of it in adorning his house or his country villa, in useful or ornamental buildings, in useful or ornamental furniture, in collecting books, statues, pictures; or in things more frivolous, jewels, baubles, ingenious trinkets of different kinds; or, what is most trifling of all, in amassing a great wardrobe of fine clothes, like the favourite and minister of a great prince who died a few years ago. Were two men of equal fortune to spend their revenue, the one chiefly in the one way, the other in the other, the magnificence of the person whose expense had been chiefly in durable commodities, would be continually increasing, every day's expense contributing something to support and heighten the effect of that of the following day: that of the other, on the contrary, would be no greater at the end of the period than at the beginning. The former, too, would, at the end of the period, be the richer man of the two. He would have a stock of goods of some kind or other, which, though it might not be worth all that it cost, would always be worth something. No trace or vestige of the expense of the latter would remain, and the effects of ten or twenty years profusion would be as completely annihilated as if they had never existed.

As the one mode of expense is more favourable than the other to the opulence of an individual, so is it likewise to that of a nation. The houses, the furniture, the clothing of the rich, in a little time, become useful to the inferior and middling ranks of people. They are able to purchase them when their superiors grow weary of them, and the general accommodation of the whole people is thus gradually improved, when this mode of expense becomes universal among men of fortune. In countries which have long been rich, you will frequently find the inferior ranks of people in possession both of houses and furniture perfectly good and entire, but of which neither the one could have been built, nor the other have been made for their use. What was formerly a seat of the family of Seymour is now an inn upon the Bath road. The marriage-bed of James the First of Great Britain, which his queen brought with her from Denmark as a present fit for a sovereign to make to a sovereign, was, a few years ago, the ornament of an alehouse at Dunfermline. In some ancient cities, which either have been long stationary, or have gone somewhat to decay, you will sometimes scarce find a single house which could have been built for its present inhabitants. If you go into those houses too, you will frequently find many excellent, though antiquated pieces of furniture, which are still very fit for use, and which could as little have been made for them. Noble palaces, magnificent villas, great Collections of books, statues, pictures, and other curiosities, are frequently both an ornament and an honour, not only to the neighbourhood, but to the whole country to which they belong. Versailles is an ornament and an honour to France, Stowe and Wilton to England. Italy still continues to command some sort of veneration by the number of monuments of this kind which it possesses, though the wealth which produced them has decayed, and though the genius which planned them seems to be extinguished, perhaps from not having the same employment.

The expense too, which is laid out in durable commodities, is favourable, not only to accumulation, but to frugality. If a person should at any time exceed in it, he can easily reform without exposing himself to the censure of the public. To reduce very much the number of his servants, to reform his table from great profusion to great frugality, to lay down his equipage after he has once set it up, are changes which cannot escape the observation of his neighbours, and which are supposed to imply some acknowledgment of preceding bad conduct. Few, therefore, of those who have once been so unfortunate as to launch out too far into this sort of expense, have afterwards the courage to reform, till ruin and bankruptcy oblige them. But if a person has, at any time, been at too great an expense in building, in furniture, in books or pictures, no imprudence. can be inferred from his changing his conduct. These are things in which further expense is frequently rendered unnecessary by former expense; and when a person stops short, he appears to do so, not because he has exceeded his fortune, but because he has satisfied his fancy.

The expense, besides, that is laid out in durable commodities gives maintenance, commonly, to a greater number of people than that which is employed in the most profuse hospitality. Of two or three hundred-weight of provisions, which may sometimes be served up at a great festival, one-half, perhaps, is thrown to the dunghill, and there is always a great deal wasted and abused. But if the expense of this entertainment had been employed in setting to work masons, carpenters, upholsterers, mechanics, etc., a quantity of provisions, of equal value, would have been distributed among a still greater number of people who would have bought them in pennyworths and pound weights, and not have lost or thrown away a single ounce of them. In the one way, besides, this expense maintains productive, in the other unproductive hands. In the one way, therefore, it increases, in the other, it does not increase, the exchangeable value of the annual produce of the land and labour of the country.

I would not, however, by all this be understood to mean that the one species of expense always betokens a more liberal or generous spirit than the other. When a man of fortune spends his revenue chiefly in hospitality, he shares the greater part of it with his friends and companions; but when he employs it in purchasing such durable commodities, he often spends the whole upon his own person, and gives nothing to anybody without an equivalent. The latter species of expense, therefore, especially when directed towards frivolous objects, the little ornaments of dress and furniture, jewels, trinkets, gewgaws, frequently indicates, not only a trifling, but a base and selfish disposition. All that I mean is, that the one sort of expense, as it always occasions some accumulation of valuable commodities, as it is more favorable to private frugality, and, consequently, to the increase of the public capital, and as it maintains productive, rather than unproductive hands, conduces more than the other to the growth of public opulence.

\* \* \*

# BOOK III

## CHAPTER IV

### HOW THE COMMERCE OF THE TOWNS CONTRIBUTED TO THE IMPROVEMENT OF THE COUNTRY

The increase and riches of commercial and manufacturing towns contributed to the improvement and cultivation of the countries to which they belonged in three different ways.

First, by affording a great and ready market for the rude produce of the country, they gave encouragement to its cultivation and further improvement. This benefit was not even confined to the countries in which they were situated, but extended more or less to all those with which they had any dealings. To all of them they afforded a market for some part either of their rude or manufactured produce, and consequently gave some encouragement to the industry and improvement of all. Their own country, however, on account of its neighbourhood, necessarily derived the greatest benefit from this market. Its rude produce being charged with less carriage, the traders could pay the growers a better price for it, and yet afford it as cheap to the consumers as that of more distant countries.

Secondly, the wealth acquired by the inhabitants of cities was frequently employed in purchasing such lands as were to be sold, of which a great part would frequently be uncultivated. Merchants are commonly ambitious of becoming country gentlemen, and when they do, they are generally the best of all improvers. A merchant is accustomed to employ his money chiefly in profitable projects, whereas a mere country gentleman is accustomed to employ it chiefly in expense. The one often sees his money go from him and return to him again with a profit; the other, when once he parts with it, very seldom expects to see any more of it. Those different habits naturally affect their temper

and disposition in every sort of business. A merchant is commonly a bold, a country gentleman a timid undertaker. The one is not afraid to lay out at once a large capital upon the improvement of his land when he has a probable prospect of raising the value of it in proportion to the expense. The other, if he has any capital, which is not always the case, seldom ventures to employ it in this manner. If he improves at all, it is commonly not with a capital, but with what he can save out of his annual revenue. Whoever has had the fortune to live in a mercantile town situated in an unimproved country must have frequently observed how much more spirited the operations of merchants were in this way than those of mere country gentlemen. The habits, besides, of order, economy, and attention, to which mercantile business naturally forms a merchant, render him much fitter to execute, with profit and success, any project of improvement.

Thirdly, and lastly, commerce and manufactures gradually introduced order and good government, and with them, the liberty and security of individuals, among the inhabitants of the country, who had before lived almost in a continual state of war with their neighbours and of servile dependency upon their superiors. This, though it has been the least observed, is by far the most important of all their effects. Mr. Hume is the only writer who, so far as I know, has hitherto taken notice of it.

In a country which has neither foreign commerce, nor any of the finer manufactures, a great proprietor, having nothing for which he can exchange the greater part of the produce of his lands which is over and above the maintenance of the cultivators, consumes the whole in rustic hospitality at home. If this surplus produce is sufficient to maintain a hundred or a thousand men, he can make use of it in no other way than by maintaining a hundred or a thousand men. He is at all times, therefore, surrounded with a multitude of retainers and dependants, who, having no equivalent to give in return for their maintenance, but being fed entirely by his bounty, must obey him, for the same reason that soldiers must obey the prince who pays them. Before the extension of commerce and manufacture in Europe, the hospitality of the rich and the great, from the sovereign down to the smallest baron, exceeded everything which in the present times we can easily form a notion of. Westminster hall was the dining-room of

William Rufus, and might frequently, perhaps, not be too large for his company. It was reckoned a piece of magnificence in Thomas Becket that he strewed the floor of his hall with clean hay or rushes in the season, in order that the knights and squires who could not get seats might not spoil their fine clothes when they sat down on the floor to eat their dinner. The great Earl of Warwick is said to have entertained every day at his different manors thirty thousand people, and though the number here may have been exaggerated, it must, however, have been very great to admit of such exaggeration. A hospitality nearly of the same kind was exercised not many years ago in many different parts of the highlands of Scotland. It seems to be common in all nations to whom commerce and manufactures are little known. I have seen, says Doctor Pocock, an Arabian chief dine in the streets of a town where he had come to sell his cattle, and invite all passengers, even common beggars, to sit down with him and partake of his banquet.

The occupiers of land were in every respect as dependent upon the great proprietor as his retainers. Even such of them as were not in a state of villanage were tenants at will, who paid a rent in no respect equivalent to the subsistence which the land afforded them. A crown, half a crown, a sheep, a lamb, was some years ago in the highlands of Scotland a common rent for lands which maintained a family. In some places it is so at this day; nor will money at present purchase a greater quantity of commodities there than in other places. In a country where the surplus produce of a large estate must be consumed upon the estate itself, it will frequently be more convenient for the proprietor that part of it be consumed at a distance from his own house provided they who consume it are as dependent upon him as either his retainers or his menial servants. He is thereby saved from the embarrassment of either too large a company or too large a family. A tenant at will, who possesses land sufficient to maintain his family for little more than a quit-rent, is as dependent upon the proprietor as any servant or retainer whatever and must obey him with as little reserve. Such a proprietor, as he feeds his servants and retainers at his own house, so he feeds his tenants at their houses. The subsistence of both is derived from his bounty, and its continuance depends upon his good pleasure.

Upon the authority which the great proprietor necessarily had in such a state of things over their tenants and retainers was founded the power of the ancient barons. They necessarily became the judges in peace, and the leaders in war, of all who dwelt upon their estates. They could maintain order and execute the law within their respective demesnes, because each of them could there turn the whole force of all the inhabitants against the injustice of any one. No other persons had sufficient authority to do this. The king in particular had not. In those ancient times he was little more than the greatest proprietor in his dominions, to whom, for the sake of common defence against their common enemies, the other great proprietors paid certain respects. To have enforced payment of a small debt within the lands of a great proprietor, where all the inhabitants were armed and accustomed to stand by one another, would have cost the king, had he attempted it by his own authority, almost the same effort as to extinguish a civil war. He was, therefore, obliged to abandon the administration of justice through the greater part of the country to those who were capable of administering it; and for the same reason to leave the command of the country militia to those whom that militia would obey.

It is a mistake to imagine that those territorial jurisdictions took their origin from the feudal law. Not only the highest jurisdictions both civil and criminal, but the power of levying troops, of coining money, and even that of making bye-laws for the government of their own people, were all rights possessed allodially by the great proprietors of land several centuries before even the name of the feudal law was known in Europe. The authority and jurisdiction of the Saxon lords in England appear to have been as great before the Conquest as that of any of the Norman lords after it. But the feudal law is not supposed to have become the common law of England till after the Conquest. That the most extensive authority and jurisdictions were possessed by the great lords in France allodially long before the feudal law was introduced into that country is a matter of fact that admits of no doubt. That authority and those jurisdictions all necessarily flowed from the state of property and manners just now described. Without remounting to the remote antiquities of either the French or English monarchies, we may find in much later times many proofs that such effects must always flow from such causes. It is not thirty years ago since Mr. Cameron of Lochiel, a gentleman of Lochabar in Scotland, without any legal warrant whatever, not being what was then eddied a lord of regality, nor even a tenant in chief, but a vassal of the Duke of Argyle, and without being so much as a justice of peace, used, notwithstanding, to exercise the highest criminal jurisdiction over his own people. He is said to have done so with great equity, though without any of the formalities of justice; and it is not improbable that the state of that part of the country at that time made it necessary for him to assume this authority in order to maintain the public peace. That gentleman, whose rent never exceeded five hundred pounds a year, carried, in 1745, eight hundred of his own people into the rebellion with him.

The introduction of the feudal law, so far from extending, may be regarded as an attempt to moderate the authority of the great allodial lords. It established a regular subordination, accompanied with a long train of services and duties, from the king down to the smallest proprietor. During the minority of the proprietor, the rent, together with the management of his lands, fell into the hands of his immediate superior, and, consequently, those of all great proprietors into the hands of the king, who was charged with the maintenance and education of the pupil, and who, from his authority as guardian, was supposed to have a right of disposing of him in marriage, provided it was in a manner not unsuitable to his rank. But though this institution necessarily tended to strengthen the authority of the king, and to weaken that of the great proprietors, it could not do either sufficiently for establishing order and good government among the inhabitants of the country, because it could not alter sufficiently that state of property and manners from which the disorders arose. The authority of government still continued to be, as before, too weak in the head and too strong in the inferior members, and the excessive strength of the inferior members was the cause of the weakness of the head. After the institution of feudal subordination, the king was as incapable of restraining the violence of the great lords as before. They still continued to make war according to their own discretion, almost continually upon one another, and very frequently upon the king; and the open country still continued, to be a scene of violence, rapine, and disorder.

But what all the violence of the feudal institutions could never have effected, the silent and insensible operation of foreign commerce and manufactures gradually brought about. These gradually furnished the great proprietors with something for which they could exchange the whole surplus produce of their lands, and which they could consume themselves without sharing it either with tenants or retainers. All for ourselves and nothing for other people, seems, in every age of the world, to have been the vile maxim of the masters of mankind. As soon therefore, as they could find a method of consuming the whole value of their rents themselves, they had no disposition to share them with any other persons. For a pair of diamond buckles perhaps, or for something as frivolous and useless, they exchanged the maintenance, or what is the same thing, the price of the maintenance of a thousand men for a year, and with it the whole weight and authority which it could give them. The buckles, however, were to be all their own, and no other human creature was to have any share of them; whereas in the more ancient method of expense they must have shared with at least a thousand people. With the judges that were to determine the preference this difference was perfectly decisive; and thus, for the gratification of the most childish, the meanest, and the most sordid of all vanities, they gradually bartered their whole power and authority.

In a country where there is no foreign commerce, nor any of the finer manufactures, a man of ten thousand a year cannot well employ his revenue in any other way than in maintaining, perhaps, a thousand families, who are all of them necessarily at his command. In the present state of Europe, a man of ten thousand a year can spend his whole revenue, and he generally does so, without directly maintaining twenty people, or being able to command more than ten footmen not worth the commanding. Indirectly, perhaps, he maintains as great or even a greater number of people than he could have done by the ancient method of expense. For though the quantity of precious productions for which he exchanges his whole revenue be very small, the number of workmen employed in collecting and preparing it must necessarily have been very great. Its great price generally arises from the wages of their labour, and the profits of all their immediate employers. By paying that price he indirectly pays all those wages and profits and thus indirectly contributes to the maintenance of all the workmen and their employers. He generally contributes, however, but a very small proportion to that of each, to very few perhaps a tenth, to many not a hundredth, and to some not a thousandth, nor even a ten-thousandth part of their whole annual maintenance. Though he contributes, therefore, to the maintenance of them all, they are all more or less independent of him, because generally they can all be maintained without him.

When the great proprietors of land spend their rents in maintaining their tenants and retainers, each of them maintains entirely all his own tenants and all his own retainers. But when they spend them in maintaining tradesmen and artificers, they may, all of them taken together, perhaps, maintain as great, or, on account of the waste which attends rustic hospitality, a greater number of people than before. Each of them, however, taken singly, contributes often but a very small share to the maintenance of any individual of this greater number Each tradesman or artificer derives his subsistence from the employment, not of one, but of a hundred or a thousand different customers. Though in some measure obliged to them all therefore, he is not absolutely dependent upon any one of them.

The personal expense of the great proprietors having in this manner gradually increased, it was impossible that the number of their retainers should not as gradually diminish till they were at last dismissed altogether. The same cause gradually led them to dismiss the unnecessary part of their tenants. Farms were enlarged, and the occupiers of land, notwithstanding the complaints of depopulation, reduced to the number necessary for cultivating it, according to the imperfect state of cultivation and improvement in those times. By the removal of the unnecessary mouths, and by exacting from the farmer the full value of the farm, a greater surplus, or what is the same thing, the price of a greater surplus, was obtained for the proprietor which the merchants and manufacturers soon furnished him with a method of spending upon his own person in the same manner as he had done the rest. The same cause continuing to operate, he was desirous to raise his rents above what his lands, in the actual state of their improvement, could afford. His tenants could agree to this upon one condition only, that they should be secured in their possession for such a term of years as might give them time to recover with profit whatever they should lay out

in the further improvement of the land; The expensive vanity of the landlord made him willing to accept of this condition; and hence the origin of long leases.

Even a tenant at will, who pays the full value of the land, is not altogether dependent upon the landlord. The pecuniary advantages which they receive from one another are mutual and equal, and such a tenant will expose neither his life nor his fortune in the service of the proprietor. But if he has a lease for a long term of years, he is altogether independent; and his landlord must not expect from him even the most trifling service beyond what is either expressly stipulated in the lease or imposed upon him by the common and known law of the country.

The tenants having in this manner become independent, and the retainers being dismissed, the great proprietors were no longer capable of interrupting the regular execution of justice or of disturbing the peace of the country. Having sold their birthright, not Eke Esau for a mess of pottage in time of hunger and necessity, but in the wantonness of plenty, for trinkets and baubles, fitter to be the playthings of children than the serious pursuits of men, they became as insignificant as any substantial burgher or tradesman in a city. A regular government was established in the country as well as in the city, nobody having sufficient power to disturb its operations in the one any more than in the other.

It does not, perhaps, relate to the present subject, but I cannot help remarking it, that very old families, such as have possessed some considerable estate from father to son for many successive generations are very rare in commercial countries. In countries which have little commerce, on the contrary, such as Wales or the highlands of Scotland, they are very common. The Arabian histories seem to be all full of genealogies, and there is a history written by a Tartar Khan, which has been translated into several European languages, and which contains scarce anything else; a proof that ancient families are very common among those nations. In countries where a rich man can spend his revenue in no other way than by maintaining as many people as it can maintain, he is not apt to run out, and his benevolence it seems is seldom so violent as to attempt to maintain more than he can afford. But where he can spend the greatest revenue upon his own person, he frequently has no bounds to his expense, because he frequently has no bounds to his vanity or to his affection for his own person. In commercial countries, therefore, riches, in spite of the most violent regulations of law to prevent their dissipation, very seldom remain long in the same family. Among simple nations, on the contrary, they frequently do without any regulations of law, for among nations of shepherds, such as the Tartars and Arabs, the consumable nature of their property necessarily renders all such regulations impossible.

A revolution of the greatest importance to the public happiness was in this manner brought about by two different orders of people who had not the least intention to serve the public. To gratify the most childish vanity was the sole motive of the great proprietors. The merchants and artificers, much less ridiculous, acted merely from a view to their own interest, and in pursuit of their own pedlar principle of turning a penny wherever a penny was to be got. Neither of them had either knowledge or foresight of that great revolution which the folly of the one, and the industry of the other, was gradually bringing about.

It is thus that through the greater part of Europe the commerce and manufactures of cities, instead of being the effect, have been the cause and occasion of the improvement and cultivation of the country.

\* \* \*

# BOOK 4

## CHAPTER II

### OF RESTRAINTS UPON THE IMPORTATION FROM FOREIGN COUNTRIES OF SUCH GOODS AS CAN BE PRODUCED AT HOME

By restraining, either by high duties or by absolute prohibitions, the importation of such goods from foreign countries as can be produced at home, the monopoly of the home market is more or less secured to the domestic industry employed in producing them. Thus the prohibition of importing either live cattle or salt provisions from foreign countries secures to the graziers of Great Britain the monopoly of the home market for butcher's meat. The high duties upon the importation of corn, which in times of moderate plenty amount to a prohibition, give a like advantage to the growers of that commodity. The prohibition of the importation of foreign woollens is equally favourable to the woollen

manufacturers. The silk manufacture, though altogether employed upon foreign materials, has lately obtained the same advantage. The linen manufacture bias not yet obtained it, but is making great strides towards it. Many other sorts of manufacturers have, in the same manner, obtained in Great Britain, either altogether or very nearly, a monopoly against their countrymen. The variety of goods of which the importation into Great Britain is prohibited, either absolutely, or under certain circumstances, greatly exceeds what can easily be suspected by those who are not well acquainted with the laws of the customs.

That this monopoly of the home market frequently gives great encouragement to that particular species of industry which enjoys it, and frequently turns towards that employment a greater share of both the labour and stock of the society than would otherwise have gone to it, cannot be doubted. But whether it tends either to increase the general industry of the society, or to give it the most advantageous direction, is not, perhaps, altogether so evident.

The general industry of the society never can exceed what the capital of the society can employ. As the number of work men that can be kept in employment by any particular person must bear a certain proportion to his capital, so the number of those that can be continually employed by all the members of a great society must bear a certain proportion to the whole capital of that society, and never can exceed that proportion. No regulation of commerce can increase the quantity of industry in any society beyond what its capital can maintain. It can only divert a part of it into a direction into which it might not otherwise have gone; and it is by no means certain that this artificial direction is likely to be more advantageous to the society than that into which it would have gone of its own accord.

Every individual is continually exerting himself to find out the most advantageous employment for whatever capital he can command. It is his own advantage, indeed, and not that of the society, which he has in view. But the study of his own advantage naturally, or rather necessarily, leads him to prefer that employment which is most advantageous to the society.

First, every individual endeavours to employ his capital as near home as he can, and consequently as much as he can in the support of domestic industry;

← concept of "the calling" put in to capitalistic terms?

provided always that he can thereby obtain the ordinary, or not a great deal less than the ordinary profits of stock.

Thus, upon equal or nearly equal profits, every wholesale merchant naturally prefers the home trade to the foreign trade of consumption, and the foreign trade of consumption to the carrying trade. In the home trade his capital is never so long out of his sight as it frequently is in the foreign trade of consumption. He can know better the character and situation of the persons whom he trusts, and if he should happen to be deceived, he knows better the laws of the country from which he must seek redress. In the carrying trade, the capital of the merchant is, as it were, divided between two foreign countries, and no part of it is ever necessarily brought home, or placed under his own immediate view and command. The capital which an Amsterdam merchant employs in carrying corn from Konnigsberg to Lisbon, and fruit and wine from Lisbon to Konnigsberg, must generally be the one-half of it at Konnigsberg and the other half at Lisbon. No part of it need ever come to Amsterdam. The natural residence of such a merchant should either be at Konnigsberg or Lisbon, and it can only be some very particular circumstances which can make him prefer the residence of Amsterdam. The uneasiness, however, which he feels at being separated so far from his capital generally determines him to bring part both of the Konnigsberg goods which he destines for the market of Lisbon, and of the Lisbon goods which he destines for that of Konnigsberg, to Amsterdam: and though this necessarily subjects him to a double charge of loading and unloading, as well as to the payment of some duties and customs, yet for the sake of having some part of his capital always under his own view and command, he willingly submits to this extraordinary charge; and it is in this manner that every country which has any considerable share of the carrying trade becomes always the emporium, or general market, for the goods of all the different countries whose trade it carries on. The merchant, in order to save a second loading and unloading, endeavours always to sell in the home market as much of the goods of all those different countries as he can, and thus, so far as he can, to convert his carrying trade into a foreign trade of consumption. A merchant, in the same manner, who is engaged in the foreign trade of consumption, when he collects goods for foreign markets, will always be glad, upon equal or nearly equal profits, to sell as great a part of them at home as he can. He saves himself the risk and trouble of exportation, when, so far as he can, he thus converts his foreign trade of consumption into a home trade. Home is in this manner the centre, if I may say so, round which the capitals of the inhabitants of every country are continually circulating, and towards which they are always tending, though by particular causes they may sometimes be driven off and repelled from it towards more distant employments. But a capital employed in the home trade, it has already been shown, necessarily puts into motion a greater quantity of domestic industry, and gives revenue and employment to a greater number of the inhabitants of the country, than an equal capital employed in the foreign trade of consumption: and one employed in the foreign trade of consumption has the same advantage over an equal capital employed in the carrying trade. Upon equal, or only nearly equal profits, therefore, every individual naturally inclines to employ his capital in the manner in which it is likely to afford the greatest support to domestic industry, and to give revenue and employment to the greatest number of people of his own country.

Secondly, every individual who employs his capital in the support of domestic industry, necessarily endeavours so to direct that industry that its produce may be of the greatest possible value.

The produce of industry is what it adds to the subject or materials upon which it is employed. In proportion as the value of this produce is great or small, so will likewise be the profits of the employer. But it is only for the sake of profit that any man employs a capital in the support of industry; and he will always, therefore, endeavour to employ it in the support of that industry of which the produce is likely to be of the greatest value, or to exchange for the greatest quantity either of money or of other goods.

But the annual revenue of every society is always precisely equal to the exchangeable value of the whole annual produce of its industry, or rather is precisely the same thing with that exchangeable value. As every individual, therefore, endeavours as much as he can both to employ his capital in the support of domestic industry, and so to direct that industry that its produce may be of the greatest value; every individual necessarily labours to render the annual revenue of the society as great as he can. He generally, indeed, neither intends to promote the public interest, nor knows how much he is promoting it. By preferring the support of domestic to that of foreign industry he intends only his own security; and by directing that industry in such a manner as its produce may be of the greatest value, he intends only his own gain, and he is in this, as in many other cases, led by an invisible hand to promote an end which was no part of his intention. Nor is it always the worse for the society that it was no part of it. By pursuing his own interest he frequently promotes that of the society more effectually than when he really intends to promote it. I have never known much good done by those who affected to trade for the public good. It is an affectation, indeed, not very common among merchants, and very few words need be employed in dissuading them from it.

What is the species of domestic industry which his capital can employ, and of which the produce is likely to be of the greatest value, every individual, it is evident, can, in his local situation, judge much better than any statesman or lawgiver can do for him. The statesman who should attempt to direct private people in what manner they ought to employ their capitals would not only load himself with a most unnecessary attention, but assume an authority which could safely be trusted, not only to no single person, but to no council or senate whatever, and which would nowhere be so dangerous as in the hands of a man who had folly and presumption enough to fancy himself fit to exercise it.

To give the monopoly of the home market to the produce of domestic industry, in any particular art or manufacture, is in some measure to direct private people in what manner they ought to employ their capitals, and must, in almost all cases, be either a useless or a hurtful regulation. If the produce of domestic can be brought there as cheap as that of foreign industry, the regulation is evidently useless. If it cannot, it must generally be hurtful. It is the maxim of every prudent master of a family never to attempt to make at home what it will cost him more to make than to buy. The tailor does not attempt to make his own shoes, but buys them of the shoemaker. The shoemaker does not attempt to make his own clothes, but employs a tailor. The farmer attempts to make neither the one nor the other, but employs those different artificers. All of them find it for their interest to employ their whole industry in a way in which they have some advantage over their

neighbours, and to purchase with a part of its produce, or what is the same thing, with the price of a part of it, whatever else they have occasion for.

What is prudence in the conduct of every private family can scarce be folly in that of a great kingdom. If a foreign country can supply us with a commodity cheaper than we ourselves can make it, better buy it of them with some part of the produce of our own industry employed in a way in which we have some advantage. The general industry of the country, being always in proportion to the capital which employs it, will not thereby be diminished, no more than that of the above-mentioned artificers; but only left to find out the way in which it can be employed with the greatest advantage. It is certainly not employed to the greatest advantage when it is thus directed towards an object which it can buy cheaper than it can make. The value of its annual produce is certainly more or less diminished when it is thus turned away from producing commodities evidently of more value than the commodity which it is directed to produce. According to the supposition, that commodity could be purchased from foreign countries cheaper than it can be made at home. It could, therefore, have been purchased with a part only of the commodities, or, what is the same thing, with a part only of the price of the commodities, which the industry employed by an equal capital would have produced at home, had it been left to follow its natural course. The industry of the country, therefore, is thus turned away from a more to a less advantageous employment, and the exchangeable value of its annual produce, instead of being increased, according to the intention of the lawgiver, must necessarily be diminished by every such regulation.

By means of such regulations, indeed, a particular manufacture may sometimes be acquired sooner than it could have been otherwise, and after a certain time may be made at home as cheap or cheaper than in the foreign country. But though the industry of the society may be thus carried with advantage into a particular channel sooner than it could have been otherwise, it will by no means follow that the sum total, either of its industry, or of its revenue, can ever be augmented by any suit regulation. The industry of the society can augment only in proportion as its capital augments, and its capital can augment only in proportion to what can be gradually saved out of its revenue. But the immediate effect of every such regulation is to diminish its revenue, and what diminishes its revenue is certainly not very likely to augment its capital faster than it would have augmented of its own accord had both capital and industry been left to find out their natural employments.

Though for want of such regulations the society should never acquire the proposed manufacture, it would not, upon that account, necessarily be the poorer in any one period of its duration. In every period of its duration its whole capital and industry might still have been employed, though upon different objects, in the manner that was most advantageous at the time. In every period its revenue might have been the greatest which its capital could afford, and both capital and revenue might have been augmented with the greatest possible rapidity.

The natural advantages which one country has over another in producing particular commodities are sometimes so great that it is acknowledged by all the world to be in vain to struggle with them. By means of glasses, hotbeds, and hot walls, very good grapes can be raised in Scotland, and very good wine too can be made of them at about thirty times the expense for which at least equally good can be brought from foreign countries. Would it be a reasonable law to prohibit the importation of all foreign wines merely to encourage the making of claret and burgundy in Scotland? But if there would be a manifest absurdity in turning towards any employment thirty times more of the capital and industry of the country than would be necessary to, purchase from foreign countries an equal quantity of the commodities wanted, there must be an absurdity, though not altogether so glaring, yet exactly of the same kind, in turning towards any such employment a thirtieth, or even a three-hundredth part more of either. Whether the advantages which one country has over another be natural or acquired is in this respect of no consequence. As long as the one country has those advantages, and the other wants them, it will always be more advantageous for the latter rather to buy of the former than to make. It is an acquired advantage only, which one artificer has over his neighbour, who exercises another trade; and yet they both find it more advantageous to buy of one another than to make what does not belong to their particular trades.

Merchants and manufacturers are the people who derive the greatest advantage from this monopoly of the home market. The prohibition of the importation of foreign cattle, and of salt provisions, together with the high duties upon foreign corn, which in times of moderate plenty amount to a prohibition, are not near so advantageous to the graziers and farmers of Great Britain as other regulations of the same kind are to its merchants and manufacturers. Manufactures, those of the finer kind especially, are more easily transported from one country to another than corn or cattle. It is in the fetching and carrying manufactures, accordingly, that foreign trade is chiefly employed. In manufactures, a very small advantage will enable foreigners to under-sell our own workmen, even in the home market. It will require a very great one to enable them to do so in the rude produce of the soil. If the free importation of foreign manufactures were permitted, several of the home manufactures would probably suffer, and some of them, perhaps, go to ruin altogether, and a considerable part of the stock and industry at present employed in them would be forced to find out some other employment. But the freest importation of the rude produce of the soil could have no such effect upon the agriculture of the country.

\* \* \*

## BOOK IV

## CHAPTER IX

It is thus that every system which endeavours, either by extraordinary encouragements to draw towards a particular species of industry a greater share of the capital of the society than what would naturally go to it, or, by extraordinary restraints, force from a particular species of industry some share of the capital which would otherwise be employed in it, is in reality subversive of the great purpose which it means promote. It retards, instead of accelerating, the progress of the society towards real wealth and greatness; and diminishes, instead of increasing, the real value of the annual produce of its land and labour.

All systems either of preference or of restraint, therefore being thus completely taken away, the obvious and simple system of natural liberty establishes itself of its own accord. Every man, as long as he does not violate the laws of justice is left perfectly free to pursue his own interest his own way, and to bring both his industry and capital into competition with those of any other man, or order of men. The sovereign is completely discharged from a duty, in the attempting to perform which he must always be exposed to innumerable delusions, and for the proper performance of which no human wisdom or knowledge could ever be sufficient; the duty of superintending the industry of private people, and of directing it towards the employments most suitable to the interest of the society. According to the system of natural liberty, the sovereign has only three duties to attend to; three duties of great importance, indeed, but plain and intelligible to common understanding: first, the duty of protecting the society from the violence and invasion of other independent societies; secondly, the duty of protecting, as far as possible, every member of the society from the injustice or oppression of every other member of it, or the duty of establishing an exact administration of justice; and, thirdly, the duty of erecting and maintaining certain public works and certain public institutions which it can never be for the interest of any individual, or small number of individuals, to erect and maintain; because the profit could never repay the expense to any individual or small number of individuals, though it may frequently do much more than repay it to a great society.

## BOOK V

## CHAPTER I

The education of the common people requires, perhaps, in a civilised and commercial society the attention of the public more than that of people of some rank and fortune. People of some rank and fortune are generally eighteen or nineteen years of age before they enter upon that particular business, profession, or trade, by which they propose to distinguish themselves in the world. They have before that full time to acquire, or at least to fit themselves for afterwards acquiring, every accomplishment which can recommend them to the public esteem, or render them worthy of it. Their parents or guardians are generally sufficiently anxious that they should be so accomplished, and are, in most cases, willing enough to lay out the expense which is necessary for that purpose. If they are not always properly educated,

it is seldom from the want of expense laid out upon their education, but from the improper application of that expense. It is seldom from the want of masters, but from the negligence and incapacity of the masters who are to be had, and from the difficulty, or rather from the impossibility, which there is in the present state of things of finding any better. The employments, too, in which people of some rank or fortune spend the greater part of their lives are not, like those of the common people, simple and uniform. They are almost all of them extremely complicated, and such as exercise the head more than the hands. The understandings of those who are engaged in such employments can seldom grow torpid for want of exercise. The employments of people of some rank and fortune, besides, are seldom such as harass them from morning to night. They generally have a good deal of leisure, during which they may perfect themselves in every branch either of useful or ornamental knowledge of which they may have laid the foundation, or for which they may have acquired some taste in the earlier part of life.

It is otherwise with the common people. They have little time to spare for education. Their parents can scarce afford to maintain them even in infancy. As soon as they are able to work they must apply to some trade by which they can earn their subsistence. That trade, too, is generally so simple and uniform as to give little exercise to the understanding, while, at the same time, their labour is both so constant and so severe, that it leaves them little leisure and less inclination to apply to, or even to think of, anything else.

But though the common people cannot, in any civilised society, be so well instructed as people of some rank and fortune, the most essential parts of education, however, to read, write, and account, can be acquired at so early a period of life that the greater part even of those who are to be bred to the lowest occupations have time to acquire them before they can be employed in those occupations. For a very small expense the public can facilitate, can encourage, and can even impose upon almost the whole body of the people the necessity of acquiring those most essential parts of education.

The public can facilitate this acquisition by establishing in every parish or district a little school, where children may be taught for a reward so moderate that even a common labourer may afford it; the master being partly, but not wholly, paid by the public, because, if he was wholly, or even principally, paid by it, he would soon learn to neglect his business. In Scotland the establishment of such parish schools has taught almost the whole common people to read, and a very great proportion of them to write and account. In England the establishment of charity schools has had an effect of the same kind, though not so universally, because the establishment is not so universal. If in those little schools the books, by which the children are taught to read, were a little more instructive than they commonly are, and if, instead of a little smattering of Latin, which the children of the common people are sometimes taught there, and which can scarce ever be of any use to them, they were instructed in the elementary parts of geometry and mechanics, the literary education of this rank of people would perhaps be as complete as it can be. There is scarce a common trade which does not afford some opportunities of applying to it the principles of geometry and mechanics, and which would not therefore gradually exercise and improve the common people in those principles, the necessary introduction to the most sublime as well as to the most useful sciences.

The public can encourage the acquisition of those most essential parts of education by giving small premiums, and little badges of distinction, to the children of the common people who excel in them.

The public can impose upon almost the whole body of the people the necessity of acquiring those most essential parts of education, by obliging every man to undergo an examination or probation in them before he can obtain the freedom in any corporation, or be allowed to set up any trade either in a village or town corporate.

It was in this manner, by facilitating the acquisition of their military and gymnastic exercises, by encouraging it, and even by imposing upon the whole body of the people the necessity of learning those exercises, that the Greek and Roman republics maintained the martial spirit of their respective citizens. They facilitated the acquisition of those exercises by appointing a certain place for learning and practising them, and by granting to certain masters the privilege of teaching in that place. Those masters do not appear to have had either salaries or exclusive privileges of any kind. Their reward consisted altogether in what they got from their scholars; and a citizen who had learnt his exercises in the public gymnasia had no sort of legal advantage over one who had learnt them privately, provided the latter had learnt them equally well. Those republics encouraged the acquisition of those exercises by bestowing little premiums and badges of distinction upon those who excelled in them. To have gained a prize in the Olympic, Isthmian, or Nemaean games, gave illustration, not only to the person who gained it, but to his whole family and kindred. The obligation which every citizen was under to serve a certain number of years, if called upon, in the armies of the republic, sufficiently imposed the necessity of learning those exercises, without which he could not be fit for that service.

That in the progress of improvement the practice of military exercises, unless government takes proper pains to support it, goes gradually to decay, and, together with it, the martial spirit of the great body of the people, the example of modern Europe sufficiently demonstrates. But the security of every society must always depend, more or less, upon the martial spirit of the great body of the people. In the present times, indeed, that martial spirit alone, and unsupported by a well-disciplined standing army, would not perhaps be sufficient for the defence and security of any society. But where every citizen had the spirit of a soldier, a smaller standing army would surely be requisite. That spirit, besides, would necessarily diminish very much the dangers to liberty, whether real or imaginary, which are commonly apprehended from, a standing army. As it would very much facilitate the operations of that army against a foreign invader, so it would obstruct them as much if, unfortunately, they should ever be directed against the constitution of the state.

The ancient institutions of Greece and Rome seem to have been much more effectual for maintaining the martial spirit of the great body of the people than the establishment of what are called the militias of modern times. They were much more simple. When they were once established they executed themselves, and it required little or no attention from government to maintain them in the most perfect vigour. Whereas to maintain, even in tolerable execution, the complex regulations of any modern militia, requires the continual and painful attention of government, without which they are constantly falling into total neglect and disuse. The influence, besides, of the ancient institutions was much more universal. By means of them the whole body of the people was completely instructed in the use of arms. Whereas it is but a very small part of them who can ever be so instructed by the regulations of any modern militia, except, perhaps, that of Switzerland. But a coward, a man incapable either of defending or of revenging himself, evidently wants one of the most essential parts of the character of a man; He is as much mutilated and deformed in his mind as another is in his body, who is either deprived of some of its most essential members, or has lost the use of them. He is evidently the more wretched and miserable of the two; because happiness and misery, which reside altogether in the mind, must necessarily depend more upon the healthful or unhealthful, the mutilated or entire state of the mind, than upon that of the body. Even though the martial spirit of the people were of no use towards the defence of the society, yet to prevent that sort of mental mutilation, deformity, and wretchedness, which cowardice necessarily involves in it, from spreading themselves through the great body of the people, would still deserve the most serious attention of government, in the same manner as it would deserve its most serious attention to prevent a leprosy or any other loathsome and offensive disease, though neither mortal nor dangerous, from spreading itself among them, though perhaps no other public good might result from such attention besides the prevention of so great a public evil.

The same thing may be said of the gross ignorance and stupidity which, in a civilised society, seem so frequently to benumb the understandings of all the inferior ranks of people. A man without the proper use of the intellectual faculties of a man, is, if possible, more contemptible than even a coward, and seems to be mutilated and deformed in a still more essential part of the character of human nature. Though the state was to derive no advantage from the instruction of the inferior ranks of people, it would still deserve its attention that they should not be altogether uninstructed. The state, however, derives no inconsiderable advantage from their instruction. The more they are instructed the less liable they are to the delusions of enthusiasm and superstition, which, among ignorant nations, frequently occasion the most dreadful disorders. An instructed and intelligent people, besides, are always more decent and orderly than an ignorant and stupid one. They feel themselves, each individually,

more respectable and more likely to obtain the respect of their lawful superiors, and they are therefore more disposed to respect those superiors. They are more disposed to examine, and more capable of seeing through, the interested complaints of faction and sedition, and they are, upon that account, less apt to be misled into any wanton or unnecessary opposition to the measures of government. In free countries, where the safety of government depends very much upon the favourable judgment which the people may form of …

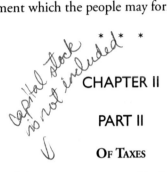

## CHAPTER II

## PART II

### Of Taxes

The private revenue of individuals, it has been shown in the first book of this Inquiry, arises ultimately from three different sources; Rent, Profit, and Wages. Every tax must finally be paid from some one or other of those three different sorts of revenue, or from all of them indifferently. I shall endeavour to give the best account I can, first, of those taxes which, it is intended, should fall upon rent; secondly, of those which, it is intended, should fall upon profit; thirdly, of those which, it is intended, should fall upon wages; and, fourthly, of those which, it is intended, should fall indifferently upon all those three different sources of private revenue. The particular consideration of each of these four different sorts of taxes will divide the second part of the present chapter into four articles, three of which will require several other subdivisions. Many of those taxes, it will appear from the following review, are not finally paid from the fund, or source of revenue, upon which it was intended they should fall.

Before I enter upon the examination of particular taxes, it is necessary to premise the four following maxims with regard to taxes in general.

I. The subjects of every state ought to contribute towards the support of the government, as nearly as possible, in proportion to their respective abilities; that is, in proportion to the revenue which they respectively enjoy under the protection of the state. The expense of government to the individuals of a great nation is like the expense of management to the joint tenants of a great estate, who are all obliged to contribute in proportion to their respective interests in the estate. In the observation or neglect of this maxim consists what is called the equality or inequality of taxation. Every tax, it must be observed once for all, which falls finally upon one only of the three sorts of revenue above mentioned, is necessarily unequal in so far as it does not affect the other two. In the following examination of different taxes I shall seldom take much further notice of this sort of inequality, but shall, in most cases, confine my observations to that inequality which is occasioned by a particular tax falling unequally even upon that particular sort of private revenue which is affected by it,

II. The tax which each individual is bound to pay ought to be certain, and not arbitrary. The time of payment, the manner of payment, the quantity to be paid, ought all to be clear and plain to the contributor, and to every other person. Where it is otherwise, every person subject to the tax is put more or less in the power of the tax-gatherer, who can either aggravate the tax upon any obnoxious contributor, or extort, by the terror of such aggravation, some present or perquisite to himself. The uncertainty of taxation encourages the insolence and favours the corruption of an order of men who are naturally unpopular, even where they are neither insolent nor corrupt. The certainty of what each individual ought to pay is, in taxation, a matter of so great importance that a very considerable degree of inequality, it appears, I believe, from the experience of all nations, is not near so great an evil as a very small degree of uncertainty.

III. Every tax ought to be levied at the time, or in the manner, in which it is most likely to be convenient for the contributor to pay it. A tax upon the rent of land or of houses, payable at the same term at which such rents are usually paid, is levied at the time when it is most likely to be convenient for the contributor to pay; or, when he is most likely to have wherewithal to pay. Taxes upon such consumable goods as are articles of luxury are all finally paid by the consumer, and generally in a manner that is very convenient for him. He pays them by little and little, as he has occasion to buy the goods. As he is at liberty, too, either to buy, or not to buy, as he pleases, it must be his own fault if he ever suffers any considerable inconveniency from such taxes.

IV. Every tax ought to be so contrived as both to take out and to keep out of the pockets of the people as little as possible over and above what it brings into the public treasury of the state. A tax may either take out or keep out of the pockets of the people a great deal more than it brings into the public treasury, in the four following ways. First, the levying of it may require a great number of officers, whose salaries may eat up the greater part of the produce of the tax, and whose perquisites may impose another additional tax upon the people. Secondly, it may obstruct the industry of the people, and discourage them from, applying to certain branches of business which might give maintenance and employment to great multitudes. While it obliges the people to pay, it may thus diminish, or perhaps destroy, some of the funds which might enable them more easily to do so. Thirdly, by the forfeitures and other penalties which those unfortunate individuals incur who attempt unsuccessfully to evade the tax, it may frequently ruin them, and thereby put an end to the benefit which the community might have received from the employment of their capitals. An injudicious tax offers a great temptation to smuggling. But the penalties of smuggling must rise in proportion to the temptation. The law, contrary to all the ordinary principles of justice, first creates the temptation, and then punishes those who yield to it; and it commonly enhances the punishment, too, in proportion to the very circumstance which ought certainly to alleviate it, the temptation to commit the crime.1 Fourthly, by subjecting the people to the frequent visits and the odious examination of the tax-gatherers, it may expose them to much unnecessary trouble, vexation, and oppression; and though vexation is not, strictly speaking, expense, it is certainly equivalent to the expense at which every man would be willing, to redeem himself from it. It is in some one or other of these four different ways that taxes are frequently so much more burdensome to the people than they are beneficial to the sovereign.

The evident justice and utility of the foregoing maxims have recommended them more or less to the attention of all nations. All nations have endeavoured, to the best of their judgment, to render their taxes as equal as they could contrive; as certain, as convenient to the contributor, both in the time and in the mode of payment, and, in proportion to the revenue which they brought to the prince, as little burdensome to the people. The following short review of some of the principal taxes which have taken place in different ages and

countries will show that the endeavours of all nations
have not in this respect been equally successful.

* mind-numbing effect of division of labor to be
counteracted w/ education

* private vices make public virtues, religious morals
inhibit wealth of Nations.

* we don't live in Smith's World, but what sort of
world do we want to inhabit?

# The Declaration of the Rights of Man and Citizen

(August 26, 1789)

The representatives of the French people, organized as a National Assembly, believing that the ignorance, neglect, or contempt of the rights of man are the sole cause of public calamities and of the corruption of governments, have determined to set forth in a solemn declaration the natural, unalienable, and sacred rights of man, in order that this declaration, being constantly before all the members of the Social body, shall remind them continually of their rights and duties; in order that the acts of the legislative power, as well as those of the executive power, may be compared at any moment with the objects and purposes of all political institutions and may thus be more respected, and, lastly, in order that the grievances of the citizens, based hereafter upon simple and incontestable principles, shall tend to the maintenance of the constitution and redound to the happiness of all. Therefore the National Assembly recognizes and proclaims, in the presence and under the auspices of the Supreme Being, the following rights of man and of the citizen:

## ARTICLES

1. Men are born and remain free and equal in rights. Social distinctions may be founded only upon public utility.

2. The aim of all political association is the preservation of the natural and imprescriptible rights of man. These rights are liberty, property, security, and resistance to oppression.

3. The principle of all sovereignty resides essentially in the nation. No body nor individual may exercise any authority which does not proceed expressly from the nation.

4. Liberty consists in the freedom to do everything which injures no one else; hence the exercise of the natural rights of each man has no limits except those which assure to the other members of the society the enjoyment of the same rights. These limits can only be determined by law.

5. Law can only prohibit such actions as are hurtful to society. Nothing may be prevented which is not forbidden by law, and no one may be forced to do anything not provided for by law.

6. Law is the expression of the general will. Every citizen has a right to participate personally, or through his representative, in its foundation. It must be the same for all, whether it protects or punishes. All citizens, being equal in the eyes of the law, are equally eligible to all public dignities, positions and employments, according to their abilities, and without distinction except that of their virtues and talents.

7. No person shall be accused, arrested, or imprisoned except in the cases and according to the forms prescribed by law. Any one soliciting, transmitting, executing, or causing to be executed, any arbitrary order, shall be punished. But any citizen summoned or arrested in virtue of the law shall submit without delay; he renders himself guilty by resistance.

8. The law shall provide for such punishments only as are strictly and obviously necessary, and no one shall suffer punishment except by virtue of a law established and promulgated before the commission of the offense, and legally applied.

9. Every man is presumed innocent until he is declared guilty; if arrest shall be deemed indispensable, all harshness not essential to the securing of the prisoner's person shall be severely repressed by law.

10. No one shall be disquieted on account of his opinions, including his religious views, provided their manifestation does not disturb the public order established by law.

11. The free communication of ideas and opinions is one of the most precious of the rights of man. Every citizen may, accordingly, speak, write, and print with freedom, subject to accountability for abuse of that freedom in cases determined by the law.

12. The security of the rights of man and of the citizen requires public military forces. These forces are, therefore, established for the good of all and not for the personal advantage of those to whom they shall be entrusted.

13. A common contribution is essential for the maintenance of the public forces and for the cost of administration. This should be equally distributed among all the citizens in proportion to their means.

14. All the citizens have a right to ascertain, either personally or by their representatives, the necessity of the public contribution; to consent to it freely; to know to what uses it is put; and to fix the proportion, the mode of assessment and of collection and the duration of the taxes.

15. Society has the right to demand of every public agent an account of his administration.

16. A society in which the observance of the law is not assured, nor the separation of powers defined, has no constitution at all.

17. Property being an inviolable and sacred right, no one shall be deprived thereof except where public necessity, legally determined, shall clearly demand it, and then only on condition that the owner shall have been previously and equitably indemnified.

# Women In Revolutionary Paris
## 1789–1795

Translated and edited by Darline Gay Levy, Harriet Branson Applewhite, and Mary Durham Johnson

### 10.
### THE DECLARATION OF THE RIGHTS OF WOMAN

Source: Olympe de Gouges, *Les Droits de la Femme* (Paris, n.d. [1791], in B.N., E* 5568).

De Gouges was a butcher's daughter from Montauban who wrote several plays and a number of pamphlets on the coming Estates General. In this work de Gouges states that the Declaration of the Rights of Man and Citizen is not being applied to women. She implies the vote for women, demands a national assembly of women, stresses that men must yield rights to women, and emphasizes women's education. She addresses *Les Droits de la Femme* to the Queen, trusting perhaps that the Queen could be converted to the cause of political rights for women and become principal spokeswoman for a feminist program. De Gouges' allegiances are complexly divided between royalty and the national legislature.

To the Queen: Madame,

Little suited to the language one holds to with kings, I will not use the adulation of courtiers to pay you homage with this singular production. My purpose, Madame, is to speak frankly to you; I have not awaited the epoch of liberty to thus explain myself; I bestirred myself as energetically in a time when the blindness of despots punished such noble audacity.

When the whole empire accused you and held you responsible for its calamities, I alone in a time of trouble and storm, I alone had the strength to take up your defense. I could never convince myself that a princess, raised in the midst of grandeur, had all the vices of baseness.

Yes, Madame, when I saw the sword raised against you, I threw my observations between that sword and you, but today when I see who is observed near the crowd of useless hirelings, and [when I see] that she is restrained by fear of the laws, I will tell you, Madame, what I did not say then.

If the foreigner bears arms into France, you are no longer in my eyes this falsely accused Queen, this attractive Queen, but an implacable enemy of the French. Oh, Madame, bear in mind that you are mother and wife; employ all your credit for the return of the Princes. This credit, if wisely applied, strengthens the father's crown, saves it for the son, and reconciles you to the love of the French. This worthy negotiation is the true duty of a queen. Intrigue, cabals, bloody projects will precipitate your fall, if it is possible to suspect that you are capable of such plots.

Madame, may a nobler function characterize you, excite your ambition, and fix your attentions. Only one whom chance has elevated to an eminent position can assume the task of lending weight to the progress of the Rights of Woman and of hastening its success. If you were less well informed, Madame, I might fear that your individual interests would outweigh those of your sex. You love glory; think, Madame, the greatest crimes immortalize one as much as the greatest virtues, but what a different fame in the annals of history! The one is ceaselessly taken as an example, and the other is eternally the execration of the human race.

It will never be a crime for you to work for the restoration of customs, to give your sex all the firmness of which it is capable. This is not the work of one day, unfortunately for the new regime. This revolution will happen only when all women are aware of their deplorable fate, and of the rights they have lost in society. Madame, support such a beautiful cause; defend this unfortunate sex, and soon you will have half the realm on your side, and at least one-third of the other half.

Those, Madame, are the feats by which you should show and use your credit. Believe me, Madame, our life is a pretty small thing, especially for a Queen, when it is not embellished by people's affection and by the eternal delights of good deeds.

If it is true that the French arm all the powers against their own Fatherland, why? For frivolous prerogatives, for chimeras. Believe, Madame, if I judge by what I feel—the monarchical party will be destroyed by itself, it will abandon all tyrants, and all hearts will rally around the fatherland to defend it.

There are my principles, Madame. In speaking to you of my fatherland, I lose sight of the purpose of this dedication. Thus, any good citizen sacrifices his glory and his interests when he has none other than those of his country.

I am with the most profound respect, Madame,
Your most humble and most obedient servant,
de Gouges

## THE RIGHTS OF WOMAN

Man, are you capable of being just? It is a woman who poses the question; you will not deprive her of that right at least. Tell me, what gives you sovereign empire to oppress my sex? Your strength? Your talents? Observe the Creator in his wisdom; survey in all her grandeur that nature with whom you seem to want to be in harmony, and give me, if you dare, an example of this tyrannical empire. Go back to animals, consult the elements, study plants, finally glance at all the modifications of organic matter, and surrender to the evidence when I offer you the means; search, probe, and distinguish, if you can, the sexes in the administration of nature. Everywhere you will find them mingled; everywhere they cooperate in harmonious togetherness in this immortal masterpiece.

Man alone has raised his exceptional circumstances to a principle. Bizarre, blind, bloated with science and degenerated—in a century of enlightenment and wisdom—into the crassest ignorance, he wants to command as a despot a sex which is in full possession of its intellectual faculties; he pretends to enjoy the Revolution and to claim his rights to equality in order to say nothing more about it.

## DECLARATION OF THE RIGHTS OF WOMAN AND THE FEMALE CITIZEN

For the National Assembly to decree in its last sessions, or in those of the next legislature:

### Preamble

Mothers, daughters, sisters [and] representatives of the nation demand to be constituted into a national assembly. Believing that ignorance, omission, or scorn for the rights of woman are the only causes of public misfortunes and of the corruption of governments, [the women] have resolved to set forth in a solemn declaration the natural, inalienable, and sacred rights of woman in order that this declaration, constantly exposed before all the members of the society, will ceaselessly remind them of their rights and duties; in order that the authoritative acts of women and the authoritative acts of men may be at any moment compared with and respectful of the purpose of all political institutions; and in order that citizens' demands, henceforth based on simple and incontestable principles, will always support the constitution, good morals, and the happiness of all.

Consequently, the sex that is as superior in beauty as it is in courage during the sufferings of maternity recognizes and declares in the presence and under the auspices of the Supreme Being, the following Rights of Woman and of Female Citizens.

### Article I

Woman is born free and lives equal to man in her rights. Social distinctions can be based only on the common utility.

### Article II

The purpose of any political association is the conservation of the natural and imprescriptible rights of woman and man; these rights are liberty, property, security, and especially resistance to oppression.

### Article III

The principle of all sovereignty rests essentially with the nation, which is nothing but the union of woman and man; no body and no individual can exercise any authority which does not come expressly from it [the nation].

### Article IV

Liberty and justice consist of restoring all that belongs to others; thus, the only limits on the exercise of the natural rights of woman are perpetual male tyranny; these limits are to be reformed by the laws of nature and reason.

### Article V

Laws of nature and reason proscribe all acts harmful to society; everything which is not prohibited by these wise and divine laws cannot be prevented, and no one can be constrained to do what they do not command.

### Article VI

The law must be the expression of the general will; all female and male citizens must contribute either personally or through their representatives to its formation; it must be the same for all: male and female citizens, being equal in the eyes of the law, must be equally admitted to all honors, positions, and public employment according to their capacity and without other distinctions besides those of their virtues and talents.

### Article VII

No woman is an exception; she is accused, arrested, and detained in cases determined by law. Women, like men, obey this rigorous law.

### Article VIII

The law must establish only those penalties that are strictly and obviously necessary, and no one can be punished except by virtue of a law established and promulgated prior to the crime and legally applicable to women.

### Article IX

Once any woman is declared guilty, complete rigor is [to be] exercised by the law.

### Article X

No one is to be disquieted for his very basic opinions; woman has the right to mount the scaffold; she must equally have the right to mount the rostrum, provided that her demonstrations do not disturb the legally established public order.

### Article XI

The free communication of thoughts and opinions is one of the most precious rights of woman, since that liberty assures the recognition of children by their fathers. Any female citizen thus may say freely, I am the mother of a child which belongs to you, without being forced by a barbarous prejudice to hide the truth; [an exception may be made] to respond to the abuse of this liberty in cases determined by the law.

### Article XII

The guarantee of the rights of woman and the female citizen implies a major benefit; this guarantee must be instituted for the advantage of all, and not for the particular benefit of those to whom it is entrusted.

### Article XIII

For the support of the public force and the expenses of administration, the contributions of woman and man are equal; she shares all the duties [*corvées*] and all the painful tasks; therefore, she must have the same share in the distribution of positions, employment, offices, honors, and jobs [*industrie*].

## Article XIV

Female and male citizens have the right to verify, either by themselves or through their representatives, the necessity of the public contribution. This can only apply to women if they are granted an equal share, not only of wealth, but also of public administration, and in the determination of the proportion, the base, the collection, and the duration of the tax.

## Article XV

The collectivity of women, joined for tax purposes to the aggregate of men, has the right to demand an accounting of his administration from any public agent.

## Article XVI

No society has a constitution without the guarantee of rights and the separation of powers; the constitution is null if the majority of individuals comprising the nation have not cooperated in drafting it.

## Article XVII

Property belongs to both sexes whether united or separate; for each it is an inviolable and sacred right; no one can be deprived of it, since it is the true patrimony of nature, unless the legally determined public need obviously dictates it, and then only with a just and prior indemnity.

## Postscript

Woman, wake up; the tocsin of reason is being heard throughout the whole universe; discover your rights. The powerful empire of nature is no longer surrounded by prejudice, fanaticism, superstition, and lies. The flame of truth has dispersed all the clouds of folly and usurpation. Enslaved man has multiplied his strength and needs recourse to yours to break his chains. Having become free, he has become unjust to his companion. Oh, women, women! When will you cease to be blind? What advantage have you received from the Revolution? A more pronounced scorn, a more marked disdain. In the centuries of corruption you ruled only over the weakness of men. The reclamation of your patrimony, based on the wise decrees of nature—what have you to dread from such a fine undertaking? The *bon mot* of the legislator of the marriage of Cana? Do you fear that our French legislators, correctors of that morality, long ensnared by political practices now out of date, will

only say again to you: women, what is there in common between you and us? Everything, you will have to answer. If they persist in their weakness in putting this non sequitur in contradiction to their principles, courageously oppose the force of reason to the empty pretentions of superiority; unite yourselves beneath the standards of philosophy; deploy all the energy of your character, and you will soon see these haughty men, not groveling at your feet as servile adorers, but proud to share with you the treasures of the Supreme Being. Regardless of what barriers confront you, it is in your power to free yourselves; you have only to want to. Let us pass now to the shocking tableau of what you have been in society; and since national education is in question at this moment, let us see whether our wise legislators will think judiciously about the education of women.

Women have done more harm than good. Constraint and dissimulation have been their lot. What force had robbed them of, ruse returned to them; they had recourse to all the resources of their charms, and the most irreproachable person did not resist them. Poison and the sword were both subject to them; they commanded in crime as in fortune. The French government, especially, depended throughout the centuries on the nocturnal administration of women; the cabinet kept no secret from their indiscretion; ambassadorial post, command, ministry, presidency, pontificate, college of cardinals; finally, anything which characterizes the folly of men, profane and sacred, all have been subject to the cupidity and ambition of this sex, formerly contemptible and respected, and since the revolution, respectable and scorned.

In this sort of contradictory situation, what remarks could I not make! I have but a moment to make them, but this moment will fix the attention of the remotest posterity. Under the Old Regime, all was vicious, all was guilty; but could not the amelioration of conditions be perceived even in the substance of vices? A woman only had to be beautiful or amiable; when she possessed these two advantages, she saw a hundred fortunes at her feet. If she did not profit from them, she had a bizarre character or a rare philosophy which made her scorn wealth; then she was deemed to be like a crazy woman; the most indecent made herself respected with gold; commerce in women was a kind of industry in the first class [of society], which, henceforth, will have no more credit. If it still had it, the revolution would be lost, and under the new relationships we would always be corrupted; however, reason can always be deceived [into believing] that any other road to fortune is closed to the woman whom a man buys, like the slave on the African coasts. The difference is great; that is known. The slave is commanded by the master; but if the master gives her liberty without recompense, and at an age when the slave has lost all her charms, what will become of this unfortunate woman? The victim of scorn, even the doors of charity are closed to her; she is poor and old, they say; why did she not know how to make her fortune? Reason finds other examples that are even more touching. A young, inexperienced woman, seduced by a man whom she loves, will abandon her parents to follow him; the ingrate will leave her after a few years, and the older she has become with him, the more inhuman is his inconstancy; if she has children, he will likewise abandon them. If he is rich, he will consider himself excused from sharing his fortune with his noble victims. If some involvement binds him to his duties, he will deny them, trusting that the laws will support him. If he is married, any other obligation loses its rights. Then what laws remain to extirpate vice all the way to its root? The law of dividing wealth and public administration between men and women. It can easily be seen that one who is born into a rich family gains very much from such equal sharing. But the one born into a poor family with merit and virtue—what is her lot? Poverty and opprobrium. If she does not precisely excel in music or painting, she cannot be admitted to any public function when she has all the capacity for it. I do not want to give only a sketch of things; I will go more deeply into this in the new edition of all my political writings, with notes, which I propose to give to the public in a few days.

I take up my text again on the subject of morals. Marriage is the tomb of trust and love. The married woman can with impunity give bastards to her husband, and also give them the wealth which does not belong to them. The woman who is unmarried has only one feeble right; ancient and inhuman laws refuse to her for her children the right to the name and the wealth of their father; no new laws have been made in this matter. If it is considered a paradox and an impossibility on my part to try to give my sex an honorable and just consistency, I leave it to men to attain glory for dealing

with this matter; but while we wait, the way can be prepared through national education, the restoration of morals, and conjugal conventions.

## Form for a Social Contract Between Man and Woman

We, _____ and _____, moved by our own will, unite ourselves for the duration of our lives, and for the duration of our mutual inclinations, under the following conditions: We intend and wish to make our wealth communal, meanwhile reserving to ourselves the right to divide it in favor of our children and of those toward whom we might have a particular inclination, mutually recognizing that our property belongs directly to our children, from whatever bed they come, and that all of them without distinction have the right to bear the name of the fathers and mothers who have acknowledged them, and we are charged to subscribe to the law which punishes the renunciation of one's own blood. We likewise obligate ourselves, in case of separation, to divide our wealth and to set aside in advance the portion the law indicates for our children, and in the event of a perfect union, the one who dies will divest himself of half his property in his children's favor, and if one dies childless, the survivor will inherit by right, unless the dying person has disposed of half the common property in favor of one whom he judged deserving.

That is approximately the formula for the marriage act I propose for execution. Upon reading this strange document, I see rising up against me the hypocrites, the prudes, the clergy, and the whole infernal sequence. But how it [my proposal] offers to the wise the moral means of achieving the perfection of a happy government! I am going to give in a few words the physical proof of it. The rich, childless Epicurean finds it very good to go to his poor neighbor to augment his family. When there is a law authorizing a poor man's wife to have a rich one adopt their children, the bonds of society will be strengthened and morals will be purer. This law will perhaps save the community's wealth and hold back the disorder which drives so many victims to the almshouses of shame, to a low station, and into degenerate human principles where nature has groaned for so long. May the detractors of wise philosophy then cease to cry out against primitive morals, or may they lose their point in the source of their citations.[1]

Moreover, I would like a law which would assist widows and young girls deceived by the false promises of a man to whom they were attached; I would like, I say, this law to force an inconstant man to hold to his obligations or at least [to pay] an indemnity equal to his wealth. Again, I would like this law to be rigorous against women, at least those who have the effrontery to have recourse to a law which they themselves had violated by their misconduct, if proof of that were given. At the same time, as I showed in *Le Bonheur primitif de l'homme*, in 1788, that prostitutes should be placed in designated quarters.[2] It is not prostitutes who contribute the most to the depravity of morals, it is the women of society. In regenerating the latter, the former are changed. This link of fraternal union will first bring disorder, but in consequence it will produce at the end a perfect harmony.

I offer a foolproof way to elevate the soul of women; it is to join them to all the activities of man; if man persists in finding this way impractical, let him share his fortune with woman, not at his caprice, but by the wisdom of laws. Prejudice falls, morals are purified, and nature regains all her rights. Add to this the marriage of priests and the strengthening of the king on his throne, and the French government cannot fail.

It would be very necessary to say a few words on the troubles which are said to be caused by the decree in favor of colored men in our islands. There is where nature shudders with horror; there is where reason and humanity have still not touched callous souls; there, especially, is where division and discord stir up their inhabitants. It is not difficult to divine the instigators of these incendiary fermentations; they are even in the midst of the National Assembly; they ignite the fire in Europe which must inflame America. Colonists make a claim to reign as despots over the men whose fathers and brothers they are; and, disowning the rights of nature, they trace the source of [their rule] to the scantiest tint of their blood. These inhuman colonists say: our blood flows in their veins, but we will shed it

all if necessary to glut our greed or our blind ambition. It is in these places nearest to nature where the father scorns the son; deaf to the cries of blood, they stifle all its attraction; what can be hoped from the resistance opposed to them? To constrain [blood] violently is to render it terrible; to leave [blood] still enchained is to direct all calamities towards America. A divine hand seems to spread liberty abroad throughout the realms of man; only the law has the right to curb this liberty if it degenerates into license, but it must be equal for all; liberty must hold the National Assembly to its decree dictated by prudence and justice. May it act the same way for the state of France and render her as attentive to new abuses as she was to the ancient ones which each day become more dreadful. My opinion would be to reconcile the executive and legislative power, for it seems to me that the one is everything and the other is nothing—whence comes, unfortunately perhaps, the loss of the French Empire. I think that these two powers, like man and woman, should be united but equal in force and virtue to make a good household. …

## 11.
## THE TRIAL OF A FEMINIST REVOLUTIONARY, OLYMPE DE GOUGES

Source: *Bulletin du Tribunal criminel révolutionnaire* (Paris, n.d. [1793]), nos. 66, 67, pp. 264–68, in Bibliothèque historique de la Ville de Paris, 104,843, vol. 2.

One of the famous victims of the Terror was Olympe de Gouges, author of the Declaration of the Rights of Woman (chapter two, above, document 10). De Gouges claimed she was happy about the Republic once she convinced herself that the King was a traitor. But in 1793 she circulated tracts critical of the Terror. In July she was arrested and imprisoned in the Abbaye for having published a document suggesting a popular referendum on the form of government France should have. After an interrogation before the Revolutionary Tribunal on 11 Brumaire (November 1, 1793), de Gouges

---

1    Abraham had some very legitimate children by Agar, the servant of his wife.

2    See Olympe de Gouges, *Le Bonheur primitif de l'homme, ou les Rêveries patriotiques* (Amsterdam and Paris, 1789).

was condemned to death. She stated that she was pregnant. That appeal, had it been accepted, would have delayed her sentence until the birth of the child. The court ordered a medical examination, and her appeal was denied. She was guillotined on 13 Brumaire.

Audience of ... 12 Brumaire, Year II of the Republic.

### Case of Olympe de Gouges.

Questioned concerning her name, surname, age, occupation, place of birth, and residence. Replied that her name was Marie Olympe de Gouges, age thirty-eight, *femme de lettres*, a native of Montauban, living in Paris, rue du Harlay, Section Pont-Neuf.

The clerk read the act of accusation, the tenor of which follows.

Antoine-Quentin Fouquier-Tinville, public prosecutor before the Revolutionary Tribunal, etc.

States that, by an order of the administrators of police, dated last July 25, signed Louvet and Baudrais, it was ordered that Marie Olympe de Gouges, widow of Aubry, charged with having composed a work contrary to the expressed desire of the entire nation, and directed against whoever might propose a form of government other than that of a republic, one and indivisible, be brought to the prison called l'Abbaye, and that the documents be sent to the public prosecutor of the Revolutionary Tribunal. Consequently, the accused was brought to the designated prison and the documents delivered to the public prosecutor on July 26. The following August 6, one of the judges of the Revolutionary Tribunal proceeded with the interrogation of the above-mentioned de Gouges woman.

From the examination of the documents deposited, together with the interrogation of the accused, it follows that against the desire manifested by the majority of Frenchmen for republican government, and in contempt of laws directed against whoever might propose another form of government, Olympe de Gouges composed and had printed works which can only be considered as an attack on the sovereignty of the people because they tend to call into question that concerning which it [the people] formally expressed its desire; that in her writing, entitled *Les Trois urnes, ou le Salut de la patrie*, there can be found the project of the liberty-killing faction which wanted to place before the people the approbation of the judgment of the tyrant condemned by the people itself; that the author of this work openly provoked civil war and sought to arm citizens against one another by proposing the meeting of primary assemblies to deliberate and express their desire concerning either monarchical government, which the national sovereignty had abolished and proscribed; concerning the one and indivisible republican [form], which it had chosen and established by the organ of its representatives; or, finally, concerning the federative [form], which would be the source of incalculable evils and which would destroy liberty infallibly.

... The public prosecutor stated next that it is with the most violent indignation that one hears the de Gouges woman say to men who for the past four years have not stopped making the greatest sacrifices for liberty; who on August 10, 1792, overturned both the throne and the tyrant; who knew how to bravely face the arms and frustrate the plots of the despot, his slaves, and the traitors who had abused the public confidence—to men who have submitted tyranny to the avenging blade of the law—that Louis Capet still reigns among them.

There can be no mistaking the perfidious intentions of this criminal woman, and her hidden motives, when one observes her in all the works to which, at the very least, she lends her name, calumniating and spewing out bile in large doses against the warmest friends of the people, their most intrepid defender.

In a manuscript seized in her home, on which she placed a patriotic title only in order to get her. poisons circulated more freely, she places in the mouth of the monster who surpasses the Messalinas and the Medicis these impious expressions—"the placard-makers, these paper scribblings, are not worth a Marat, a Robespierre; in the specious language of patriotism, they overturn everything in the name of the people; they appear to be serving propaganda and never have heads of factions better served the cause of kings; at one and the same time they serve two parties moving at a rapid pace towards the same goal. I love these enterprising men; they have a thorough knowledge of the difficult art of imposing on human weaknesses; they have sensed from the beginning that in order to serve me it was necessary to blaze a trail in the opposite direction; applaud yourself, Calonne, this is your work."

Lastly, in the work in question one sees only provocation to the reestablishment of royalty on the part of a woman who, in one of her writings, admits that monarchy seems to her to be the government most suited to the French spirit; who in [the writing] in question points out that the desire for the republic was not freely pronounced; who, lastly, in another [writing] is not afraid to parody the traitor Isnard and to apply to all of France what the former restricted to the city of Paris alone, so calumniated by the partisans of royalty and by those of federalism.

On the basis of the foregoing exposé the public prosecutor drew up this accusation against Marie Olympe de Gouges, widow Aubry, for having maliciously and purposefully composed writings attacking the sovereignty of the people (whose desire, when these were written, had been pronounced for republican government, one and indivisible) and tending towards the reestablishment of the monarchical government (which it [the people] had formally proscribed) as well as the federative [form] (against which it [the people] had forcefully protested); for having had printed up and distributed several copies of one of the cited works tending towards these ends, entitled, *Les Trois urnes, ou le Salut de la patrie*; for having been stopped in her distribution of a greater number of copies as well as in her posting of the cited work only by the refusal of the bill-poster and by her prompt arrest; for having sent this work to her son, employed in the army of the Vendée as *officier l'état major*; for having, in other manuscripts and printed works—notably, in the manuscript entitled *La France sauvée, ou le Tyran détrôné* as well as in the poster entitled *Olympe de Gouges au Tribunal Révolutionnaire*—sought to degrade the constituted authorities, calumniate the friends and defenders of the people and of liberty, and spread defiance among the representatives and the represented, which is contrary to the laws, and notably to that of last December 4.

Consequently, the public prosecutor asks that he be given official notice by the assembled Tribunal of this indictment, etc., etc.

In this case only three witnesses were heard, one of whom was the citizen bill-poster, who stated that, having been asked to post a certain number of copies of printed material with the title *Les Trois urnes*, he refused when he found out about the principles contained in this writing.

When the accused was questioned sharply about when she composed this writing, she replied that it was some time last May, adding that what motivated her was that seeing the storms arising in a large number of *départements*, and notably in Bordeaux, Lyons, Marseilles, etc., she had the idea of bringing all parties together by leaving them all free in the choice of the kind of government which would be most suitable for them; that furthermore, her intentions had proven that she had in view only the happiness of her country.

Questioned about how it was that she, the accused, who believed herself to be such a good patriot, had been able to develop, in the month of June, means which she called conciliatory concerning a fact which could no longer be in question because the people, at that period, had formally pronounced for republican government, one and indivisible, she replied that this was also the [form of government] she had voted for as the preferable one; that for a long while she had professed only republican sentiments, as the jurors would be able to convince themselves from her work entitled *De l'esclavage des noirs*.

A reading was provided by Naulin, the public prosecutor's substitute, of a letter written by the accused to Herault-Séchelles in which principles of federalism are found.

The accused replied to this fact that her intention had been, as she had said already, pure and that she wanted to be able to show her heart to the citizen jurors so that they might judge her love of liberty and her hatred of every kind of tyranny.

Asked to declare whether she acknowledged authorship of a manuscript work found among her papers entitled *La France sauvée ou le Tyran détrôné*, she replied yes.

Asked why she had placed injurious and perfidious declamations against the most ardent defenders of the rights of the people in the mouth of the person who in this work was supposed to represent the Capet woman, she replied that she had the Capet woman speaking the language appropriate for her; that besides, the handbill for which she was brought before the Tribunal had never been posted; that to avoid compromising herself she had decided to send twenty-four copies to the Committee of Public Safety, which, two days later, had her arrested.

The public prosecutor pointed out to the accused, concerning this matter, that if her placard entitled *Les Trois urnes* had not been made public, this was because the bill-poster had not been willing to take it upon himself. The accused was in agreement with this fact.

Questioned about whether, since her detention, she had not sent a copy to her son along with a letter, she said that the fact was exact and that her intention concerning this matter had been to apprise him of the cause of her arrest; that besides, she did not know whether her son had received it, not having heard from him in a long while and not knowing at all what could have become of him.

Asked to speak concerning various phrases in the placard entitled *Olympe de Gouges, défenseur de Louis Capet,* a work written by her at the time of the former's trial, and concerning the placard entitled *Olympe de Gouges au Tribunal Révolutionnaire* as well, she responded only with oratorical phrases and persisted in saying that she was and always had been a good *citoyenne,* that she had never intrigued.

Asked to express herself and to reply precisely concerning her sentiments with respect to the faithful representatives of the people whom she had insulted and calumniated in her writings, the accused replied that she had not changed, that she still held to her same opinion concerning them, and that she had looked upon them as ambitious persons.

In her defense the accused said that she had ruined herself in order to propagate the principles of the Revolution and that she was the founder of popular societies of her sex, *etc.*

During the résumé of the charge brought by the public prosecutor, the accused, with respect to the facts she was hearing articulated against her, never stopped her smirking. Sometimes she shrugged her shoulders; then she clasped her hands and raised her eyes towards the ceiling of the room; then, suddenly, she moved on to an expressive gesture, showing astonishment; then gazing next at the court, she smiled at the spectators, etc.

Here is the judgment rendered against her.

The Tribunal, based on the unanimous declaration of the jury, stating that (1) it is a fact that there exist in the case writings tending towards the reestablishment of a power attacking the sovereignty of the people [and] (2) that Marie Olympe de Gouges, calling herself widow Aubry, is proven guilty of being the author of these writings, and admitting the conclusions of the public prosecutor, condemns the aforementioned Marie Olympe de Gouges, widow Aubry, to the punishment of death in conformity with Article One of the law of last March 29, which was read, which is conceived as follows: "Whoever is convicted of having composed or printed works or writings which provoke the dissolution of the national representation, the reestablishment of royalty, or of any other power attacking the sovereignty of the people, will be brought before the Revolutionary Tribunal and punished by death," and declares the goods of the aforementioned Marie Olympe de Gouges acquired for the republic. ...

Orders that by the diligence of the public prosecutor this judgment will be executed on the place de la Révolution of this city [and] printed, published, and posted throughout the realm; and given the public declaration made by the aforementioned Marie Olympe de Gouges that she was pregnant, the Tribunal, following the indictment of the public prosecutor, orders that the aforementioned Marie Olympe de Gouges will be seen and visited by the sworn surgeons and doctors and matrons of the Tribunal in order to determine the sincerity of her declaration so that on the basis of their sworn and filed report the Tribunal can pronounce according to the law.

Before pronouncing his judgment, the prosecutor summoned the accused to declare whether she had some observations to make concerning the application of the law, and she replied: "My enemies will not have the glory of seeing my blood flow. I am pregnant and will bear a citizen or *citoyenne* for the Republic."

The same day [12 Brumaire], the health officer, having visited the condemned, recognized that her declaration was false.

... The execution took place the same day [13 Brumaire] towards 4 p.m.; while mounting the scaffold, the condemned, looking at the people, cried out: "Children of the Fatherland, you will avenge my death." Universal cries of "Vive la République" were heard among the spectators waving hats in the air.

*complexities of race & gender

LaVergne, TN USA
27 December 2009
168034LV00002B/1/P